NIETZSCHE AND METAPHYSICS

ALSO PUBLISHED IN THE SERIES

Nietzsche and Metaphysics

PETER POELLNER

OXFORD
UNIVERSITY PRESS

OXFORD

UNIVERSITY PRESS

Great Clarendon Street, Oxford OX2 6DP

Oxford University Press is a department of the University of Oxford.
It furthers the University's objective of excellence in research, scholarship,
and education by publishing worldwide in

Oxford New York

Athens Auckland Bangkok Bogotá Buenos Aires Calcutta
Cape Town Chennai Dar es Salaam Delhi Florence Hong Kong Istanbul
Karachi Kuala Lumpur Madrid Melbourne Mexico City Mumbai
Nairobi Paris São Paulo Singapore Taipei Tokyo Toronto Warsaw

and associated companies in Berlin Ibadan

Oxford is a registered trade mark of Oxford University Press
in the UK and certain other countries

Published in the United States
by Oxford University Press Inc., New York

British Library Cataloguing in Publication Data

Data available

Library of Congress Cataloging in Publication Data
Poellner, Peter.
Nietzsche and metaphysics / Peter Poellner.
—(Oxford philosophical monographs)
Includes bibliographical references.
1. Nietzsche, Friedrich Wilhelm, 1844–1900—Metaphysics.
2. Nietzsche, Friedrich Wilhelm, 1844–1900—Influence.
3. Metaphysics. I. Title. II. Series.
B3318.M5P64 1995 193—dc20 95-13035
ISBN 0-19-823517-8
ISBN 0-19-825063-0 (pbk.)

Typeset by Best-set Typesetter Ltd., Hong Kong
Printed in Great Britain
on acid-free paper by
Bookcraft Ltd
Midsomer Norton, Somerset

Meinen Eltern

ACKNOWLEDGEMENTS

Many of the ideas and arguments of this book are based on a D.Phil. thesis written, as it seems to me now, a long time ago. Above all, I should like to thank Leszek Kolakowski, whose encouragement, patience, and sympathetically critical attention were of great help in the genesis of that study. I should also like to thank those members of the Philosophy Department of the University of Warwick who have commented on and suggested improvements of parts of the book, or discussed ideas contained in it with me. In particular, I have attempted to take account of a number of specific criticisms of various arguments by A. Phillips Griffiths, Michael Luntley, and Martin Warner. Whether my responses to them are adequate is of course not for me to decide. I have also profited from helpful comments by Patrick Gardiner and Timothy Sprigge on earlier versions of the study. Finally, I should like to thank the following friends and colleagues with whom I have, over the years, had many conversations about the issues with which this book is concerned: Antonia Caputo, Peter Dube, Simon Kriss-Rettenbeck, John McGovern, Fania Oz-Salzberger, and Christine Scheicher.

P.P.

University of Warwick
March 1994

CONTENTS

ABBREVIATIONS

A. WORKS PUBLISHED BY NIETZSCHE

AC — *Der Antichrist (The Antichrist)*, prepared for publication 1888.

EH — *Ecce Homo,* prepared for publication 1888.

FW — *Die Fröhliche Wissenschaft (The Gay Science)*, Books I–IV, 1882; Book V, 1887.

GD — *Götzendämmerung (Twilight of the Idols)*, 1889.

GM — *Zur Genealogie der Moral (On the Genealogy of Morals)*, 1887.

GT — *Die Geburt der Tragödie (The Birth of Tragedy)*, 1872.

JGB — *Jenseits von Gut und Böse (Beyond Good and Evil)*, 1886.

MAM — *Menschliches, Allzumenschliches (Human, All-too-Human)*, 1878–80.

MR — *Morgenröte (Daybreak)*, 1881.

NcW — *Nietzsche contra Wagner,* prepared for publication 1888.

UzB — *Unzeitgemässe Betrachtungen* (in four parts) (*Untimely Meditations*).

UzB I — *David Strauss*, 1873.

UzB II — *Vom Nutzen und Nachteil der Historie (Of the Use and Disadvantage of History)*, 1874.

UzB III — *Schopenhauer als Erzieher (Schopenhauer as Educator)*, 1874.

UzB IV — *Richard Wagner in Bayreuth,* 1876.

W — *Der Fall Wagner (The Case of Wagner)*, 1888.

Z — *Also sprach Zarathustra (Thus spoke Zarathustra)*, 1883–85.

B. OTHER WRITINGS OR COLLECTIONS OF WRITINGS BY NIETZSCHE

GOA — *Werke* (Grossoktavausgabe).

KGW — *Werke: Kritische Gesamtausgabe* (Complete Critical Edition of Nietzsche's Works), edited by G. Colli and M. Montinari.

PT   *Philosophy and Truth,* selections from Nietzsche's notebooks of the early 1870s, including the essay 'On Truth and Lie in a Non-Moral Sense'. Translated and edited by D. Breazeale.

WM   *Der Wille zur Macht* (*The Will to Power*), selections from Nietzsche's notebooks of the 1880s. First published in this form 1906.

A NOTE ON TRANSLATIONS
AND REFERENCES

All translations from Nietzsche's writings in this study are my own, except those from WM, which are by W. Kaufmann and R. J. Hollingdale (with some modifications), and those from PT, which are by D. Breazeale. Translations from works by other authors, if their titles are given in German, are also mine.

The last numeral in references to Nietzsche's writings signifies the paragraph, note, or fragment, except with works where this would have been unhelpful, namely GT, UzB, and Z, as well as in references to GOA. In these latter cases, the last numeral signifies the *page* of the relevant edition.

In the cases of GT, UzB, and Z, two page references are always given, the first being to the relevant volume of the *Kritische Gesamtausgabe*, the second to the English translations listed in the bibliography.

References to *Nachlass* notes in KGW are (in this order) to section, volume, notebook, and note or fragment (e.g. KGW VII.1.6.8).

I have only referred to GOA in a few instances, when I failed to locate the respective note or fragment in KGW.

I

Introduction

This book offers a critical interpretation of Friedrich Nietzsche's thought on two traditionally central disciplines of philosophy: epistemology and metaphysics. It will confine its field of study largely to what is perhaps not entirely appropriately called Nietzsche's 'mature' philosophy, which is contained in his writings produced after 1882, that is, in the third and final major phase of his philosophical career.[1] It is during this period that he developed most of the ideas which are usually associated with his name and for which he is best known. References to his earlier views will here be confined to the bare minimum of what seems to me essential for an adequate understanding of his later philosophy, or to those earlier ideas which anticipate the latter.

Any study of Nietzsche has to take up some position or positions on a very fundamental question concerning the nature of the work of this controversial thinker. It has often been remarked that his *oeuvre* occupies a peculiar position in the line of those writers in the European tradition who have called themselves philosophers or who have had this label applied to them by large sections of the educated public. It is characterized by the fact that there is not only a wide divergence of views concerning what he said or meant to say, or concerning the value of what he said. Both of these types of disagreement are, after all, widespread with regard to virtually every major philosopher in the tradition. Rather, the disagreement here seems to be about what the status of Nietzsche's writings is, i.e. what genre or discipline they belong to.

It is a commonplace that academic philosophers have often been reluctant to recognize him as a philosopher at all. This is true especially of the professionals in the Anglo-American academic

---

[1] I shall generally follow the conventional division of Nietzsche's philosophical activity into three main periods, a division which is, I believe, well-founded (see below). Cf. e.g. Karl Löwith, *Nietzsches Philosophie der ewigen Wiederkehr des Gleichen* (Stuttgart, 1950), 22–6.

world; but even on the continent of Europe he has frequently been regarded as marginal to the concerns of 'genuine' philosophers. It is not difficult to see why. There is, in the works he published himself, relatively little that would qualify as a respectable argument of one of the sorts standardly recognized as such by most philosophers. To be sure, Nietzsche here makes many apparent claims concerning philosophical questions—for example, that the concept of a thing in itself is a contradiction in terms, or that there are no 'subjects', or that all our commonsense and scientific 'truths' are false. But these statements are usually made without much elucidation of precisely *which* concept, say, of a thing in itself, or of the subject, he is rejecting, and without patiently explaining, and defending against objections, his reasons for rejecting it. Often he seems to attack in summary fashion a number of views under the same heading, while his reasons for doing so, to the extent that they are discernible at all, seem to apply at best to some of these views, frequently to those which few contemporary philosophers feel committed to holding anyway (e.g. the construal of objects as properties inhering in substrata which persist throughout any changes of the objects' properties; or the notion of the self as a mental substance, a substratum of mental states and acts; or the idea of a Kantian or Platonic timeless realm of 'being' distinct from the empirical world of continuously changing, pragmatically identified and individuated particulars).

Moreover, it is often pointed out that even if one ignores Nietzsche's provocative and rhetorically overstated paradoxes (e.g. to the effect that all our knowledge is false), there still seem to remain a plethora of contradictions and confusions in his statements on just about any issue. We are told by him that the causes of human emotional or affective states are hidden from us (e.g. KGW VII.3.34.46), while also being informed that these causes are various 'physiological' conditions (e.g. GM iii.15, 17). In yet other passages, it is claimed that '[t]here are neither causes nor effects' (WM 551), which would appear to render both of the above statements misconceived. We hear that the idea of a constitution in itself, i.e. of any item of reality being characterized by intrinsic essential properties, is 'nonsense' (WM 583A), while also reading that 'life itself is *essentially* appropriating, violating, overpowering of the alien and of that which is weaker [. . .] because life is simply will to power' (JGB 259). Alongside remarks announcing mysteriously that 'there is no "truth"' (WM 616, cf. WM 540)—at least as regards first-order statements about the world—we find others which suggest that there are a great many truths concerning, for example, human psychology—concerning the motives human beings have for embracing certain views or ideals. This list could be extended at some length. But it may suffice to show that those philosophers who dismiss Nietzsche as hopelessly confused have good prima facie reasons for doing so.

Against such a dismissal, a minority of apologists have argued that it rests on a misunderstanding of what Nietzsche is doing. Attempts in such quarters at vindicating his enterprise have generally taken one of two forms. They have either endeavoured to show that a suitably subtle interpretation of his apparent claims, with appropriate elaborations and qualifications, can remove their seeming absurdities and inconsistencies, and yet leave a substantial remainder of philosophical thought which is both original and worth taking seriously—taking seriously, that is, given the minimum standards of acceptability recognized among most of those thinkers who would generally (and not merely by one or another marginal intellectual sect) be regarded as philosophers, such as the 'classical' or canonical philosophers of the Western tradition from Plato to Kant. Such attempts at rendering Nietzsche's thought philosophically respectable, regardless of whether or not they are successful in their own terms, often have issued in what seems to this reader a somewhat disappointing result. The more they have succeeded in weeding out his rhetorical exaggerations, unqualified summary condemnations, and careless formulations, the less that is both distinctive and interesting has tended to remain in his thought thus purified. This is particularly true of those aspects of his work which are the subject matter of the present study. It emerges on such interpretations, for example, that Nietzsche anticipated Wittgenstein in pointing out that grammar sometimes misleads us into certain philosophical misconceptions, or that he advocates a naturalized approach to epistemology, based on provisional and revisable hypotheses subject to empirical confirmation or disconfirmation, or that he rejects the concept of facts the obtaining of which might be radically recognition-transcendent. All of these claims have a basis in Nietzsche's writings, but there does remain the suspicion that the points he is taken to be making have been formulated more clearly, and argued for more perspicuously, by Wittgenstein, Popper, and various contemporary anti-realists.

It is partly for reasons such as this and partly because such interpretations seem to excise, or leave as idle embellishment, so much of what is characteristic of his writings that other partisans of Nietzsche reject any such attempt to make him 'respectable'. The very features which render these writings unacceptable to more traditionally minded thinkers are here taken to embody precisely the essence of Nietzsche's 'critique' of that tradition. Such features are, for example, the aphoristic, allusive, and sometimes elusive character of many of the works published by himself, their often highly rhetorical—relative to philosophical conventions—style, the frequently personal, *ad hominem*, nature of his attacks, their irony, sarcasm, and irreverence, and finally, the very inconsistency of many of his pronouncements with one another. All or some of these characteristics are seen as constituting the heart of his 'critique' of the 'ascetic' practices of traditional philosophy: its concern with definitions, with logical argument, with consistency, with clarity and explicitness, and its preference for the literal over the metaphorical (both of these terms, of course, being defined in terms of—historically changing—standard usage). It seems to this reader that at least some of these points also have a warrant in Nietzsche's texts. But it is equally clear that an interpretation which focuses mainly or even exclusively on these aspects of his writings, while it may or may not be interesting in its own right, has some difficulty if it wishes to convince us either that what Nietzsche is doing has any relevance to the more traditional concerns of philosophy, or that it can be seen as a critique of these concerns or of particular ways of pursuing them. For it would seem that merely doing something *different* (even if under the same name) from what philosophers have been doing no more constitutes a *critique* of philosophy, or of particular philosophies, than watching films represents a critique, or engages in any interesting way with, a generally more rule-governed and, if you wish, 'ascetic', activity like playing the classical piano. This is not to say that watching films may not sometimes, and for some people always, be more enjoyable than piano playing. But it is hard to see how an activity or a position can be seen as engaging with or criticizing another, unless it makes statements or employs methods which can be recognized as *relevant* and worth taking seriously by those ostensibly addressed by it. It will be a central hermeneutic hypothesis guiding the present interpretation of Nietzsche that he does really wish to engage critically with those whom he persistently appears to criticize.

It is, no doubt, perfectly respectable to refuse such a critical engagement—there are many people, after all, who, in most circumstances, do not experience a particular fascination with the traditional questions of epistemologists and metaphysicians. And it is quite consistent to consider, as Richard Rorty does in his more recent writings, the appropriate response to those questions to be simply 'the recommendation that we in fact *say* little about these topics, and see how we get on', for 'our purposes would be served best by ceasing to see truth as a deep matter'.[2] This is arguably Nietzsche's own 'method' in *parts* of his published writings. But it requires only little reflection to see that for this recommendation to exercise any attraction at all—at least in civilizations in which the very concept of culture is still strongly, if often subliminally, linked with the tradition Rorty polemicizes against (and was so even more in Nietzsche's time)—it needs to be complemented by a convincing and insightful account of *why* 'the nature of truth' is irrelevant to 'our purposes', and indeed an account of *what* purposes 'truth' has been supposed to be essential to since Socrates inaugurated the quest for it. But as soon as we attempt to tell such a story, as Nietzsche does, we would seem to be back on familiar territory— for we cannot embark upon it without, among other things, offering a plausible description both of 'our purposes' and of precisely what concept of truth is supposedly irrelevant to them. We shall pursue these points further at a later stage. For the moment, I should like to mention another consideration which seems to me pertinent to an assessment of Nietzsche's work.

The various responses mentioned so far are largely characteristic of the reception of his work within the Schools. But Nietzsche is one of those thinkers whose readership and influence has, over the last century or so, extended very far beyond the confines of academic philosophy and indeed has probably been greater outside than within. It is hardly disputable that this influence has been at least partly due to the fact that he has been perceived as making insightful substantive claims about a variety of issues that have

---

[2] Richard Rorty, *Contingency, Irony, and Solidarity* (Cambridge, 1989), 8.

been, at one time or another, of concern to many people. These include, arguably, his analysis of modern European culture as 'decadent', his account of 'pessimistic religions' as symptoms of 'weakness' and usually expressive of *ressentiment*, as well as the connections he draws between the general cultural conditions he analyses and criticizes and what might be called an intellectual paradigm characteristic, according to him, of most Western thought since Plato, a paradigm he labels the 'ascetic ideal'. It is these apparently substantive claims about the world, as well, of course, as Nietzsche's alternative 'ideals' which he sets against European 'decadence', which have been largely responsible for his great popular influence and his wide readership. Any interpretation which is to be of interest beyond the confines of those institutions whose occupational concerns lie in the study or production of written words is well advised to take account of this fact. It is certainly *possible*, given sufficient determination and a sufficiently strong will to ignore many things he says, to read Nietzsche as being concerned exclusively with a certain thesis about the role of metaphors in language, or as not making any substantive claims at all, or as merely parodying and playing with various elements of available 'discourses', but such a reading would not only leave the specificities of very large areas of his writings unaccounted for or under-interpreted, it would also render him uninteresting to most of his readers, who have felt that he has something to say on issues which are of importance to them (in contradistinction to issues which *ought* to be of importance to them according to one or another philosophical or literary school).

Nevertheless, each of the standard responses to Nietzsche's work I have outlined seems to me to capture an important element of his thought—that is to say, each of them, properly understood, is warranted by the texts. It will be argued in this study that—for example—the last-mentioned, 'popular', reading of Nietzsche as primarily concerned with questions of value and as a 'philosopher of culture' is in an important sense indeed correct. He announces as one of his main tasks the 'calling into question' (GM iii.24) of certain values and theories of value which he believes have dominated Western civilization since Plato. Prominent among them are those theories which have construed the good as a real property, either inherent *in rebus* or subsistent *ante res*. Such theories have generally conceived of the good for human beings as involving the recognition of, and the acting for the sake of, such 'objective' values. Moreover, the historically most influential variants of this type of theory—Platonism, Aristotelianism, and mainstream Christianity—have held that the *telos* of human beings lies ultimately in the intuitive, contemplative grasping of a real subsistent Good *ante res* (see Chapters 5.1 and 5.3). Human life and human actions themselves are seen here as being of value to the extent that they participate in such an objective good, or aspire towards it— it is thus, in this sense, an 'external', ontologically perceiver-independent good which is regarded as giving value to and 'justifying' human life and actions. As we shall see in Chapter 3.2, Nietzsche argues obscurely but ingeniously that the basic thought, or better, mode of experience, which expresses itself in such theories has also informed many practices and evaluative hierarchies which prima facie seem quite unrelated to it. In particular, the value that has been accorded in Western culture to 'truth' sought for its own sake (either in metaphysics or in science) is, according to the later Nietzsche, historically *and* logically closely connected with it. Indeed, for him, both the belief in objective or real value and what he calls the 'will to truth' manifest a more general psychological disposition which he designates the 'ascetic ideal'. This ideal usually involves a particular sort of self-deception (*Selbstbetrügerei*, GM i.13) referred to by Nietzsche as *ressentiment*. *Ressentiment* is a condition in which a certain apparent good is desired by an individual avowedly for its own sake, but in fact in order to 'negate' or denigrate something else which is perceived as hostile or oppressive to that individual. The 'other' which the ascetic ideal, according to Nietzsche, negates or devalues, whether in the form of religion narrowly defined, or realist ethics, or in the form of the 'will to truth', is 'life' (GM iii.11)—which means, among other things, that realm of continuously changing, sensible particulars which confronts us in everyday experience. Obviously, all of these claims and the concepts they involve require, and will be given, considerable explanation and elaboration. I have introduced them here in outline merely to indicate that I consider them to be at the very centre of the later Nietzsche's philosophical concerns and that the 'popular' reading, to the extent that it recognizes this (as it generally does), will be vindicated in this study.

The apparently psychological—even psychologizing—character of the claims just mentioned is shared by many other reflections of

Nietzsche's on epistemological and metaphysical questions. In a philosophical climate in which the distinction between psychological and logical issues has become something of an orthodoxy, this may be taken to disqualify them as prime examples of *ignoratio elenchi*. However, it will be maintained here that—whether accepted or not—these reflections are far from irrelevant. For Nietzsche's most interesting arguments in this area belong (to use a later distinction) not to genetic, but to descriptive psychology or phenomenology (cf. JGB 23 and 186, where he characterizes his task as 'psychological' and, in the first instance, 'descriptive'). Prominent among those of his claims which are both psychological and of epistemological relevance is his analysis of the standards of validation accepted by metaphysicians—and some philosophical anti-metaphysicians—as determined by their independently identifiable 'ruling drives'—their dominant desires (WM 677, see Chapter 4.4). The characteristic rhetorical, sometimes pamphlet-like, sometimes frivolous, often 'anti-philosophical' style of much of the work Nietzsche himself published is, it will be argued here, explicable partly as a result of these psychological tenets concerning the role of 'ruling drives' in philosophy and concerning the will to truth as the 'core' of the ascetic ideal, and partly from his own values which, with some important qualifications, are radically opposed to the dispositions which are represented by that ideal. The published works thus frequently manifest his refusal to take seriously the—according to him—pretence to 'cold, pure, divinely unconcerned dialectics' (JGB 5) of philosophers:

I fight all the tartuffery of false scientific manners [*Wissenschaftlichkeit*]:

1. in the demonstration, if it does not correspond to the genesis of thoughts;

2. in the claims to methods that are perhaps not yet possible at a certain stage of science;

3. in the claims to objectivity, to cold impersonality, where, as in the case of all valuations, we describe ourselves and our inner experiences in a couple of words. (WM 424)

Among the values and dispositions which Nietzsche's published works not only advocate, but exemplify through their style and manner of composition, are a passionate intensity, an affirmation of the flux of appearances, irony towards the 'tartuffery' of piety (including the piety of 'false scientific manners'), a provocativeness

which deliberately courts rejection, misunderstanding and misap-
propriation, an independence which cultivates the heroic posture
of 'standing alone', but also, very noticeably, a psychological
'honesty' (*Redlichkeit*) which does not attempt to blur distinctions
but insists on them and strives to make them explicit, often by using
concrete historical or literary examples. To this extent, his published works are indeed often closer to 'literature' than to philosophy as traditionally conceived, and it is also correct to say that
the literary character of those works is essential to Nietzsche's
endeavour. But both the philosophers who dismiss him for this
reason and the anti-rationalist apologists who wish to appropriate
him on the same grounds tend to ignore the fact that these 'literary'
aspects of his work are, in part, based on psychological and epistemological claims (concerning the 'will to truth' and the standards of
validation employed in philosophy) whose truth, in some recognizable and fairly substantial sense, they presuppose and for which he
has reasons which can be identified, and sometimes reconstructed,
such as to be recognizable as *relevant* (and perhaps as plausible) by
those against whom they are directed. To be sure, any such grounds
he may have for any of his claims must be problematic in the light
of his own pronouncements concerning the role of 'ruling drives' in
philosophy. It has often been observed that there seems to be a self-
referential paradox in saying, for example, that 'all philosophical
positions are held on the strength of standards of validation whose
relevance is relative to their adherents' dominant drives/desires/
values'. What, in that case, is the status and the force of this
statement itself? We shall examine this and related issues at length
in Chapters 4.3 and 4.4. Here as elsewhere it will be seen that
logical argument is as important to Nietzsche's enterprise as its
literary aspect—indeed, the latter is in an important sense based on
the former.

One occasionally hears it said that any interpretation which sees
'traditional' philosophical argumentation as crucial to what
Nietzsche is doing thereby renders his work subject to the very
'ascetic ideal' he attacks. But a careful reading of the texts shows
that what he criticizes in what he calls the ascetic ideal is ultimately
not traditional forms of argumentation, but rather the overriding
value accorded by that ideal to the attaining of truth, ostensibly for
its own sake (see Chapter 3.2). Indeed, if he were to 'criticize' and
reject such argumentation *per se* as 'ascetic', he would hardly be a

very interesting thinker. In order not to fall subject to his own criticism, he would have to confine himself to statements and *schwärmerische* effusions which *could* not be cast in the form of what would normally be regarded as a plausible, or even a valid, argument. As most of us know, prolonged exposure to ostensibly assertoric discourses of this nature tends to be far from stimulating. To the extent that they succeed in retaining our interest at all, it is because we continue to hope that some of the statements[3] made or implied are plausible (i.e. likely to be true) on the strength of criteria we normally employ (which are the only ones we have).

In the present study it will be argued that the characteristic features of Nietzsche's work can only be interestingly explained with reference to his belief in the truth (in a sense to be elucidated) of certain psychological and epistemological 'hypotheses'. It therefore falls largely within the second category of responses to his work I have mentioned—what one might call the reconstructionist response. It is to this extent quite unapologetically an exercise in 'philosophical labouring' (JGB 211). It should be evident from what has been said so far that such an interpretation relates only to *one* aspect of his work—although a very fundamental one—and that it does not commit one to the idea (false, I believe) that Nietzsche's main concern is to establish the truth of various philosophical theses. Rather, such an approach is quite compatible with the recognition that his ultimate concerns are not theoretical ones; but they arguably *involve* certain theoretical positions, and these are the subject matter of the present study.

Besides the psychologico-epistemological considerations which, I have maintained, lie at the centre of Nietzsche's later thought, there are a great many other apparent claims and arguments which seem to relate more directly to the traditional epistemological and metaphysical quandaries of philosophy. Many of these are only hinted at or stated bluntly in the works published by himself, but they occupy a proportionally much larger space, and are given rather more explanation, in his notebooks.[4] For this reason, a study

---

[3] e.g. statements of the form that such-and-such a mode of thinking is inimical to 'life'.

[4] These notebooks comprise, for the relevant period alone, six volumes of the new *Kritische Gesamtausgabe*, G. Colli and M. Montinari (eds.) (Berlin, 1967–), of his writings. A selection of some of the notes and fragments contained in them was first published under the title *Der Wille zur Macht* by Nietzsche's sister in 1901. The later, extended, edition of this selection, which first appeared in 1906, has been

of Nietzsche's thought on these issues which ignores the notebooks seems to me to deprive itself of its most extensive and potentially valuable source of material. Equally, of course, a reading which concentrates exclusively on the notebooks, or parts of them (as Heidegger does),[5] and does not continuously check and compare what is said in them with the published works, is questionable as an interpretation of *Nietzsche's* thought. The present study will make extensive use of the *Nachlass*, while attempting to avoid the inadequacies of that kind of approach. One very noticeable fact about the many notebook entries relating to epistemological and metaphysical questions in particular is that, despite their fragmentary character, they are generally more argumentative in a traditional sense and less 'rhetorical' than the corresponding passages in the published works. This seems to me to be one of the most important *textual* (i.e. other than philosophical) grounds supporting the interpretation offered here: Nietzsche believes he has *reasons*, which could in principle be recognized by the addressees of his criticisms, for being as ironical and dismissive about many traditional philosophical endeavours as he frequently is in the published works. Often these reasons are only presented with any degree of clarity in the notebooks.

So what are the ideas on epistemology and metaphysics we find in the later Nietzsche? There is, to begin with, a pervasive sceptical strand of thought. I subsume under this heading his remarks to the effect that various theories and beliefs about the world—both quite specific and highly general ones—are either not rationally justifiable or indeed incoherent or unintelligible. Among the targets of his criticisms here are a certain conception of the subject (as either mental substance or transcendental subject), the doctrine of substance *qua* substratum in which properties inhere, the belief in powers in 'external' objects, certain construals of volitional efficacy, the physics of mechanistic atomism, and the belief in the

published in a fairly reliable English translation as *The Will to Power*, W. Kaufmann (ed.) (New York, 1968). Most of the commentaries available in English, if they discuss notebook material at all, refer almost exclusively to the notes contained in this selection. As I shall hope to show, this has had detrimental effects on the interpretation of Nietzsche's thought concerning the issues we will be concerned with.

[5] Martin Heidegger, *Nietzsche* (Pfullingen, 1961), 2 vols. For Heidegger's extravagant claims concerning the importance of the notes contained in *Der Wille zur Macht*, see esp. i. 15–20.

explanatory character of Newtonian or Boscovichean forces. But there are also more general sceptical arguments concerning the rational justifiability of *any* beliefs about the nature of what we are accustomed to call the external world. Many of Nietzsche's arguments in these matters are highly interesting but not entirely original—they often have precedents in Descartes, Hume, Berkeley, Schopenhauer, and Lange. His criticism of 'force', for example, involves a particular conception of explanation—a fact interpreters have not always been alert to—and is clearly inspired by his reading of Boscovich, Schopenhauer, and contemporary philosophies of science like Fechner's and Lange's. The sceptical arguments mentioned above will be the subject of Chapter 2. Some of the issues raised there are still widely discussed today and I shall address Nietzsche's most comprehensive sceptical ideas partly by drawing upon, and defending them against, more recent views which are inimical to them (Chapter 2.3).

There is another type of sceptical thinking in Nietzsche which he also applies to most of the items of belief mentioned above and which has no such historical precedents. It might be characterized in general terms as proceeding from the assumption of the practical utility of these beliefs, together with certain other premises, to the conclusion that they are unlikely to be true. This sceptical argument from utility, as I shall call it, is closely connected with various claims we find in his writings concerning 'conditions of existence' within which human beings have had to maintain themselves, and which have constituted constraints on the evolution of their 'organs of knowledge'. These naturalizing epistemological ideas and their relation, if any, to modern evolutionary epistemology will be discussed in detail in Chapters 4.1 and 4.2. It will emerge there, among other things, that the 'evolutionary' strand of thought is incompatible with some of his other sceptical reflections. But such incompatibilities by themselves (obviously) neither force us to dismiss both nor any particular one of the incompatible statements. Which of them, if any, we accept depends rather on the cogency of these claims considered separately. (To say this is by no means to ignore the fact that the concept of cogency becomes itself problematic in Nietzsche.)

Some of Nietzsche's sceptical arguments involve a distinction (which he draws explicitly) between two conceptions of truth. There is a sense of 'truth'—which I, following him (WM 515), will call conditional truth—which is predicated of statements[6] that ideally satisfy the criteria of acceptability employed in formal or natural science. But he sometimes acknowledges another sense of 'truth'—metaphysical truth (WM 519)—which would pertain to propositions that describe reality, or some part of it, by predicating intrinsic properties of it which it, either always or at some particular time, 'in itself' has, and which may conceivably be different from those predicated in conditionally true propositions. However, we also find a prominent strand of thought in the later writings which denies the very intelligibility of the concept of metaphysical truth which is presupposed by Nietzsche's more comprehensive sceptical reflections. This element in his later philosophy may appropriately be called anti-metaphysical or anti-essentialist (although these labels by themselves are not very informative). It is often referred to, but rarely does one find a clear exposition of what exactly it amounts to, or indeed by what reasoning Nietzsche arrives at it. Yet the notebooks in particular give us, I shall argue, fairly good indications as to what this reasoning is. I shall attempt to show in Chapter 3.1 that it proceeds, not from an investigation into the second-order concept of truth, but rather from an analysis of concepts like 'real object' and 'essence' or 'nature' as relative to the representations, interests, and concerns of affective 'subjects' (who are neither Kantian or Schopenhauerian transcendental subjects nor attribute-supporting substrata of mental states). For Nietzsche, it is unintelligible to speak of 'objective reality' without at least implicit reference to interest-involving subjective perspectives within which what are called real objects appear or could appear. I shall attempt to elucidate his arguments to this effect through a detailed analysis of a number of *Nachlass* fragments and through contrasting these with various alternative accounts of 'objective reality' as found in Locke and Kant and in more recent philosophers inspired by Kant. It will be seen that Nietzsche—

---

[6] Throughout this study, I shall follow ordinary usage in speaking of statements, assertions, claims, beliefs, or judgements as being (putatively) true or false. But I shall also often apply these terms to propositions. There has been much debate in recent philosophy of logic and of language as to whether the truth bearers are intensional items (such as propositions, or Fregean thoughts, or types of Husserlian intentional acts), or rather types or tokens of sentences. While I shall generally proceed on the former assumption, the point is not central to many of the issues we shall be discussing and much of what will be said could be rephrased in a linguo-centric idiom.

questionably—takes the rejection of the concept of a non-relational constitution in itself, and hence of 'metaphysical truth', to follow from his analysis of objective reality.

Given this rejection of the very notion of metaphysical or absolute truth which is involved in his sceptical arguments, the question will arise what status the latter are to be accorded within his later philosophy. It will be suggested that Nietzsche is not a sceptic and that the role of his sceptical ideas should be understood as part of his endeavour to undermine and discredit the 'ascetic ideal' and its adherents. In other words, they can be seen as attempts to show that, even if the concept of absolute truth were intelligible, specific claims to truth in this sense, at least as regards a putative 'external' or objective sphere, are not rationally justified and probably not rationally justifiable. However, none of his sceptical arguments depend on his views concerning the ascetic ideal and they can consequently in principle be addressed without reference to these.

Many of Nietzsche's ideas mentioned so far relate to what philosophers usually call the objective or external world. But it is well known that the majority of his reflections—certainly in the published works—are concerned with what he himself often refers to as 'inner experience'. We find a great many apparent claims in these writings about human desires, intentions, and emotions—i.e. about items which traditionally have been taken to be or to involve mental states of a certain character. His many pronouncements concerning the ascetic and Christian ideals, to the extent that they invoke the concept of *ressentiment* (and hence of self-deception), also appear to include certain tenets about the specific nature of various 'inner experiences'. Moreover, his works contain an analysis of human agency in terms of what he calls a will to power, and this phrase expresses, at least in one of its senses, a psychological concept (it will be examined in Chapter 4.3). All of these claims are prima facie problematic if Nietzsche intends either his sceptical or his anti-essentialist ideas to apply to 'inner experience'. If his scepticism relates also to the latter, what warrant is there, for example, for his assertions to the effect that the Christian ideal always, and the 'will to truth' usually, involve *in fact ressentiment*, i.e. self-deception? More fundamentally, what sense is there in saying that *x* is *really y* (e.g. that the ascetic ideal is *really* a symptom of 'weakness') if the notion of a constitution in itself is itself 'nonsense'? These questions are particularly pressing if, as the present interpretation will suggest, Nietzsche's remarks on the ascetic ideal and the will to truth represent the fulcrum of his later philosophy. The issue concerning the nature of inner experience is further complicated by the fact that he in many places seems to advocate the anti-Cartesian and proto-Freudian thesis that there are causally efficacious occurrences which are both distinctly psychic or mental (e.g. FW 357) and radically unconscious, that is, neither present nor accessible to self-consciousness. We shall have to ask not only whether this supposition is coherent, but also whether it is compatible with his anti-essentialism and whether, given his own epistemological criticisms, he could have any evidence for the claims he seems to make concerning the character of these unconscious processes. All of these issues will be discussed in Chapter 5.

In the final chapter we shall turn to an examination of one of the most puzzling and controversial aspects of his later philosophy—the apparent metaphysics which is presented, in outline, in many of the *Nachlass* fragments and adumbrated in some passages in the published works. This 'metaphysics' seems to involve an ontology of interacting 'quanta of force' which are characterized exclusively by relational properties. It is introduced in some places as an explanatory hypothesis which, Nietzsche suggests, is required to supplement and 'complete' (WM 619) the victorious Newtonian or Boscovichean dynamist physics of fields of force. The reason why such a metaphysical complement might be thought to be needed is that these physics are, to Nietzsche, not explanatory at all—for they leave the *modus operandi* of 'force' unspecified. (Needless to say, such statements involve a particular conception of explanation; see Chapter 2.1.) Nietzsche designates the effective force which constitutes the force-quanta in his apparent ontology as 'will to power'. It is evident that *if* this concept is indeed to provide an explanatory complement to the 'descriptions' of Newtonian and post-Newtonian physics, it has to provide a specification of what precisely the efficacy of force-quanta consists in. It is not an easy task to find such a specification in Nietzsche, but it will be argued that some of the *Nachlass* notes supply important clues in this respect which admit of further elaboration (see Chapter 6.1).

Finally, we shall address two central questions raised by the *soi-disant* metaphysics of the will to power. First, we will have to ask whether it is coherent. It is clear that the notion of 'quanta' which are constituted exclusively by continuously changing relational properties accords well with Nietzsche's anti-essentialism (his denial of metaphysical truth, in the sense in which this term is used here). On the other hand, it is far less obvious whether this conception is itself an intelligible (hence explanatory) one. Secondly, we need to ask what the *point* of offering an apparently explanatory metaphysical hypothesis could be for Nietzsche, given his views concerning what the desire for such explanations is indicative of, and in the light of his statements elsewhere concerning the 'naïvety' of all such explanatory attempts.

It can be seen even from this brief outline of the following discussion of Nietzsche's ideas on epistemology and metaphysics that his thought regarding these matters is highly complex. It contains a number of different lines of thought, some of which are not easily reconciled with one another. This study will follow the reconstructionist approaches in that it will endeavour to clarify and elaborate upon Nietzsche's often fragmentary remarks. Unlike some of the interpretations which have pursued a similar aim, it will also go beyond exposition and critically examine each of the clearly identifiable major strands in his later philosophy on these matters in some detail. I shall concur with the recent anti-rationalist readings of Nietzsche that at least some of the inconsistencies in his thought cannot be eliminated without thereby also excising elements of his philosophy which play a major role in it and are prominent in the texts. I shall also agree that we can learn from these inconsistencies—although *what* can be learnt from them is, I believe, rather different from what some of these interpretations have suggested.

If one surveys the recent literature on the later Nietzsche's ideas on epistemology and metaphysics, it is noticeable that, to the extent that it has attempted to render them consistent, it has been forced to ignore at least some prominent and recurrent aspects of his work. This seems to me to be also true, despite their merits, of each of the three major recent studies in English which deal centrally with the issues under consideration here: Richard Schacht's *Nietzsche* (1983), Rüdiger Grimm's *Nietzsche's Theory of Knowledge* (1977), and Maudemarie Clark's *Nietzsche on Truth and Philosophy* (1990). While I shall refer to them at various points in the text, it is perhaps apposite to give a brief discussion of their main theses here, which may help to acquaint the non-specialist reader with some of the central issues at stake in recent debates on Nietzsche's philosophy.

Schacht interprets Nietzsche as an epistemologist and a philosophical 'cosmologist' (p. 188) concerned with establishing what the 'world's basic nature' is (p. 202)—in other words, as a thinker whose project lies in the mainstream of Western philosophy since the Greeks. He sees Nietzsche's criticisms of various concepts employed by metaphysicians not as sceptical in nature, nor ultimately as anti-rationalist or anti-metaphysical (that is, as rejecting the very idea of 'the world's basic nature'). Rather, Nietzsche intends to replace these inadequate conceptions by an 'explanatory hypothesis' which, although neither final nor 'rigorously demonstrable' nor 'completely adequate to reality' (p. 200), yet can make a good claim to represent a more apt, just, or adequate (pp. 99, 104) characterization of the basic nature of reality than the available rival theories. Its aptness is sharply to be distinguished from purely pragmatic considerations such as 'value for life' (p. 201) and rather consists in its putatively identifying 'certain fundamental characteristics' of reality 'which do not change in nature but only in expression' (p. 197). To say this is of course to accept 'that there is something [. . .] which may or may not be comprehended at all adequately' (p. 104). Reality is distinct from our interpretations of it (p. 189) and Nietzsche's alleged claim to be characterizing with relative adequacy the 'states of affairs in the world' (p. 108) thus preserves 'something of the basic idea underlying the correspondence account of truth' (ibid.). As to the criteria of adequacy relevant here, Schacht maintains that Nietzsche's cosmology of the will to power is relatively more adequate than rival theories on the grounds that it is distinguished by parsimony of explanatory principles as well as by its 'fit' with experience and by the fact that it is not affected by the criticisms various rival cosmologies are subject to—in particular, the argument from utility (e.g. p. 137; the label is not used by Schacht). According to him, Nietzsche considers the task of the 'coming philosophers'—and his own—to be ultimately a very traditional one: what is to be of primary concern to them is the attainment of truth, which is 'an adequacy-relation between characterizations of reality and the character of that reality on a more fundamental level than others are willing and able to reach' (p. 110).

Schacht's study is an impressively comprehensive and scholarly work, and yet he does not seem to me to take full account of a number of important aspects of Nietzsche's later writings, a circumstance which arguably has deleterious consequences for his general interpretation of them. He pays little attention to the crucial third book of *Zur Genealogie der Moral*, in which Nietzsche identifies the will to truth as the 'core' of the ascetic ideal and formulates his task as that of calling into question the value of truth and of the belief that 'truth is divine' (GM iii.24). However these statements are to be precisely understood, they seem difficult to reconcile with Schacht's fundamental claim that the overriding concern of Nietzsche's 'coming philosophers' is the quest for truth (unless this claim is very heavily qualified). Secondly, Schacht does not accept that there is a general sceptical line of thought in the later Nietzsche. While it is easy to see the rationale for such a denial—the incompatibility of these sceptical ideas with other things Nietzsche says—their presence seems to me too pervasive (e.g. FW 374, KGW VII.3.36.30, WM 473) for them to be ignored without distorting his thought. On the other hand, Schacht seems to me to be rather too generous towards some of Nietzsche's critical arguments against various traditional theories. He accords a central place to what I have called the argument from utility and appears to endorse it. Here it will be argued, by contrast, that this and related arguments represent one of Nietzsche's weakest critical strategies. Further problems arise with Schacht's construal of the will to power as an explanatory 'cosmological' hypothesis intended to characterize certain unchanging aspects of the 'world's basic nature'. This does not allow him to account convincingly for Nietzsche's remarks concerning the way 'ruling drives' and 'taste' are bound up with *all* 'interpretations of the world', including the one apparently suggested by himself (e.g. WM 418 and 677, FW 39), nor for his statements to the effect that concepts like that of an 'essence' or a constitution in itself are 'nonsense'. Whatever the exact import of these remarks, Nietzsche is clearly making a stronger point than the somewhat obvious one that the objects of *ordinary experience* 'have the properties and indeed the identities they do only by virtue of the relations in which they stand to other such "things" and to us' (p. 141). But even assuming that the will to power really is the basis of an explanatory cosmological theory, Schacht seems to me to construe this notion in such a way that, on

Nietzsche's own conception of explanation, it would *not* be explanatory. Since Schacht denudes terms like 'will' and 'power' of many of their usual connotations and interprets the will to power simply as a 'dispositional tendency' towards 'ordering transformation' (pp. 220, 228–9), this notion can hardly be said to explain change, but merely offers an extremely general description of it. It does not tell us anything about *how* change is effected. To say that there is a dispositional tendency towards ordering transformation is no more to explain change than the fact that opium makes one fall asleep is explained by saying that there is a *virtus dormitiva* in opium.

Rüdiger Grimm's study emphasizes precisely those aspects in Nietzsche's writings which Schacht finds most difficulty in accounting for. He concentrates on those remarks (especially in the *Nachlass*) in which Nietzsche seems to maintain that the very concept of a basic or ultimate nature of the world is unintelligible (e.g. pp. 62–3). Far from retaining the essentials of the correspondence theory of truth, Nietzsche (according to Grimm) rejects this theory and embraces instead a different account of truth according to which 'the criterion of truth is the enhancement of the feeling of power' (WM 534). Nietzsche's claim is that 'I call something "true" if it increases my will to power, my "Machtgefühl". Conversely, something is "false" if it decreases my will to power' (p. 19). Consequently, a belief can be 'true' for one person whose 'will to power' it increases, and 'false' for another person whom it 'weakens'. A belief may thus be 'true' and 'false' for different individuals at the same time, or for the same individual at different times (p. 27). This applies also to Nietzsche's own apparently metaphysical doctrine that 'the world is will to power' (p. 28).

There are clearly passages in Nietzsche which permit the sort of construal Grimm gives them. However, the philosophical problems with such an interpretation are considerable. One obvious objection is that it requires us to accept that two human beings can have the same thoughts (say, 'there are trees'), but these thoughts would actually *be* true (rather than just mistakenly considered to be true) for one, but not for the other. This would involve the dubiously coherent, and at any rate overwhelmingly implausible, assumption that, while they can think the same thoughts and communicate with one another, they actually find themselves confronted with different 'objective realities'. One might reply to this objection that

Nietzsche (on Grimm's reading) just defines truth in such a way that the truth-conditions of a proposition or thought about the world do not just involve some state of affairs obtaining or being 'given' in sensory or quasi-sensory experience. They also involve its being apprehended in a manner which includes a certain subjective hedonic character, which Nietzsche calls a 'feeling of power'. This would perhaps allow him to say that the same proposition, thus identified, might be 'true' for one individual and 'false' for another, or 'true' *and* 'false' for the same individual at different times. To say that it is true at a given time is simply to say that the state of affairs it represents is experienced in such a way as to be associated with a 'feeling of power'. Grimm is not entirely explicit as to whether he would accept this paraphrase, or something like it, but some of his statements suggest that he would. He says, for instance, that on Nietzsche's view 'we call something true' because 'we *experience* some increase or enhancement of our will to power' (p. 22, my emphasis), and that each organism is '*its own standard* for determining the growth or increase of its power' (ibid., my emphasis). The problems of such a view are obvious. It would, in effect, not allow us, or Nietzsche, to make a distinction which we make all the time, namely between 'seems true now' and 'is true'. If the proposition 'human beings are able to fly by flapping their arms at moderate speed' was entertained by me yesterday and seemed to enhance my 'feeling of power', then it *was* true (for me) yesterday; if the same proposition is entertained by me now after I have performed the experiment by jumping from a second floor window, and if it now, as is to be expected, makes me feel rather weak, it *is* false (for me) now. If Nietzsche were to operate with some such radically revisionist concept of truth, his criticisms of various metaphysical, epistemological, and ethical views would all be instances of the type 'it seems to me now that *p*', for example, 'it seems to me now that correspondence truth is incoherent' or 'it seems to me now that the ascetic ideal is a symptom of weakness'. If he were saying no more than that, none of his statements would conflict or compete with anything other philosophers or indeed theologians have maintained—he would not even engage with their claims (cf. Chapter 6.3). Thus, this interpretation of Nietzsche's ideas on truth is a good illustration of the more general point I made earlier: if he radically rejected the concepts of truth and argumentation traditionally employed by philosophers, nothing of what he said would even constitute a *criticism* of their theories and practices—he would simply be doing something different.

Grimm does not seem to be explicitly aware of this difficulty, but some of his formulations indicate that he does wish to avoid the conclusions which have been pointed out above. For he sometimes paraphrases Nietzsche's view rather differently, suggesting that a belief is 'true' for an individual if it *actually* serves to increase the power of the individual who holds and 'implements' it (pp. 19, 27, 28). One problem with this alternative definition is that it is circular—the *definiendum* is assumed in the *definiens*, for it in effect explicates '*p* is true' as 'the belief that *p* is true will increase my power'. Moreover, whether a belief which I now hold really will serve to increase my power in the future—i.e. whether it is useful in a certain sense—is usually entirely independent of any 'feelings' with which it may now be associated for me. It generally depends on the belief's involving or being based on propositions which correctly predict future events, and the criteria of correctness in question here seem to have nothing to do with any 'feelings of power' on my part. It therefore appears that 'truth' as a certain kind of utility (increasing power) presupposes another, more fundamental, concept of truth involving the satisfaction of certain conditions—for example, empirical confirmability or predictive success—which, it appears, can be explicated without reference to any such notions as 'feeling of power'. Whether this really is the case will be the subject of our discussions in Chapters 3.1, 4.3, and 4.4. One of the questions obviously pertinent to these discussions will be what expressions like 'feeling of power' and indeed 'will to power' actually mean in Nietzsche. Grimm's statements, since they do not pursue these conceptual issues in much detail, give us little help here. But it would certainly seem that he himself employs a concept of truth more substantial than, and at variance with, that (or those) he ascribes to Nietzsche when he maintains (questionably) that 'the' correspondence theory of truth is inconsistent (p. 50), or that 'the traditional concept of truth constrains life, hampers it from fully expressing its ownmost possibilities' (p. 25). Does he really mean to say no more than that entertaining the thought 'the correspondence theory of truth is inconsistent' is associated, at the time of writing, with an increased feeling of power on his part? And, circularity apart, does he not wish to express more than the expectation that believing the statement 'the traditional concept of truth constrains life [in general]' will increase his power in the future?

Maudemarie Clark's recent book on Nietzsche in some respects shares the concerns of the present study more than the interpretations previously mentioned. Her project is very much a philosophical-critical one and she, as it were, approaches Nietzsche from the 'outside', interrogating his statements from a point of view which, in her case, is strongly influenced by recent pragmatist and anti-realist philosophers. The well-known danger of this kind of non-contextual approach is that it more often than not does violence to the texts. Unfortunately, I do not think that Clark has succeeded in entirely avoiding this danger. Her most original and startling exegetical claim is that Nietzsche's views on truth and metaphysics changed dramatically between *Jenseits von Gut und Böse* and *Zur Genealogie der Moral* (e.g. p. 96). Before that point he held, according to her, 'the thesis that human knowledge falsifies reality' (ibid.). However, as he began to realize the consequences of his rejection of the concept of a thing in itself (p. 109), he saw that it implied that 'our best empirical theories' cannot be 'radically false' (p. 124, cf. p. 54). Much depends here, of course, on precisely what concept of a 'thing in itself' Nietzsche is taken to have rejected in his last writings. According to Clark, he remains committed to what she calls common sense realism, that is, to the view that 'the world is independent of the actual *existence* of knowers' (p. 45). The world 'exists whether or not there is any knowledge of it' and it has 'a nature or constitution whether or not anyone actually knows what it is' (ibid.). Nietzsche's critique of the thing in itself amounts rather to a rejection of 'metaphysical realism', a theory which is characterized by Clark in a number of different formulations. It is said to be the view that 'the world's nature is independent of what *can be known of it*' (ibid.). In another formulation, she suggests that, for the metaphysical realist, the truth about the world may not only transcend what can be known by our finite cognitive capacities—which common sense realism would also accept—but may also be such that 'our best standards of rational acceptability' are irrelevant to it. Such standards are, for instance, a theory's 'simplicity, coherence, explanatory power, predictive success' (p. 86). The later Nietzsche's critique of the notion of a thing in itself amounts, for Clark, to a denial of the 'possibility that a theory that gave *us* everything else we could want from a theory [. . .] might nevertheless fail to be true' (p. 86, my emphasis).

Clark's reading is ingenious, but it is subject to serious exegetical and philosophical objections. With respect to the former, it is very questionable whether Nietzsche would have changed his views as drastically as she suggests between 1886 and 1887 without there being any explicit acknowledgement of this anywhere in the texts. This is particularly unlikely in view of the fact that comparably significant earlier changes (after *Unzeitgemässe Betrachtungen* and *Die fröhliche Wissenschaft*) were repeatedly acknowledged and announced by him. Moreover, since we find in the notebook entries of 1887 and 1888 many notes in which he continues to attack 'common sense realism' (see Chapter 3.1) or to express radically sceptical ideas, Clark's reading would force us to conclude that Nietzsche continued to hold views in his notebooks which he rejected in his published writings—a somewhat unattractive hypothesis. Here as elsewhere in her study she seems to me hampered by her decision to use as her source exclusively the works published by Nietzsche himself. This has particularly detrimental effects for her treatment of his attack on the thing in itself. There is only one statement in the later published works to the effect that this concept is incoherent (JGB 16), and it is so brief and unexplained as to allow, by itself, for almost any interpretation. The *Nachlass*, by contrast, contains a large number of entries on this subject, and the relevant notes give us some enlightenment about Nietzsche's reasons for his claim and about which concept precisely is the object of his criticism. I shall argue in Chapter 3.1 that, in the light of these notes, Clark's reading is not tenable.

Philosophically, one problem with Clark's reading is that her two formulations of the doctrine Nietzsche is said to reject are not equivalent. With respect to the first formulation, it is doubtful whether anyone, including Kant, has avowedly held the view that the world's nature is 'independent of what can be known' by any *possible* knower. Her second formulation seems to imply that, for Nietzsche, there could be no truths which are not related to *our* cognitive interests and to the obtaining of which our ('shared') standards of rational acceptability might be irrelevant. The standards she actually mentions are some of those employed in natural science—most importantly, predictive success ('explanatory power'

in natural science largely *is* predictive power). But *if* it is intelligible
to suppose that the world has 'a nature or constitution whether or
not anyone actually knows what it is' (p. 45), then it is not clear
why this nature might not conceivably include features which are
not related to our (contingent) cognitive interests and hence not
capturable by means of the sort of theory she seems to have in
mind. These features might, for example, resemble secondary qualities to the extent that they are irrelevant to the prediction of events.
And there might conceivably be knowers with superior cognitive
capacities who, while being uninterested in prediction (since their
existence might not depend in the way ours does on successful
prediction), might yet have some kind of cognitive access, via
various quasi-perceptual states, to those qualitative features of
reality which elude us and to which the standards of rational
acceptability Clark mentions are simply irrelevant. If her reading of
Nietzsche were correct, he would have to maintain that it is incoherent to say that those conceivable beings have knowledge about
the world. This is a very unattractive position, but even if Nietzsche
did hold it, the conclusions from it which Clark attributes to him
would be illegitimate. She takes him to conclude from his rejection
of the thing in itself, as interpreted by her, that our best (present)
theory about the world *could* not be radically false (e.g. p. 98). But
this simply does not follow—Descartes's demon might have the
same cognitive interests we have and share the standards of rational
acceptability Clark lists (cf. Chapter 2.3).

Despite these serious problems in her interpretation, Clark's
study has many virtues. It is closely argued, and it offers, in particular, detailed and perceptive analyses of several texts, including
Nietzsche's early essay 'On Truth and Lie in a Non-Moral Sense',
which has received much attention in recent years. With regard to
this essay she shows convincingly that linguo-centric and anti-
rationalist interpretations such as Paul de Man's have failed to
grasp its point.[7] When Nietzsche in this early essay calls truth a
'host of metaphors' he is, as the immediate context shows very
clearly, not making a claim about literal or figurative *language*, but
about *perceptual contents*.[8] His illustration of Chladnian sound
figures in the sand makes it quite evident that Nietzsche, the philo-

---

[7] M. Clark, *Nietzsche on Truth and Philosophy* (Cambridge, 1990), 63–93. Cf.
Paul de Man, *Allegories of Reading* (New Haven and London, 1979), 103–18.
[8] Clark, *Nietzsche on Truth and Philosophy*, 78.

logist, is here using the term 'metaphor' itself metaphorically to denote what would normally or standardly be called an isomorphism (cf. Chapter 4.2).

Perhaps a few more words on de Man's academically fairly influential readings are in order, if only because one sometimes encounters similar remarks in other writings. Discussing Nietzsche's first book, *Die Geburt der Tragödie*, de Man maintains that 'all the authoritative claims that it seems to make can be undermined by means of statements provided by the text itself' (p. 117). Hence, 'the entire system of valorization at work in *The Birth of Tragedy* can be reversed at will' (p. 118). Nietzsche's discourse is 'fundamentally ironic' (p. 116) and 'resembles the endlessly repeated gesture of the artist "who does not learn from experience and always again falls in the same trap". What seems to be most difficult to admit is that this allegory of errors is the very model of philosophical rigor' (p. 118).

Let us grant de Man his central exegetical claim that this early work of Nietzsche's really does undermine its own statements— although a historically more aware reading, which took account of the textually attested influence of F. A. Lange's *Geschichte des Materialismus* on Nietzsche during the period in question, might come to a somewhat different conclusion. De Man hints that this fact would have relevance for philosophical discourse in general, for, he suggests, in *Die Geburt der Tragödie* we find 'the very model of philosophical rigor'. Yet, nothing in what de Man says goes to show any such thing. For the traditional philosopher, Nietzsche's statements conflicting with each other would simply show that he was an incompetent thinker. And such a philosopher might add that this estimation is confirmed by Nietzsche's style in that work, which is very far indeed from what would normally be called rigorous by philosophers. (Nietzsche himself later partly concurred with this estimate. In his 'Attempt at a Self-Criticism', added in 1886, he called it an 'impossible' and *schwärmerisches* book, 'without any will to logical cleanliness'.) Nietzsche's alleged self-undermining in *Die Geburt der Tragödie* or elsewhere *might* have some of the general relevance de Man wants to claim for it if, in each of the apparently incompatible pairs of statements, both thesis and antithesis could be proved to be true on independent grounds— somewhat in the manner Kant attempted, with questionable success, in his Antinomies—but de Man does not even begin such a task. The mere *presence* of 'incompatible, mutually self-destructive [*sic*] points of view' (p. 131) in Nietzsche, which is all de Man can be said to have shown even on a charitable reading, would be neither worrying nor interesting to traditional philosophy. De Man's approach thus has the weaknesses which so often beset anti-rationalist interpretations of Nietzsche: it claims a general critical relevance for his work, but its mode of interpretation in practice succeeds precisely in depriving it of any such relevance.

Throughout this introduction and indeed throughout this book it is assumed that there are some interpretations of Nietzsche's work which are clearly more adequate to it than others. This is quite compatible with the acknowledgement that there may not be a *unique* correct interpretation of them. However, this rather modest and seemingly unexceptionable claim appears to be denied by some of his readers. At the end of his essay on Nietzsche,[9] Jacques Derrida suggests that 'it is always possible' that the totality of Nietzsche's text 'means nothing at all or that it has no decidable meaning' (pp. 131–3). The reason for this appears to be that Nietzsche's texts—like most other sequences of written words—are 'detached [. . .] not only from the milieu that produced [them], but also from *any intention or meaning on Nietzsche's part*' (p. 125, my emphasis). Hence, 'the meaning [. . .] remain[s] in principle inaccessible' (ibid.). 'What if *Nietzsche himself* meant to say nothing, or at least not much of anything, or anything whatever?' (pp. 125–7, my emphasis). For all we know, the totality of Nietzsche's apparent statements may have been intended as parodies, even though this may not be announced or even hinted at anywhere in the texts. But even if it were thus announced, we would not know whether such a communication might not be a 'dissimulation' and, hence, entirely misleading (cf. pp. 135–7). Whatever the text *appears* to say may not be what is meant by Nietzsche, and this 'is tantamount to saying that there is no "totality of Nietzsche's text"' (p. 135). It is a consequence of this approach that the text—any text—is incapable of resisting any 'interpretation' whatever, since, by appealing to a possible but inaccessible 'intention or meaning' (p. 125) on the author's part, we may simply circumvent or neutralize what the texts on a certain '*stratum* of readability' (p. 129) *say.*

---

[9] Jacques Derrida, *Spurs. Nietzsche's Styles* (Chicago and London, 1979).

The critical assumptions betrayed by Derrida's statements[10] in this particular essay are highly peculiar and are in fact closely related to what is usually called the intentional fallacy. According to this critical approach, we have established the 'real' meaning of the text if our interpretation of it coincides with the intentions of the historical individual that produced it. But, Derrida's remarks suggest, these intentions are inaccessible—the text is 'detached' from them (p. 125)—hence it is possible that the meaning also remains 'in principle inaccessible' (ibid.).

Since the present study does not share these critical assumptions, it does not recognize the points made in Derrida's essay as a problem. It also does not share the model of human communication that essay embodies, a model which both systematically assumes dissimulation and seeks to arouse the suspicion of its presence (see esp. p. 137). There are indeed interesting questions which might be asked about the concept of 'freedom' adumbrated by Derrida, but to pursue them would lead beyond our present concerns.[11]

It is certainly arguable that we can only interpret a string of visual marks as a text to the extent that we, explicitly or implicitly, suppose them to have been produced intentionally. But the only intentions in which we are usually interested in the interpretation of philosophical or literary texts are those which are implied by the meanings of the words and sentences constituting them, and these meanings in turn are determined by public usage rather than by inaccessible and possibly diverging private intentions on the part of a historical individual (i.e. of the 'real' as opposed to the 'implied' author).[12] Where we have reason to suspect that non-standard or technical or non-assertoric usages are involved, these reasons, as

[10] I shall read Derrida's apparent assertions relating to the interpretation of Nietzsche's texts as precisely that—assertions. Some of his remarks hint somewhat heavy-handedly that they could also be read as parodic (p. 137). However, it is only as assertions that they have any relevance for the interpretation of texts other than *Spurs* itself.

[11] 'The hermeneutic project which postulates a true sense of the text is disqualified under this regime. Reading is *freed* from the horizon of the meaning or truth of being, *liberated* from the values of the product's production or the present's presence' (p. 107, my emphases). Nietzsche, who had a life-long interest in the psychology of different types of *Gelehrten*, as well as in the significance of the preoccupation with (negative) freedom in much modern thought (cf. WM 442, 776), would undoubtedly have found these remarks intriguing in both respects.

[12] It is true that we do often suppose the intentions of the author implied by a literary or philosophical text—who is of course a construct—to be rather similar to

well as our interpretations of those usages, require substantial and specific evidence in the texts themselves. That the meanings of words and sentences can, in the sense I have indicated, often (indeed with relatively recent texts in our native language *usually*) be 'read off' by us, because of our acquaintance with their normal usage, is admitted by Derrida himself (p. 129). It is only *because* of this knowledge on our part that we can recognize some usages as parodies and that 'dissimulation' becomes possible—it is only *possible* to dissimulate because words have standard, public, meanings which the dissimulator can, and needs to, utilize for his purposes.[13] When, in the following, I shall speak of an interpretation of 'Nietzsche', I shall mean, as most of his readers have done, an interpretation of the totality of his (later) texts in terms of meanings which are—usually—accessible, for they are embodied in a public language. It is on account of what these texts *say*, rather than for the occasions they may offer for associative 'liberated' word-play, that for more than a century most of Nietzsche's readers, including the writer of the present pages, have found them stimulating and of continuing interest.

those of its real author, but this assumption is neither essential, nor is its truth required, for interpreting the text as having a determinate meaning.

[13] Cf. Bernard Harrison's illuminating discussion of this and related issues in his *Inconvenient Fictions* (New Haven and London, 1991), esp. 137–40.

2

Scepticism

Nietzsche's reflections on epistemological and metaphysical questions are usually considered, with some prima facie plausibility, to fall into two distinct groups. There are those in which he *criticizes* various views that have been held in the history of philosophy concerning the nature of metaphysical reality and the nature and scope of our knowledge. On the other hand, he also appears to put forward *positive* tenets about these matters which, it might seem, he intends to replace the inadequate conceptions criticized by him.

Statements belonging to the first category pervade Nietzsche's writings of all periods with remarkable consistency (although they do undergo significant development), while his apparent positive claims are not only more sparse, but also change dramatically at various points in his philosophical career. Moreover, at least some of them are, on the face of it, difficult to reconcile with the negative strictures which he arrives at in the critical strand of his thinking. For these reasons, it seems most appropriate to begin these inquiries with an extensive discussion of the critical aspects of his later thought and to proceed from this to an interpretation and assessment of his apparent positive tenets, since it is arguably only in the light of the former that we can hope to grasp the latter's import and purpose.

The critical reflections which will primarily concern us in this study are those in which Nietzsche raises a variety of objections against the claim that we possess knowledge, either probable or certain, of a metaphysical kind—knowledge about that which exists in itself in some ultimate sense. These objections, which are usually found in their most developed form in the writings of the later period, can also roughly be divided into two broad groups which I propose to call 'sceptical' and 'anti-metaphysical' arguments respectively. In the light of recurrent disputes in the literature concerning Nietzsche's attitude to metaphysics, this classification may be thought to beg the question; I shall endeavour to vindicate it in what follows.

The two groups of arguments correspond roughly to what have traditionally been regarded as two necessary conditions for the application of the concept of knowledge. For a belief to qualify as knowledge it has usually been thought necessary that it be both justified and true. The sceptical line of thought in Nietzsche might be characterized as consisting in the attempt to show that we cannot in fact justify, or at least not rationally justify, many of the beliefs that commonly have been regarded as true by major philosophical traditions and by many non-philosophers. But we shall also subsume under this heading his assertions to the effect that certain widespread beliefs regarding the ultimate constitution of things not only cannot be rationally supported, but are in fact unintelligible.

The second strand of thought referred to above is directed against the notion of truth which is involved in the concept of knowledge when understood in a metaphysical sense. For Nietzsche, to assert that a statement is true because it represents a metaphysically substantial 'fact' or because what it states 'is the case' is ultimately incoherent. The reason why 'truth', if it is intended to have metaphysical import, fails to be intelligible when analysed properly is that the corresponding notion of 'something being the case' involves such concepts as 'nature in itself' and 'essence', and these, according to Nietzsche, are 'contradictory impossibilities'. It is evident that this anti-metaphysical line of thought in Nietzsche is considerably more radical—and also more original—than the sceptical arguments mentioned earlier. Let us, however, turn our attention to the latter group first. It will occupy the remainder of this chapter. Questions concerning the relation between these two major strands in Nietzsche's thought will be addressed at various later stages (esp. in Chapters 3.2, 5.3, 6.3).

1. SUBSTANCE AND CAUSE

Due to the 'aphoristic' nature of much of Nietzsche's later philosophy and to the fact that many of his epistemological reflections in particular are to be found only in fragments in his notebooks, there is neither an immediately evident structure connecting his various sceptical remarks, nor a textually obvious single origin or place of departure for his criticisms. Any order which a discussion like the present one necessarily imposes on them is, therefore, to some extent arbitrary. But it may be thought not entirely inappropriate to consider at the outset some of Nietzsche's remarks on one of the traditionally most central concepts in metaphysics—substance. The term 'substance', of course, has been given a number of related but different meanings in the course of the history of philosophy, and it or its synonyms have been thought indispensable for a variety of reasons. Aristotle, with whom the expression originates, uses it to mean the individual concrete thing,[1] the permanent substratum underlying the changing qualities of things,[2] and the logical subject of propositions.[3] At the founding moment of modern philosophy, Descartes reaffirms the centrality of substance. He defines it, first, as that in which properties inhere, although it can itself only be known by these properties: 'for by means of our natural light we know that a real attribute cannot be an attribute of nothing'.[4] In a second definition, he states that 'the notion of *substance* is just this—that which can exist by itself, without the aid of any other substance'.[5]

While the rationalist tradition subsequently continues to accord central importance to substance, it becomes a target of attack for the empiricists. Locke denies that we have any clear idea at all when we talk of substance, 'the general name "substance" being nothing but the supposed, but unknown, support of those qualities we find existing, which we imagine cannot subsist *sine re substante*, without something to support them, we call that support *substantia*'.[6] Yet we have 'no idea of what it is, but only a confused, obscure one of what it does'.[7] Hume, finally, following the empiricist approach rather more consistently than Locke, declares that 'the idea of a substance [. . .] is nothing but a collection of simple ideas [i.e. ideas of empirical qualities], that are

---

[1] Aristotle, *Categories*, 2ª11.   [2] Ibid. 4ª10.

[3] Aristotle, *Metaphysics*, 1029ª8.

[4] R. Descartes, *The Philosophical Works of Descartes*, E. S. Haldane and G. T. R. Ross (eds.) (Cambridge, 1931–4), ii. 53.

[5] Ibid. 101.

[6] J. Locke, *An Essay Concerning Human Understanding*, in *The Works of John Locke* (London, 1874), II.xxiii.2.

[7] Ibid. II.xiii.19.

united by the imagination, and have a particular name assigned to them'.[8]

Nietzsche's criticism of substance in the second of the three Aristotelian senses—substance as substratum, to which we shall confine ourselves for the moment—proceeds along very similar lines.[9] He denies that we have any contentful idea of something that is supposed to remain of an object, a 'thing', once its qualities which are perceived as affecting the observer and other objects are abstracted from it: 'If I think of the muscle apart from its "effects", I negate it [. . . .] A "thing" is the sum of its effects, synthetically united by a concept, an image' (WM 551).[10] It is grammar which misleads us into thinking that, apart from the (changing) qualities, effects, or 'powers' of a 'thing', there is some permanent, unchanging and unknown, seat or bearer of these properties in which an object's qualities inhere and from which its powers emanate:

A quantum of force is just such a quantum of drive, will, efficacy—rather, it is nothing but precisely this driving, willing, effecting itself, and only under the seduction of language [. . .] which understands and misunderstands all effecting as conditioned by something that effects, by a 'subject', can it appear otherwise [. . .] there is no such substratum; there is no 'being' behind the doing, effecting, becoming; 'the doer' is only superinvented [*hinzugedichtet*] to the doing. Basically, ordinary people duplicate the doing when they speak of lightning that flashes; this is a doing-doing: [. . . .] The natural scientists are no better when they say 'force moves, force causes' and such like. (GM i.13)

Nietzsche's criticism of the notion of substance as the seat or bearer of the manifold of properties apprehended as an object is not just that we have no experience of such a substratum in the external objects in which we believe it to be present (although we might be able to conceive of it). It is rather, as becomes clear from the first quotation above, that under scrutiny the concept turns out to be empty or unintelligible—what we *mean* by a 'thing' is the sum of its

---

[8] D. Hume, *A Treatise of Human Nature* (Oxford, 1978), 16.

[9] For his criticism of substance as the individual concrete thing (as conceived by atomist materialism), see S. 2 of this chapter. His views concerning substance as that which can exist by itself will be discussed in Chs. 3.2 and 6.2.

[10] Nietzsche does not make the traditional distinction here between the intrinsic properties which are said to constitute an object (its primary qualities, in Lockean terminology) and its powers which manifest themselves as 'effects' on other entities or on observers. The reasons for his refusal to make such a distinction will emerge in Ch. 2.2.

properties and once we abstract from these we merely succeed in 'negating' the object altogether. We may infer from these remarks and similar ones that the unintelligibility of the notion of a substratum derives from the fact that substrata are supposed to be *both* items which are logically distinct from the properties of an object *and* such as to be, in principle, uncharacterizable by any monadic predicates (i.e. without intrinsic properties). As generally in the critical strand in Nietzsche's later philosophy, the position implicit in these remarks is not just an *epistemological* empiricism, but a radical empiricism of meaning (see Chapter 3.1).[11]

What are the consequences of this anti-rationalist (and anti-Kantian) line of thought? Up to this point, they seem hardly very dramatic. Many thinkers since Hume, even if attached to realist metaphysics, would agree with Nietzsche's arguments. Arguably, they do not, by themselves, preclude the possibility of the 'independent' existence of the objects regarded as real by common sense and by science. To be sure, 'substance' has often been called upon to explain how, given the relative and variable character of an object's qualities as they appear to different observers, or to one observer at different times, it can nevertheless be said to exist in some sense 'in itself', that is, self-identical, unconditioned by and independent of a perceiving or conceiving subject. 'Substance' was supposed to confer this objectivity and independent existence on the object. But it might be, and often has been, argued that objectivity in this sense can be vouchsafed without having recourse to such problematic notions by thinking of the object as simply a bundle of qualities subject-independently co-instantiated at particular times and places. If the object is to be thought as a relatively enduring one—as many physical things usually are—further specifications need of course to be added, such as spatial and qualitative continuity of 'its' successive temporal phases. And we can, so the argument might continue, in favourable conditions cognitively latch on to what is thus objectively (non-perspectivally) the case by identifying the object ostensively and describing it by attributing characteristics to it which are constitutive of it irrespective of

---

[11] Nietzsche is likely to have been influenced in his criticism of substance by F. A. Lange. Lange proposed to replace the Aristotelian notion of objects as qualities inhering in a substratum by a construal of them as clusters of (continually changing) spatio-temporally co-instantiated properties. (F. A. Lange, *Geschichte des Materialismus* (Iserlohn, 1866), 93.)

whether we or any other 'subjects of knowledge' are aware of it, thus dispensing with substance while preserving independent existence.[12] As we shall see in due course, for Nietzsche, solutions of this kind are spurious because they rest upon the incoherent notion that an object can 'in itself' have, or rather be constituted by, non-perspectival properties.

There are a number of remarks in Nietzsche's writings suggesting a psychological hypothesis regarding the origins of the inadequate concept of substance as substratum. According to these, the idea of (absolutely or relatively) permanent substrata in the objects can be understood psychologically as derived from the assumption of an unchanging self or soul underlying our various experiences and causing our actions. The belief in substance is nothing but that belief projected onto objects:

The oldest and longest psychology was at work here [. . .] all events were a doing, all doing consequence of a will, the world became a plurality of doers, a doer (a 'subject') was imputed to all events [. . . .] The thing itself, to say it once more, the concept thing a reflex merely of the belief in the self [*Ich*] as cause. (GD, 'The four great errors', 3; cf. also WM 485)

The fact that one can ascribe one's various mental states to oneself gives rise to the notion of a mental substance (or indeed of a Kantian transcendental subject) distinct from them and causing at least some of these states: 'hitherto one believed as ordinary people do, that in "I think" there was something of immediate certainty, and that this "I" was the given *cause* of thought' (WM 483). For Descartes, since he could not doubt that he was doubting, the proposition 'I am thinking' (or 'I am conscious') was known with certainty whenever he entertained it. But, Nietzsche insists, Descartes's conclusion that there is a *res cogitans* does not follow from the argument in the second *Meditation*:

'There is thinking: therefore there is something that thinks': this is the upshot of Descartes' argumentation. But that means positing as 'true a priori' our belief in the concept of substance—that when there is thought there has to be something 'that thinks' is simply a formulation of our grammatical custom that adds a doer to every deed. (WM 484)

It is clear from this, as well as from the note cited below and many others, that Nietzsche's criticism is directed not only against the

---

[12] For an example of this type of view, see A. Quinton, *The Nature of Things* (London, 1973), esp. 28–9, 38–9, 66–71, 134–9.

rationalist notion of a *res cogitans*, but also against Kant's and Schopenhauer's idea of a transcendental subject which logically cannot be characterized in terms of any intrinsic properties and which is yet supposed to be distinct from what for Kant are 'its effects', for Schopenhauer its non-causal correlates—the unified contents of experience.[13] However, Nietzsche nowhere engages with the Kantian arguments claiming to establish the indispensability of such a transcendental subject. Interestingly, his objection against mental substances and transcendental subjects does not quite parallel his argument against substrata in objects. Objects cannot have substances over and above their properties because nothing remains of the concept of an object once we subtract the latter. But in the case of the soul, Nietzsche maintains, more cautiously:

'The subject' is not something given, it is something added and invented and projected behind what there is.—Finally, is it necessary to posit an interpreter behind the interpretation? Even this is invention, hypothesis. (WM 481)

The soul as the substratum of conscious episodes (like 'thinking' and 'interpreting') is itself an interpretation, a 'hypothesis', for which there are neither a priori grounds nor, obviously, any evidence—it is not 'something given'. But Nietzsche does not argue against it on the grounds that there is nothing to what we customarily call the self apart from conscious episodes.

[13] Cf. Kant's statements in I. Kant, *Critique of Pure Reason* (Basingstoke and London, 1990): 'This principle of the necessary unity of apperception [. . .] reveals the necessity of the synthesis of the manifold given in intuition, without which the thoroughgoing identity of self-consciousness cannot be thought. For through the "I", as simple representation, nothing manifold is given; only in intuition, which is distinct from the "I"[!], can a manifold be given' (B 135). The 'synthesis of the manifold given in intuition' is described by Kant as an '*act* of the subject' (B 154, my emphasis). That subject's 'existence is already given thereby, but the mode in which I am to determine this existence, that is, the manifold belonging to it, is not thereby given' (B 158, note).

Schopenhauer's theory of a transcendental subject is clearer, but in the light of Nietzsche's remarks no less problematic: 'That which knows all things and is known by none is the *subject*. [. . .] Like all objects of perception, [the body] lies within the forms of all knowledge, in time and space through which there is plurality. But the subject, the knower never the known, does not lie within these forms; on the contrary, it is always presupposed by these forms themselves, and hence neither plurality nor its opposite, namely unity, belongs to it. We never know it, but it is precisely that which knows whenever there is knowledge. (A. Schopenhauer, *The World as Will and Representation* (New York, 1966), i. 5.)

To be sure, his criticism of substance rules out as unintelligible any conception of the self as the 'owner', 'bearer', correlate, or cause, itself without intrinsic properties, of conscious experiences—such a subject would precisely be a ' "doer" [. . .] superinvented to the doing' (GM i.13). Nevertheless, for Nietzsche, it is not nonsensical to speak of a self distinct from these experiences. Indeed, as we shall see, one of his positive tenets appears to be that the conscious empirical self represents merely a terminal phenomenon, the result of occurrences which are mostly unconscious.[14]

Besides substance, there is yet another central concept of traditional metaphysics which, Nietzsche suggests, is the result of a transference of an ostensible 'inner fact' onto 'external' objects—the concept of causality. Indeed, both projections are intimately connected. What do we mean, in common parlance, by the word 'cause'? 'That something can be constituted in such a way that, when it is assumed [*gesetzt*], thereby something else must also be necessarily assumed' (KGW VII.3.34.70). An event or set of events which is the cause of another is a sufficient condition for the latter to occur. But, moreover, the ordinary understanding of 'cause' involves the notion of an 'effective thing' (WM 552) whose effective forces or powers are released in certain conditions, thus bringing about, that is, necessitating or compelling, certain changes in other objects. The common pre-reflective understanding of a cause is of a thing which, by virtue of its *nature*, manifests under given circumstances a force or power which necessitates certain events in the environment of the cause.

It was, of course, again David Hume who delivered the original and most influential blow against this conception of causation, asserting that the supposed necessity of the relation of cause and effect resides 'in the mind, not in objects'. The only connections we in fact perceive between objects and events are those of contiguity and constant conjunction and it is only through the repeated experience of concomitant changes in objects, i.e. through 'custom', that we come to form the idea of a necessary connection between these changes and of 'powers' in one object which produce modifications in another: 'Either we have no idea of necessity, or necessity is nothing but that determination of the thought to pass from

---

[14] For a discussion of various aspects of Nietzsche's alternative conception of the 'subject', see Chs. 5.2, 6.1, and 6.2.

causes to effects and from effects to causes, according to their experienc'd union'.[15]

On this point, too, Nietzsche's argument is reminiscent of Hume's, yet there are also substantial differences:

We have no 'sense for the *causa efficiens*': here Hume was right; habit (but not only that of the individual!) makes us expect that a certain often-observed occurrence will follow another [. . . .] That which gives the extraordinary firmness to our belief in causality is not the great habit of seeing one occurrence following another but our inability to interpret events otherwise than as events caused by intentions. It is belief in the living and thinking as the only effective force—in will, in intention—it is belief that every event is a deed, that every deed presupposes a doer, it is belief in the 'subject'. (WM 550)

Nietzsche here agrees with Hume that 'we have absolutely no experience of a cause' (WM 551) in what we call the external world, if a cause is taken to involve a 'capacity to produce effects' (ibid.). We only observe successions of changes in the objects. Yet it is not only individual 'habit' which gives rise to the strong expectation that future sequences of events will resemble those experienced in the past. Our ubiquitous tendency to reason inductively (and to do so successfully) cannot adequately be explained along strict empiricist lines and Nietzsche's parenthetical remark suggests an evolutionary explanation instead. While the evolutionary elements in Nietzsche's thinking are themselves fraught with problems (see Chapter 4), his suspicion against the Humean account of the psychological genesis of inductive thinking has been widely shared among more recent philosophers.[16]

---

[15] Hume, *A Treatise of Human Nature*, 166.

[16] Evidently, Hume's account assumes the possibility of frequently observing instances of conjunctions which are obviously similar. As William James, among others, pointed out long ago (W. James, *Principles of Psychology* (New York, 1950), ii. 634 f.), in reality the sequences of events observed by us are often not at all similar in any obvious or relevant way, and we only detect the relevant similarities after examining the sequences more closely, isolating the respective cause-effect system from external interferences, etc. More recently, Karl Popper has remarked in a similar vein that the detection of causal regularities is not, *pace* Hume, self-explanatory, since what needs to be accounted for is our ability to focus, out of all the similarities among any two objects or events, on the causally relevant ones (K. Popper, *Conjectures and Refutations* (London, 1963), 46–8). Both James and Popper propose evolutionary explanations of our success in identifying causal sequences.

More importantly, in the present context, Nietzsche suggests that the expectation of an invariable concomitance of instances of the relevant types of events does not capture everything we mean when talking of causes and effects. We cannot help thinking of a cause as that which brings about, 'effects', or necessitates its effect, and this notion of power in objects is the result of an anthropomorphizing transference of the idea of an efficacious will onto them:

Causality is created only by thinking compulsion into the process. A certain 'comprehension' is the consequence, i.e., we have made the process more human, 'more familiar': the familiar is the familiar habit of human compulsion associated with the feeling of force. (WM 664)

The ordinary concept of a cause owes its explanatory power—that element in it which makes us feel we have 'understood' or 'comprehended' a sequence of events—exclusively to this transference of volition onto objects: 'Our "understanding of an event" has consisted in our inventing a subject which was made responsible for something that happens [. . .]: *causa efficiens* and *causa finalis* are fundamentally one' (WM 551).

The idea recurs time and again in Nietzsche's writings that comprehension and its correlative, explanation, consist essentially in establishing analogies between unfamiliar types of events or objects and empirically familiar ones—i.e. in 'reducing', in this sense, the former to the latter. It is an idea with long-standing precedents, having been adopted programmatically by the critics of late medieval Aristotelianism from Galileo onwards. The Aristotelians, according to them, had 'explained' the familiar and well-known by the unfamiliar and obscure—material objects by substantial forms and change by occult powers—while the correct philosophical and scientific procedure should be the reverse. Analogy became the paradigm of explanation with the mechanists of the seventeenth and eighteenth centuries and came to be seriously threatened only with the advent of the apparent *actio in distans* of Newton's universal gravitation (see Section 2 of this Chapter). Robert Boyle, one of the paragons of mechanism, can be cited as representative of many philosophers and probably the majority of scientists even up to the late nineteenth century, when he says that 'to explicate a phenomenon [is] to deduce it from something else in nature more known to us than the thing to be explained by it'.[17] The known *explicans*, for Boyle as for many like-minded thinkers, was to be matter characterized by its essential properties of solidity, extension, and mobility. But from the days when the inadequacy of classical mechanism came to be seen as an inescapable fact—a process which had started with Newton and culminated in the last decades of the nineteenth century—natural scientists have increasingly come to be content with a rather more modest conception of explanation: 'explaining' a phenomenon at the most basic level of explanation is now, in scientific practice if not always in the philosophy of science, usually understood to mean subsuming the phenomenon in question under appropriate universal propositions describing 'laws of nature' of the form 'all A's are (concomitant with) B's'.[18] What remains of the naïve concept of causation here is the invariable correlation of events of one type and events of another type, supporting the universal 'all A's are B's',[19] which in turn entails singular causal statements of the relevant sort. 'Explaining' some particular event *x*, on this model, means identifying *x* as an A and knowing the relevant universal 'all A's are B's'. We are then in a position to deduce the cause of *x* from the conjunction of *x* and the 'law'. For Nietzsche, conceptions of explanation of this general type are unacceptable:

> *Cause and effect*—'Explanation' we call it: but it is description that distinguishes us from older stages of knowledge and science. We describe better—but we explain just as little as all previous ones [. . . .] The series of 'causes' stands in front of us much more completely in every case, we reason: this and this has to precede if that is to follow—but thereby we have *comprehended* nothing. The quality, for instance, in any chemical process appears now as ever as a 'miracle', just as any locomotion; no one has 'explained' impact. (FW iii.112)

Explanation proper, it is implied here, would consist in more than the framing of theories and experimental laws which succeed in correlating one type of phenomenon with another in however quantitatively precise a manner; it would involve a comprehension

---

[17] R. Boyle, 'The Origins of Forms and Qualities', in M. A. Stewart (ed.), *Selected Philosophical Papers* (Manchester, 1979), 67.

[18] For a classical statement, see E. Nagel, *The Structure of Science* (London, 1961), 15–28. Cf. also Ch. 2.2 below.

[19] This is of course a highly simplified schema. The consequents in causal sequences often have several possible antecedent conditions or sets of conditions, not all of which may be known to us.

of the 'quality' in the cause which 'compels' (cf. WM 664), or brings about, the effect.[20]

Historically, there have been three major approaches to the problem of causation, each of which might be thought to comply with this ideal of explanation by going beyond the mere 'description' of contingent regularities.[21] The first of these involves the claim that there are necessitating powers in objects and that, *pace* Hume, we can gain cognitive access to these. According to another approach, we can legitimately understand causal sequences in objects as analogous to our own intentional activity. We are acquainted with causal necessitation through the direct knowledge we have of the efficacy of our own volitions, and causation in objects operates in a manner essentially similar to these. Finally, there is the doctrine of 'internal relations', according to which physical objects are *logically* interconnected in the sense that an object's nature or essence includes various relational properties, specifically causal ones. Nietzsche, as we have seen, rejects the first of these explanatory approaches—he insists that we have no experience of powers in the 'external world', but only of successions of events. As regards the two theories mentioned last, we shall see that he adumbrates a radical version of the doctrine of internal relations and, at least in some passages, also suggests a variant of 'volitionism'.

But as for his criticism of our common, pre-reflective idea of causation, we may ask what it can be said to achieve and what it is intended to achieve. It is helpful, in order to understand Nietzsche's intention behind his argument, to compare it again with Hume's criticism and, more particularly, with the conclusions which have usually been drawn from the latter. Those who have acknowledged the cogency of Hume's argumentation have frequently concluded from it that the naïve concept of causation stands in need of a revision which would cleanse it of its occult ingredients. But it has also often been argued that any such revision in accordance with

[20] Modern 'Humeans' often reply to this demand that it is misguided, since there simply *is* no such quality, no 'causal power'—it is not merely a case of our being ignorant of it. There is no *reason* why innumerable events in the universe occur in what appears to be a law-governed manner—they just do. The sheer extraordinariness of this claim—that it is a mere brute fact, an accident, that these apparently universal regularities obtain—has been rightly emphasized by G. Strawson (*The Secret Connexion* (Oxford, 1989), 20–31).

[21] See also H. R. Harré and E. H. Madden, *Causal Powers* (Oxford, 1975).

Hume's strictures is bound to deviate from the pre-critical notion of cause and effect to such an extent as to be a radically different concept. A brief review of various problems that have standardly been identified in the 'Humean' regularity account of causation may help to bring out some of the issues associated with the dispute which are most relevant in our context.

To begin with, the asymmetry commonly perceived to hold in the relation between cause and effect would seem to have to be considered, on such a construal, as unfounded. For it appears that the ordinary notion of causal priority is distinct from mere temporal priority and is in fact based on the anthropomorphizing analogy of spontaneous intervention, that is, on our conception of ourselves as agents who act without being themselves determined in their actions by causal antecedents: 'we [say] that X is causally prior to Y where, if an intervention had been applied to X, Y would have been different, but not vice versa'.[22] Secondly, the need to distinguish between accidentally true universal statements and laws of nature forces the 'Humean' to adopt differentiating criteria which, it could be argued, are quite at variance with non-philosophical customary beliefs. How can the regularity account of causation distinguish between a genuine law of nature and an accidentally true universal, such as 'all men in this room are over six feet tall'?

One of the standard answers given to this problem is that, in the latter case, the objects to which the predicate is applied are typically restricted to a certain limited spatio-temporal region. A basic law-like universal, by contrast, is said not to be thus restricted; its objects are not 'required to be located in a fixed volume of space or a given interval of time'.[23] This criterion rules out by stipulation basic laws applying only for a finite period of time in a closed sub-region of space. The problem with it is that it may disqualify those universals generally recognized as laws, too; for the validity of, say, the laws of radioactive disintegration or planetary motion may well be spatio-temporally restricted, although obviously less so than our example of an accidentally true universal.[24] In any case, a definition of basic laws of nature along these lines would appear to conflict with the common belief that there could conceivably be such laws,

---

[22] J. L. Mackie, *The Cement of the Universe* (Oxford, 1974), 180.
[23] Nagel, *The Structure of Science*, 59.
[24] Cf. Harré and Madden, *Causal Powers*, 30.

which are valid only for certain kinds of phenomena in a sub-region of space and during a restricted interval of time.[25]

A similar point applies to another suggested demarcating criterion, according to which a genuine (basic) law is distinguished from an accidentally true generalization by the fact that the evidence for it is not identical with its scope of prediction and that the latter is open to further extension in a genuine law.[26] This makes it a matter of definition that there cannot be basic causal laws which apply only to a closed set of instances. Like the spatio-temporal criterion of demarcation, it rules out a priori the possibility of interpreting statements about closed sets of regularly concomitant events as specifying basic causal regularities, rather than collocations, or a combination of basic laws and collocations. The hypothesis that some things might suddenly and without cause change their behaviour for a certain span of time such that their causal relations with each other are altered for the duration of that interval, is on this account necessarily false—it is *not* false because this could even in principle be shown by the evidence, nor because the regularity theory by itself implies the impossibility of uncaused changes, or because there are independent reasons for refusing to countenance this as a logical possibility, but simply by virtue of the definition of causal relations.

Many people would perhaps have considerable doubts concerning the likelihood of such an occurrence, and some—for instance, Kantians—might deny the very coherence of the supposition of an uncaused change in the causal relations between types of events. But arguably few, if any, non-philosophers would be prepared to reject the hypothesis that there might be basic causal correlations obtaining in a closed set of instances as *necessarily* false on account of the meaning of the term 'causation'.

What these considerations suggest is that the idea of causation as something over and above regular succession, namely as some power in the objects which *explains* their conjunction, is rather more firmly lodged in our structure of beliefs than modern 'Humeans' appear to think. As Nietzsche rightly maintains, we naturally tend to regard an account as explaining, rather than describing, a given occurrence if it enables us to 'comprehend' it, and we would think of the latter as accomplished when we have

[25] Cf. Mackie, *The Cement of the Universe*, 207.
[26] Nagel, *The Structure of Science*, 63.

attained an intuitive grasp of, or acquaintance with, whatever quality it is that 'compelled' it to happen. Many of Nietzsche's attacks are directed against putative explanations of this kind. However, the point of these attacks, as of his sceptical arguments in general, is rather different from that of Hume's scepticism, despite the similarities between some of the observations made by both philosophers. Nietzsche's persistent endeavour to undermine and discredit any of our ostensible explanations of phenomena can only be adequately understood in the light of what he thinks the desire for explanation and comprehension in this sense to be indicative of. We shall examine the rationale of Nietzsche's scepticism in detail further below. For the present, it suffices to remark that it is consistently directed against what we naturally and spontaneously regard as explanation proper, by contrast to what Nietzsche terms the description of phenomena. What I have attempted to show in the preceding paragraphs in my discussion of the 'Humean' account of causation and some of its familiar problems is that Nietzsche is correct in identifying the everyday intuitive notion of explanation implicit in ordinary discourse with the knowledge of (qualitative) natures and modes of operation.

The naïve concept of causation, according to Nietzsche, is anthropomorphic, since in it the alleged experience of the causal effectiveness of our own will is transferred onto objects. The question here naturally arises: is there really such an experience? Are we indeed familiar with efficacy or power in our own volitions? Nietzsche denies this in a number of places, both in the writings he published and in the *Nachlass*. In *Götzendämmerung*, he declares:

Of these three 'inner facts' by which causation seemed to vouch for itself, the first and most convincing one is that of the *will as cause*; [. . . .] By now, we have thought better of it [. . . .] The 'inner world' is full of mirages and will-o'-the-wisps: the will is one of them. The will no longer moves anything, consequently no longer explains anything—it accompanies processes, it may also be absent. (GD, 'The four great errors', 3)

What is the nature of the occurrence which we usually take to be an efficacious act of will or a volition? Nietzsche suggests two answers to this question which are not mutually exclusive. In a fragment included in *Der Wille zur Macht* we find the remark that 'we have misunderstood the feeling of strength, tension, resistance, a muscu-

lar feeling that is already the beginning of the act, as the cause'
(WM 551). In another note he suggests that 'when we do something
there arises a feeling of force [*Kraftgefühl*], often even before the
deed, occasioned by the idea of what is to be done (as at the sight
of an enemy or an obstacle to which we feel ourselves equal): it is
always an accompanying feeling. We instinctively think that this
feeling of force is the cause of the action, that it is "the force"' (WM
664).

Nietzsche's first point has some plausibility—there is indeed a
tendency to confuse the feeling of muscular effort with the volitional effort which we believe to be causally responsible for our
movements on at least some occasions. It is equally plausible to
maintain that this is a misunderstanding and that volitional effort,
if it is indeed effective at all, is quite distinct from any muscular
feelings we may have. William James remarked, a few years before
Nietzsche's note was written:

It is needless [. . .] to say what absolutely different phenomena these
two efforts [muscular and volitional] are, or to expiate upon the
unfortunateness of their being confounded under the same generic name.[27]

But if the so-called experience of volition is not a muscular feeling,
what is it? Nietzsche's second remark identifies it as a feeling of
force or strength (*Kraft*) which often accompanies the 'idea of what
is to be done', i.e. an either prevenient or concomitant mental
representation of the action. The same note also suggests that
feelings of this kind arise only when we judge ourselves to be equal
to the proposed task, that is, if we regard the mental representation
as of an action which is indeed possible for us. 'Volition', on this
account, would consist in the idea of the action represented with a
certain kind of qualitative 'flavour' *sui generis* which Nietzsche
terms a 'feeling of force', depending in turn on the judgement that
the projected action is feasible. We are not concerned here with a
further elaboration of the particular brand of volitional theory
which is the object of Nietzsche's criticism. What is important in
our context is rather that Nietzsche in the same passage declares the
notion of the *Kraftgefühl* as motive power to be spurious: 'the force
we feel "does not set the muscles in motion". "We have no idea, no
experience, of such a process".' (WM 664), and: 'There is no such

---

[27] W. James, 'The Feeling of Effort', in *Collected Essays and Reviews* (London,
1920), 202.

thing as "cause"; some cases in which it seemed to be given us, and in which we have projected it out of ourselves in order to understand an event, have been shown to be self-deceptions.' (WM 551). We have derived the concept of cause as effective power from what is supposedly most familiar to us; but under closer scrutiny we discover that even in so-called volitional activity we do not experience any mechanism or mode of operation by which conscious episodes 'set in motion' the limbs of the body. Here, too, 'we experience only that one thing follows upon another' (WM 664). Causal efficacy thus seems no less elusive in the paradigm case of volition than in 'external' events.

But Nietzsche's sceptical observations regarding our alleged acquaintance with efficacy in volition are not as unambiguous and unqualified as they may have appeared so far in this exposition. Indeed, his lack of clarity on this issue is part of a cluster of central ambiguities on crucial points which have proved most recalcitrant to straightforward interpretation and which have given rise to such a wide variety of conflicting exegeses. For the sceptical statements on which I have concentrated so far seem to be directly contradicted by a number of passages in which he does recognize introspective knowledge of a type of efficacy which he also designates as 'will' or, more specifically, as 'will to power'. This 'will' is to be distinguished from the representation cum feeling of force which, according to him, constitute the spurious act of will or volition as ordinarily conceived:

From a psychological point of view the concept 'cause' is our feeling of power resulting from the so-called act of will—our concept 'effect' the superstition that this feeling of power is the motive power itself—[. . .]

If we translate the concept 'cause' back to the only sphere known to us, from which we have derived it, we cannot imagine any change that does not involve a will to power [. . .]

Should we not be permitted to assume this will as a motive cause in chemistry, too?—and in the cosmic order? (WM 689)

Here, a distinction is drawn between a 'feeling of power' which has usually been mistaken for the motive power and, on the other hand, a 'will' which we can 'imagine' and 'should be permitted to assume' as a universal efficacious cause. We are not concerned at this point with the apparent panpsychist (or 'panvolitionist') implication of this note, nor indeed with the precise mode of operation of the will referred to in it.[28] What is of relevance here is merely that Nietzsche does recognize in this as well as in some other passages,[29] contrary to the remarks quoted earlier, a causal efficacy or power of some kind, a 'will' with which, it is claimed, we are introspectively familiar.

Do any of these mutually exclusive lines of thought represent Nietzsche's final view on this matter? It would seem textually highly questionable to attribute to him one of them at the expense of the other—for he ultimately refuses to commit himself to either. This emerges fairly clearly from an important passage in *Jenseits von Gut und Böse* which can be taken rather more confidently to express his considered view than the often provisional notes in the *Nachlass*:

> Ultimately, the question is whether we really recognize the will as *efficacious*, whether we believe in the causality of the will: if we do so—and, at bottom, the belief in *this* is precisely our belief in causality itself—then we *have* to make the attempt to assume the causality of the will hypothetically as the only one. 'Will' can of course act only on 'will'—and not on 'matter' (on 'nerves' for example): enough, one must venture the hypothesis that will acts upon will wherever 'effects' are recognized—(JGB 36)

Even here, Nietzsche does not commit himself unreservedly to saying that 'the will' is effective—although he proposes to 'venture the hypothesis'. There is a distinct sense of a certain arbitrariness in this option, conveyed both by the hypothetical construction of the central sentence in this passage and by Nietzsche's use of the verb *glauben (an)*:—if we *believe in* the efficacy of the will, then we 'have to' extrapolate from this belief.

In some passages of his later works and in many notes in the *Nachlass*, Nietzsche himself seemingly accedes to a view which presupposes some kind of efficacy of the will; he 'ventures the hypothesis' of the will to power as the motive cause 'in the cosmic order'. Whether this hypothesis does amount to a resolution of the ambiguity discussed here will be the subject of the final chapter.

2. ATOMS AND FORCE

We have seen that Nietzsche in some places genetically explains the belief in effective causation (power, necessitation) as derived from

---

[28] See Ch. 6.1 for a discussion of this.
[29] e.g. WM 490, 658; FW 127; JGB 19; KGW VIII.1.1.30.

the ostensible 'inner fact' that the will moves. But besides causation in objects and the idea of substrata underlying the manifold properties of objects, there is yet another related misconception that has arisen from a transference of something 'inner' onto the 'external' world—the enduring material thing (see e.g. WM 635).

According to some remarks, the materialist conception of substance as 'matter', a non-mental, subject-independent reality characterized by either relatively or absolutely invariant specific instantiations of certain generic properties—extension, mobility, and solidity or impenetrability—which it is said to possess in itself is also psychologically derivative from the belief in an enduring mental substance, the 'self'. The particular target of his criticism is the theory of matter which arguably has been most influential and widely-held among modern (post-Cartesian) philosophers and scientists: corpuscularianism. On this theory, matter is an extended substance composed of minute elements or corpuscles, also called atoms. All qualities of perceptible material things are reducible to the qualities of these elements (Locke's primary qualities) or to the 'textures' or arrangements of the elements (secondary qualities), giving rise to ideas in the perceiver which do not resemble the qualities in the objects themselves (unlike the ideas of primary qualities). The elements are supposed to possess only qualities which are essential to matter as such, namely some determinate extension (figure and size), motion or rest, and solidity (impenetrability). Solidity, which distinguishes matter from empty space, is conveyed to the senses as hardness but it is distinct from the latter in that all perceptible hardness is only relative solidity. Ordinary-sized objects are penetrable (or divisible) because of the interstices between the corpuscular elements, but these elements themselves are absolutely solid and rigid. Thus, the idea of absolute solidity is ostensibly arrived at by analogy with felt (relative) hardness.[30]

Mechanists like Boyle attempted to explain all modifications of matter in terms of interactions—impact and pressure—of these corpuscles. But, as Lange observed in his *Geschichte des Materialismus*,[31] with the general acceptance of the Newtonian concept of force, which proved refractory to mechanical reduction—to an explanation in terms of pressure and impact among atoms—the assumption of such ultimate extended particles for the

---

[30] Cf. P. Alexander, *Ideas, Qualities and Corpuscles—Locke and Boyle on the External World* (Cambridge, 1985), 140.
[31] Lange, *Geschichte des Materialismus*, 359–71.

purpose of explaining natural phenomena came increasingly to be seen as superfluous. Dynamist theories of matter began to challenge the hitherto predominant mechanical-corpuscularian ones. For Nietzsche, the assumption of corpuscles or atoms is not only obsolete (as it was for Lange), but 'refuted':

> As regards materialist atomism: it belongs to the best-refuted things there are [. . .] thanks primarily to the Pole Boscovich who, together with the Pole Copernicus, has so far been the greatest and most victorious opponent of appearances. For while Copernicus persuaded us to believe, contrary to all the senses, that the earth does _not_ stand firm, Boscovich taught us to abandon the belief in the last thing of the earth that 'stood firm', the belief in 'substance', in 'matter', in the earth-residue and particle-atom. (JGB 12)

> When I think of my philosophical genealogy I associate myself [. . .] with the mechanist movement (reduction of all moral and aesthetic questions to physiological ones, of all physiological to chemical ones; of all chemical to mechanical ones)— but with the difference that I do not believe in 'matter' and consider Boscovich to be one of the great turning points, like Copernicus [. . .] (GOA xiv.353)

Nowhere in his writings does Nietzsche attempt a refutation of the theory of extended atoms himself, yet he repeatedly refers to Boscovich's arguments in complete agreement, so that it is fair to say, as Anni Anders does, that 'Boscovich had become a building block in Nietzsche's own philosophy'.[32]

The Jesuit philosopher Roger Joseph Boscovich argued in his _Philosophiae Naturalis Theoria_ that the assumption of direct contact between two rigid spheres in the phenomenon we call impact is in contradiction with the law of continuity and ought therefore to be abandoned.[33] He illustrated his argument by the following thought-experiment.

Assume two spheres _a_ and _b_ moving at six and twelve degrees velocity respectively in the same direction, the faster sphere (_b_) moving, initially at some distance, behind the slower one (_a_). If, at 'impact', a direct contact takes place between the two spheres, _a_ has to change its velocity, i.e. become accelerated, instantaneously and discontinuously, for otherwise there would be interpenetration— which is ruled out by the hypothesis that the two bodies are, like

---

[32] K. Schlechta and A. Anders, _Friedrich Nietzsche—Von den verborgenen Anfängen seines Philosophierens_ (Stuttgart-Bad Cannstadt, 1962), 136.

[33] R. Boscovich, _A Theory of Natural Philosophy_ (Chicago, 1922), 46 f.

atoms, perfectly solid. But such an instantaneous change of velocity by a finite increment violates the law of continuity, which is inductively very well confirmed, as it is found to apply to all other natural phenomena. (In fact, in Newtonian physics, if a discontinuous instantaneous change in velocity were admitted, the force required for this acceleration would have to be infinite.) Boscovich concludes that the change of velocity in the phenomenon of 'impact' does not come about instantaneously by direct contact but rather takes place *continuously* a short span of time *before* the apparent contact. The velocity change can in fact only be accounted for, according to Boscovich, by the assumption of a repulsive force which acts at very small distances between any two bodies. This force increases asymptotically as the distance diminishes, so that for infinitesimal distances the value of the force approaches infinity, thus ruling out the possibility of contact between the centres of force. For large distances, Newton's laws of gravitation remain (approximately) valid so that one has to postulate a transition, at a certain distance, of the repulsive force between any two bodies into an attractive force. In fact, certain physical and chemical phenomena (such as cohesion) suggest a number of such points of transition from repulsive to attractive force and vice versa at definite, but as yet unknown, distances from any given centre of force.

What is important in our context is the following conclusion Boscovich draws from this hypothesis. Since the repulsive force between two bodies approaches infinity as the distance between them decreases, the constituents of matter cannot be composite or continuous, but must be perfectly simple and at some distance from each other. For otherwise, one would have to assume that the repulsive force does not act between the elements of matter although it does act between composites made up of these elements, a highly implausible assumption as it contradicts the principle of homogeneity. But if the elements of matter must be perfectly simple and indivisible *in principle*, Boscovich continues, they cannot be extended. To be sure, the Peripatetics admitted elements which were supposedly simple and indivisible and yet had extension, but:

this idea is quite overthrown by [the principle] of induction [. . . .] For we see, in all those bodies that we can bring under observation, that whatever occupies a distinct position is itself also a distinct thing; so that those that occupy different parts of space can be separated by using a sufficiently large force; nor can we detect a case in which these larger bodies have any part that occupies different parts of space at one & the same time, & yet is the same part. Further, this property by its very nature is the sort for which it is equally probable that it happens in magnitudes that we can detect by the senses & in magnitudes which are below the limits of our senses.[34]

As we can see from this passage, what Boscovich 'refutes' is not really the theory of atoms—its untenability is in fact assumed in his premises. Rather, what he shows is the inconsistency of the pressure and impact model of causation with the atomist theory and with certain other, prima facie very plausible, principles of Newtonian physics. In any case, it is in this manner that Boscovich arrives at his conception of unextended physical points as the ultimate constituents of matter. These points are distinguished from geometrical points by the fact that they possess the real property of inertia and that they are surrounded by forces of the kind described above. The mass of a body is, for Boscovich, 'precisely the same thing as the number of points that go to form a body'.[35] This is obviously quite different from the Newtonian concept of mass as 'quantity of matter'. In fact, since Boscovich's points have no volume, consequently no mass in the Newtonian sense, they also cannot exert a 'force' as this term is used by Newton. Boscovich's forces are, strictly speaking, accelerations. If matter consists of aggregates of unextended points surrounded by forces, material things as ordinarily conceived—as regions of space filled, either partly or wholly, by solid 'stuff'—are *phenomena*, but they are, to use Leibniz's phrase, *phaenomena bene fundata*. In Locke's terminology, matter, in itself, has no primary qualities which distinguish it from empty space and which are the basis of a material object's tertiary qualities, its 'powers' to make 'a change in the bulk, figure, texture and motion of *another body*'.[36] The forces—such as gravitational force—which appear to 'emanate' from material objects distinguishable from them on account of the latter's primary qualities are, in fact, not ontologically dependent on any such qualities distinct from them; rather, material objects *consist* exclusively of such forces.

Boscovich points out that all the modifications to which we believe matter to be susceptible, including motion according to Newton's laws, can be explained by his hypothesis as well as by the

---

[34] R. Boscovich, *A Theory of Natural Philosophy*, 85.   [35] Ibid. 277.
[36] Locke, *An Essay Concerning Human Understanding*, II.viii.23.

assumption of an extended stuff-like substance, while avoiding the difficulties to which corpuscularian mechanism is subject. The fact that we *perceive* bodies as extended and (relatively) solid is not a decisive objection:

> when a body approaches close enough to our organs, my repulsive force [. . .] is bound to excite in the nerves of those organs the motions which, according to the usual idea, are excited by impenetrability and contact; & that thus the same vibrations are sent to the brain, and these are bound to excite the same perception in the mind as would be excited in accordance with the usual idea.[37]

I have summarized Boscovich's dynamist theory of matter at such length here not only because Nietzsche seems to have considered his critique of the corpuscularian account of matter conclusive, but also because, as we shall see, Boscovich's reduction of matter to centres and fields of force forms an essential part of the background from which Nietzsche's own dynamist 'hypothesis' emerges and against which it has to be understood.[38]

Boscovich regards his attractive and repulsive forces, or rather, propensities of acceleration, as philosophically unproblematic. He concedes that we may as yet be ignorant as to the *causes* of these forces, but there is nothing obscure or mysterious about the forces themselves: 'for everybody knows what approach means, and what recession is; everybody knows what it means to be indifferent, & what having a propensity means; & thus the idea of a propensity to approach, or to recede, is perfectly distinctly obtained'.[39] For Boscovich, force is both *real*[40] and ultimate, that is, irreducible to mechanical phenomena, since these phenomena themselves are to be 'explained' by forces. Nietzsche, while accepting Boscovich's criticism of the explanatory hypothesis of mechanist atomism, follows Schopenhauer and Lange in denying any explanatory power to both the Newtonian and the Boscovichean concepts of force:[41]

[37] Boscovich, *A Theory of Natural Philosophy*, 109.
[38] Anders has argued that Nietzsche, who read Boscovich's work in 1873, had his attention drawn to it by T. Fechner's *Über die Physikalische und Philosophische Atomenlehre* (Leipzig, 1864). Fechner, who held a theory similar to Boscovich's, in turn had been discussed by Lange in his *Geschichte*. See Schlechta and Anders, *Friedrich Nietzsche*, 128.
[39] Boscovich, *A Theory of Natural Philosophy*, 95.   [40] Ibid. 113.
[41] Schopenhauer's talk of a 'force of impenetrability' (*The World as Will and Representation*, i. 122) suggests that he, too, accepted a dynamist conception of

One cannot 'explain' pressure and impact themselves, one cannot get free
of the *actio in distans*:—one has lost the belief in being able to explain at
all, and admits with a wry expression that description and not explanation
is all that is possible, that the dynamic interpretation of the world with its
denial of 'empty space' and its little lumps of atoms, will shortly come to
dominate physicists [. . .] (WM 618)

The postulation of a force which cannot be reduced to the mechanical phenomena of pressure and impact involves the acknowledgement that bodies 'attract' or 'repel' each other via regions of space
not occupied by anything possessing, in itself, properties analogous
to those we ordinarily perceive in physical objects—like solidity—
and distinguishing them, for us, from empty space. Physical objects
seem, in this sense, to act on each other 'at a distance', a distance
which, in the case of gravitational force, may be as great as millions
of miles.

The doubts about whether an ostensibly explanatory notion
involving *actio in distans* in this sense actually does provide any
insight into the nature of the phenomena accounted for by it did, of
course, originate long before Schopenhauer. Newton himself, when
he introduced the concept of universal gravitation into physics,
refused to 'feign hypotheses' regarding its causes, yet he believed in
the existence of such causes and did not regard *actio in distans* as
an acceptable ultimate explanatory concept. In a letter to Bentley he
wrote:

That gravity should be innate, inherent, and essential to matter, so that one
body may act upon another at a distance through a vacuum, without the

matter in terms of forces, in contradistinction to the traditional conception of an
extended substance which we find in Locke and other atomists. But he maintained
that scientific (or 'etiological') explanation does not enlighten us as to the qualitative
nature of force. It is concerned with 'only the *How*, not the *What* of the phenomenon, only its form, not its content' (ibid. 121–2). The forces of natural science are
qualitates occultae, signifying 'just the causal nature of the cause at the point where
this causal nature is etiologically no longer explicable at all' (ibid. 112). Thus, what
remains beyond the reach and concern of science is 'the definite mode of operation
of things, the quality, the character of every phenomenon' (ibid. 121), or, in another
formulation, 'the specific mode of a thing's action, in other words, the very manner
of its existence, its being or true essence' (ibid. 124).
    Lange noted that the concept of force had increasingly replaced the simple,
'intuitively clear' (*anschaulich*) pressure and impact models of classical mechanist
materialism. But 'force', if regarded as physically real, is unintelligible (*widersinnig*)
(*Geschichte des Materialismus*, 360). 'We hear that force is not a pushing God, but
we do not hear how it manages to transmit movement from one material particle to
another through empty space. Ultimately, we are only given one myth for another'
(ibid. 371).

mediation of anything else, by and through which that action and force may be conveyed from one to another, is to me so great an absurdity, that I believe no man, who has in philosophical matters a competent faculty of thinking, can ever fall into it.[42]

But it is George Berkeley's essay 'On Motion' which provides the philosophical *locus classicus* for the argument which was later to be taken up and developed by Schopenhauer and Nietzsche. According to Berkeley, force is not a known quality distinct from motion, it is rather an 'occult quality'.[43] 'Gravity' and 'attraction' do not furnish us with an understanding of the 'nature of motion itself' but are part of a 'mathematical hypothesis'[44] which enables us merely to establish the 'successions of sensible things, noting by what laws they are connected'.[45]

Terms like 'force', 'attraction', and 'repulsion', as used in physics, appear to designate a known mode of operation, a 'mechanism', while in fact they refer either merely to correlations of masses, distances, and accelerations, or to some unknown type of entity, whatever its real essence may be, which, if it were known, would explain these correlations. Thus, Nietzsche maintains: '"Attraction" and "repulsion" in a purely mechanistic sense are complete fictions: a word. We cannot think of an attraction divorced from an intention' (WM 627).

Functional correlations by themselves, which describe 'laws of nature' and are expressed in mathematical formulae in which one variable is designated as 'force', are not explanatory:

The calculability of the world, the expressibility of all events in formulas— is this really 'comprehension'? (WM 624)

It is an illusion that something is *known* when we possess a mathematical formula for an event: it is only designated, described; nothing more. (WM 628)

Here again, Nietzsche re-affirms the notion of explanation, as opposed to description, which we have already encountered in his remarks on the 'Humean' regularity account of causation. He refuses to identify the explanation of an event with its subsumption under some quantitative law of functional dependence, expressed

---

[42] Cited in M. Jammer, *Concepts of Force* (Cambridge, Mass., 1957), 139.
[43] G. Berkeley, 'Of Motion', in M. R. Ayers (ed.), *Philosophical Works* (London, 1993), 256.
[44] Ibid. 259.   [45] Ibid. 275.

in 'the formulas of mathematics—with which, as one must emphasize again and again, nothing is ever comprehended, but rather
designated and recorded [*verzeichnet*]' (WM 554).[46]

Extrapolating from Nietzsche's views as expounded here, we can
surmise that he would regard the disputes between 'realist' and
'positivist' construals of natural science, which came to dominate
philosophy of science in the early twentieth century, as often missing the point. It is not that he would urge us, in the manner of
philosophers of science like Mach and Duhem, to regard science as
a positivistic enterprise concerned with the economical correlation,
classification, and recording of phenomena. Nietzsche's approach
in this matter is not prescriptive. Rather, he would maintain that to
the extent that natural science employs terms apparently referring
to putative entities the intrinsic nature of which is obscure to us—
like force—it is to all intents and purposes *in fact* positivistic, even
if some scientists and philosophers of science believe the contrary,
because it tells us nothing about the qualitative nature of the items
whose 'reality' it asserts.[47]

Let me recapitulate once again the notions of 'comprehension'
and 'explanation' implicit in Nietzsche's remarks. We could only

[46] The essence of this view is expressed, somewhat obscurely, even in the early
unpublished essay 'Über Wahrheit und Lüge im Aussermoralischen Sinn' (1873):
'After all, what is a law of nature as such for us? We are not acquainted with it in
itself, but only with its effects, which means in its relations to other laws of nature—
which in turn are known to us only as sums of relations. Therefore all these relations
always refer again to others and are thoroughly incomprehensible to us in their
essence' (PT 87).

[47] One standard objection levelled by the scientific realist against positivistic
construals of the modern scientific enterprise is that scientific theories often give rise
to the supposition that there are various entities (genes, atoms, etc.) which, although
originally unobserved, can subsequently be detected through conducting suitable
experiments and/or through the use of more advanced scientific instruments. On the
positivistic account of (modern) scientific theories as mere calculating devices, these
discoveries would seem inexplicable and 'miraculous'.

This argument does not affect Nietzsche's remarks. The theoretical 'entities'
which we are said to discover eventually by suitable procedures are again phenomena (e.g. spots on a screen, or tracks in a cloud-chamber) whose underlying nature
is unknown to us. The Nietzschean sceptical critic of standard scientific realism need
not deny that there may be real perception-independent items of *some* sort corresponding to certain variables in scientific equations which as yet have not been
correlated with observable phenomena, but which at some stage in the future may
be successfully correlated with observables. What he does deny is that such newly
discovered correspondences usually enlighten us about the intrinsic qualitative
nature of these entities.

truly be said to comprehend an event, or to be able to explain it, if we could derive its occurrence from some qualitative aspect(s) of the nature of the objects involved. These aspects, which would obviously have to include their causal powers or forces, could in turn only justifiably be claimed to be known or comprehended if they were 'familiar' (cf. FW 355) to us, that is, if we could contentfully 'imagine' them (WM 621), or were acquainted with them intuitively in a perceptual or quasi-perceptual manner, or if they could plausibly be understood as materially analogous (similar) to such 'familiar' qualities.

The notion of comprehension (and explanation) as a knowledge of natures or essences in this sense not only conforms, as I said earlier, to ordinary, pre-philosophical beliefs, but also to what has been claimed by the major part of the European philosophical tradition.[48]

The mechanists thought they could explain change by appeal to what they believed to be 'familiar' qualities such as the force of impact exerted by one solid body upon another—corpuscles were imagined like tiny billiard balls moving about and frequently colliding. It may be objected against Nietzsche's sceptical reflections on Boscovichean and Newtonian forces—'an empty word'—that such forces, too, can be conceived as 'resembling' certain experienced (intuitively known) qualities. Boscovich's forces are, after all, supposed by him to be the causes of precisely those experiences in the subject which mechanists like Locke thought due to intrinsically solid 'stuff'. Does this not suggest that the intrinsic nature of force is at any rate no *less* familiar than the latter would be? It has been

---

[48] It was common to the Aristotelians and their mechanist critics, can be found in the writings of the rationalists as well as in Locke, Berkeley, and (controversially) Hume, and has, although frequently abandoned in the 20th cent., been defended by, among others, Pierre Duhem and Edmund Husserl (cf. E. Husserl's *The Crisis of European Science* (Evanstown, 1970), 51–2, and P. Duhem, *The Aim and Structure of Physical Theory* (Princeton, 1954), e.g. 19).

J. B. Cohen has argued in his *The Newtonian Revolution* that it was primarily the success of Newton's theories which was responsible for the subsequent acceptance, among scientists, of 'a standard of sufficiency for the acceptability of [. . .] explanations that did not require an explanation of the forces or other causes of observed effects' (p. 113). He adds: 'Newton's insistence that it is enough to predict the celestial and terrestrial motions and the tide of the seas was, in fact, less a battle-cry of the new science than a confession of failure. For what Newton was saying in essence is that his system should be accepted in spite of his failure to discern the cause or even to understand universal gravity' (p. 131).

argued, for example, that the nature of force can perfectly well be conceived as the 'objective correlate' of certain experiences, such as the 'feeling of strain':

> Force is not supposed to be our feelings of strain; it is simply supposed that the strains which we feel are forces, or are indications of forces. It is of course absurd to suppose that the sun feels a strain when it pulls the earth; but this is absurd, not because the sun could not be subject to a strain, but because—having no mind—it cannot feel a strain or anything else. It is thus perfectly consistent for a man to describe forces as the sort of factors in nature which reveal themselves to us directly as our feelings of strain [. . .][49]

The problem with this kind of approach seems to be, ultimately, that while we tend to think that we can conceive of the 'objective correlate' of 'feelings' like the sensation of hardness as a quantity of matter being intrinsically solid, voluminous, and of a certain shape—although we shall see that Nietzsche will deny the coherence of this common-sense belief, too—it seems rather more difficult to think of the 'objective correlate' of 'feelings of strain' as in itself characterized by qualities which could in any way 'resemble' the latter.

Boscovich's forces are claimed to be 'real', yet they are neither in themselves stuff-like (solid) nor characterizable by mental predicates. Nietzsche argues that our putative conception of such items, in abstraction from what are said to be their 'effects' (actual or possible), is spurious, consisting exclusively of negations.[50]

In this section I have argued that Nietzsche follows Boscovich in maintaining that the most elementary and seemingly unproblematic mechanical phenomena involve action at a distance in the pre-twentieth-century sense of this expression. He also accepts Boscovich's analysis of matter into extensionless point-centres surrounded by fields of force. But he denies that either Boscovich's or

---

[49] C. D. Broad, *Scientific Thought* (London, 1923), 162–3.

[50] It is partly because forces do not have any qualities identifiable apart from their 'effects' that they are frequently characterized as 'real' fields of potential which, while having (apart from extension) no *actual* properties by themselves, are said to be constituted by their *potential* to act in a specifiable manner, at every point of the field, on objects introduced into it. The quasi-Boscovichean claim that all physical objects might ultimately consist of such fields of potential appears to lead to an infinite regress (cf. John Foster, *The Case for Idealism* (London, 1982), 67–72). A closely analogous problem arises with Nietzsche's theory of interacting 'quanta of force' or 'power quanta' (see Ch. 6.2).

Newton's concept of force is explanatory: '[a] force we cannot imagine is an empty word' (WM 621). We do not know the intrinsic nature of these forces; all we do know are their supposed 'effects' (WM 620).

3. SCEPTICISM GENERALIZED: THE PROBLEM OF JUSTIFICATION

Among Nietzsche's critical remarks concerning claims to metaphysical knowledge, in the sense of true and (recognizably) justified beliefs[51] about reality as it is in itself, there are some which are of a more fundamental and general nature than the criticisms of very specific conceptions and doctrines we have looked at so far. These criticisms would still permit us to claim knowledge of the nature of what philosophers usually call the external world if we had good reasons to attribute to it qualitative characteristics at least analogous to qualities with which we are experientially acquainted or which we can 'imagine'. The question which naturally arises here is: what would count as 'good reasons' in this context? Sceptics have traditionally argued that even if we had found a representation of reality which was empirically contentful and coherent and which, furthermore, satisfied all the standards of validation which we ordinarily, in non-philosophical contexts, apply to knowledge-claims, this representation might nevertheless be false. What would be the conditions in which we would be justified in rejecting this sceptical challenge? Let us hear Nietzsche:

[51] In recent philosophy, there have been various attempts to analyse 'knowledge' in such a way that, for a belief to qualify as knowledge, a justification of it which is normally recognized or recognizable by normal human inquirers *as* a justification is no longer required even as a necessary condition. (See e.g. Robert Nozick, *Philosophical Explanations* (Oxford, 1981), 167–96. I shall always use the terms 'justification' and 'rational justification' in the above sense, which might be called weakly internalist.) Such 'externalist' construals of knowledge are unfortunately of little help for settling disputes in fields of inquiry—such as philosophy—in which there have always been a multitude of conflicting claims to knowledge. There are indeed well-known objections against a conception of knowledge which makes the truth of a belief and its rational justification into sufficient conditions for that belief to constitute knowledge (Gettier cases). But it would, I believe, be widely conceded, even by thinkers impressed by these objections, that rational justification in the above traditional sense seems to have *some* bearing on the likelihood of a belief's being true. The intuition that this is so is all that is required for the central argument of this section.

One is unjust against Descartes if one calls his appeal to the trustworthiness of God facile. Indeed, only on the assumption of a God morally constituted like us is 'truth' and the quest for truth something that promises success and has any sense to begin with. (KGW VII.3.36.30)

As every student of philosophy knows, Descartes begins his *Meditations* with the unsettling suspicion that the familiar world— 'the heavens, the earth, colours, figures, sound, and all other external things'[52]—his knowledge of which previously seemed to him most assured, might in fact be illusions inspired by a deceitful demon. Descartes lays these suspicions to rest by discovering in himself the idea of a 'supreme God, eternal, infinite, immutable, omniscient, omnipotent, and creator of all things',[53] whose veracity he cannot doubt. He concludes from his possession of this idea, in conjunction with various other premises which he finds he cannot doubt, that such a perfect being exists and that consequently his doubts concerning what appeared to him to be an 'external world' of physical objects are unfounded.

Descartes's way back from doubt via his arguments for the existence of God has of course turned out to be less compelling to most of his readers than the original doubts themselves. One might conclude from this lack of success that, since God cannot be relied upon to guarantee the truth of a large class of our beliefs, a self-criticism of our 'faculty of knowledge' is required to determine the extent and the limits of our knowledge. For Nietzsche, any such enterprise is doomed to failure. This does not mean, however, that he regards all beliefs as open to doubt. In at least some places, he concedes that various beliefs are 'irrefutable' (WM 535) because they are constitutive of intelligible language and thought:

We cease to think when we refuse to do so under the constraints of language; we barely reach the doubt that sees this limitation as a limitation. Rational thought is interpretation according to a scheme that we cannot throw off. (WM 522)

It is plausible to assume that the expressions 'constraints of language' and 'rational thought' here stand for various formal structures of thought codified in the laws of classical logic— Nietzsche specifically mentions in this context the law of identity

---

[52] R. Descartes, *Meditations on the First Philosophy*, in *Philosophical Works*, i. 148.
[53] Ibid. 162.

and the law of non-contradiction (WM 516), although his point would presumably apply also to rules of inference such as *modus ponens*. We 'cease to think' when abandoning these and consequently can neither criticize nor 'refute' them—their validity is presupposed in anything we would recognize as an argument, including a sceptical one. In a number of notes, Nietzsche suggests an evolutionary account of our acquisition of these structures of thought (see Chapter 4.1) and he also, in some remarks, appears to do precisely what the above quotation implies cannot be done—to question the 'adequacy to reality' of the logical constraints of language. I will offer an interpretation of these passages later.

However, leaving aside our belief in the axioms and rules of inference of logic, there are many other apparently less fundamental beliefs which prima facie can intelligibly be called into question. We can doubt, according to Nietzsche, whether our awareness of objects and events as situated in a one-directional time and a three-dimensional objective space 'corresponds to' reality (cf. FW 374, MR 117). This implies, at least, that it can be subject to doubt whether any of the qualities we attribute to the 'external' world are really instantiated as we normally think them, or at any rate some of them ('primary qualities'), to be. What would be required for us to *know* to be the case in this respect what we, or most of us, ordinarily believe to be the case?

The intellect cannot criticize itself, simply because it cannot be compared with other species of intellect and because its capacity to know would be revealed only in the presence of 'true reality', i.e., because in order to criticize the intellect we should have to be a higher being with 'absolute knowledge'. (WM 473)

Nietzsche's argument here recalls Hegel's objection against Kant's critical enterprise.[54] We can only either justify or reject as illegitimate our beliefs *in metaphysicis* (including negative claims of the kind often incautiously made by Kant) if we *have* relevant knowledge. The epistemological criticism would require, Nietzsche suggests, a comparison of the perceptual data cum conceptual framework which constitute our interpretation of reality, with reality itself. This would involve what is for us impossible (assuming

---

[54] G. W. F. Hegel, *Vorlesungen über die Geschichte der Philosophie* (Stuttgart, 1965), iii. 555, and *Phänomenologie des Geistes* (Hamburg, 1952), 64–5. Cf. also J. Habermas, *Erkenntnis und Interesse* (Frankfurt, 1968), 354.

that we are finite beings), namely the adoption of a point of view external to the constitutive features of our, or indeed of any finite, partial 'perspective'—a 'God's eye' view. According to the fragment quoted above, the sceptical predicament is irresolvable for any finite subject of knowledge who, having access to the world 'by [its] perspectival forms [of cognition] and only by these' (FW 374), due to its very limitedness, cannot rule out the possibility of its non-logical beliefs being comprehensively erroneous. For those parts and aspects of reality not accessible to any given finite subject of knowledge might conceivably render these beliefs 'illusory'. It is precisely this putative possibility which traditional sceptical hypotheses are intended to illustrate. (Henceforth I shall generally refer to them as the sceptical 'picture' to avoid the scientific connotations of 'hypothesis'.) Descartes conjectured that all his beliefs about what he normally regarded as an external world of material objects causally affecting him might be false and that the real cause of his perceptual states and of his beliefs (the deceiving demon) might be very different from what he had habitually assumed. In the modern version of this picture it is conjectured that 'I' might in fact be a brain in a vat of nutrients, electrically stimulated in such a way that it mistakenly experiences itself as a complete human being in standard human surroundings.[55] Of course such stories seem fantastic. Indeed, it is in the nature of the sceptic's supposition that it runs counter to our ordinary intuitions. But it is important to remember that they are merely intended as examples illustrating that there are indefinitely many prima facie conceivable ways in which the causes of our beliefs about the 'external world' might differ radically from what 'we'[56] usually take them to be.

[55] See H. Putnam, *Reason, Truth and History* (Cambridge, 1981), Ch. 1. The updating of Descartes's picture of the malicious demon into a scientist producing illusory experiences in a brain through electrical stimulation may render it, perhaps, more accessible to the modern reader, but it may also give rise to the misleading impression that it is essential for the argument that the manner in which the illusions are created be specified and be, to some extent, analogous to the techniques of manipulation and deception with which we are familiar. This impression is misleading because, according to the sceptic's picture, our belief in the efficacy of such techniques may ultimately be just as illusory as any putative knowledge regarding the external world.

[56] It is probably advisable to be more cautious concerning the extension of this 'we' than philosophers writing on scepticism usually are. I intend it to refer to the majority of post-Enlightenment Westerners who, arguably, normally regard most of their beliefs about the external world as ultimately caused by mind-independent

Nietzsche suggests that only a 'being with "absolute know-ledge"', by which I take him to mean an omniscient knower, would be justified in rejecting the sceptical hypothesis, for such a being would by definition be, and know itself to be, 'in the presence of "true reality"'. Where metaphysical knowledge is concerned, a subject would have to know everything in order to know anything.

It may be thought that something rather less than omniscience is required for a subject to know, in the sense indicated earlier, whether some proposition is (non-logically) true or false. To mention only a few alternative proposals, one might for example argue that we know that *p* if *p* is either (*a*) a 'self-justifying' proposition, i.e. one not *requiring* further justification, or (*b*) if *p* can be derived by means of self-justifying rules of inference—candidates would be the rules of inference of classical deductive and inductive logic—from premises which are self-justifying.[57] A question that arises here is, naturally: what is a 'self-justifying' proposition? One way of understanding this expression—the Cartesian way—is to say that a proposition is self-justifying if the subject that entertains or contemplates it cannot doubt its truth while it is contemplating it. But many philosophers would say that something different is required. A proposition may invariably appear indubitable to one person whenever she thinks of it, but not to another. For this and other reasons, there is a strong inclination to argue that the justification, or at any rate the *rational* justification, of knowledge-claims must involve the agreement of different inquirers. If one accepts this point, one might think of interpreting 'self-justifying' as follows: (i) a proposition is self-justifying if and only if it would be taken to be indubitable by any subject who, by our standard criteria in these matters, would be considered by us to be a human being, and who understands it. On this interpretation, we would evidently arrive at an extremely stringent conception of 'self-justifying' and, consequently, of 'rational justification' and 'knowledge'.

A weaker interpretation of 'self-justifying' (ii) would require only that the great majority of competent (human) inquirers—that is, of

objects the intrinsic nature of which bears *some* relevant resemblance, although perhaps fairly remote, to their perceptions of them.

[57] My construal of knowledge here is a broadly foundationalist one. But this is not essential to the main argument of this section. It can readily be seen that the questions raised by Nietzsche would also arise, *mutatis mutandis*, if one chose to adopt a coherentist account.

those who understand the thought(s) in question and who have engaged sufficiently in the relevant sort of investigation—would regard it as indubitable. On a still weaker model of knowledge one might drop the demand for indubitability altogether and only demand that (iii) all, or, still more modestly, (iv) the great majority of competent inquirers would *accept* certain propositions and rules of inference as basic, which by virtue of such acceptance would count as 'self-justifying'.

On all the various construals of 'rational justification' mentioned here, convergence of opinion is essential. Some philosophers might take exception to this, while others are likely to raise objections against the model implied by at least the fourth construal of 'self-justifying' as being too weak. What matters, it may be said, is not so much whether some proposition or rule of inference is generally accepted, but whether they are, respectively, empirically confirmed and reliable. With respect to the first worry, we may certainly choose to define 'rational justification' in a way which does not require convergence of opinion among competent inquirers, and which is yet more restrictive than the principle 'anything goes'. However, such alternatives seem to be of little use in the epistemological matters at issue here, since they allow for an indefinite number of conflicting positions to be 'rationally justified' and, as far as this requirement is concerned, to constitute knowledge. But is not the very point of making rational justification a condition of knowledge to provide some means of adjudication between conflicting claims? Rational justification without convergence of opinion is, in this respect, a concept without a use. As for the second objection, it seems clear that concepts like empirical confirmation and reliability, as standardly used in this context, involve agreement among competent inquirers. A statement reporting the outcome of some experiment in physics is not empirically confirmed unless it is agreed to be so by most competent inquirers, and the same goes, on any useful understanding of 'reliability', for the putative reliability of some method or rule of inference. There may indeed be methods of inquiry which are as a matter of fact reliable although no one is aware that they are. But, here also, it is not clear of what use reliability in *this* sense might be in settling scientific or philosophical disputes.

But why should rational justification be relevant to knowledge in the first place? Surely because most of us consider a belief more likely to be true if it can be rationally justified at least in the weakest sense mentioned than if it cannot. Now, as emerges clearly from passages like JGB 11, Nietzsche would not agree with this. For him, even if we were able rationally to justify a thought considered to be non-analytic in the most stringent of the senses suggested, we would have no good reason to regard it as true. It might be rationally justified and yet it would not be rational to believe it to be *true*. For the rest of this section I shall attempt to clarify this apparently self-contradictory point of Nietzsche's.

It is, I think, fairly undisputed that there are no non-analytic propositions which emerge as knowledge on construals (i) and (ii) of the epistemically basic items, and it is questionable whether any would do so on construal (iii). But some people would probably maintain that there are promising candidates for knowledge on our fourth, weakest, interpretation. Among them, they would claim, are many of the experimental reports of scientists and many of the well-confirmed, that is, successfully predictive, 'laws' established by the natural sciences. We may also perhaps include here, using 'proposition' in a somewhat loose sense, the rules of inference—such as induction—accepted by most practising scientists (even though some philosophers of science have difficulties with them).

Results which are obtained by the application of the epistemic methods of natural science would normally count as paradigm cases of rationally justified beliefs. Examples are the mutually confirming observational results established by different observers in suitably standardized experimental conditions, or certain universal propositions describing putative law-like regularities which have proved successful in predicting such experimental results.

Sometimes it is even claimed that there is a conceptual relation between a belief's satisfying the standards of acceptability enshrined in the methods of modern science, and the 'truth' of that belief. Of course, few would maintain that, say, the agreement of all existing observational reports on the outcome of some frequently repeated physical experiment logically entails the truth of these reports. It is logically possible, though very unlikely, that all those observers happened to be suffering from similar perceptual abnormalities when observing their experiments. Nevertheless, the occurrence of such agreement would certainly normally be considered to make the truth of the reports in question more probable than lack of agreement. And assuming that all human observers of some physical experiment, *whenever* it is performed, agreed on its results (on 'the data'), it might even be claimed that it is difficult to understand what could be meant by saying that their mutually confirming reports might be false. Arguably, 'truth' as used in ordinary non-philosophical contexts, and predicated of statements about the world, receives its meaning by virtue of its application in a range of paradigm situations—which involve 'direct' observation in suitable conditions and intersubjective confirmation—so that it is simply unintelligible to say that a statement which meets *all* the relevant criteria might not be true in this sense.[58]

Similarly, no one would wish to argue that the invariable success, hitherto, of some experimental law or of a more general theory entails the truth of either of them. But let us assume that a theory always predicted phenomena within its domain with the desired degree of accuracy—that it never failed. Let us also suppose that it accounted better than any other possible theory—in terms of predictive success, simplicity, etc.—not only for the data which happened to be available to the inquirers at the time, but for all the relevant data which human observers could, in principle, avail themselves of by cognitive means which are accessible to them through (what we usually take to be) their own powers. Would it not be unintelligible to say that such a theory might nevertheless be false?

According to the remarks of Nietzsche's we are presently discussing, not only would it be *intelligible* to say that such an 'ideal' theory is not true, we would not even have any rational justification to regard it as *likely* to be true. Equally, even if all actual or possible human observers,[59] and all conceivable observers of a similar cognitive constitution, were to agree in their judgements concerning 'observational data'—for example, the outcomes of different realizations of the same type of experiment—this would not even make the truth of these judgements probable. It seems clear that these claims of Nietzsche's, if they are not to be blatantly incompatible

---

[58] A related point was made by Gilbert Ryle. Ryle argued that not all experiences we take to be perceptual ones can be illusory, because in order for there to be illusory 'perceptions' there have to be some veridical ones, just as there have to be, at some point, genuine coins in currency if there are to be counterfeit coins. (G. Ryle, *Dilemmas* (Cambridge, 1954), 93 f.)

[59] The expression 'human observers' is used here in accordance with our ordinary criteria of identification. It consequently—if we take Nietzsche's point—licenses no inferences regarding the metaphysical nature of what it refers to.

with at least one frequent ordinary, non-philosophical usage of the word 'truth', and indeed if they are not to be self-contradictory, must involve a distinction between different senses of 'truth'.

There are a number of notes in the *Nachlass* in which such a distinction is explicitly drawn (WM 515, 584—both written in 1888). In WM 515, he speaks of some Kantian 'synthetic a priori' judgements (those about space) as 'conditional truths'. In the following, I shall use this expression more widely to designate those 'rationally justified' propositions which ideally satisfy the criteria of acceptability enshrined in the methods of natural science (methods which arguably are themselves rationally justified at least in the weakest of our four suggested interpretations). An example of such a conditional truth has been given above: a theory which, besides satisfying various other *desiderata*, never fails to predict with the desired degree of accuracy the phenomena within its domain.

Nietzsche contrasts with 'conditional truth' the notion of *Wahrheit an sich*, which could be translated as 'truth in itself', or perhaps better, 'truth as such'. I shall be referring to this as metaphysical, or absolute, truth (Nietzsche himself uses the former expression in WM 513). To elucidate what metaphysical truth is, it seems helpful to recall the sceptic's picture—a demon deceiving the Cartesian ego, or a super-scientist manipulating a brain in a vat. Here a subject of knowledge is assumed who is 'in the presence of "true reality"' and from whose privileged point of view human beliefs can be recognized as false. Undoubtedly, this subject is conceived in analogy—although possibly a very remote analogy—to what we think of as human subjects. On the sceptic's supposition, both the psycho-physical entity which I normally regard as myself and other 'human beings' may be seen not to exist from the perspective of the privileged, 'undeceived', observer (the demon, the super-scientist, or Nietzsche's 'higher being with "absolute knowledge"'). All my beliefs about the 'external world' are false, and all the methods I normally use to attain 'knowledge' of it turn out to be systematically misleading—they do not engage with reality at all! In this scenario, what seems to determine the application of the concept of truth is the experiences and beliefs of the hypothetical 'undeceived' knower. Thus, to say, for example, that the proposition 'there are square objects' is (metaphysically) false is to say that no instantiations of the property of squareness—items which are sufficiently similar or materially analogous to those *we* normally designate as square—figure among objects of belief of the hypothetical undeceived observer. Many people would say that what a sentence like 'there are square objects' asserts to be the case, when understood in this metaphysical sense, may be the case independently of any actual or possible observer. We shall discuss Nietzsche's views on this matter later. The point to be made here is simply that an analysis like the one suggested here, if it is coherent, is *sufficient* for the sceptic's purposes.[60]

In any case, it is something very much like the distinction between two senses of truth elaborated here which underlies Nietzsche's frequent pronouncements to the effect that our truths *could be* falsehoods.[61] In the light of this distinction, the sceptic's claim, which is also Nietzsche's claim in the passages under discussion, can be restated as follows. A belief about the world may be rationally justified, indeed it may be optimally rationally justified, that is, it may be conditionally true; but there is nevertheless no rational justification for thinking that it is metaphysically true, or that it is likely to be true in this sense. Hence it also does not qualify as knowledge in the relevant sense. Note that the standards of rational justification which we ordinarily employ, or which we at least supposedly employ in paradigmatically rational pursuits such as science, are not questioned here. Nietzsche, unlike Hume, is not concerned, for example, with questioning the justifiability of induction. Rather, the claim is that according to these very criteria of rational justification we have no good grounds to think that conditionally true beliefs are also metaphysically true.

Since the time in which Nietzsche wrote there have been numerous fundamental objections against the procedure of the 'Cartesian sceptic', especially, but by no means exclusively, from philosophers working in the analytic tradition. While it is obviously not possible in a study of this nature to attempt to mention all or even most of these, it may be useful to address at least some of the more influential critical responses to the sceptical problem. If nothing else, this may help to bring the character and import of Nietzsche's own sceptical remarks into clearer focus.

---

[60] It is therefore not the case, as has sometimes been maintained, that the sceptical predicament is only statable on realist assumptions about the physical world.

[61] It is not being denied here that he sometimes goes further and says that our truths *are* falsehoods. (Both versions occur, e.g., in JGB 11.)

One objection which used to be raised frequently has in effect already been answered above. Does not, it may be asked, the sceptic's supposition involve the adoption of radically different standards for what is to count as knowledge from the ones that are 'ordinarily' used, and does it not therefore impose unduly, indeed impossibly, high requirements on the justification of claims to knowledge?[62] While this question would have to be answered affirmatively when asked of Descartes' doubts, it does not, I believe, affect the sceptical problem as such, and it is not pertinent to Nietzsche's remarks. Certainly, the sceptic proposes, or elicits, an understanding of 'knowledge' and 'truth' which is different from the understanding of these terms implicit in many everyday usages and in a scientific context. But the difference, as we have seen, lies in the hypothetical adoption, or projection, of a point of view (a perspective) different from our own, one which is *ex hypothesi* unattainable for us in principle by (what we take to be) our own powers, and from which our beliefs might be seen to be false. It does *not* lie in a revision of our ordinary *standards of rational justification* (such as inductive confirmation). Quite the contrary; the sceptic's point is parasitic on them, since he argues that, in terms of these very criteria of rational justification, we have no grounds upon which to reject his supposition. Admittedly, we also have no such grounds upon which to believe that the sceptic's picture represents correctly what is the case, as its critics have generally been eager to point out. But the assertion of the unavailability of evidence either way, far from undermining the sceptic's point, only paraphrases it. In Nietzsche's words, the 'intellect cannot criticize itself': it cannot rationally assess the possibility of comprehensive illusion because the familiar procedures by which we normally support or criticize claims regarding putative matters of fact cannot get a grip here, *all* our observations being compatible with the sceptic's picture.

This last point is important if we are not to misconstrue the sceptical predicament as it has sometimes been. W. V. Quine, for instance, maintains that the sceptical challenge 'arises from within natural science',[63] but that it would only become a problem if science ceased to be, in its own terms, successful:

[62] Cf. J. L. Austin, 'Other Minds', in *Philosophical Papers* (Oxford, 1961).
[63] W. V. Quine, *The Roots of Reference* (La Salle, 1973), 2.

Experience might, tomorrow, take a turn that would justify the sceptic's doubts about external objects. Our success in predicting observations might fall off sharply, and concomitantly with this we might begin to be somewhat successful in basing predictions upon dreams and reveries. At that point we might reasonably doubt our theory of nature in even its broadest outlines.[64]

These lines seem to me to manifest a fundamental misunderstanding of what the sceptic is saying. To begin with, it is not the case that the sceptical challenge 'arises from natural science', either as a matter of fact or of logic. Neither Descartes in the first *Meditation* nor Nietzsche in the remarks we have quoted arrive at their sceptical suggestions presupposing any scientific data or theories. They do not even mention science. Moreover, the sceptic's supposition can be understood, if it can be understood at all, by anyone without any knowledge of any scientific theories, although one will only understand it if one has at least a basic grasp of what counts as 'rational justification' in science as well as in many everyday situations.

It is also incorrect to say that the sceptic's claim, if it were true, would imply that 'our theory of nature' would fail in its predictions. The sceptic is not committed to any beliefs concerning the course 'our' experience will in fact take. It is quite compatible with his supposition that the world as experienced by 'us', our notional world, consists of phenomenal entities of various types, all change among which takes place in accordance with invariable laws which can be stated in the form of differential equations. It is thus not denied by the sceptic, nor need it be denied by him, that some theories 'work'—are predictively successful—and others do not. One only needs to recall Descartes's own illustration of his point, or its modern version, the brain in a vat, to see that it is integral to the sceptic's picture that, if it were true, the world as experienced by the 'deceived' subject would be qualitatively indistinguishable from its character-as-experienced if that picture were false. It is a feature of the situation as described by the sceptic that it neutralizes empirical evidence.[65] For every item of evidence would, in that situation, be

[64] W. V. Quine, 'Reply to Stroud', cited in B. Stroud, *The Significance of Philosophical Scepticism* (Oxford, 1984), 232.

[65] 'The point of all sceptical hypotheses is the claim that everything in our experience could be exactly the way it is now, even if the world were completely different from the way we take it to be.' (Peter Bieri, 'Scepticism and Intentionality', in E. Schaper and W. Vossenkuhl (eds.), *Reading Kant* (Oxford, 1989), 79.)

part of the illusion the deceived subject is under. Of course, if what the sceptic suggests as a possibility, or an essentially analogous situation, is in fact the case, it would have to be possible, in practice, for our experience to take a different course in the future from what we normally expect. But this does not mean that we would have to be able to disabuse ourselves of illusion by what we think of as our own powers.

But if empirical evidence is really irrelevant in the sense indicated, the question may be asked whether the sceptic's picture does indeed portray a real possibility; in other words, whether it is really coherent. Various arguments denying this have been fairly influential in recent philosophy.

One such line of argument, originating in some of Wittgenstein's remarks, runs roughly as follows. If what the sceptic projects as a possibility were the case, the deceived subject would in fact be solitary, since what he normally thinks of as other human beings like himself actually would not exist. This would mean that the language he supposedly uses to formulate his doubts would be private to himself (for there would not *be* anybody else). But such a language, it is claimed, is impossible. For anything that can intelligibly be called a language involves the use of symbols according to rules. But there can be no language which involves only private 'rules' (known only to the solitary subject). The subject's memory is not sufficient to make possible a consistent use of symbols, i.e. one which could be said to exemplify a rule.[66] For

---

[66] Like some interpreters of Wittgenstein, I shall assume that all that is required of a person for her to be correctly said to be following a rule is that she gets a 'practice' right—e.g. that she sincerely claims to be in pain when and only when she in fact is in pain. There is nothing over and above getting it consistently right that she needs to do or to know in order to be 'following a rule'.

The view that rule-following is only possible if the ostensible practice in question is a public one seems to amount to the supposition that it is only intelligible to say that someone 'gets it right' if the rightness at issue—for example, the consistent use of the same symbol to designate type-identical phenomena—can be monitored by someone other than the symbol-user. Otherwise, it is maintained, there would be no difference between 'is right' and 'seems right'. In this general form this view is highly implausible. An old-style scientist experimenting in his laboratory before the advent of modern scientific teamwork was surely capable of giving a name to a new phenomenon and applying it consistently to occurrences of the same type throughout a whole series of experiments. He may also conceivably have applied such a name inconsistently and therefore 'got it wrong', although he would not have been aware of his mistake—but there would still have been a difference between 'is right' and 'seems right'. Both of these scenarios are not only intelligible but presumably have actually occurred. Naturally it will be replied here either that the publicity

there to be rules at all, it has to be possible for their observance or violation to be checked publicly, that is, by someone other than the ostensible language user. But this is made impossible by the Cartesian picture of a solitary subject. Hence, if the sceptic's hypothesis can be formulated at all, it is false.

There are many subtle variants of this type of argument to which the above statement undoubtedly does not do justice. But for our purposes it may suffice. A number of worries might be raised about the 'private language argument' in particular, such as that the possibility of a public ('independent') check on and possible correction of a subject's use of symbols involves *essentially* a reliance on private memory-contents just as any consistent private usage would.⁶⁷ But the fundamental objection I would like to consider is against the effectiveness of the general transcendental line of argumentation of which the above is an example. Such arguments generally proceed from the premiss, conceded by the sceptic, that there is language (or experience, or experience of a certain sort), and from the further premiss that *if* there is language (or experience, etc.), then some condition x must be satisfied, to the conclusion that x is satisfied. In the present case, x is, allegedly, that there are language users other than the subject in question who can provide an independent check on the rule-governedness or otherwise of the subject's putative linguistic behaviour.

It has been pointed out that such arguments at best license the conclusion that the alleged condition must be *believed* by the subject to be satisfied, not that it actually *is* satisfied.⁶⁸ Nietzsche himself might be thought to be gesturing towards a similar point

requirement only demands the relevant phenomena to be *in principle* publicly accessible, or perhaps that not all the symbol-users' deployment of signs could be of this private nature even in practice. But once it is conceded that it *makes sense* to speak of someone following a rule, or getting it right, in a situation which is *in fact* private (like our reclusive scientist in his laboratory), one begins to wonder about the status of these claims. Can they then really constitute anything more than hypotheses concerning the contingent limitations of human cognitive capacities, such as the fallibility of memory? It would only be *unintelligible* to speak of a person following a private rule if one could not coherently assume her to be in principle capable of determining the conditions of satisfaction of any statements involving a privately devised symbol for a phenomenon that is *de facto* accessible only to her. In that case even our reclusive scientist would not be experimenting but merely doodling.

⁶⁷ See e.g. Stanley Rosen, *Nihilism* (New Haven, 1969), 15–17. For some further remarks on Wittgensteinian arguments, see Ch. 3.1.

⁶⁸ Barry Stroud, 'Transcendental Arguments', in *The Journal of Philosophy* 65 (1968), 241–56.

when he says, in connection with Kantian synthetic a priori judgements, that even if they must be believed to be true, they may still be false (JGB 11—admittedly, the force of the 'must' in Nietzsche's remark is different from that apparently intended by most advocates of transcendental arguments). The objection needs to be interpreted with care. It may be taken to mean that, while the sceptic's supposition might be true, we cannot (in some not very clear sense of 'cannot') believe that it is. From this the conclusion might be drawn that one cannot coherently be a sceptic.[69]

To me the point of the objection seems to be a different one. It is that the best a transcendental argument can establish is that the world *as experienced* must have certain ('phenomenal') features, not that the *world* must have them. If it is countered that, *pace* Kant and standard realism, the notion of a 'world' in contradistinction to the world *qua* object of experience for us is unintelligible, this is quite a separate point, involving the acceptance of some version of the verification principle. With respect to the specific case of the private language argument as an attempted refutation of 'Cartesian' scepticism, one could say that by itself it shows at most that the experience of the subject must be such as to allow for other (apparent) subjects like him who seem to him to share a language with him. But this is quite compatible with the sceptical scenario of illusion—for these other apparent other subjects may 'really' not exist at all. They may be just one more element in the illusory world of the deceived subject. In fact, since the sceptic usually supposes that the world-as-experienced, the notional world, of the deceived subject is at present no different from what it would be if it really were as it appears to be, he takes account of the private language objection in advance. In conclusion, it seems that what transcendental arguments of this sort show, if their premises are accepted, is not that the sceptical picture is incoherent, nor that it is (in some sense) impossible to believe that the world might be radically different from how it presents itself to 'us', but only that the world as it does present itself to 'us', our phenomenal world if you like, has to be of a certain very general character. And this the sceptic can accept with equanimity.

Another objection against general, 'Cartesian', scepticism concerning the external world has found some favour more recently.

[69] Cf. R. C. S. Walker, 'Transcendental Arguments and Scepticism', in Schaper and Vossenkuhl, *Reading Kant*, 73.

For the sceptical scenario to be stable, it must be possible for us to refer to that 'real world' which, if the sceptic is right, we might be cognitively cut off from. However, some philosophers have argued that 'we must [. . .] take the objects of a belief to be the causes of that belief'[70] and that, therefore, it cannot be the case that the causes of our beliefs might be radically different from what we believe them to be. Contrary to the sceptic's implicit assumptions, what a belief *is*—i.e. what it is about—is determined by what it is caused by.

For slightly different reasons, but to similar effect, Hilary Putnam has argued that the supposition that I might be a brain in a vat (a radically deceived subject) is self-refuting, for if I were a brain in a vat, I could not say that I am, for I could not refer to objects, including vats, in the 'real' world, the world of the manipulating super-scientist, at all. I could not, for example, refer to trees in the world of the scientist, but only to my perceptual images or, alternatively, to the electrical impulses causing them, since there would be no causal connection between my use of 'tree' and real trees.[71]

The central tenet of this 'causal theory of reference', which runs counter to some very deep-seated intuitions about reference most of us have, is, roughly, that what we are talking or thinking about—the object of reference—is not determined by what description we would give of the object (or kind of object) to which we intend to refer by a given symbol. What we are referring to in using a given symbol is not, or need not be, what we take ourselves to be referring to. Rather, we are referring, possibly unbeknown to us, to whatever (kind of) object is related to our use of a symbol by an 'appropriate' causal chain.

The theory might be said to represent a continuation of a dominant tendency of analytic philosophy in its initial phase: the endeavour to expose as impossible or incoherent certain ways of using

[70] Donald Davidson, 'A Coherence Theory of Truth and Knowledge', in E. LePore (ed.), *Truth and Interpretation* (Oxford, 1986), 317–18. I shall not inquire in detail into what Davidson's reasons for this claim might be. As Bieri ('Scepticism and Intentionality') notes, they involve a questionable transition from the (plausible) claim (*a*) that the *identification*, by an interpreter, of the beliefs of a speaker depends on the assignment to the speaker of a certain range of possible causal origins of his beliefs, to the claim (*b*) that the *identity* of a belief (what it is about) depends on its *real* causal origins.

[71] Putnam, *Reason, Truth, and History*, 14.

language which, in the *iudicium* of the world, have almost invariably been thought to be perfectly legitimate and unproblematic. But it could also be seen as a culmination of the anti-Cartesian tendency of much modern thought. While Freud (and, on some interpretations, Schopenhauer and Nietzsche) declared that the individual has no special authority to judge what she really feels or desires, the 'causal' theorists claim that she doesn't even have any special authority to judge what she is thinking about. That authority resides, rather, with the 'expert'—not the psychoanalyst in this case, to be sure, but rather, in general, with the causal theorist of reference, and in any particular case, with the historian and, ultimately, with some *future* physicist or neurophysiologist.

It would lead us too far beyond our immediate concerns to discuss the causal theory of reference in any detail—especially as this would necessitate a fairly elaborate engagement with problematic cases which, it is claimed, suggest the inadequacy of the traditional intentionalist account.[72] In our context it is sufficient to raise some questions concerning the status of the theory.

It may certainly be more plausible to construe the (intended!) referent of tokens of an expression on some occasions as, say, the (type of) item to which the expression was originally applied—whatever beliefs about the referent the present user of the expression may have. But this is quite different from, and does not entail, the exceedingly strong claim that it is *impossible* to refer to a (type of) entity by giving a description of it unless there is an 'appropriate' causal chain linking the utterance of the expression

---

[72] The considerations in this regard which seem prima facie most plausible tend to involve none too clear, but at any rate questionable, assumptions concerning the intentional contents which are expressed in the use of indexical and demonstrative words. It is maintained that when I say 'everything which is like *this* liquid stuff in front of me is water', the intentional content 'in my head' is not sufficient to pick out the natural kind I am referring to. By extension of the argument to this effect, one would have to claim that when I say, with the normal and characteristic sense of fully conscious understanding, '*I* am bored', my apparent understanding of what I mean and who I am referring to is not sufficient to individuate the particular item (me) I am actually referring to, for a *Doppelgänger* of mine living in a twin galaxy type-identical to ours might have precisely 'the same' (type-identical) mental content when saying these words, and yet he would be referring to himself rather than to me. It seems evident to me, and I suspect to anyone not in the grip of a philosophical theory, that any account which entails that when I say 'I am bored' I cannot normally tell who I am referring to, myself or a hypothetical *Doppelgänger* of mine in a twin galaxy, or both, by a mere awareness of what is 'in my head'—what I am conscious of and *as* I am conscious of it—*must* be based on an inadequate account of the intentional contents expressed in the utterance of indexicals like 'I'.

and its referent. This latter thesis is hardly an empirical one—especially since its very point is that we need not, in determining the referent of an utterance of some expression, necessarily take account of the sort of evidence most of us would consider to be primarily relevant—namely, what the speaker thinks she is referring to. But if it *were* an empirical thesis, it, and the ostensible evidence for it, would of course themselves come within the purview of the sceptic's doubts.

What we seem to be dealing with is, rather, a metaphysical theory, a 'metaphysics of reference'. In the absence of cogent a priori arguments which establish that it is the only coherent construal of the referential relation, we are entitled to ask why we should accept it.[73] This is, of course, a question the sceptic also will wish to ask: 'how do you know this?' It is evident that, as far as the sceptic is concerned, the causal theorists' metaphysics of reference lacks rational justification in any of the senses we have mentioned. Leaving aside other worries such a theory raises—such as the fact that it appears to involve a changing of the subject through redefining what we commonly mean by 'reference'—it simply begs the question against the sceptic. Certainly, there are many metaphysical theories which, if true, would rule out scepticism. For of course the sceptic must make some assumptions to formulate his hypothesis. His point is precisely that such theories, while some of them might conceivably be true, have not 'rationally' been shown to be true and that, if the evidence of the history of philosophical controversy is anything to go by, it is rather unlikely that any of them ever will. If the sceptic is consistent, he will, in the face of an objection like the causal theory of reference—granting for the moment that it is not unviable for other reasons—simply retreat to a second-order scepticism. He will, in other words, concede that it is *possible* that, contrary to what most of us spontaneously think, the sceptic's point is not coherently statable. But he will add that in terms of the most widely accepted canons of rational justification we have no good reasons to think that it is not.

Another, rather older, kind of objection against scepticism is content to rest its case with what might be called the intuitive plausibility of the commonsensical thought that at least some of our

---

[73] It is hardly sufficient merely to dismiss the traditional 'intentionalist' account as a 'magical' theory of reference (Putnam, *Reason, Truth, and History*), since this is really no more than a tendentious restatement of Brentano's claim that intentionality is *sui generis*.

most firmly held beliefs concerning matters of fact (such as perceptual beliefs about objects presented to us in suitable observational
conditions) are true, or very likely to be true, in an absolute sense.
G. E. Moore may have been making some such point when he
claimed that, while he could not *prove* various propositions about
the 'external world',[74] he was nevertheless more certain that he
knew them to be true than he was certain that any of the assumptions the sceptic needs to make in setting up his scenario of illusion
are true.[75] We shall examine such arguments from intuitive plausibility when discussing some of the claims associated with evolutionary epistemology. Since the conclusions to be reached in that
discussion apply, in essence, to the present case also, I shall forgo a
more detailed treatment here.

But I should like to consider one final response to the sceptical
problem as raised by Nietzsche. It is, strictly speaking, not a response at all, but a rejection of the question. One recent writer, for
example, concludes a discussion of 'Cartesian' scepticism with the
statement that it may be impossible to refute the sceptic, but that
the question he raises is ultimately simply 'uninteresting'.[76] Probably the best-known recent exponent in the English-speaking world
of such a dismissal of the sceptical question is Richard Rorty. In
Rorty's case, it is of course part of a more general rejection of
metaphysics. In earlier writings, he was still prepared to see something 'deep and romantic'[77] in the 'Kantian [...] worry about
whether the words we use have any relation to the way the world
actually is in itself'[78] (although he seemed to regard this worry as
essentially different from Descartes's in the first *Meditation*). More
recently, however, he has suggested that 'our purposes would be
served best by ceasing to see truth as a deep matter'.[79] It is not that
metaphysical or indeed sceptical questions can be shown to be
incoherent;[80] the suggestion is rather that 'we might want to stop
doing those things [e.g. worry about the way the world actually is

---

[74] G. E. Moore, 'Proof of an External World', in *Philosophical Papers* (London,
1959), 150.
[75] Moore, 'Four Forms of Scepticism', in *Philosophical Papers*, 226.
[76] Michael Devitt, *Realism and Truth* (Oxford, 1984), 52.
[77] Richard Rorty, *Consequences of Pragmatism* (Brighton, 1982), 181.
[78] Ibid. 179.   [79] Rorty, *Contingency, Irony, and Solidarity*, 8.
[80] 'On the view of philosophy which I am offering, philosophers should not be
asked for arguments against, for example, the correspondence theory of truth or the
idea of the "intrinsic nature of reality". The trouble with arguments against the use
of a familiar and time-honoured vocabulary is that they are expected to be phrased
in that very vocabulary. They are expected to show that central elements in that

in itself] and do something else'[81]—the something else consisting primarily in what he calls self-creation.

There is, of course, little point in arguing with such an expression of preference. However, we may note that Rorty does not even begin to provide a plausible explanation (nor, perhaps, does he wish to) of *why* metaphysical questions and beliefs have been as central as they have been in Western thought at least since Plato and, arguably, in the self-understanding of Western (and not only Western) civilization more generally. In this, it would appear that he has simply failed to understand the 'conversation of Europe', to use a phrase he frequently invokes. As for scepticism, he seems to regard it as largely a sterile academic question perpetuated by Anglo-American philosophy professors and of little interest to anyone else.[82] While it undoubtedly *sometimes* has played this role, it is no more convincing to explain the persistence of sceptical questions as the result of a conspiracy of academic philosophers than was the Enlightenment explanation of the persistence of religion as due to clerical conspiracies. Nietzsche, of course, was not a philosophy professor, nor did he share this particular type of humanistic Enlightenment optimism.[83]

The *locus classicus* for a rejection of the sceptic's point as in some sense illegitimate or 'inappropriate' is Heidegger's *Sein und Zeit*. For Heidegger, the 'scandal of philosophy' is not, as it was for Kant, that no one had yet succeeded in demonstrating the reality of the 'external world', but that 'such proofs have time and again been expected and attempted'.[84] For '*Dasein*'—by which he means that being which he claims is phenomenologically prior to the philosophical distinction of subject and object founded upon it—'*Dasein* rightly understood resists such demonstrations because it always already *is* what subsequent proofs consider it necessary to demon-

---

vocabulary are "inconsistent in their own terms" or that they "deconstruct themselves". But that can *never* be shown.' (Ibid.)

   [81] Ibid. 9.   [82] Rorty, *Consequences of Pragmatism*, 176 f.

   [83] Rorty's Enlightenment optimism is also very noticeable in his persistent appeals to 'our purposes', 'our common European project', the 'purposes *we* share', etc.— assuming that these locutions are not *merely* (as they undoubtedly *also* are) persuasive devices. Even his characterization of truth as 'whatever emerges from the conversation of Europe' (*Consequences of Pragmatism*, 173) assumes that something will emerge, that there will be, or is likely to be, convergence of opinion. Nietzsche would have regarded this expectation (except with respect to science) as naïve, and the hypothetical outcome as undesirable.

   [84] Martin Heidegger, *Sein und Zeit* (Tübingen, 1986), 205.

strate to it'.[85] In other words, phenomenologically, 'we' always are in an 'external' world, hence there is simply no need to *prove* the reality of the latter. Such proofs 'presuppose a subject which is to begin with world-less or, respectively, not sure of its world, and which in effect first has to assure itself of a world [. . . .] After the breaking apart of the original phenomenon of being-in-the-world, an assemblage of the left-over remnant, the isolated subject, and a "world" is then effected'.[86]

It is not easy to evaluate these imperious assertions or indeed to discern what Heidegger thinks follows from them. For one thing, it is questionable whether they represent an adequate description of the sceptical problem even in its original Cartesian form. Neither Descartes nor many of those who have taken his problem seriously have presupposed a 'world-less' subject—a subject that is not sure of '*its* world' or of '*a* world' (my emphases). Descartes says expressly at the beginning of the third *Meditation*: 'I will eliminate from my thoughts all images of bodily things, or rather, since this is hardly possible, I will regard all such images as false, vacuous, and worthless'. In Heideggerian terms, Descartes realizes that he cannot but see himself as in *a* world, but he proposes to inquire into the status of this 'phenomenal' world, wondering whether it is real or illusory ('false'). The idea of an experiential 'world' which is not real is by no means ruled out by Heidegger's own approach, which explicitly distinguishes these concepts.[87]

More generally, it seems that most of those who have taken scepticism seriously would concede that, certainly, most of the time we experience ourselves as being 'in a world'. They may also agree with Kant that there can only be subjects potentially conscious of themselves as subjects if they find themselves 'in' a world of what they can think of as objects which are 'other' or 'external' to themselves—although they may not usually be aware of them in this extremely general (and, according to Heidegger, etiolated) mode of presentation.[88] They might also well admit that most of the time most of us do not adopt a philosophical or contemplative stance or attitude towards this 'phenomenal' world, making fully explicit our beliefs about it and wondering whether all of these

---

[85] Ibid.   [86] Ibid. 206.   [87] Ibid. 211, first para.

[88] For example, they may in the first place and most often (*zunächst und zumeist*) be aware of some of these objects as 'tools' or 'stuff' (*Zeug*) which is ready to hand (*zuhanden*).

beliefs might be false. Nevertheless, they would argue that as a matter of evident phenomenological fact we *can* become conscious of ourselves as subjects confronted by an 'external' world—otherwise we simply could not *understand* terms like 'subjective' and 'objective', 'self' and 'other', which we all understand, not merely *qua* philosophers, but in our 'average everydayness'. Once we are conscious of ourselves in this way, and once we *do* adopt a philosophical or contemplative attitude, it seems both intelligible and—for some—important to raise questions of the kind the sceptic is asking. Consequently, so the reply might continue, Heidegger is simply missing the point.[89]

The question to ask Heidegger is, in the end, why *Dasein* 'rightly understood' should 'resist' the very terms of the sceptical problem. Is it that these terms simply are intrinsically incoherent, so that it cannot in principle make intelligible sense to ask whether all our beliefs about the 'external world' are false and whether, therefore, our 'world' is merely an 'illusory' one? Such a claim would certainly require considerably more argumentative support than we find for it in Heidegger.

Alternatively (and perhaps more plausibly), Heidegger might be interpreted as enjoining us to resist the adoption of a mode of being-in-the-world in which the sceptical question could arise for us. That question is, as far as he is concerned, 'inappropriate' or 'inadequate'[90] in the sense that it is symptomatic of '*Dasein*'s falling'.[91] Heidegger himself of course strenuously denied issuing or implying such quasi-moral evaluations and enjoinders,[92] but here as elsewhere it is very difficult to interpret these denials as anything other than disingenuous.

In any case, it is certainly true that sceptical questions can only arise and be of interest to us once we are in a certain 'mode' of relating to the world—if we adopt a certain attitude to it. Similarly, and no more trivially, whether we find such questions interesting will depend on what our interests are. As we shall see, Nietzsche, unlike many who are inclined to dismiss sceptical questions as 'uninteresting' or 'inappropriate', attempted a subtle analysis of the interests and concerns which might give rise to them.

---

[89]   Cf. Ernst Tugendhat, *Der Wahrheitsbegriff bei Husserl und Heidegger* (Berlin, 1970), 263.

[90]   Heidegger, *Sein und Zeit*, 207. Heidegger's term '*unangemessen*' conveniently can mean either.

[91]   Ibid. 206.   [92]   e.g. ibid. 167.

3

Beyond Scepticism: 'For—There Is No "Truth"'

1. REALITY AND INTEREST

I suggested earlier that Nietzsche's criticisms of the idea that we possess knowledge—in the sense of true and rationally justified beliefs—about reality fall roughly into two groups. Those in the first category call into question the justifiability, in terms of the standards of rational justification I have mentioned, either of various fairly specific or of rather more general claims to metaphysical knowledge (an example of the former kind would be 'accelerations of physical objects are brought about by a force which is neither material nor mental in character, but whose intrinsic nature is nevertheless known to us'; an example of the latter type is 'there is an external world independent of my states of awareness of it'). The second line of criticism, which will be the subject of the following pages, is directed at the very concept of what I have called metaphysical truth, which has been taken for granted in the sceptical considerations to which we have addressed ourselves up to now.

Although this anti-metaphysical line of thought in Nietzsche contains ideas which have parallels in the writings of other philosophers—particularly Schopenhauer, and the idealists in general—its upshot is considerably more radical than, and indeed contrary to, the conclusions drawn by them. According to the interpretation suggested here, this anti-metaphysical strand of thought—the attack on the notion of metaphysical truth—is one of the most central and distinctive elements in Nietzsche's later philosophy, and thus an understanding of it is crucial to any adequate assessment of his work as a whole. However, the caveat should immediately be added here that the ideas to be discussed in this section are incompatible with other statements of his, an examination of which we shall defer to the following chapter. Sometimes one can even find mutually incompatible thoughts on these issues within the same note or passage. Nevertheless, it is important to isolate and pursue in some detail the remarks which will be considered here, not merely on textual-historical grounds, but for the more important philosophical reason that they contain his most forceful arguments for certain claims concerning truth which are the main basis for his reputation as a radical thinker on the traditional questions of metaphysics.

The analysis of metaphysical truth which emerged in the earlier discussion of the sceptical scenario of illusion explicated truth in this sense, rather vaguely (and ultimately circularly), as a property of propositions (or judgements, beliefs, etc.) in which qualities or relations are predicated of reality or parts of it as it appears to an 'undeceived' subject. More commonly, of course, the reference to such a subject is thought to be dispensable at least in those cases where the relevant objects are 'non-mental' in character. A proposition is regarded as true if it corresponds, in a sense notoriously difficult to explicate satisfactorily, to the structure of reality, mental or non-mental, as it is in itself.[1] In other words, a type of metaphysical realism is advocated according to which many objects (such as those we call physical objects) exist and have a structure or constitution independently of whether we or any other mind-endowed beings have ever existed to perceive them. The entities in question are accorded 'objective existence', a phrase which is usually elucidated by a string of negations: they are *not* constituted by our (or anybody else's, e.g. God's) knowledge of them, *nor* by our (or anybody else's) imposition of concepts, categorial frameworks, or theories.[2]

In Nietzsche's writings, there are many passages in which he suggests that the very notion of a subject-independent entity having properties or 'structure' in itself is incoherent. Even among his early notes we find remarks like the following:

We can say nothing about the thing in itself, for we have eliminated the standpoint of knowing, i.e. of measuring. A quality exists *for us*, i.e. it is measured by us. If we take away the measure, what remains of the quality?

---

[1] For one fairly recent version of this venerable view, see M. Devitt, *Realism and Truth* (Oxford, 1984), 36.
[2] Cf. ibid. 13.

What things are is something that can only be established by a measuring subject placed alongside them [. . .] (PT 37)

A similar point seems to be made in various later fragments and sometimes idealist consequences are explicitly drawn:

'Things that have a constitution in themselves'—a dogmatic idea with which one must break absolutely. (WM 559)

'In the development of thought a point had to be reached at which one realized that what one called the properties of things were sensations of the feeling subjects: at this point the properties ceased to belong to the thing.' The 'thing-in-itself' remained. [. . .]

'The thing affects a subject'? Root of the idea of substance in language, not in beings outside us! The thing-in-itself is no problem at all! Beings will have to be thought of as sensations that are no longer based on something devoid of sensation. (WM 562)

Nietzsche repeatedly asserts that the statement that there are, or might be, objects which have a structure or an intrinsic set of properties which are not essentially properties for a subject, i.e. which could conceivably be instantiated without there being a subject to perceive them, to be 'affected' by or 'concerned' with them, is 'absurd' and 'nonsensical' (WM 583, 558). It would appear that his argument to this effect, which occurs in various formulations in the notebooks, is, at least in part, the classical idealist one maintaining the inconceivability, and hence impossibility, of a determinate, non-perspectival, and in this sense, 'objective' or absolute reality, which was originally put forward, rather ambiguously, by Berkeley, and which was taken up (among others) by Schopenhauer.[3] In its most compelling terms it may perhaps be put as follows: all conceivable instantiated properties (including 'primary' ones) are properties thus instantiated for, or from the 'point of view of', a subject; we cannot concretely and contentfully conceive of, or imagine, any actually existing entity which does not imply a feeling, or perceiving, or conceiving subject or 'mind' to whom it appears from a certain perspective as having a determinate property or set of properties. The more fully we attempt to spell out the conception of some entity as actual at a given time—i.e. as instantiating, at that time, some property or properties—while not being actual *for* any subject, any point of view, or 'perspective'

[3] G. Berkeley, *The Principles of Human Knowledge*, part I, para. 23. Schopenhauer, *The World as Will and Representation*, i. 14, 27; ii. 5, 486–7.

whatever, the more clearly we come to see that the task is unaccomplishable. We may speak, of course, of objects which are actual while not thus implying any subjective perspective whatever, just as we may speak of the greatest finite number or of round squares, but if we really endeavour to bring home to ourselves the meaning of what we have said, we shall invariably fail to do so in a coherent manner. As Schopenhauer puts it:

it is an idea that may, of course, be conceived in the abstract, but not realized. The endeavour to achieve this, the attempt to think the secondary without the primary, the conditioned without the condition [. . .] fails every time, much in the same way as the attempt fails to conceive an equilateral right-angled triangle.[4]

Similarly, Nietzsche declares:

To think away the subject—that is to represent [*vorstellen*] the world without a subject: is a contradiction: to represent without representation! (GOA xi.185)[5]

Nietzsche's formulation here is rather vague and does little to enlighten us as to where exactly the contradiction is supposed to lie. Indeed, prima facie it invites the same interpretation that is standardly given of Berkeley's apparently similar argument. On this reading, we cannot 'represent'—i.e. perceive or conceive of—anything that is actual without being perceived or conceived of by a 'subject' on the grounds that we are precisely asked to represent the object in question to ourselves and thus, once we do so, it *ipso facto* cannot be unrepresented: it cannot be not perceived or conceived of by anyone. If the argument were to be read thus it would certainly

---

    [4] Schopenhauer, *The World as Will and Representation*, ii. 486–7.
    [5] These remarks were written in 1880–1, i.e. during Nietzsche's so-called middle period, but we shall see that they are entirely in conformity with later ideas of his. Notwithstanding his criticism of the notion of the subject as a mental substance or substratum 'underlying' experiences, he himself continues to use this term (cf. also WM 490, 560, 569), and indeed the expressions 'soul' (e.g. JGB, part 9, *passim*) and 'person' (KGW VIII.3.23.3.4), albeit in a modified sense which will be further elucidated in Ch. 6.2. I shall also continue to use the term 'subject', but place it sometimes in inverted commas to remind the reader of the difference of what it signifies from, say, Cartesian, Kantian, or Schopenhauerian conceptions. Nietzsche rejects any construal of the self as either a transcendental subject or as a *res cogitans*. But this does *not* imply, for him, that talk of subjects (or for that matter of souls or persons) is either useless or misconceived—it only means that such talk requires a different interpretation from those he has criticized (see Ch. 2.1. Also Volker Gerhardt, 'Die Perspektive des Perspektivismus', in *Nietzsche-Studien*, 18 (1989), 270–6).

deserve its notoriety.[6] Indeed, if it were accepted in this sense it would entail rather more than those who have advocated it would have wished, namely that no one can conceive of an object that is actual yet not conceived of by *himself*, and that therefore (granting the further step) no such object can exist.[7] Yet, we seem to have no difficulty in conceiving of there being objects which we have never thought of. The reason why we are able to do this is, clearly, that we can distinguish between the *object* conceived and the object *as conceived by us*.[8] When we conceive of an object by means of some mental representation (which may, but obviously need not, involve a visual image or series of such images) we can, and in many cases do, abstract from, or 'discount', certain features of our mental representation, such as, for instance, the property of now-being-thought-of-by-me. Indeed, unless we were able to do this, we could not even distinguish the object conceived from the act of conceiving it. Only some properties featuring in the mental representation are standardly attributed to the object by means of a certain kind of attention given to these properties and of a certain intentional directedness, arguably familiar to all of us, but difficult to describe more precisely, with which these properties, and only these, are attributed to 'reality' beyond our representation.[9] Thus we can conceive of an object being actual, yet unconceived by us (indeed we can intelligibly speak of objects which would exist even if we had never been born). More generally, we can imagine objects without imagining, thinking of, or attending to the subjects by whom they are represented and their relevant states of consciousness. In *this* sense, we can imagine, even visualize, the unseen.[10]

Why is it then, according to Nietzsche, a 'contradiction' to speak of 'represent[ing] the world without a subject'? In order to understand what he is claiming here, we need to pay closer attention to his repeated pronouncements to the effect that what an object is, its

[6] It is questionable whether even Berkeley intended it to be interpreted along these lines, although his formulation certainly suggests this gloss. Cf. A. C. Grayling, *Berkeley: The Central Arguments* (London, 1986), 113–17.

[7] Franz Brentano, *Psychology from an Empirical Standpoint* (London, 1973), 93.

[8] A point also made by Brentano (ibid.), and often since.

[9] T. L. S. Sprigge, *The Vindication of Absolute Idealism* (Edinburgh, 1983), 118. Sprigge's discussion of the argument is the most thorough and searching known to me. My own exposition is generally indebted to it.

[10] Cf. B. Williams, *Problems of the Self* (London, 1973), 34–7.

'whatness' or essence, is something that can only be established, indeed only contentfully conceived, from some determinate perspective or point of view (or sets of perspectives or points of view). The perspective, needless to say, need not be a visual one. Rather, what is designated by this term in this context is simply the determinate manner in which the object appears in perception or conception. For example, if I visually imagine a building, I imagine it from some point of view (or successively, from several). Similarly, if I represent to myself an object in a purely tactile sensory mode, its contours will be represented as resistances to a tactile approach from a certain angle or point (or points): in other words, from a certain 'perspective'. When Nietzsche rhetorically exclaims: 'As if a world would still remain after one deducted the perspective!' (WM 567) he is saying, arguably, that *unlike* certain other characteristics of the mental representation of some object, we cannot 'discount' the perspectival, and thus subject-implying,[11] character of it without the representation ceasing to represent anything in a contentful manner. It is because we cannot do this that every contentful conception of an object involves subject-implying (perspectival) characteristics and it is in this sense that we cannot 'represent the world without a subject'.[12] One should perhaps add at this point that Nietzsche includes in the perspectival, subject-

[11] It would seem fairly clear that the concept of perspective or viewpoint (WM 556) which, in Nietzsche's sense, is essentially linked to concepts like 'concern' and 'interest' (see below), also implies 'subjective'. A 'viewpoint' which involves concerns or interests is *ipso facto* 'subjective', at least in a minimalist sense of the latter expression. This has been rightly emphasized by Volker Gerhardt: 'one must not overlook the fact that perspectives [in Nietzsche's sense] require *subjects* who relate to something other than themselves' ('Die Perspektive des Perspektivismus', 266–8). This does of course not yet commit one to any very specific philosophical conception of the subject. Nietzsche himself explicitly links 'subjectivity' and perspectival 'interpretation' in WM 560: 'That things possess a constitution in themselves quite apart from interpretation and subjectivity is a quite idle hypothesis: it presupposes that interpretation and subjectivity are not essential, that a thing freed from all relationships would still be a thing'.

[12] Some philosophers might be inclined to concede Nietzsche's point with respect to the *qualities* of an object, but would maintain that we can at least conceive certain abstract structures we believe them to possess—such as quantitative relations of functional co-variation—in a non-perspectival way. While Nietzsche does not explicitly address this objection, we may surmise that he would contend that his point applies both to qualities and to formal relational properties in so far as the latter are themselves contentfully conceivable. In any case, the quasi-Pythagorean notion that what is 'objectively real' is 'number', i.e. numerical indices which are not indices *of* some quality or qualities, is dismissed by him as 'nonsensical' (WM 564: 'The reduction of all qualities to quantities is nonsense').

implying, character of an object the aspect of it under which it always (necessarily) is of some degree of 'concern' to a subject, so that, for him, it is meaningless to speak of a really existing object that is of no concern to *any* subject: 'something that is of no concern to anyone *is* not at all' (WM 555). We shall discuss this suggestion in more detail below.

But let us first turn to some objections against the general Nietzschean (and idealist)[13] claim that all conceivable objects have subject-implying properties and that, therefore, it is 'absurd' to suggest that there might be objects which are not objects for some subject. Even if one accepts the premiss that we are indeed incapable of representing to ourselves an object which does not possess any subject-implying properties, this fact, it might be said, would only show a psychological incapability on our part, but it would not license the conclusion that such an object could not possibly exist—the limits of conceivability in the sense in which we have used this term need not coincide with the limits of possibility. To this it might be replied that while it may be true that 'subjective', psychological inconceivability does not entail impossibility, it is at any rate the only criterion we have for considering some ostensible state of affairs to be impossible. Does not the only ground we have for regarding some proposition which purports to describe a state of affairs in the actual world and which is of the form '*p* and not-*p*' as necessarily false, and the state of affairs it purportedly represents as impossible, lie in the fact that we find it 'subjectively' more and more difficult and puzzling to combine its component meanings, the better we come to understand them, in the manner we are asked to combine them?[14] To be sure, it may be asked

[13] In saying that there is an affinity between Nietzsche's view and idealism, I am of course not suggesting that he is committed to a phenomenologically implausible and metaphysically problematic version of the 'veil of ideas' doctrine. When perceiving what we call physical objects, we do not 'immediately' perceive 'ideas' residing non-spatially 'in' an extensionless 'mind' or 'thinking substance'. On the contrary, we *directly* apprehend items which appear as having three-dimensional spatial characteristics, as both Kant and Schopenhauer insisted (*contra* Berkeley). The element of idealist thought I have attributed to Nietzsche is rather that there can only be real objects if there are subjective perspectives from which (or to which) they appear or could appear. (For further discussion of the idealism-phenomenalism issue, see below). It is this element of idealism which was also accepted by phenomenologists like the later Husserl (see e.g. E. Husserl, *Cartesian Meditations* (The Hague, 1977), esp. 83–8).

[14] Sprigge, *The Vindication of Absolute Idealism*, 128. In the light of some of Nietzsche's remarks on logic (e.g. WM 516) it is, of course, questionable whether he

whether our sense of puzzlement or incomprehension when asked to entertain the notion of some entity without perspectival properties is as strong as that felt when we are asked to conceive of, say, an object which is both square and not-square at a given time. Nietzsche appears to assert that it is. Indeed, as we have seen, he seems to claim that it is a straightforward 'contradiction' to say that 'an object *a* exists unrepresented'. Thus he says that 'we possess the concept "being", "thing", only as a relational concept' (WM 583 A) and elsewhere he states, a little misleadingly but quite unambiguously in the particular respect which concerns us here: ' "It exists" means: I feel myself as existing in opposition to it' (KGW VIII.1.5.19). Leaving aside for the moment some of the problematic aspects of this remark, the central point could be interpreted as saying that 'being' simply *means* 'being felt' (or, more generally, being represented) and that it is, therefore, self-contradictory to speak of an 'unrepresented actually existing object'. This invites the question whether we do not have some understanding of 'being', even of 'being an object', which is more fundamental than, or at any rate independent of, our understanding of predicates such as 'being represented' or 'being an object of consciousness'. Is it really, as Nietzsche seems to suggest, an analytic truth, which becomes evident after sufficiently attentive reflection, that whatever 'is' is 'being represented', i.e. that we would not apply the term 'real' to putative entities or properties whose nature could not be contentfully conceived?[15] Even if Nietzsche's argument (as I have interpreted it) concerning the perspectival character of any conceivable object is accepted, might one not intelligibly maintain, without giving an entirely idiosyncratic construal to 'existence', that an object may exist although its nature is not contentfully conceivable by us, or indeed by any subject the nature of which can itself, in the relevant respects, be thus conceived (henceforth I shall refer to this as 'a possible subject')? Could one not, for instance, intelligibly hold a very much weaker view than Nietzsche's concerning the representational implications of notions

could advance such an argument. But if those remarks are to be taken seriously, it is doubtful whether he could meaningfully say anything at all (see Ch. 4.5).

[15] The conceivability requirement, as I understand it, allows in principle for entities whose nature can only be conceived by analogy—however, even the analogues which provide the 'content' of such conceptions would, so Nietzsche's remarks imply, be essentially characterized by perspectival properties.

like existence, being, or actuality—which, like Nietzsche, I have been using synonymously here—and say that some 'object in general = x' may exist even though none of its intrinsic (non-relational) properties are knowable by any possible subject, provided that some such subject, if it were actualized and suitably located, would have representational states whose nature was dependent on the (inconceivable) intrinsic character of x? To be sure, once it is conceded that it makes sense to speak of actual but in principle (i.e. to any possible subject) inconceivable properties of objects, it is difficult to see why one should not abandon the representational condition altogether. One would then hold a strong version of metaphysical realism according to which some 'object in general = x' might exist (be actual) even though it were such that (*a*) none of its properties could be known by any possible subject,[16] and (*b*) the nature of the representational states of any such subject would not be dependent in any circumstances on the (in principle inconceivable) character of x.[17]

Nietzsche's remarks imply that, in order for us to make sense of such a view—which, for him, only appears to be intelligible to those who think about the matter superficially—we would have to have an intuition of 'actuality' which was prior to and thus independent of the predication of specific, hence subject-implying, properties. This, according to him, we do not have, and 'actuality' or 'existence' can therefore not be an intelligible primitive concept, but rather needs to be elucidated by other concepts of the kind suggested by him. It is evident that his line of thinking relies heavily on the unstated premiss that a necessary condition for an adequate grasp of the concepts at issue in the argument (such as the concept of an object) is the ability to contentfully conceive of, or imagine, by means of what I have called a representational content, an instantiation of such a concept.

[16] Such a subject, of course, would have to be defined without explicit or implicit reference to actual objects supposedly represented by it: i.e. it would not be permissible in this context simply to introduce an 'omniscient knower' to refute this version of realism.

[17] The two versions of realism outlined in this paragraph and the preceding one are not only rejected by Nietzsche and classical idealism, but also, it appears, by more recent 'anti-realist' philosophers (in a, to my mind, somewhat oblique and elusive idiom): 'it is difficult to resist the idea that any intelligible statement could, if it were true, be known to be so by some creature suitably placed in time and space and endowed with appropriate faculties of perception and thought.' (M. Dummett, *Frege: Philosophy of Language* (London, 1973), 465.)

Of course, Nietzsche holds no more than Berkeley or Schopenhauer that, because all objects are essentially subject-implying or perspectival, they are therefore dependent on 'us' in the sense that we can determine the course and nature of our experience quite at will. On the contrary, he acknowledges that we do experience patterns of qualities as resistances (*Widerstände*) or inhibitions (*Hemmungen*) to our will which we cannot remove simply by volitional fiat—unlike, say, certain images conjured up by the imagination and terminated simply by what is standardly called an act of will, an instance of what we believe to be volitional agency. The very concept of the objectively real, as we ordinarily apply it, refers to those representational contents which we interpret as *affecting* us or to those possible representational contents which we believe would 'affect' us if certain conditions (appropriate positioning in space and time, sufficient strength of our representational powers) were satisfied.[18] By 'representational content'—an expression not used by Nietzsche—we may here understand the 'object side' of representational states—such as dreaming, imagining, or perceiving—which involve some kind of qualitative, sensory, or quasi-sensory or, more generally, intuitive 'filling'. A representational content is what such a state is said to be *of*. Thus, for example, when I imagine touching a solid cube of such-and-such a size, solidity, and surface structure, it is these instantiated properties, as apprehended from a certain perspective, which constitute the representational content of my representational state.

What is regarded as 'objectively real' are some of those actual and possible representational contents which we cannot (or could not) freely remove, control, or dispose of by mere 'acts of will'—of which an example has been given above—i.e. which (would) inhibit or offer resistance to us in this sense (KGW VIII.1.2.77, WM 533).[19] What Nietzsche's argument so far, if accepted, would of

---

[18] Cf. A. Quinton, *The Nature of Things* (London, 1973), 293.

[19] There are some types of representational contents which 'resist' our 'will' but which we do not regard as objective, namely 'bodily' sensations in their phenomenal character. Nietzsche's view does, as we shall see, allow that sensations *qua* sensations having a certain phenomenal what-it-is-likeness, may be regarded as 'real', but of course they cannot in this mode of presentation be considered to be *objective*. Yet he offers no criteria by which to distinguish such contents from the objectively or 'externally' real. This is not to say that his theory could not be supplemented so as to account for this distinction without drawing on Kantian considerations regard-

course rule out is that we experience these patterns of *Widerstände* because we are causally affected by properties pertaining to non-subject-dependent objects having a structure or constitution in themselves. Whatever the correct explanation of the recalcitrant nature of aspects of our experience, it cannot be found in that type of metaphysical realism—for it is, according to Nietzsche, unintelligible. The concept of 'objective reality', far from explaining *why* we tend to be more concerned with certain features of our experience than with others ('because the former correspond to what is objectively real') in fact can only be elucidated with the help of such notions as interest, concern, and experienced resistance:

> But we have only drawn the concept 'real, truly existing' from the 'concerning us'; the more we are affected in our interest, the more we believe in the 'reality' of a thing or an entity. 'It exists' means: I feel myself as existing in opposition to it [*an ihm*] [. . . .] So, 'being' is grasped by us as that which acts on *us*, that which *proves itself through its efficacy*. (KGW VIII.1.5.19)[20]

Nietzsche's point in this important note from the *Nachlass* may perhaps be interpreted as follows. Philosophers have sometimes

ing the order among the succession of representational contents. Such considerations by themselves would in any case be irrelevant to this particular distinction, for our bodily sensations might succeed one another according to an invariable pattern or order without thereby ceasing to be subjective.

[20] Nietzsche here clearly rejects a position which M. Clark calls 'common sense realism' and attributes to him, namely the view that both the existence and the 'nature of the world is independent of the actual *existence* of knowers and representations' (*Nietzsche on Truth and Philosophy*, 45). There are a plethora of other notes in the *Nachlass*, some written in the very last year of Nietzsche's philosophical activity, in which he quite explicitly and unambiguously attacks this view (e.g. WM 555–6, 559–60, 567–8, 583 A, 625). On Clark's reading, Nietzsche rejects only what she calls 'metaphysical realism', according to which 'the world's nature is independent of what *can be known of it*' by 'any possible knower' (Clark, *Nietzsche on Truth and Philosophy*, 45–6). I suspect that very few philosophers, if any, would avowedly subscribe to such a version of realism anyway, and one wonders why Nietzsche should have taken the trouble of repudiating it, as he is supposed to have done, so strenuously. *Pace* Clark, as the references listed above make clear (and as I have argued throughout this section), according to Nietzsche, accepting 'common sense realism' commits one, whether one realizes this or not, to what Clark calls 'metaphysical realism', i.e. to precisely the view that there are entities with properties (namely non-subject-implying ones) which are inconceivable, and *a fortiori* unknowable, by 'any possible [conceivable] knower'.

Incidentally, if Nietzsche's criticism of 'things in themselves' were to be read as Clark suggests, it would not even affect Kant's notion of a *Ding an sich* as intended by him, for the nature of the *Ding an sich* was not supposed by Kant to be unknowable by 'any possible knower'. A being with intellectual intuition could, for Kant, know things as they are in themselves.

maintained, inspired by Kant's arguments, that a subject can only ascribe experiences to itself if it possesses the concept of an experience in general, and that the possession of this concept in turn requires a distinction between how things seem and how they 'objectively' are.[21] Nietzsche is concerned, in the above passage and elsewhere, with the equally fundamental question, which also occupied Kant, of what could be meant by saying that 'this is how things objectively (really) are'. As already suggested, he seems to maintain that the idea of objective reality essentially involves that of actual or possible 'affections' of a subject. The remarks quoted above, as well as some other passages (WM 533, GM iii.12, last para.) imply strongly, if somewhat obscurely, that a subject's possession of this latter concept requires that that subject be able to think of itself as a being with interests or desires—one such interest might be, for instance, the avoidance of pain—which it thinks itself as capable of pursuing in at least some cases through something like volitional (i.e. self-moving, 'spontaneous') agency. (I take the latter point to be implied by his talk of 'performance', 'struggle', and 'resistance' in WM 533, and of 'inhibitions' in KGW VIII.1.2.77.) It is tempting to interpret the affection or efficacy of which Nietzsche speaks in this context as *consisting in* the resistance or indifference to what the subject thinks of as its volitional agency of some of the representational contents in its experience.[22]

Thus, according to the present interpretation of Nietzsche's remarks, if we did not have interests and desires (or 'will', in his quasi-Schopenhauerian terminology), believing ourselves capable of realizing these at least sometimes through something like volitional agency, we would not be able to distinguish between the self

---

[21] Cf. P. F. Strawson, *The Bounds of Sense* (London, 1975), 107.

[22] Nietzsche's analysis of what it is for something to be a real object 'external' to the 'self' in terms of the interpretation by a subject of certain elements in its experience as affections would seem to imply the view, which is contrary to some of his statements discussed earlier (Ch. 2.1), that we do in fact have a contentful idea of efficacy or power, consisting in the resistance of some of the representational contents in our experience to volitional agency, or to our 'will' (see also Ch. 6.1). His argument, implying that our conception of objective reality involves the notion of causal efficacy, recalls Schopenhauer's tenet that the concept of causality is a priori in the sense of being a condition of our possessing the concept of objects external to us: 'only by the passing of the understanding from the effect to the cause does the world stand out as perception extended in space, varying in respect of form, persisting through all time as regards matter. For the understanding unites space and time in the representation of matter, that is to say, of effectiveness' (*The World as Will and Representation*, i. 12).

and real objects 'external' to it, and consequently would not possess the concept of objective reality distinct from our 'subjective' experiences. We might say that, for Nietzsche, it is a condition of the possibility of a subject's possessing the concept of objective reality not that there be relatively persisting and re-identifiable things constructible from certain elements of that subject's experience, nor that there obtain among many of these elements largely invariant or even immutable causal relations, but that it encounters resistances to what he calls its will. For Nietzsche, unlike Kant, the interpretation of patterns of resistance which we encounter as appearances of enduring, re-identifiable objects (rather than as, say, a flux of events) is not a necessary ingredient in our notion of the objective. However, according to him, it is only as beings with interests who regard themselves as capable of volitional agency that we can have anything like our conception of an objective, 'external', reality at all.[23]

He is of course not merely making the trivial point that only a subject that is active in *some* minimal sense of that term can employ any concepts at all—concept-employment being after all an activity at least in the sense of a process, an event or a series of events—and that only such a subject can thus, *a fortiori*, have a notion of objective reality. Rather, as I have interpreted his remarks, they include the claim that if we analyse the concept of the objectively real, we shall find that *part* of what we mean by '*x* is objectively real' is '*x* is independent of, in the sense of resistant to, some

---

[23] Several years after Nietzsche, W. Dilthey developed in some detail the 'assumption that the essence [*Kern*] of the experience of resistance, hence of the reality of objects[!], is constituted by the consciousness of an impulse of the will and of intention, and then by the obstruction of the intention, i.e. by two volitional states' (p. 102). Dilthey maintained that the conceptual part of his thesis was supported by numerous case studies from medical practice. Patients who had temporarily suffered from an abnormal absence of desires and 'stirrings of the will' (*Willensregungen*) afterwards reported a concomitant disappearance of any sense of the reality of the objects presented to them in that state (pp. 117–24). Dilthey concluded: 'If one could conceive of a man who was only perception and intelligence, then this intellectual apparatus would perhaps contain all manner of means for the projection of images: but all of this would not make possible a distinction between the self and real objects' (p. 130). (W. Dilthey, 'Beiträge zur Lösung der Frage vom Ursprung unseres Glaubens an die Realität der Aussenwelt', in *Gesammelte Schriften*, V (Leipzig and Berlin, 1923). A somewhat similar position was also developed by Max Scheler. (See his *Erkenntnis und Arbeit* (Frankfurt, 1960) and 'Idealismus-Realismus' in *Späte Schriften* (Bern, 1976).) My reconstruction of Nietzsche's view differs in various important points of detail from both Dilthey's and Scheler's theories.

subject's apparent agency'. Thus, 'objectively real' is, for Nietzsche, elliptical. It would be more accurate to say that '*x* is objectively real for, or relative to, some subject'—but that subject has to be of a certain kind. We can imagine, Dilthey suggests, a 'perceiving mind' that was confronted with, or exposed to, a stream of images in thoroughgoing order and regularity, but that lacked any of the characteristics subsumed by Schopenhauer under his concept of the will—any desires, emotions, or any sense of itself as an intentional agent. If this assumption is indeed coherent, we can also imagine that, whenever this mind is aware of a red image, the sentence 'occurs' to it, as if infused via some divine telepathic inspiration, that 'this is red', and that this sentence is present to its awareness and accompanied by a sense of understanding just as we have it when we think 'this is red', looking at a similar image. However, for both Nietzsche and Dilthey, it could *not* understand 'this is objectively real' unless it also had interests and desires and a sense of itself as a 'spontaneous', quasi-volitional agent. Anything like our distinction between what is 'subjective' and what is 'objectively real' simply would be impossible in such a case. With however much orderliness numerically different representational contents might succeed one another 'according to a rule', allowing in principle for the 're-identification of particulars', every representational content would, for such a mind, be just that: one more image. (As will be argued below, Nietzsche would not even accept what I have assumed here for the purposes of illustration, namely that a subject could in principle at least *individuate* representational contents without interests and desires governing the individuation and classification. His denial of this implies that on his view—unlike Dilthey's—the concept of a desireless subject is incoherent.)[24]

On the other hand, it could be argued that we can quite well imagine a subject whose experiential world contains very little order—few regularities of succession among its representational

----

[24] I have attributed to Nietzsche the claim that (i) desires, interests, or values, and (ii) the ability of the subject to think of itself as a volitional (free, spontaneous) agent, are necessary conditions for that subject both (*a*) to individuate experience-contents, and (*b*) to possess something like our concept of objective *reality*. Even for someone generally sympathetic to Nietzsche's approach, it may seem questionable whether (ii) really is a necessary condition of (*a*). Might I not be aware of numerically and qualitatively distinct items in my experience even if I could not consider myself as an agent?

contents which hold independently of what it thinks of as its own agency, and few continuities allowing for re-identification of numerically identical particulars—while having various interests (e.g. avoidance of certain colour patterns which it experiences as painful), and also the ability to regard itself as an agent. The reason why it can think of itself as an agent is that some of the 'objects', or representational contents, it encounters behave in its experience rather like our own idle imaginings do in ours (that is, they are responsive to some of our wishes, those we call intentions), while others behave more like tables and chairs do with us (i.e. rather unresponsive in this respect)—with the difference that they frequently and inexplicably disappear and are replaced by other 'objects'/contents according to no apparent rule. Such a subject could arguably nevertheless in principle have a grasp, however rudimentary, of the meaning of 'subjective' and of the notion of 'objective reality' contrasted with it. While this may seem implausible to some, I suspect that this is because of one's tending to import into the hypothesis various assumptions and beliefs we have about the quite contingent limitations of specifically human cognitive powers (such as a weak, fallible memory).

The central point which the above thought experiment is intended to illustrate is this. On the present construal, the difference between a broadly Kantian account of objective reality and that which I have attributed to Nietzsche—and which was also held, in its essentials, by Dilthey and Scheler—is ultimately a disagreement about what we *mean* when we say that something is objectively real. It may be interjected here that the 'conditions of the possibility' of an objective world assumed by Kant were supposed by him to be 'necessary' in some sense *other* than conceptual necessity. But it is difficult to see what other relevant sense there might be, except an ultimately psychological necessity, conditional upon the truth of various assumptions concerning a given subject's contingent psychological limitations. And, to repeat, it seems to be precisely such suppositions which often give to various more recent 'transcendental arguments' a, to my mind, ill-deserved air of plausibility.

To return to Nietzsche. We may further illustrate his general point by a rather pedestrian example drawn from our everyday encounter with the 'objective world' of common sense. What makes me believe that there is a closed door in front of me which does not merely 'seem' to be there? Should I have the intention to go out of the room, the closed door will, in a certain sense, 'resist' this intention, and it differs in this respect from a door which—as we say—I merely imagine to be there. The 'real' door is, in other words, systematically indifferent to my simply wishing, indeed 'willing' or 'intending', it to disappear or to be absent, in contrast to an object which I would call imaginary.[25]

A similar point could be made—with some qualifications we shall come to presently—regarding qualities apprehended by senses other than touch. I believe that the table which I see in front of me is a 'real' table because, if I turn my eyes away from it and then turn them back, I will again see the table no matter whether I wish to see it there or not. The world which we ordinarily consider to exist 'objectively' and externally to us is thus a system of resistances which we either experience as actual or which we would expect to encounter in various roughly specifiable circumstances (these experiences of resistance must of course not be simply identified with *sensations* of various kinds, e.g. tactile ones—a point also made by Scheler and William James). The above-mentioned phenomenological characteristics of what we consider to be real objects had of course been noted by philosophers prior to Nietzsche—for instance, by Descartes, Locke, and Berkeley—but, with the partial exception of the latter, they did not draw his radical conclusion that 'objective reality' can only be explicated with recourse to them.

Let us now turn to a second aspect of the passage I quoted earlier (KGW VIII.1.5.9). Nietzsche seems to imply in it what he states more explicitly elsewhere (WM 588), namely that our concept of objective reality as analysed by him allows, *in principle*, for grades or degrees, in other words that it is only contingently the case that for us, or at least for most moderns, objective reality is an all-or-nothing affair. Clearly, not every representational content in a subject's experience which is resistant to its will in the sense suggested earlier is equally credited by it with being objectively real. Rather, it is, according to him, those recalcitrant elements in its

---

[25] We may here take any intention to move one's body in a way which would involve a sensory encounter with the object if the object were real, but which simply ignores, or involves the attempt to ignore, the object as a special case of wishing or 'willing' it to be absent. For an account of what it might mean to speak of willing with respect to objects where willing is generally ineffective, see T. L. S. Sprigge, *Facts, Words and Beliefs* (London, 1970), 288–97.

experience which affect its interest most strongly which are interpreted thus.

Perhaps his meaning here can be brought out more clearly by considering, again by way of example, Locke's distinction between primary and secondary qualities. On a Nietzschean view, *one* part of the explanation why a Lockean primary quality such as solidity has traditionally been accorded real existence in the objects while this privilege has usually been withheld from the qualities he designated secondary ones (e.g. colour) would presumably be that the former is associated with, indeed constitutive of, those aspects of our experience which normally affect most of us most forcefully and pervasively and which are for this reason of greatest concern to us. It has been suggested, not unconvincingly, that this centrality of the Lockean primary qualities in our experience and their correspondingly great concern to us is largely due to the fact that they involve the sense of touch—or more precisely, of tactile pressure—in a way secondary qualities do not.[26]

It will of course be replied at this point that the basis for something like the Lockean distinction is rather more simple: primary qualities, suitably interpreted, are involved in the scientific explanation of phenomena, while secondary qualities do not enter into these—they are 'explanatorily idle'. (As some philosophers might put it: 'they don't do any work for us'. Secondary qualities are, so to speak, the undeserving poor of metaphysics.) Nietzsche, it seems to me, could concede this without prejudice to his main point. He could reply that what, according to him, we have *de facto* come to regard as 'explanation' in science since Newton's refusal to feign hypotheses—the discovery of ever more comprehensive laws and theories describing regularities of concomitance and succession among phenomena and the subsumption of particular occurrences under familiar types of regularities for the purpose of prediction and control—is itself, with respect to its status as explanation, dependent on certain fairly obvious interests of subjects like us. It is only in so far as we have a vital interest in predicting and manipulating various events and 'objects' which figure or might figure in the course of our experience that we consider certain universal propositions enabling us to do so to be 'explanatory', that is, to be answering the questions we desire to ask. To argue that those

[26] J. Bennett, 'Substance, Reality, and Primary Qualities', in C. B. Martin and D. M. Armstrong (eds.), *Locke and Berkeley* (Notre Dame, 1968), 117.

representational contents, like perceived instantiations of colour, which do not play a part in 'explanations' of this kind are *therefore* not 'objectively real' is evidently to introduce a criterion of reality which is dependent upon certain interests subjects like us, even though in slightly varying degrees, generally have (or so I shall presume). Why, one might ask, attempting to ignore these particular interests for a moment, should it be relevant for determining the 'objective reality' of instances of type x that numerical indices for the arguments of x figure in certain functional equations useful for prediction? The perspectivalness or interest-dependence of such a criterion of reality becomes obvious if one considers the following analogy. A future science of the mind might conceivably make any appeal to episodic states of consciousness obsolete for the prediction of human behaviour. Would this compel us to deny the *reality* (which is of course not *objective* reality anyway) of occurrent states of consciousness like fear or anger or love? *If* Nietzsche's account were applicable to items which are not object-like (such as states of consciousness in their phenomenal nature), his answer presumably would have to be: that depends on the interests of the inquirers or, to introduce another term he often uses in this context, on their values.

Another illustration of the line of reasoning which, I have suggested, underlies Nietzsche's remarks may perhaps be helpful here. Many of us tend to regard a 'secondary' quality like colour as not being really 'in the objects', arguably because colour does not play any part in scientific explanations of phenomena and because, furthermore, we can manipulate the colours objects appear to have by applying those explanations in appropriate ways.

Now, usually our visual and tactile experiences are mutually congruent to a remarkable extent in the following sense: the boundaries of objects as they present themselves to us in different sensory modes, e.g. as discontinuities of colour and as resistance to touch, tend to coincide in these various modes. But suppose that our experiences of colour particulars and tactile particulars were generally not congruent in this manner, but rather diverged from one another frequently and systematically, and that no conventional account couched in terms of the 'primary' qualities of objects had succeeded in explaining this fact. Let us also assume that we had resigned ourselves to accepting that no explanation of this kind was possible. We would then be confronted with two synchronic but diverging patterns of 'resistance', in Nietzsche's terms. In one sensory modality, there would be our tactile experiences, while in another, we would be aware of a variety of non-solid patterns of colour expanses the boundaries of which would not coincide with the former. Would we, in those circumstances, regard ourselves as living in two different 'objective realities' irreducible to each other? On Nietzsche's account, this would not necessarily be the case. What we would acknowledge as being objectively real in this hypothetical case would be determined by, and ultimately not specifiable independently of, our dominant interests and concerns. Having the kind of interests subjects like us do in fact seem to have, it might be thought likely that we would regard as real those observable and theoretical entities which would either figure in our tactile experiences or in the 'explanatory' generalizations by means of which we could predict and, to some extent, exert control over the contents of those experiences.[27] But it is also conceivable, on a Nietzschean view, that we would, in such circumstances, explicitly distinguish between different levels, orders, or degrees of objective reality.

Once it is recognized that what counts as an explanation for a subject depends on that subject's interests and 'values' it can also readily be seen—although we shall not pursue this point in any detail here—how Nietzsche's explication of 'objective reality' could be defended against certain objections arising from the consideration of phenomena like dreams and hallucinations. These, it might be said, constitute obvious counter-examples against the kind of account adumbrated by him, since in them we are confronted with patterns of resistance which are *not* accorded objective reality by us (or, at any rate, by most modern Westerners), thus suggesting that Nietzsche's criteria are, at the very least, not sufficient. However, if we are prepared to acknowledge (with B. Williams)[28] that there is an explanatory asymmetry between what we normally call veridical experience on the one hand, and hallucinatory and dream-experience on the other, and if it is the case that an account which

---

[27] As R. Norman has pointed out, we would normally call an apparent object which we can feel but not see an invisible object, but we would refer to one which we can see but not feel as an illusion or a hallucination ('The Primacy of Practice: "Intelligent Idealism" in Marxist Thought', in G. Vesey (ed.), *Idealism—Past and Present* (Cambridge, 1982), 161–2).

[28] B. Williams, *Descartes—the Project of Pure Enquiry* (Harmondsworth, 1978), 309 f.

we consider explanatory is one which answers to our satisfaction questions which are of importance to us, given the interests that subjects like us generally have, then it may readily be seen that Nietzsche could account for the distinction under discussion in his own terms. What makes us regard dream experiences as non-veridical is not that they are necessarily less coherent with one another than those experiences we call veridical—for they need not be—but that we believe them to be 'explicable', which means, in part, controllable by applying theories, sometimes very rudimentary ones, from waking life. The latter thus, as it were, 'reaches into' dream experience, while the reverse is generally not the case. As Nietzsche's remarks would lead us to expect, it is this difference, and the corresponding difference in the degree to which our interests are affected in dream and waking experience respectively, that accounts for the fact that we accord objective reality to (some of) the contents of the latter, but not of the former.

Another line of criticism might be thought to create more serious difficulties. Doesn't Nietzsche's approach, as I have interpreted it, involve the following two assumptions which are rather questionable both from a textual and from a philosophical point of view? First, that there are 'acts of will' by means of which some 'subject' may initiate events *ab novo*. Secondly, that there could conceivably be self-conscious subjects prior to the constitution, relative to them, of an external, objective sphere. Is such a supposition not rather problematic, particularly in the light of a number of well-known Kantian and post-Kantian arguments to the contrary?

With respect to the first objection, we should remember that Nietzsche's statements concerning volitional acts are by no means exclusively negative (cf. Chapter 6.1). But, in any case, what his account of the objectively real, according to the present reading, requires is not that there actually *are* causally efficacious acts analogous to what philosophers have traditionally called acts of will, but that the 'subject' for which there is an objective, external world must be able to *think of itself* as capable of something like volitional agency. What this in turn requires is arguably no more than that some of the contents in the subject's experiential world change in accordance with the sort of sincere wishes that are not checked by countervailing desires or considerations and that we call 'intentions' if they occur with respect to representational contents that do normally change in accordance with them. Whenever our experiential world changes according to our intentions in this sense, we regard ourselves as having acted 'freely' or 'voluntarily', and it is freedom of the will in this limited sense which is sufficient in the present context. As Nietzsche remarks, 'free' here means 'without a *feeling* of being compelled' (KGW VII.3.34.250, my emphasis).

Concerning the second point it might be replied that, regardless of whether Kant and those who have followed him are right in this matter or not, Nietzsche is no more committed to the absolute priority of the subject than Schopenhauer is in the first book of *The World as Will and Representation*. He might very well concede that just as there can be no 'real objects' without a 'subject' that has desires or, in his terms, interests or values, so there can be no such potentially self-conscious subject without what it takes to be an external, objective sphere. Nietzsche does, as far as I am aware, not explicitly say this, but nothing in what he does say rules out such a response, and this would seem to be sufficient to deflect the criticism.[29]

This is perhaps the appropriate place to interpose some remarks about the relation between Nietzsche's and Schopenhauer's views concerning objects and objective reality. For this purpose it is important to distinguish two aspects of Nietzsche's position as we have elaborated it. Nietzsche maintains, first, that the individuation and classification of representational contents is only possible for a subject that has what he refers to variously as 'interests', 'values', 'will', or 'affects' (for the latter locutions, see GM iii.12, last para.). Secondly, only such a subject can have something like our concept of objective *reality*. That these are two different theses can be easily seen by considering cases of vivid imagining or daydreaming in which one clearly does individuate 'objects' without, usually, according objective reality to them. Now, Schopenhauer makes it quite clear that, for him, the individuation and classification of objects is possible for a subject considered in abstraction from its

---

[29] Another objection against the sort of view I have attributed to Nietzsche appears to be raised by Martin Heidegger: 'the experience of resistance, that is, the discovery of that which resists one's endeavour, is ontologically only possible on the basis [*auf dem Grunde*] of the disclosedness of the world' (Heidegger, *Sein und Zeit*, 210). While these and similar statements by Heidegger are indeed 'not very precise' (Scheler, 'Idealismus-Realismus', 263), their apparent point seems to be adequately countered by Scheler's reply: 'certainly: the sphere of the external world is disclosed, but *in* [or: *through*] its resistance' (ibid. 322).

(phenomenal) 'will'. He declares, for example, that 'for the purely knowing subject as such, this body [its own] is a representation like any other, an object among objects'[30] and repeats, a little later: 'the knowing subject is an individual precisely by reason of this special relation to this one body which, considered apart from this [i.e. apart from his awareness of the will in himself], is for him only a representation like all other representations.'[31] Nietzsche evidently goes further than Schopenhauer on this point, as for him no individuation/classification of objects, or 'representations' in Schopenhauer's terminology, is possible without the 'will'. Concerning the second thesis, some remarks Schopenhauer makes *en passant* might be read as anticipating Nietzsche. Thus he says that, if we were not also aware of ourselves in our aspect as affective or volitional beings, the world of representations 'would inevitably pass by us like an empty dream, or a ghostly vision not worth our consideration'.[32] But his statements in this context seem rather too cursory to inspire confidence in the conclusion that his view here is actually the same as Nietzsche's.

It may be asked what distinguishes Nietzsche's analysis of objective reality from plain phenomenalism. First, there is his emphasis on the crucial role of the subject's interests or 'values' without which, according to him, anything like our notion of an objective reality, a reality external to the 'self', would be impossible. As I have interpreted him, his claim is not merely the now frequently accepted one that reality does not impose any particular way of classifying the data of experience; it is, rather, that 'we' tend to classify those data according to our interests, and that there is no classificatory scheme that might usefully be called the correct one independently of the specific interests of the classifier(s). Nietzsche, of course, agrees with this, but he suggests, at a more fundamental level, that the very concept of objective reality is to be analysed as 'objective and real *relative to*' some 'subject(s)' that has interests or 'values' and can regard itself as capable of realizing or satisfying these in something analogous to what we think of as our volitional agency.

A second point which distinguishes the account suggested by Nietzsche's remarks from (ontological) phenomenalism is that it is not committed to the claim that there is nothing to the ordinary

[30] Schopenhauer, *The World as Will and Representation*, i. 99.
[31] Ibid. 103.   [32] Ibid. 99.

objects of sense perception, such as trees and mountains, other than actual or possible perceptions of ours, or of observers like us. For him, these objects may certainly consist in more than the experience-contents, actual or to be expected, of observers of a certain type. There may well be, as far as the logic of the Nietzschean account up to this point is concerned, something actual about the world which makes subjunctive conditionals of the form 'if I were to do x now, I would see y' true (conditionally true, in Nietzsche's sense). However, that something cannot be an object—a material thing—existing in itself. Nietzsche's view seems in fact to be closer to idealism than to ontological phenomenalism: in so far as we consider an item to be objectively real (actual) while unrepresented by us, we—whether we are fully and explicitly aware of this or not—consider it to be represented by *some* 'subject' (although this is, given what has been argued so far, not a *sufficient* condition for it to be considered objectively real). However, since his statements are elusive and ambiguous on this point, this interpretation can only be offered tentatively.

Nietzsche's analysis of objective reality may appear to be inconsistent with the sceptical argument discussed earlier. The privileged 'undeceived' observer in that argument, as well as the objects he perceives, do *ex hypothesi* not figure in the perceptual experience of the subject(s) deceived by him. Hence it might seem that, on Nietzsche's account, they cannot be real for those subjects and the sceptical predicament simply cannot arise for them. This conclusion would be too hasty. Still, the question needs to be asked why, in the sceptical picture, we should credit the hypothetical 'undeceived' knower (the demon, the super-scientist, or Nietzsche's 'being with absolute knowledge') with having access to truths about objective reality, while being prepared to consider our own point of view to be subject to systematic illusion. What makes that hypothetical 'other world' 'real'?

how do we arrive at the idea that our world is *not* the true world?—it could be that the other world is the 'apparent' one (in fact the Greeks thought of, e.g., a *shadow kingdom*, an *apparent existence*, beside true existence). [. . .] It is symptomatic that such a distinction should be at all possible—that one takes this world for the 'apparent' one and the other world as 'true'. (WM 586)

To accept (as the sceptic does), as a logical possibility, that the perceptual beliefs of ours, or of any observers like us, might be systematically false *means* to be willing to entertain the conjecture that there might be a kind of perceptual awareness, (*a*) the contents of which differ radically from ours, and (*b*) which appears preferable or more valuable to us than our own, even though it may, even in principle, be unattainable for us by (what we take to be) our own powers. For Nietzsche, to repeat, 'values' (interests, concerns) are a condition of the possibility of objective reality. If we did not regard the perspective of the deceiving demon (or the super-scientist) to be preferable to, or more valuable than, that of the 'deceived' subject, we would not necessarily deny the *occurrence* of the former's experiential episodes, but we would, according to him, deny that any of their experiences represented anything objectively real, i.e. that they referred to anything but illusory objects (just as the sceptic does not deny the occurrence of experiences on the part of the deceived subject, but suggests that all their representational contents—including the subject's own body as perceived by him, his position relative to other apparent objects in space, etc.—might be illusory).

What could the interests be which might induce us (or indeed any 'subject') to acknowledge a type of awareness as being more valuable than our own, even if such an awareness were *ex hypothesi*, i.e. in principle, unattainable by any cognitive methods or techniques at our disposal? We shall see below that a very similar question arises, or should arise, also for the realist metaphysician who believes that material objects exist independently of being represented. One might argue that what makes, on the sceptic's supposition, the deceiving demon's beliefs 'true' (more valuable, given our concerns), and our own 'false', is the fact that the former enjoys a power we do not possess—he is after all assumed to be manipulating our own experiences, although we are not cognizant of this. In that case, what would make the judgements of that knower true and ours false would be the fact that the former are more conducive to a certain kind of manipulative and controlling activity, that is, to the exertion of power. What this would seem to amount to is a *definition* of the truth of a belief at least partly in terms of its conduciveness to the exertion of power by the 'subject' holding that belief.

Nietzsche's general view allows also for interests other than what might broadly be called technological and manipulative ones, which might lead us to regard some (supposed) 'other world' as 'real'—for instance, aesthetic values. However, if *no* such 'ulterior' interests or values determined a person's supposition or belief that some radically other perceptual or quasi-perceptual awareness represents or might represent *reality*, this supposition becomes thoroughly mysterious and indeed unintelligible—at least if one grants Nietzsche's premiss that the truth of the relevant judgements of some hypothetical other, 'undeceived', knower cannot consist in their mirroring, or being isomorphous to, or in some weaker sense corresponding to, the structure of material objects or of metaphysical facts as they are in themselves, independently of any subject's awareness and concern.

One important implication of Nietzsche's reasoning is that for beings experiencing different 'sensations', encountering different patterns of resistance, and having different interests and concerns, there would indeed be different 'objective realities'. Nietzsche himself says, a little incautiously:

It is obvious that every creature different from us senses different qualities and consequently lives in a different world from that in which we live. Qualities [i.e. qualities as perceived by us] are an idiosyncrasy peculiar to man; to demand that our human interpretations and values should be universal and perhaps constitutive values is one of the hereditary madnesses of human pride. (WM 565)

And he concludes from this that 'There are many kinds of eyes. Even the sphinx has eyes—and consequently there are many kinds of "truths", and consequently there is no truth' (WM 540).

For a strong metaphysical realism, certain propositions about objects and their properties are metaphysically true irrespective of whether any conscious subject entertains or believes them or is in a position to obtain evidence for them. Nietzsche contends, on the contrary, that 'the insect or the bird perceives an entirely different world from the one that man does, and that the question of which of these perceptions of the world is the more correct one is quite meaningless' (PT 86).

The example given here by Nietzsche—which, although taken from an early notebook, is quite in keeping with the general line taken in his later writings—is hardly capable of sustaining his point. For although it is generally accepted among biologists that organisms of different species live in sometimes dramatically different *Umwelten*, that is, that the range of perceptual stimuli registered by them varies dramatically, the realist, while conceding this, may still maintain that all these phenomenal 'worlds' are nevertheless selective representations of the same ontologically independent objective reality, the world as described by natural science and, less adequately, by common sense (cf. Chapter 4.5). He is also likely to add that science is capable of explaining *why* organisms of some species perceive the world differently from the way we do. But however different the perceptions of an insect may be from ours (if indeed it is permissible to attribute perceptions to an insect), it still lives in the same world. If it is not equipped to register the stimuli associated with the approach of a car, it will nevertheless be hit by it, just as we would if we happened to find ourselves in its place. Therefore, so the reply might continue, it is located in the same, unitary, objective reality as we are, a reality which is, at least partly, accessible to description by metaphysically true statements. So it seems that Nietzsche's argument from differences among the perceptual capacities of empirical organisms of different species fails to warrant his conclusion. And it is, of course, not surprising that empirical findings of the sort mentioned by him do not succeed in establishing his 'transcendental' (in my interpretation: conceptual) point. However, perhaps a more compelling argument could be devised which does have some similarity to Nietzsche's, but does not rest on such empirical considerations.

Let us assume for this purpose a quasi-monadic mind, or experiencing 'subject', who is, from our point of view, disembodied. If we wish, we may locate this quasi-monadic mind at a particular point in physical space. Let us also suppose him to be continually confronted with a stream of experiences of some kind. In order to take at least some account of Kantian worries about the unity of apperception and the sort of experiences allegedly required for it, we may even assume them to contain a succession of phenomenal elements—say, coloured, three-dimensional shapes—which he interprets as appearances of enduring, re-identifiable objects, any changes in which occur in accordance with invariable laws. One of these objects he particularly associates with himself as his 'body'. We may also perhaps assuage certain Wittgensteinian qualms by stipulating that he thinks of himself as communicating in some language with what appear to him to be other individuals like him who seem occupied, among other things, with keeping a check on his use of language. For the purpose of the argument, little hinges on the nature of the contents of this mind's consciousness, except that we require it to be incapable of experiencing, or being 'affected' by, the specific spatio-temporal pattern of extended objects (of resistances in Nietzsche's sense) which we find ourselves confronted with. Being from our point of view—though not from its own—disembodied, it is not affected, restricted, hampered, or supported by the same *Umwelt* of 'material objects' against which we partly define ourselves.

It may be objected that the existence of such a mind is in fact impossible—mental states requiring some physical substrate to be realized in. But not only does this objection presuppose the acceptance of a particular metaphysics, it should also be obvious that it is beside the point. The purpose of thought experiments like the present one is to tell us something about our concepts, and about the structure of our beliefs and values, and they can perform this role provided that we, their addressees, continue to find them intelligible, irrespective of whether the state of affairs they project is *de facto* possible on the assumptions made by the adherents of one or another metaphysical view. If we grant the intelligibility of this thought experiment—and I cannot see any cogent reason why we should not[33]—we can rephrase Nietzsche's statement as follows: it is *conceivable* that there are 'subjects' who experience themselves as affected by an entirely different 'objective reality' from the one that we do, and the question whether their beliefs or ours would be 'true' in some absolute, non-subject-relative sense is entirely meaningless.

Ordinary metaphysical realism with respect to material objects has it that certain thoughts about them are true regardless of whether there are any knowers who believe them or are capable of establishing their truth. For a realist of this type, the disembodied mind in our thought experiment is simply ignorant of all meta-

[33] The question of how we could verify the existence of such a subject is a quite separate one. It may be said that we could not even intelligibly suppose there to *be* such a subject unless *we*, beings whose cognitive powers are inherently limited, had, or could develop, without changing our nature, methods or techniques to verify or confirm its existence. But this claim not only runs counter to a stubborn and persistent *consensus gentium*, it is also one of the more fantastic instances of philosophers' sleight-of-hand dogmatism. Another question which seems to me irrelevant here is whether we could possess the concepts of other subjects at all unless at least some of them were—from our point of view—embodied. A Nietzschean would have no difficulty conceding this point.

physically true propositions about material objects. Nietzsche reasons, on the contrary, that it is senseless to insist that a subject which is not 'affected' by (and thus, not interested in or concerned with) some set or arrangement of properties which are, in some sense, 'instantiated', and whose existence is not in any way bound up with them, is, so to speak, systematically ignorant of the (metaphysical) truth of thoughts to the effect that these properties 're-ally', or 'objectively', are so instantiated.

It is to be expected that whether one finds this argument compelling depends on what one thinks the ontological status of those properties is. For Nietzsche, they cannot but be constituted by the contents of perceptions (or, in his language, interpretations), if they are to be actual. But what if one does not accept Nietzsche's premises—if one thinks it intelligible to suppose that those objects which, in our thought experiment, are perceived by us but not by the monadic mind, exist or subsist, in some to us contentfully inconceivable manner, in themselves? One may then be inclined to reply that the disembodied mind is indeed systematically ignorant of what is objectively real.

In principle, it is also possible to reject Nietzsche's idealist premises while nevertheless accepting his analysis of objective reality. Thus one may deny that the assumption of objects which have a constitution or nature in themselves—i.e. which can be characterized without reference to any actual or possible subject—is 'nonsensical', and yet hold that whatever is objectively *real* has this status by virtue of its relation to some such subject(s) and its interests or values. Such a view would of course involve a significant conceptual revision for most of us. It would force us to accord a kind of intermediate ontological status between reality and non-existence to those putative objects which, while not 'affecting' any subject and being characterizable without reference to any such actual or possible affections, might yet subsist in some sense in themselves. They would be rather like the denizens of the 'shadow kingdom' of which Nietzsche speaks in WM 586. Thus, on this view, it would be possible to concede that the objects perceived by us, but not by the quasi-monadic mind in our thought experiment, might indeed subsist in some manner in themselves, but that they would nevertheless not be objectively real for that mind. He would not, on account of his ignorance of these objects, be ignorant of any truths about objective *reality*.

Even if one finds *both* this intermediate position and Nietzsche's idealist premisses unacceptable and insists on a more conventional realist view as outlined in the last paragraph but one, our thought experiment should bring out one thing very sharply, and I consider this to be the main virtue of it and indeed of Nietzsche's argument. If 'objective reality' (and with it, truth) is prised off in this manner from the experiences, interests and concerns of any 'subject of knowledge', then the question obtrudes itself: of what importance or relevance could knowledge of objective reality in *this* sense possibly be to anyone? What does our monadic mind lack that might conceivably matter to him if he were informed of it? Or why should it matter to *us* whether we are like him or whether the objects we perceive exist 'independently' of us? What is at stake when philosophers argue vigorously for or against a 'realist' view of material objects?

I indicated at the beginning of this section that Nietzsche never commits himself to the views examined above—or, for that matter, to most of his other apparently metaphysical claims—with complete conviction, although he pursues them at some length throughout his notebooks and is clearly attracted by them. There are a number of reasons for his persistent prevarications and ambiguities in this respect. One of them, which is not always recognized by readers who are misled by the frequent bellicosity of his style, is an—among philosophers—unusually modest sense that our intuitions on these matters are often too tenuous to allow us to embrace with what he would call intellectual cleanliness any particular position with a great degree of confidence. (Cf. his remarks on the hubris of metaphysicians in MR 539.) Another reason has to do with the answers he eventually arrives at to a question which is raised in a very acute and self-conscious way by the arguments discussed in this section: what is at stake in such metaphysical disputes? As Nietzsche frequently reminds us, throughout the history of Europe, at least from Plato onwards, it has generally been assumed, by philosophers and non-philosophers alike, that the attainment of truth is greatly desirable. Great intellectual (and occasionally physical) battles have been, and continue to be, fought in which the combatants have either claimed to be defending truth against 'error' or 'superstition', or at least, in justification of their struggle, have claimed to be, unlike their opponents, in the possession of truth. If the 'truth' in question is indeed supposed to be definable without recourse, ultimately, to what Nietzsche calls a subject's values, this conspicuous feature of various historical conflicts would certainly seem perplexing. In order to explain it, one would have to stipulate a strong and pervasive desire for truth (in the relevant metaphysical sense) which is not reducible to any other interests and concerns. As we shall see in the next section, it is precisely this putative desire—the 'will to truth'—which Nietzsche thinks requires rather more phenomenological analysis than it has traditionally been given.

I have argued that Nietzsche explicates our notion of objective reality as relative to subjects who have interests or 'values', can think of themselves as capable of volitional agency, and who (would) experience themselves as 'affected' (resisted) by the contents of (some of) their representations which they either actually have or would have if various further conditions were satisfied. It appears, therefore, that the concept of objective reality as elucidated by him presupposes another, more fundamental notion of 'being' which is applicable to whatever it is that 'feel[s itself] as existing' against that which concerns it and resists its efforts (cf. KGW VIII.1.5.19). Indeed, without such a concept it is not clear how we (and Nietzsche—see WM 569, WM 490) could even speak of subjects *qua* subjects as 'existing' at all. It is difficult to avoid the conclusion that this more fundamental concept of being would have to characterize it as 'feeling' or, more generally, as 'awareness'. While Nietzsche sometimes appears to acknowledge this implication of his claims,[34] he more often does not seem to take notice of the fact that his own account involves a more basic analysis of reality in terms of complex episodes of experience which at any given instant have a determinate nature. It is partly by generally ignoring this implication that he proceeds to draw conclusions from his arguments which have both intrigued and perplexed commentators.

As we have seen, the denial of the conceivability of objects constituted by instantiations of non-subject-implying or non-perspectival properties is not peculiar to Nietzsche's thinking.

---

[34] In WM 569, Nietzsche points out, quite in keeping with the logic of his position as interpreted here, that *if* objects are to be regarded as existing independently of the perceptions of *any* 'subjects' they are said to affect (as we arguably do regard them in our pre-reflective metaphysics of common sense), they would have to be conceived as subjects themselves. Such a view of the nature of the objects would obviously not be a phenomenalist, but rather a panpsychist one (cf. also WM 582).

Idealist philosophers have traditionally argued along essentially similar lines. The conclusion which idealists have generally drawn from this kind of reasoning—if they were not, like Schopenhauer in some passages, inconsistent at this point—is that reality *an sich* is consciousness. That which really and independently exists, substance in one of the traditional senses of this term, can only be understood as 'mind' or *Geist*. Nietzsche, on the contrary, draws the rather different and more radical conclusion that not only the notion of a thing, i.e. a material object, existing in itself, but, more fundamentally, the very idea of something being characterized by an intrinsic 'essential nature' which constitutes it as what it is is incoherent:[35] ' "Absolute reality", "being-in-itself" [is] a contradiction' (WM 580). There are a substantial number of passages both in the published writings of his last active years and in the *Nachlass* which indicate that Nietzsche believes himself to have shown not only that object-like entities which are not objects of awareness, interest, and concern are impossible, but that there can be no non-relational being, no existent characterized by an intrinsic 'essential nature' at all:[36]

There are no 'facts-in-themselves', for a sense must always be projected into them before there can be 'facts'.

The question 'what is that?' is an imposition of meaning from some other viewpoint. 'Essence', the 'essential nature', is something perspectival and already presupposes a multiplicity. At the bottom of it there always lies 'what is it for *me*?' (for us, for all that lives etc.).

A thing would be defined once all creatures had asked 'what is that?' and had answered their question. Supposing one single creature, with its own relationships and perspectives for all things, were missing, then the thing would not yet be 'defined'.

In short: the essence of a thing is only an *opinion* about the 'thing'. Or rather: 'it is considered' is the real 'it is', the sole 'this is'. (WM 556)

The 'in-itself' is even an absurd conception; a 'constitution-in-itself' is

---

[35] Cf. R. Grimm, *Nietzsche's Theory of Knowledge* (Berlin, 1977), 62: 'Nietzsche denies that it is meaningful to speak of an "ultimate nature of things"; this is most often expressed as an assertion to the effect that there *is* no ultimate nature of things.'

[36] The term 'essential nature' is here used in a wide sense, encompassing the Platonic Forms, Aristotelian substantial forms, and the notion that any entity has, at any one time, some intrinsic determinate property or properties which characterize it as what it really is (at that time). What I shall call Nietzsche's anti-essentialism is directed against *all* of these.

nonsense; we possess the concept 'being', 'thing', only as a relational concept—(WM 583 A)

The concept 'truth' is nonsensical. [. . .] There is no 'essence-in-itself' (it is only relations that constitute an essence—) (WM 625; cf. WM 568, 557, 558)

If there is nothing that has a constitution-in-itself, then there can be no statements about the world which in any way adequately characterize or 'correspond to' anything as it is in itself. In other words, there can be no metaphysically true assertions in the sense in which we have used this term so far (cf. WM 625). Every existent or real entity exists only for, or in relation to, something else; its properties are exclusively relational ones and its being is relative in this sense. Consequently, for Nietzsche, 'there is no truth' (WM 540)—no thoughts which are true by virtue of predicating properties of some x which x has 'in itself'. The claim that the concept of truth in *this* sense is incoherent is found in numerous places in the writings of the final period (frequently as the assertion that 'there is no truth', e.g. WM 13, 15, 616), and the need to reject it is stated in a well-known passage in *Götzendammerung* under the heading 'How the "true world" finally became a fable': 'The true world we have abolished: which world remained? the apparent one perhaps? . . . By no means! *with the true world we have also abolished the apparent one!*'

The dichotomy of mere phenomena on the one hand, and reality itself on the other, of the way things appear 'to us' (or other 'subjects') and their intrinsic constitution, vanishes once the latter concept is seen as 'nonsensical' (i.e. strictly speaking as incoherent rather than as without any sense). Needless to say, this does not imply the obsolescence of the distinction between true and false statements, veridical and illusory perceptions, etc., *within* the world as it shows up for us.

Central as the denial of a 'true world', of metaphysical facts, and of essential natures is in Nietzsche's later philosophy, it needs to be emphasized that it does not follow from his analysis of all actual, instantiated properties as dependent on awareness and interest. For this analysis is clearly compatible with a more conventional idealist position which acknowledges the possibility of true propositions about the intrinsic nature or constitution of experiential states or acts (including their contents) *qua* such states or acts. To be sure,

Nietzsche's emphasis on the role played by interest, concern, and what he calls the 'projection' of 'sense' and the 'imposition of meaning' in our attribution of objective reality to elements in our experience has, I believe, no close parallels in the mainstream of the idealist tradition and can perhaps be seen as anticipating (and possibly influencing) certain tenets of the phenomenological school, particularly the concern of the latter with the intentional nature of consciousness and, in later developments, its emphasis on the primacy of affectivity. But such an analysis does not entail the denial of essential natures and of the notion of a constitution in itself, although Nietzsche appears to think it does, judging by the remarks we have cited above. Thus, on the present interpretation, he illegitimately concludes from the unintelligibility of (one variant of) realism or of *things* in themselves—which is all his reasoning, if valid, has demonstrated—the incoherence of the notion of intrinsic natures, and thus arrives at a position according to which all being is relational. The notes in which he apparently develops his idea of the will to power into an ontology could be seen as outlining a 'metaphysics' based on this very premiss: that nothing exists in itself and that whatever 'is' is constituted exclusively by its relations to other beings whose 'natures' in turn consist entirely of relational properties. We shall have occasion to examine Nietzsche's elaboration of this conception, and to discuss the question of its coherence in detail, later (Chapter 6.2).

But let me first return to another question which preoccupies Nietzsche throughout his philosophical career, but attains particular prominence in the writings of his last years and is intimately connected with his criticism of the notion of a reality *an sich*. It is what one might call a question of philosophical anthropology: what is the origin and the significance of the desire for metaphysical truth and for knowledge of truth thus conceived—in Nietzsche's terminology, for 'absolute' or 'unconditional' knowledge?

2. THE WILL TO TRUTH AND THE ASCETIC IDEAL

If objective reality for subjects of a given kind consists in certain patterns of experienced or experienceable resistances interpreted as affections by them, then knowledge of objective reality could be said to amount for them in part to the exact establishment of the laws or regularities of co-variation obtaining among these patterns of resistances and affections. This is indeed what Nietzsche regards as the task of science:

> We want to introduce the exactness and the rigour of mathematics into all the sciences as far as this is possible, not in the belief that in this way we shall know the objects, but in order thereby to *establish* [*festzustellen*] our human relation to the objects. Mathematics is only a means for the general and ultimate [*letzte*] knowledge of man. (FW 246)

Science is thus seen as a tool by which to codify and extend our repertoire of what are perforce perspectival truths for ultimately practical purposes:

> Against this, one has to *insist* on what concepts and formulae can only be: means of communication [*Verständlichung*] and of calculability, the aim is practical applicability: the reasonable limit that man may make use of nature.

> Science: the domination of nature for the purposes of man—eliminate the surplus of fantasizing of metaphysicians [and] mathematicians: (KGW VII.2.25.308; cf. also WM 610, GOA xii.4, and GOA xiii.83)

But if science *qua* science is exclusively concerned with perspectival truths, what is the significance of the desire—which has played such a prominent part in the intellectual history of Europe—for metaphysical truth about what reality might be like 'in itself'? What sense can be made of the belief that there might conceivably be true propositions, the truth of which subjects might never be able to ascertain or find evidence for—*vide* Descartes's hypothesis, or the monadic mind in the previous section—and which it would nevertheless be important for them to know? To put this question slightly differently: why should it matter to us whether the patterns of 'affections' we are capable of experiencing, and the beliefs concerning objects which go with them, correspond to, or adequately represent, or are materially analogous to, those objects 'as they really are'—even if the latter notion made sense? After all, 'there is absolutely no escape, no side- and by-ways into the *real world*! We are in our web, we spiders, and whatever we catch in it, we can catch nothing at all but what can be caught precisely in *our* web' (MR 117). In short, the question which preoccupies Nietzsche is why, given the apparent irrelevance of metaphysics to man's practical—in particular, scientific and technological—dealings with the world-as-experienced-by-us, there should have been, throughout the history of philosophy, such a pervasive desire not to suffer from illusion, not to be deceived, about the 'ultimate nature of things': '—Descartes is not radical enough for me. With regard to his desire to have something certain and "I do not want to be deceived" it is necessary [to] ask "why *not*?"' (KGW VII.3.40.10).

The later Nietzsche, in his writings from *Die Fröhliche Wissenschaft* to *Antichrist*, tends to associate the apparent desire to know reality as it is in itself—the supposedly irreducible aspiration to attain to metaphysical truth—with certain other psycho-physical characteristics:[37]

Whoever is incapable of laying his will into things, lacking will and strength, at least lays some *meaning* into them, i.e. the faith that there is a will in them already. [. . .] The philosophical objective outlook can therefore be a sign that will and strength are small. For strength organizes what is close and closest; 'men of knowledge', who desire only to ascertain what is, are those who cannot *fix* anything *as it ought to be*. (WM 585 A)

According to a dominant strand in Nietzsche's later philosophy, the desire to know, avowedly for its own sake, what is true in a metaphysical sense is definitive of the *homo religiosus* or, to use his own term, of the individual who is subject to the 'ascetic ideal'. Many of the remarks in which he expresses this view are obscure, but they are arguably both capable of clarification and of considerable philosophical interest.

It is in the last part of the third book of *Zur Genealogie der Moral* (paras. 23–8) that Nietzsche develops the thesis that the 'love of truth', that is, the desire cognitively to attain to the real nature of things (ostensibly) for its own sake, is the central element of the religious mentality:

Wherever else the intellect is at work today rigorously, powerfully, and without counterfeiting, it is absolutely devoid of the ideal—the popular expression for this abstinence is 'atheism'—*except for its will to truth*. But this will, this *residue* of an ideal is, if you will believe me, that ideal itself, entirely esoteric, divested of all externalities, and thus not its residue but rather its *core*. (GM iii.27)

Here Nietzsche appears to define the ('ascetic', or religious) ideal in such a way as to allow it to be ascribed even to those who embrace

[37] This association is not present in the writings of the middle period (*Menschliches, Allzumenschliches* and *Morgenröte*). It is one of the most distinctive features of Nietzsche's later philosophy.

'atheism'.[38] This is of course bound to provoke the question: what are the criteria which permit such an identification of the 'will to truth' with the religious impulse? Nietzsche's own statements on this point are sometimes rather ambiguous and indeed misleading, but one interpretation they suggest is that there are at least three characteristics which the desire for absolute or metaphysical truth and what I have called the religious impulse (the ascetic ideal) have in common. It seems that each of them separately would, for Nietzsche, warrant his assimilation of one to the other, even though often several or indeed all of these characteristics are found conjointly.

In the first place, the person who aspires to metaphysically true beliefs, ostensibly for no other reason than that they *are* true in this sense, seems to consider the state of having attained to such truths as an intrinsic good. In so far as he values his dispositional ability to present such truths to his awareness, one may plausibly assume that he does so because he values those states themselves in which he actually attends to, or 'contemplates', metaphysical truths. In entertaining and believing propositions which supposedly represent reality or some part of it as it is in itself (granting this to be a coherent notion), the believer might be said, in Kantian terms, to attain cognitively to the unconditioned and to be contemplating it.

Nietzsche detects a very significant analogy between this desire to contemplate the 'unconditioned' and the good avowedly aspired to by the believers of various narrowly religious doctrines—notably of the central Christian tradition and its philosophical predecessors (Platonism). For 'man's happiness', his true good, as conceived by the classical philosophical representatives of this tradition, consists precisely in the 'vision' of unconditioned reality—the latter being

---

[38] Cf. the following note: 'The relation of religion to nature once used to be the reverse: religion coincided with the *popular conception* of nature. Nowadays the popular conception is the materialist one. Consequently, those elements of religion which exist today have to talk to the common people in a materialist idiom' (KGW VII.1.4.221). A. Danto, *Nietzsche as Philosopher* (New York, 1965), therefore rightly distinguishes between a narrow and a wide sense of 'religion' in Nietzsche. One may be an 'atheist' in the narrow sense (rejecting, for instance, any revealed religion) and yet be religious in the wide sense. On the other hand, there are some systems of belief traditionally referred to as religious which, as Nietzsche himself stresses, fall outside the range of phenomena he subsumes under the concept of the ascetic ideal. This is particularly true for the beliefs of the pre-Socratic Greeks as they are portrayed in Homer.

identified with God, who is the *ens realissimum* (everything else existing only derivatively, and thus in a conditioned manner, by the power of God's will, which is continually required to maintain created things in existence).[39]

Of course, there are differences between the general desire for truth and the rather more specific aspiration towards the 'vision of the Divine Essence'. In particular, the believer of the relevant 'narrowly' religious doctrines aspires to a quasi-perceptual, intuitive state ('vision', *contemplatio Dei*), a kind of immediate awareness of what is ultimately real as it is in itself. Many of those who have claimed to desire truth for its own sake have been content with rather less—for instance, a partial intuitive representation of the ultimate constituents of reality by analogy with items 'directly' accessible to empirical observation or introspective awareness, or a knowledge of the laws operating among these constituents. Yet in both cases 'reality' is regarded as something the cognitive participation in (or 'possession' of) which renders the state in which such participation or cognitive grasping is attained—the state of having true beliefs about it—valuable in itself. To the extent that the attainment of such a state is seen as 'objectively' good in the sense of to be desired by all human beings, the pursuit of metaphysics is regarded as incumbent upon man if he is to achieve happiness, or to satisfy his real interests, or to realize his *telos*.

Now, why should the possession of true beliefs about reality-in-itself, the 'contemplation of being', be considered to be valuable, no matter what being or reality is like (again: assuming such locutions to be ultimately intelligible)? Nietzsche suggests that the belief in a good of this kind is explicable psychologically and sociologically as a remnant or after-effect of the Platonic-Christian assumption that *esse et bonum convertuntur*, that reality is in itself of a certain character, although this assumption is generally no longer held explicitly and consciously by most modern advocates of metaphysical endeavours:

It is still a *metaphysical belief* on which our belief in science is based—we modern knowers, we atheists and anti-metaphysicians, we also take *our* fire from the flame that was ignited by the belief of millenia, that Christian belief which was also the belief of Plato, that God is the truth, that truth is *divine* . . . But what if precisely this is becoming more and

[39] See e.g. Thomas Aquinas, *Summa Theologiae* (London, 1963–81), Ia IIae, 3. 8.

more incredible, if nothing proves to be divine anymore, unless it be error, blindness, lie—if God himself proves to have been our most long-standing lie? (GM iii.24)

We need not occupy ourselves at this point with the assumption seemingly implicit in the last sentence concerning what reality is actually like—it is evident that any such assumptions must be highly problematic for Nietzsche to make. We shall also leave aside for the moment the issue of science, which will be addressed below. What interests us here is only one question pointed to by this passage. Unless reality is supposed to be of a certain very specific character—as in traditional Christianity—why should the possession of metaphysically true beliefs about it be considered to be desirable or even, as it often has been by philosophers, as of supreme importance?

A second feature on account of which Nietzsche identifies the desire for truth for its own sake as the 'core' of the ascetic ideal is connected with what I would call the subjective aspect of the psychological state that, apparently, is desired both by the 'narrowly' religious believer and by the metaphysician. Not only are both, as explained above, concerned with the same generic object— the nature of reality-in-itself—they also both envisage, ideally, a condition of final attainment in which their desire is satisfied once and for all. The religious believer does not, ultimately, value the *quest* for God, but rather the achieved vision of God which 'so [. . .] fulfil[s] a man's whole desire that nothing is left beside for him to desire'.[40] In other words, what he aspires to is a state of desireless rest, a 'contemplative' condition in which he is 'eternally' free of further desire, dissatisfaction, and thus also of change. Similarly, according to Nietzsche, the individual motivated by the 'will to truth' typically does not value the pursuit of truth for its own sake, but its attainment. *Qua* metaphysical inquirer, she values the achieved static condition of desireless possession or contemplation of 'the truth'. Thus, in both cases we are confronted with an aspiration towards a non-active (in the Scholastic sense), contemplative condition in which all desire is absent (or 'fulfilled'), i.e. in which its object has been achieved once and for all. The Christian notion of the *unio mystica* and its analogues in other religions are merely special cases, although very revealing ones, symptomatic of

---

[40] See e.g. Thomas Aquinas, *Summa Theologiae* (London, 1963–81), Ia IIae, 1. 5.

a certain type of human disposition that also manifests itself in the metaphysician's wanting 'truth for its own sake'—a disposition to which the good appears as a condition of rest finally achieved in which 'nothing is left beside [. . .] to desire'.[41] If this disposition is less apparent in a metaphysician's case, this may be either because she quite obviously is not interested in truth for its own sake (see Chapter 4.4), or because she at any rate does not accord exclusive or overriding importance to this specific good. However, the more she sincerely values the possession of truth for its own sake, the more clearly the resemblance to the 'narrowly' religious believer emerges.[42] In Nietzsche's words, both envisage the greatest good as a 'return and homecoming to the ground of things, as breaking free of all delusion, as "knowledge", as "truth", as "being", as liberation from any goal, any wish, any activity, as a beyond good and evil' (GM iii.17).

The third characteristic which leads Nietzsche to identify the metaphysician's will to truth and 'narrowly' religious belief as special cases of the more general psychological disposition he calls the ascetic ideal differs markedly from the first two. There the similarity emerged as a result of a phenomenological analysis of the desire for (metaphysical) truth, avowedly for its own sake. Here we encounter a psychological phenomenon which, Nietzsche suggests, is typically *associated* with the will to truth, while also being constitutive of the religious mentality in the narrow sense. For the religious believer, the nature of reality is such as to call for and legitimate certain pursuits and activities as appropriate for a given type of created being, while prohibiting others. This belief is frequently shared by the person who values truth in a metaphysical sense. This is how one can interpret Nietzsche's remark that 'whoever is incapable of laying his will into things [. . .] at least lays some *meaning* into them, i.e. the belief that there is a will in them already. [. . .] The philosophical objective outlook can therefore be a sign that will and strength are small' (WM 585 A). The metaphysician, according to Nietzsche, tends to believe that 'reality' calls for, or

---

[41] Cf. KGW VII.2.26.308: 'the real end of all philosophizing [is] the *intuitio mystica*'.

[42] Among the classical philosophers of the modern period, Spinoza would provide a particularly clear illustration of Nietzsche's point. But even Descartes, for all his practical–technological concerns elsewhere, sometimes professes to the 'ascetic ideal'. See *Discourse on Method*, in *The Philosophical Works of Descartes*, i. 82.

provides an authoritative justification for, certain modes of life, practices, and attitudes as to be adopted by *all* humans. One such practice, we may suppose, is the pursuit of truth itself. Others would presumably depend on what the nature of reality is taken to be by the respective metaphysician. A Christian theist would obviously hold specific kinds of action (e.g 'charitable' ones) to be called for on account of what is metaphysically the case. But, similarly, a scientific realist, or a Freudian (or, for that matter, a Schopenhauerian), while *rejecting* value realism, may believe, and not a few arguably have believed, that, since the world 'really' is of a certain character, certain practices and pursuits are 'better' or, in some idioms, more 'rational'—the latter being used here partly as a term of praise—than others, *irrespective* of the contrary preferences or desires people may actually experience.[43]

For example, the ancestor worship of certain 'primitive' tribes may in this light be considered to be irrational in the sense indicated, and therefore as to be disapproved of or even, where possible, to be eradicated, irrespective of whether such practices are regarded by their practitioners as conducive to their well-being and in accord with their conception of the good life. If they involve false beliefs about the nature of the world, this fact by itself is thought to render them generally inferior to other forms of life involving true beliefs. A characteristic way in which this form of the ascetic ideal

---

[43] The proposal by some recent philosophers that, if materialism is true, we 'ought to' eliminate the mentalistic idiom of 'folk psychology' for this reason alone might be thought to supply a good illustration of Nietzsche's point. The preferences or desires mentioned above include those which non-self-deceived individuals would avow if challenged, or—assuming that they are ignorant of relevant circumstances which are in practice empirically recognizable by human beings—desires which they would avow were they acquainted with these circumstances. We may also include here those desires of self-deceived individuals which they experience without acknowledging them, but which they would explicitly acknowledge if they could divest themselves of their self-deceptions. (For a discussion of self-deception, see Ch. 5.3.) However, any appeal to putative 'real' desires which are not experienced or experienceable *at all* in any of these senses, and which a subject could only, if at all, be persuaded to have if she *first* accepted certain metaphysical propositions, is itself a manifestation of the ascetic ideal. An example of this would be a certain type of religious doctrine which maintains that the 'natural' desires which human beings actually experience are invariably contrary to what they ought to be according to the doctrine, and that they will only, if at all, experience any of the desires they ought to have, and become able to perform any of the actions they ought to perform, once they accept the truth of the doctrine in question (for a good illustration of this sort of argument, see Locke, *An Essay Concerning Human Understanding*, I.iii.13).

finds expression is in statements like 'if there were no truth, people would be free to do just anything'. 'Reality' (and thus 'truth') are thought to exert some kind of quasi-moral constraint on what human beings can legitimately do or desire.

One may of course ask: what if the tribespeople engaging in those practices are not primarily concerned with the truth *per se* of the beliefs connected with them, or indeed with theoretical inquiry in general, but with the (in their eyes) otherwise better or more elevated character they give to the life of the community—say, through a sense of common purpose and solidarity, or a sense of meaning even in suffering, created partly by a shared and unquestioned set of rituals? It is even arguable that some of the presumed goods associated with those practices depend essentially on the latter *not* being made into objects of critical inquiry, but rather on being regarded as 'natural givens'. (The early Nietzsche was acutely aware of such correlations.) Still, it may be replied that the realization of these alleged goods is conditional upon the belief in the truth of certain propositions about the world. A certain ritual, for example, will only attain its end of conveying to its participants a sense of their attunement to the will of the deities to whom it is addressed as long as the participants continue to believe in the existence of those deities. More generally, a person evidently cannot take himself to be acting for the sake of an actual good which he does not believe exists (see Chapter 5.1).

However, it certainly *is* possible to believe that goods are realized in attitudes, practices, or modes of life which one is also convinced are based on false beliefs—one may even take those goods to override or outweigh the erroneousness of the latter. It is also possible to believe that these overriding goods do not, or not exclusively, consist in any beneficial external *consequences* of those attitudes, practices, or modes of life, but are intrinsic to them. This is arguably what Nietzsche has in mind when he insists time and again in his later writings that 'the falsity of a judgement is for us not necessarily an objection against it; this is perhaps the point where our new language sounds most alien' (JGB 4). Applying these points to our earlier example, we may say that it is certainly conceivable that an individual—say, a tribe member who has been initiated into the secrets of the dominant Western *Weltanschauung*—may become convinced of the falsity of many of his original beliefs and those of his group, and yet judge that it is desirable for other members of the tribe to retain these beliefs on account of the goods he considers to accrue from them, but not from their rivals, to the tribe—which goods appear to him to be greater than either the possession of the corresponding metaphysically true beliefs or the goods embodied in the practices he has found related to those beliefs. Whether he would be right in this would be difficult—though not in principle impossible—to decide in a particular case. Such adjudication would usually require, among other things, a thorough inside knowledge of, and participation in, the rival beliefs and practices. (This is rather different from the traditional procedure of anthropologists, i.e. 'observing' those beliefs and practices.)

In any case, such a choice would be illegitimate and reprehensible for adherents of the ascetic ideal of the type presently under discussion. Such individuals, according to Nietzsche, characteristically ask for legitimation or 'authority' for their (and others') actions and, in general, their (and others') mode of life, from the supposed fact that it is in conformity with the nature of reality, rather than being content with, or openly acknowledging, the brute fact that such-and-such is what they (or others) happen to desire. We need not concern ourselves here with the question whether or how such metaphysical legitimation might be possible. But even a cursory look at history, and at the manner in which ostensibly greater access to truth, i.e. superior rationality (this concept being here defined without essential reference to the desires of those concerned), has frequently been invoked by individuals or groups to justify certain actions against the 'unenlightened'—for example, in colonial enterprises—should be sufficient to convince us that the psychological point Nietzsche is making is at any rate not entirely fanciful.[44]

---

[44] For the role often played in this attitude by what I shall call the heroic posture—'to accept the truth unflinchingly, whether one likes it or not'—see Chs. 4.4 and 5.3.

As one might expect from Nietzsche's argument, his point seems to apply not only to cases where actions have been explicitly justified by recourse to supposed 'objective' value properties, but also to those instances—arguably far more frequent in recent history—where individuals, governments, or other institutions have sought to legitimate aggressive actions on the basis of the ostensibly 'irrational' ('superstitious', etc.) nature of their victims' beliefs in particular divinely ordained ('objective') moral taboos and sanctions.

Somewhat more sophisticated are justifications of such actions which argue that the ends inadequately pursued in the practices of the unenlightened are really the

On the other hand, it seems that the attitude in question here, as indeed the psychological disposition discussed before it, need not necessarily involve the (for Nietzsche, unintelligible) belief in metaphysical truths about a supposed objective reality in itself. It may also be found where a more modest conception of truth, at least largely in line with Nietzsche's strictures, is prevalent. Someone may, for instance, agree with Nietzsche that objective reality, and true beliefs about it, cannot coherently be conceived without reference to subjects with specific affective and volitional properties *to whom* this reality appears or may appear. He may accept that science provides us with propositions which are, or are likely to be, at best true for us (perspectivally true) in the sense suggested in the previous section. But he may also believe that the possession of such perspectival truths is desirable for its own sake and also that what reality-for-us is like has practical implications of the sort described above. Thus, the ancestor worship in our example might be considered 'irrational' by him and hence as either dispensable or even as reprehensible, given the nature of reality-for-us and quite irrespective of either metaphysical quandaries or the experienced desires of those engaging in those practices. Clearly, someone holding a view of this kind may still distinguish between either his own or other people's desires and what they *ought* to do, irrespective of those, in the light of what reality is like. The 'asceticism' which lies in the belief that oneself or others *ought* to act in conformity with the nature of reality (rather than their possibly quite contrary desires) may, in other words, also characterize individuals who reject the concept of absolute or metaphysical truth at least with respect to 'objective reality'.

It is tempting to conjecture that Nietzsche realizes this when he suggests that there is a historical/psychological and a logical con-

---

same as those pursued more efficiently by applying one's own beliefs in suitable ways. It is, for instance, conspicuous that European anthropologists during the age of Empire mostly attempted to construe the religious beliefs and practices of native peoples as either exclusively or primarily magical—i.e. as bad technology. Interestingly, Nietzsche, for all his virulent attacks on religion, never suggests such a crude and obviously inadequate explanation of it—partly, no doubt, because he himself had been educated into an intense, and relatively traditional, religious subculture, and thus knew the phenomenon from the 'inside'.

It may be objected that the legitimating strategies I have mentioned were usually little more than pretexts disguising rather more concrete commercial and colonial interests. That may be so, but some of them could only function successfully as pretexts to the extent that the 'will to truth' had a hold on their addressees.

nection between the specifically Christian ('narrowly' religious) form of the ascetic ideal and the high regard in which scholarly and scientific attitudes and endeavours (*Wissenschaftlichkeit*) have been held in European culture. Successful scholarly and scientific work demands a kind of 'self-denial', enjoining the *Wissenschaftler* to pay obeisance to the 'facts' in her respective discipline even if those happen to conflict with her own interests and desires (see GM iii.27). Such deference to the presumptive facts, irrespective of its consequences, can only appear commendable, Nietzsche suggests, to a person who has embraced the Christian virtues of truthfulness and 'self-denial', even though she may no longer accept the metaphysics which was originally associated with these virtues. His claim here is prima facie not very convincing, at least when applied to the natural sciences, since the adequacy of (modern) scientific hypotheses and theories is judged in large part by their predictive success (see Chapter 4.2) and hence, ultimately, by their conduciveness to the satisfaction of certain evidently non-ascetic interests. But an individual may, and many arguably do, value the discoveries of science as at any rate perspectival truths-for-us the possession of which they either regard as valuable in itself or as having practical implications of the kind suggested earlier. Either attitude would be considered 'ascetic' by Nietzsche.

It should by now be clear why he chooses the label 'ascetic' for the type of aspiration—the ideal—we are analysing. It generally involves the evaluative privileging of a static, achieved, restful possession of knowledge (either of the 'unconditioned' or, in the case mentioned last, of reality-for-us), as opposed to the ever-renewed practical engagement with the world as it presents itself in everyday experience. Alternatively, or in addition to this, it may involve the belief in certain moral or quasi-moral constraints imposed by 'reality' upon whatever desires an individual ought to have or to act upon. Without embarking in any detail on a phenomenology of everyday life, it should nevertheless be fairly uncontroversial to say that the 'objective' world in which we live our practical lives confronts us as a world of particulars continually undergoing change (albeit rarely *radical* change). Our empirical selves seem to consist to a considerable extent of more or less volatile and changing perceptions, thoughts, and 'passions' which are never so completely satisfied as to let us attain a state of desireless 'mental' rest (Schopenhauer's point), and which, furthermore, may conflict in various ways with what the experts tell us is 'the truth' about the world. In so far as a person is subject to the ascetic ideal, she will either disregard or, in more extreme cases, reject entirely these characteristics of everyday experience which Nietzsche simply calls 'life'. The 'will to truth' represents in this sense a desire for an 'other-world', a 'beyond' (*Jenseitigkeit*; GM iii.24, 25). What manifests itself in it is a wish to escape from, or at least to go beyond, that domain of 'life' and to be 'something else, somewhere else' (*Anders-sein*, *Anderswo-sein*; GM iii.13).[45]

Some of the issues raised above warrant and require, I believe, a far more elaborate independent discussion. But since our concern is a more general examination of Nietzsche's later thought, such a discussion cannot be pursued here in a way which could hope to be adequate to the subject. Yet we should not leave it without mentioning that in some passages in *Jenseits von Gut und Böse* and *Zur Genealogie der Moral* Nietzsche appears to propose an account of the connection between the ascetic ideal and the desire for truth which is at variance with the interpretation given here. This account has been developed in some detail by a recent commentator, Maudemarie Clark.[46] According to her interpretation of Nietzsche, adherence to the ascetic ideal means valuing something *because* it involves a denial of what she somewhat question-beggingly calls 'natural, earthly, or material existence' or 'natural human existence'.[47] Only if someone values truth because he values self-denial is he ascetic. For example, one may value the truths of science on account of the technological benefits attainable by applying the results of scientific investigations and one would, in this case, not be subject to the ascetic ideal. However, according to Clark's reading of Nietzsche, many of those who value science as the road to truth value it precisely *because* it requires them to deny their 'natural' desires—such as the desire for a providential order devised by a benevolent God—and they *eo ipso* espouse the ascetic ideal. Metaphysicians on the other hand, that is, those who possess or think they possess a notion of truth in an absolute or metaphysical sense and believe that knowledge of it is important, may be called ascetic

---

[45] Nietzsche emphasizes that this kind of asceticism differs in kind from the ascetic constraints imposed by individuals on some of their 'passions' (e.g. sexual desire) with the avowed aim of thereby being better able to pursue the objects of other passions (see GM iii.8). To what extent this is the case will emerge later.

[46] Clark, *Nietzsche on Truth and Philosophy*, 159–203. [47] Ibid. 161–2.

for different reasons. They believe that 'genuine' knowledge (of the 'true world') must be a priori rather than empirical, as well as that the empirical world is illusory and that truth must be completely independent both of human cognitive capacities and of human interests. Here also, 'the ascetic ideal's devaluation of natural human existence underlies these propositions'.[48] Metaphysicians espouse these views in order to denigrate 'life'.

Let me address this last point first. Nietzsche does indeed in some places (such as JGB 2 and GM iii.12) make comments on metaphysicians of very particular schools (Kantians and Platonists) which can be interpreted along the lines suggested by Clark. But they can hardly constitute his main reason for identifying the 'will to (metaphysical) truth' *generally* as the 'core' of what he calls the ascetic ideal. For obviously, there have been many philosophers who have both operated with a concept of metaphysical truth and thought it important to gain access to truth in this sense without claiming either the empirical world to be mere illusion or the proper method of metaphysics to be purely a priori. Such a claim would, for instance, fit neither Locke nor Berkeley nor a modern scientific realist. And it is difficult to see why simply believing that there is a reality which has a constitution in itself independently of whether human beings know it should by itself be ascetic.

Turning to Clark's reading of Nietzsche's statements about science, while not denying that some of his remarks seem to license at least certain elements in her interpretation, I find it again hard to believe that these remarks thus construed should really constitute his central argument. If they did, he would certainly be a less important philosopher than I have so far in this study taken him to be. For if he merely wanted to point out that a person is ascetic who values science solely in order thereby to denigrate or deny certain 'natural' human desires, he would not exactly have shown much analytical insight. In any case, I would surmise that there are very few human beings who value natural science because some of its results—on a particular interpretation which Nietzsche frequently attacks—conflict with the belief in the existence of a benevolent God and divine providence and thus require, if accepted, the abandoning of such cherished human beliefs and desires.[49] Such a person

---

[48] Clark, *Nietzsche on Truth and Philosophy*, 177–8.

[49] Admittedly, in the published works from the middle period onwards, Nietzsche repeatedly states or implies precisely this: that the discoveries of science are incom-

would *ex hypothesi* not value science if, as is logically possible, it had led to discoveries which *supported* those beliefs and desires. There surely cannot be many people of whom this counterfactual is true. The formulations in *Zur Genealogie der Moral* make it very clear that Nietzsche thinks of himself as making explicit and calling into question an attitude, a psychological disposition, which is (or was at his time) almost universal in European culture. If Clark's interpretation were correct, this estimation of the significance of his insights would have been, to put it mildly, somewhat exaggerated.

More generally, the main problem with this reading is that it renders the connection between the will to truth and the ascetic ideal (*a*) contingent and (*b*) such that it clearly applies only to very few individuals even in Nietzsche's own time. This makes it entirely incomprehensible why he should consider the former to be the 'core' of the latter. This claim only becomes remotely plausible if either the description of the ascetic ideal logically involves characteristics which are also constitutive of the will to truth (this is the case with the first two criteria we have mentioned), or, more weakly, if it can plausibly be maintained that it is at least generally associated with psychological features which are also characteristic of the latter (our third criterion). If the ascetic ideal is to be understood, as Clark proposes, as the demand for self-denial because and in so far as such denial 'devalues' the 'natural human condition', then it would appear that it could express itself equally in many different forms of human behaviour and the distinctive relation identified by Nietzsche between that ideal and the will to truth would be lost entirely.

The preceding discussion may be thought by some not to belong to the concerns of philosophy but, if anywhere, to a

patible with various 'narrowly' religious beliefs and that 'intellectual cleanliness' requires the latter to be relinquished for this reason (e.g. MR 33, 103; MAM ii.2.20; FW 151; AC 15). However, as we have seen (Chs. 2.2 and 2.3), the thrust of many of his own arguments, especially those characteristic of the later period, by no means supports such incompatibilist claims. The question arises therefore: how are we to understand them, especially when they occur in the later published works? One might conjecture that Nietzsche himself did not realize that many of his own reflections tend to undermine these claims. But it is probably more plausible to suppose that he uses the latter merely as polemical ploys against 'narrowly' religious believers without subscribing to them himself. This conjecture recommends itself particularly with respect to the very last works of 1888, in view of their rather 'unphilosophical', obviously polemical and pamphlet-like character.

phenomenological psychology. By contrast, Nietzsche would argue, and I would be inclined to agree, that a strict separation between these respective fields of inquiry would reduce philosophy to an activity on a par with, say, horse racing or playing chess—which, while it might have some virtues, is not the role accorded to it either by the classical philosophers of the tradition, or by the founders of universities, or by the majority of educated laymen in most European or Europeanized cultures. One of the traditionally central concerns of philosophers has been the investigation of values. Philosophers have either thought it their task, not only to analyse the meaning of 'good', but to adjudicate between different proposed values, including those embodied in various forms of organized pursuits such as scholarship and science, or have regarded such adjudication to be the task of other disciplines or institutions (for example, constitutional assemblies or electorates in the case of certain values relevant to public life). But in *either* case their position on these matters has been based on various assumptions concerning human nature or at least concerning the nature of the putative goods at stake in the activities and pursuits in question. Since all, or at least all culturally significant, activities fall under the purview of its investigations, it cannot, without falling short of what traditionally has been thought of as one of its main tasks, avoid asking the question 'what good is at stake?' also about itself, in particular about its traditionally 'first' discipline, the 'queen of the sciences'—metaphysics. And this is precisely what Nietzsche does.

Of course, one may pose two different kinds of question concerning the point of an activity. Neither of them is dispensable for the philosophical task we are speaking of. One may ask: what is the *objective* of, say, chess or metaphysics? The answer would be, presumably, checkmating the opponent in the former case and attaining to true beliefs about reality in itself in the latter. But one may also ask: why should one desire this objective; what *good* is it? And here the answer in the case of chess might be, for instance, that the desired good consists in exercising one's analytical prowess or, perhaps, simply in dispelling boredom. (It is clear that playing chess is only contingently linked to these goods—they might equally be attained by any number of other means.) In the case of metaphysics we have discussed part of Nietzsche's answer at length above.[50] One may play chess or do mathematics without concerning oneself with the question of what the good of either activity is. But given the essential concern with values of philosophy as traditionally conceived, and given its universal and hence self-reflexive character, one cannot be a philosopher in this traditional sense without attempting to give some answer to the questions raised by Nietzsche. What distinguishes him from many of his predecessors is not that he poses a new question, but that he addresses it more explicitly and, of course, more critically.

Nietzsche, more radically than most of those predecessors, calls into question the will to truth. According to him, the ascetic ideal, and thus the will to truth, is a 'symptom' of 'degenerating life' and of the 'sickliness' (*Krankhaftigkeit*) of those who represent it. The 'weak' (*die Schwachen*) cannot but experience as oppressive the 'deceitful and changing' nature of the world of their everyday experience, its general character of 'appearance, change, becoming, death', and the inevitable frustration of many of their 'natural' passions. The ascetic ideal constitutes their characteristic reaction to the specific nature of their encounter with 'life'.

In assessing Nietzsche's argument, it is obviously important to try to clarify what he means by 'weakness' here. There seem to be three separately sufficient criteria for the application of this term in his later works. First, he applies it to the 'lower orders' in traditional pre-modern aristocratic societies which are dominated by the virtues of excellence—'imprudent' courage in warfare, physical prowess, etc.—of the ruling élite (cf. GM i.10 and 14; AC 21). Secondly, he uses 'weakness' to characterize those whom he calls, in a fairly straightforward sense close to ordinary usage, physiologi-

---

[50] It needs to be emphasized that Nietzsche is only concerned here with an analysis of the good desired by those—like some of the classical philosophers of the tradition and many professional and non-professional philosophers since—who apparently have valued truth 'for its own sake', or who have at any rate thought it important, either for themselves or for all human beings, to discover it. He is quite aware that one may also embark on metaphysics as one may play chess: to demonstrate one's analytical prowess or to dispel boredom or to gain fame or simply because 'doing philosophy' happens to be one's job. This is of course the approach characteristic of a type which Nietzsche calls the 'scholar' (*der Gelehrte*). One may also pursue metaphysics because one considers correct answers to its questions essential for the progress of the specialist, particularly the natural, sciences (Descartes, for one, seems to have thought this). But there should be few, these days, who believe this.

cally 'ill-constituted' and 'sickly' (GM iii.14, 15; WM 283). Thirdly, and perhaps most importantly, he defines weakness through the notion of *ressentiment* (esp. GM i.10). This crucial concept can perhaps best be elucidated by means of a contrast with the disposition Nietzsche calls noble (*vornehm*). The noble individual as described by him characteristically possesses a spontaneous sense of his own value, a serene awareness of himself as 'happy' or privileged by fortune or nature (which does not necessarily, or even usually, involve a propensity towards complacent self-contemplation). Nietzsche emphasizes that this sense of self-value is largely unaffected by what many people would regard as undesirable external circumstances: the 'noble' individual shows 'indifference and contempt' towards security, comfort, and even his own physical survival (GM i.11). If he recognizes 'external' or object-like goods, they will strike him directly and indeed 'naïvely' (GM i.10) as worthy to be admired or as to be loved—although he does not *eo ipso* regard them as to be loved by *everyone*.

By contrast, the individual who is subject to *ressentiment* does not arrive at his specification of value, and his sense of his own worth, in this naïve and spontaneous manner, but rather by way of a prior opposition to an 'other' who is experienced by the subject of *ressentiment* more or less painfully as in some to him significant way stronger, or more powerful, or better,[51] and who is resented by him possibly, but not necessarily, for this reason alone. His dislike or hatred of an 'other', a not-self, precedes and conditions his explicit awareness and conception of good or value, which is merely a reactive construction,[52] drawn in opposition to whichever values happen to be represented by the 'other' who is

---

[51] If the object of *ressentiment* is experienced in this latter mode of presentation, this will not be explicitly acknowledged by the subject of *ressentiment* to himself. See below.

[52] *Ressentiment* involves a specific type of reactiveness, but not every 'reactive' behaviour expresses or constitutes *ressentiment*. A person who is attacked in the street at night and who hits back at his attacker may certainly be said to be reactive, but he is not *ipso facto* in a condition of *ressentiment*. Similarly, a protracted but unexpressed and impotent desire for revenge for an insult received is also reactive, but not yet an instance of *ressentiment*. The latter is a specific form of self-deception about values, and any putative account of it which is couched in an idiom that cannot capture something like our everyday concept of self-deception—which involves reference to purposes as well as to consciousness—also fails to capture, let alone illuminate, the complexity and specificity of the phenomenon Nietzsche is analysing. (For one particularly confused attempt of this kind, see Gilles Deleuze, *Nietzsche and Philosophy* (London, 1983), 21 f.)

hateful to the individual of *ressentiment* for prior and independent reasons:

Every ideal presupposes *love* and *hatred*, *admiration* and *contempt*. Either the positive emotion is the *primum mobile* or the negative emotion. For example, in all *ressentiment* ideals *hatred* and *contempt* are the *primum mobile*. (KGW VIII.2.10.9)

The real, though unacknowledged, purpose for which the values or goods apparently recognized by the individual of *ressentiment* are embraced by him, or accorded the particular importance they appear to have for him, is to procure for himself a sense of worth and superiority over the enemy, the 'other' whom he resents. Unlike the noble individual, he does not 'really' recognize the goods he professes to acknowledge, or value them to the extent he claims to, but merely uses them to disparage the object of his resentment— hence *ressentiment* is a form of self-deception: '[w]hile the noble man lives in trust and openness towards himself [. . .] the man of *ressentiment* is neither honest nor naïve nor open and straightfor- ward towards himself. His soul *squints*' (GM i.10).

The values self-deceivedly embraced in the condition of *ressentiment* can only achieve their purpose if they are regarded by their adherents as *universally* desirable, that is, as having a claim to the allegiance even of those others ('evil', 'unregenerate', 'irrational' ones) whom to denigrate and thus diminish in thought they were invented, or accepted, or granted overriding importance, by the subject of *ressentiment* in the first place.[53] All *ressentiment* attitudes thus involve a belief that some ostensible good or other—e.g. justice, or some formal moral principle such as the principle of universalizability itself—'ought' to be recognized by everyone. But Nietzsche also suggests, more controversially, that any belief in goods which ought to be acknowledged by all human beings in-

[53] Cf. Max Scheler's analysis of the phenomenon in his detailed study of *ressentiment*: 'The formal structure of the expression of *ressentiment* is here always the same: something, A, is affirmed, esteemed, praised, not for the sake of its intrinsic quality, but with the intention—which remains without linguistic ex- pression—to negate, denigrate, put blame on something else, B. A is "played off" against B' (M. Scheler, *Das Ressentiment im Aufbau der Moralen* (Frankfurt, 1978), 25).
If our interpretation above is correct, Nietzsche does not define the strength of an individual in terms of the actual success of that individual in a struggle for power. Consequently, the charge of self-contradiction against his idea of a historical victory of the weak seems misconceived (this charge is levelled against Nietzsche by Danto, among others: *Nietzsche as Philosopher*, 186).

volves *ressentiment*. (I shall discuss his argument to this effect, as well as his claim that *ressentiment* can, in a manner of speaking, 'create' values, in Chapter 5.3.) According to Nietzsche, *ressentiment usually* accompanies weakness in one of the first two senses mentioned above, but is not invariably found conjointly with them (cf. his remarks on the psychology of Jesus; AC 29–34). In many passages he asserts or implies, moreover, that there is a causal correlation between the characteristics referred to by 'weakness' in those senses and *ressentiment*: the latter is generally a reaction to the painful awareness of the superior power of another on the part of individuals who are incapable of responding to it either by emulation or by engaging in openly acknowledged hostility. Nevertheless, Nietzsche does not regard 'social' and 'physiological' weakness as even jointly sufficient conditions for *ressentiment*; nor, presumably, are they necessary conditions, either jointly or separately, although his remarks are not explicit on this question.

Two elements, then, are constitutive of the type of complex state Nietzsche calls *ressentiment*. First, the to some degree painful apprehension by the subject of *ressentiment* of an 'other' as in some respect superior and as dislikeable or hateful at least partly for this reason, and, secondly, the advocacy by the subject of certain values which are, contrary to his avowals, not really acknowledged by him for their own sake, but in order to diminish or denigrate or reduce in thought the object of *ressentiment*. Derivatively, one can speak of a *ressentiment* disposition, designating a propensity to experience 'not-selves' predominantly in this manner. Nietzsche's formulations sometimes suggest a further element of self-deception in the phenomenon of *ressentiment*. He seems to imply that the subject of *ressentiment* is not only self-deceived concerning his commitment, or the strength of his commitment, to certain ostensible values (e.g. humility, justice, peacefulness, prudence, rationality, etc.), but also about his real attitude towards those characteristics of the 'other' to which these values are opposed (e.g. pride, prowess in warfare, physical strength, an 'imprudent' and carefree impulsiveness, etc.). He seems to suggest that the subject of *ressentiment* himself in fact recognizes these latter qualities as good or desirable (in varying degrees, we may assume), but does not openly acknowledge this fact to himself, either because he himself lacks them, or because the 'other' who is resented possesses them in greater measure. While this additional element of self-deception may be present in states of *ressentiment*, it seems to me that the label can be applied even where it absent. However, some element of self-deception is essential to *ressentiment*. Where a person self-consciously merely pretends to hold certain values either in order to induce guilt in (an)other individual(s) or to present them in an unfavourable light to third parties, the term would not be appropriate.

It emerges clearly from Nietzsche's description that, according to him, the absence or presence, in varying degrees, of the *ressentiment* disposition plays a part in determining under which aspects or descriptions an 'other' will be explicitly noticed or predominantly attended to.[54] For example, the products of a penchant for extravagant public building projects on the part of a powerful social superior may be apprehended by one person simply under the aspect of 'making public space more aesthetically pleasing', while another individual may tend to describe them predominantly as wasteful, useless, pompous, overbearing, and so forth. If these judgements are actualizations of a *ressentiment* disposition—which of course they need not be—they will involve an approval of ostensible virtues such as frugality, sobriety, modesty, etc., which are not really valued by the subject, or not to the extent it is claimed, either for their own sake or as means towards the attainment of *other* goods, but rather (self-deceivedly) as means to disparage or reduce the object of *ressentiment*. The latter is essential to the correct description of the end sought by the subject of *ressentiment*—a sense of superiority over the 'other' through his 'diminution in thought'. It should be added that both the 'noble' and the *ressentiment* disposition are ideal types, to borrow an expression of Weber's. In actual individuals *both* may often be found, according to Nietzsche, in different degrees and contexts.

The weak cannot but experience the everyday world with which they are confronted primarily as a source of suffering. They charac-

---

[54] Cf. Scheler's observation that the *ressentiment* disposition directs 'even instinctive attention—which is independent of the sphere of the voluntary—to such phenomena in the environment as may provide material for the typical forms of these affective processes. Even the forming of perceptions, expectations, and memories is co-determined by these attitudes. They select from the phenomena they encounter automatically those elements and aspects which might justify [. . .] these emotions and affects, and suppress others' (Scheler, *Das Ressentiment im Aufbau der Moralen*, 31).

teristically respond to this suffering by endeavouring to escape from or, in a certain sense, 'overcome' that world. The usual manifestation of this endeavour is the ascetic ideal and the conception of the good which it embodies. That ideal, we recall, tends to involve the aspiration towards a static, restful, possession of 'knowledge', as opposed to the active engagement with the empirical world of changing phenomena and the multifarious affections of the will associated with it. It is also frequently connected with the belief in the universal legitimacy or desirability of some states or activities conferred upon them by 'the nature of reality'. The ascetic ideal is, according to Nietzsche, invariably an expression of the 'instinct of [self-]protection and of healing' of the weak, suffering, and—when it is put forward as to be aspired to by all human beings—of the *ressentiment*-ridden man. Wherever it is powerful, we are therefore entitled to infer the sickliness of those among whom it is powerful (GM iii.13). Nietzsche, in the writings of the last period, is notoriously eloquent and strident in expressing his detestation of and contempt for weakness if, and to the extent that, it involves *ressentiment*.

here a *ressentiment* without parallel rules, that of an unsatisfied instinct and will to power which desires to become master, not over something pertaining to life, but over life itself, over its deepest, strongest, most basic conditions; here an attempt is made to use strength to block up the sources of strength, here the gaze is directed biliously and maliciously against physiological flourishing itself, in particular against its expression: beauty, joy [. . .]. (GM iii.11)

The weak seek to escape from or to 'overcome' what Nietzsche calls 'life' in general because it is an incessant source of suffering for them. But the weakness of *ressentiment* involves, moreover, a hatred directed specifically at *other humans*. It is not, I think, part of Nietzsche's *definition* of *ressentiment* that the not-selves which are its objects should necessarily be other human beings. But it is conspicuous that he *always* presents it as a relation between human beings. He never suggests that it might be directed either at lower organisms or at objects which we take to be inanimate. The significance of this is twofold. First, it implies the recognition—certainly not new, but perhaps worth reiterating irrespective of whether one accepts Nietzsche's general analysis—that the affective and evaluative life of beings like ourselves is largely shaped, positively or negatively, in our encounter with other beings whom we regard as being significantly like ourselves. Secondly, it confirms, should it need confirmation, our interpretation of *ressentiment* as a form of self-deception about values. It can only fulfil the functions Nietzsche attributes to it if its objects are capable of an at least potentially self-conscious awareness of value.

Nietzsche maintains—and this is presumably an empirical claim—that *ressentiment* is generally aimed at the—on his definition—strong or noble individuals who do not suffer from the fluctuating and unstable world of everyday experience but rather joyfully 'affirm' (*bejahen*) it. The well-constituted, the strong, and the beautiful are typically the objects of *ressentiment*, the primary purpose of which with regard to them is to induce in them a sense of *guilt* about precisely those qualities which enable them to live in serene harmony with themselves and to affirm 'life' (we shall have more to say about this inducement of guilt in Chapter 5.3). To the extent that the weakness of *ressentiment* attempts to undermine and diminish the life-affirming character of the *Wohlgeratenen*, it is a danger to life in its most successful manifestation. This train of thought leads Nietzsche to his notorious conclusion that 'the sickly ones [*die Krankhaften*] are the great danger to man: *not* the "beasts of prey". Those who have come out wrong, who are crushed, broken, from the very start—they are the ones, the *weakest* are the ones, who most undermine life among men, who most dangerously poison and call into question our confidence in life, in man' (GM iii.14).

We have seen that, for Nietzsche, the ascetic ideal, if it is held with sincerity rather than in a self-consciously pragmatic way as a means to exert power over those who do believe in it, is invariably a symptom of the 'sickliness' of those who are subject to it. Consequently, his own desire not to acknowledge weakness—and his contempt for the weakness of *ressentiment* in particular—quite naturally lead him to question the symptom of these conditions, the ascetic ideal, and the latter's 'core', the aspiration to metaphysical truth. He says expressly:

From the moment when the belief in the God of the ascetic ideal has been denied, *there is also a new problem*: the problem of the *value* of truth.— The will to truth requires a critique—let us herewith determine our own task—, the value of truth is to be called into question as an experiment. (GM iii.24)

I argued earlier that Nietzsche's denial of the coherence of the concept of absolute or metaphysical truth—his rejection of the notion of a reality as it is in itself—is not entailed by his criticism of a certain variant of realism. Some of his remarks suggest strongly that this denial is, psychologically, inspired by his contempt for the *ressentiment* of those who insist on the importance of 'truth', or indeed on the supposedly universal claims of any putative good on all human beings irrespective of the desires they may actually experience, and by his own preference for the kind of strength which does not endeavour to escape from the passions and struggles of 'life' into the 'other-world' of the contemplation of metaphysical truth:

> It is of cardinal importance that one should abolish the *true* world. It is the great inspirer of doubt and devaluator in respect of the world *we are*: it has been our most dangerous attempt yet to assassinate life [. . .] (WM 583 B)

The present reading of Nietzsche's attitude to the desire for truth in his writings after *Morgenröte* is strongly at odds with an interpretation which has been quite influential in the English-speaking world—that of Walter Kaufmann. According to Kaufmann, even the later Nietzsche considers the possession of truth as essential to human well-being and 'does not condemn *Geist* and the passion for truth but declares "truth" to be "divine"'.[55] It is difficult to follow Kaufmann at this point, for the immediate context of the statement which he cites and which he claims sums up the philosopher's attitude to the will to truth (FW 344) renders it fairly clear that Nietzsche has strong reservations about precisely the belief that 'truth is divine':

> that Christian belief which was also the belief of Plato, that God is the truth, that truth is *divine* . . . But what if precisely this is becoming more and more incredible, if nothing proves to be divine any more, unless it be error, blindness, lie—if God himself proves to have been our most long-standing lie? (FW 344)

As we have seen above, Nietzsche is even more forthright and explicit in his rejection of the will to truth in other passages. And in so far as he himself has paid homage to the idols of truth and truthfulness—particularly in the middle period of his philosophical

---

[55] W. Kaufmann, *Nietzsche—Philosopher, Psychologist, Antichrist* (Cleveland and New York, 1966), 308.

career—he includes himself among the idol-worshippers whom he berates.[56]

There are, indeed, a number of passages even in his last works in which Nietzsche does praise 'science' and 'truthfulness', opposing these to attitudes like 'mendaciousness', 'faith', and 'conviction' (e.g. AC 52 and 54—but note AC 56!). Remarks like these do indeed seem to conflict with the statements which we have discussed and which have been accorded centrality in the present interpretation of Nietzsche's later work. However, as I have already suggested, they can often be taken as rhetorical ploys used by him in his polemics against 'narrowly' religious versions of the ascetic ideal. A similar reading recommends itself with respect to his concern with scepticism. His 'scepticism' should not be regarded as the disappointing fruit of a thwarted search and desire for metaphysical truths. Especially in the light of his thoughts on the ascetic ideal, it seems more appropriate to interpret it as one of several strategies by means of which he attempts to discredit the endeavours of those who are subject to that ideal.

But such a reading, which aims at reconciling Nietzsche's rejection of the 'will to truth' *qua* central constituent of the ascetic ideal with an apparent concern with truth noticeable in many of his utterances, cannot plausibly account for all of the latter, nor for all of his polemical attacks on the 'dishonesty' of his opponents. The great majority of these attacks are directed against the accounts given by the partisans of the ascetic ideal—i.e. according to Nietzsche, by almost all philosophers since Plato and, of course, by theologians—of 'inner experience', in particular of *human motivation*. One of his chief preoccupations in his writings from *Menschliches, Allzumenschliches* on appears to be the replacement of these accounts by a more adequate one. To the extent that this is indeed his purpose, it would certainly seem that he, too, is inspired by a will to truth at least in this particular domain. Such a desire would, however, only render his psychological analyses pragmatically inconsistent with his rejection of the ascetic ideal if their objective could be correctly described in terms of any of the features which, we have argued, are constitutive of that ideal. We shall see later (Chapter 5.3) that it cannot plausibly be so described.

[56] Cf. GM iii.24: 'Perhaps I know all this too much from close by: that venerable philosophers' asceticism [. . .] that wanting to stop with the factual . . .'

More importantly, perhaps, it seems that Nietzsche's psychological method, if it is intended to uncover the *real* motives behind various kinds of human actions and beliefs, not only betrays a desire for truth on the part of the investigator, but also requires that, at least in this particular domain, true statements can be made about the intrinsic nature of certain psychological or 'physiological' conditions.

4

Truth, Survival, and Power

We have so far discussed several critical strands of thought in Nietzsche, each of which is designed to undermine our belief in our possession of knowledge, in the sense of rationally justified true beliefs, about the world as it 'really' or 'in itself' is. Not only can we not rationally justify as being metaphysically true any of our beliefs about what we call the external world. Rather, a dominant line of argument in the later Nietzsche's writings attempts to show that the very concept of absolute or metaphysical truth is ultimately unintelligible, since it involves the 'nonsensical' notion of entities having intrinsic natures or constitutions in themselves. Now, clearly one cannot be both an anti-essentialist in this sense and a sceptic with respect to our supposed knowledge of metaphysical truths, since this kind of scepticism involves the very construal of truth whose intelligibility is denied.

It will be argued here that this *ad hominem* criticism does not really affect Nietzsche, for it would be naïve to believe that he himself actually subscribes to all the considerations and positions he presents or adumbrates. In the particular case of his sceptical arguments, the most fruitful way of understanding them would seem to be as instruments or tools which he employs in his struggle against the ascetic ideal—an ideal which he regards as pernicious for reasons I have already indicated and which I shall have to say more about later (Chapter 5.3). We can understand them, that is, as saying that even if 'metaphysical truth' were intelligible, knowledge of it would be unattained and probably unattainable, if by 'knowledge' we mean true beliefs which are rationally justified. Consequently, the metaphysical claims made by the philosophical representatives of the ascetic ideal—Platonist, Cartesian, Berkeleian, materialist, or whatever—could not be substantiated in terms of standards of justification which they themselves typically subscribe to, even if these claims were intelligible. I propose that this is a useful way of interpreting Nietzsche's sceptical arguments which is in accord with his concerns and intentions as manifested in his writings, and which enables us to assess each of them on its own merits without feeling compelled to search for an interpretation which would render them consistent with other claims he appears to make. It seems fairly clear that such a logically consistent interpretation of all, or even most, of his statements cannot be found, even if one restricts one's attention to any one period of his philosophical career.[1] This does not mean, however, that we ought to abandon the requirement for consistency for each of these arguments and positions considered separately. Nor does it mean that we may not be able to find a consistent unity of *purpose* behind this variety.

The first part of the present chapter will be concerned with a sceptical line of argument quite distinct from those that have been mentioned so far. It proceeds from the empirical premiss that many, perhaps most, of our beliefs—commonsensical or scientific ones about objects, as well as religious or moral ones—manifestly fulfil various practical purposes in our lives and it infers from this, in conjunction with certain other premisses, the improbability of any of these beliefs being metaphysically true (even assuming the concept of metaphysical truth to be an intelligible one).

Many of the arguments and observations Nietzsche makes in this context could be interpreted as advocating a type of naturalized epistemology—more specifically, a sceptical variant of an 'evolutionary' theory of knowledge. We shall turn to these first. In the later parts of the chapter (sections 3–5), we will address ourselves to the *positive* tenets Nietzsche appears to develop in connection with the thesis that our beliefs are practical tools for dealing with the world.

1. NIETZSCHE AND EVOLUTIONARY EPISTEMOLOGY

The meaning of 'knowledge': here, as in the case of 'good' or 'beautiful', the concept is to be regarded in a strict and narrow anthropocentric and biological sense. [. . .] The utility of preservation—not some abstract-theoretical need not to be deceived—stands as the motive behind the development of the organs of knowledge. (WM 480)

---

[1] Cf. R. Margreiter, *Ontologie und Gottesbegriff bei Nietzsche* (Meisenheim, 1978), 3.

Nietzsche conjectures in many places throughout his later writings—especially in the *Nachlass* and in some passages of *Die Fröhliche Wissenschaft* and *Jenseits von Gut und Böse*—that what we take to be our knowledge of the world has developed contingently under the constraints of an external environment within which human beings have had to assert themselves in a struggle for survival and for power. The very categorial framework of human knowledge, which Kant attempted to codify, represents, according to these conjectures, a set of canons of interpretation which has proved useful in a 'struggle for existence' (a Darwinian concept which Nietzsche rarely uses, for reasons which will become clear later): 'innumerably many beings who reasoned differently from the way we reason [*schliessen*] now, perished [. . .]' (FW 111).

According to this view, the categorial framework of our experience is necessary (and known a priori) only for individuals at a relatively late stage of the development of the 'species', but was contingent prior to this. 'Necessary' here means, as it did for Lange, psychologically inescapable in that we cannot conceive of a reality which would not display the features predicated in judgements to which this term is applied. Thus Nietzsche, like Lange, gives a naturalized interpretation to the Kantian doctrine that all experience 'necessarily'—in some not very perspicuous sense—has certain very general structural features, because without them what he calls experience would not be possible at all. Nietzsche suggests that all our experience has certain psychologically necessary, general characteristics because the 'species' to which we belong would have perished in a hostile environment had its members experienced the world differently.

In the light of these ideas, Nietzsche might be ranked among the first proponents of what came to be labelled 'evolutionary epistemology', a philosophical tendency which enjoyed great popularity from the 1870s onwards[2] and which is, in its neo-Darwinian version, commanding considerable support today.[3] Although his related ideas differ in crucial respects from the Darwinian approach, it will be useful to discuss them initially in the context of

[2] See D. T. Campbell, 'Evolutionary Epistemology', in P. Schilpp (ed.), *The Philosophy of Karl Popper* (La Salle, 1974), i. 437 f. Campbell points out that by the 1890s evolutionary assumptions in epistemology were commonplace.

[3] See e.g. Karl Popper, *Objective Knowledge* (Oxford, 1972); K. Lorenz, *Behind the Mirror* (London, 1977); G. Vollmer, *Evolutionäre Erkenntnistheorie* (Stuttgart, 1975) and *Was können wir wissen?* (Stuttgart, 1985), 2 vols.

this dominant strand of evolutionary epistemology. One advantage of this procedure is that it will facilitate spelling out the implications of a position which Nietzsche himself presents in often somewhat general and vague terms. Moreover, we thereby become able to appreciate what bearing, if any, his reflections have on a naturalized approach to epistemological problems, which finds many adherents in our time.

Evolutionary epistemology starts from the 'hypothetical' premiss that the subject of knowledge is to be identified with the empirical organism studied by biology and physiology. Historically, a milestone in the development of this naturalistic approach was F. A. Lange's *Geschichte des Materialismus*, a work which was avidly read by the young Nietzsche and in which the Kantian distinction between phenomena and things-in-themselves is re-interpreted in the light of empirical data afforded by the physiological study of the nature of our cognitive apparatus.

A central assumption shared by most versions of evolutionary epistemology is that the cognitive apparatus of any organism, including humans, registers primarily those features of reality which the organism needs to take account of in order to survive in its environment. Charles Darwin argued in *The Origin of Species*[4] that the environment of any species of organisms acts, in the course of generations, as a selective check on the mutations of whatever characteristics are responsible for the hereditary features of the individual members of that species (these characteristics were later identified more precisely by the science of genetics). Those features produced by the mutations in question which are not useful or even harmful with respect to the individual's adaptation to its environment are likely to disfavour that individual in the 'struggle for existence' and to diminish its chances of producing numerous offspring. In the course of a number of generations, the better adapted types will have ousted and replaced the less well-adapted ones which compete with them for limited food, shelter, and sexual partners in a given habitat. The pivotal role of utility for adaptation (biological utility) in the formation of new characteristics in organisms becomes apparent in Darwin's own classic formulation of the thesis:

---

[4] Nietzsche probably first became acquainted with Darwinism through Lange's *Geschichte des Materialismus* (cf. Schlechta and Anders, *Friedrich Nietzsche*, 55). He seems to have studied Darwin's ideas with great interest. His library contained a number of books specifically on the subject.

in all cases natural selection will ensure that modifications [. . .] shall not be in the least degree injurious; for if they became so, they would cause the extinction of the species [. . . .] What natural selection cannot do, is to modify the structure of one species, without giving it any advantage, for the good of another species.[5]

It is not difficult to see how a theory of this kind might be applied to all the characteristics of the phenotype of a species, including its cognitive apparatus (the 'organs of knowledge', in Nietzsche's terminology). In this particular application, too, biological utility is the central explanatory concept. According to a theory of knowledge constructed along Darwinian lines, 'what we experience is [. . .] only just sufficing for our practical purposes; we have developed "organs" only for those aspects of reality of which, in the interest of survival, it was imperative for our species to take account, so that selection pressure produced this particular cognitive apparatus.'[6] We realize the extent of the influence of evolutionary thinking on Nietzsche if we compare this remark by the modern Darwinian, Konrad Lorenz, with some of Nietzsche's statements in the *Nachlass*:

It is improbable that our 'knowledge' should extend further than is strictly necessary for the preservation of life [. . .] (WM 494)

[. . .] we have senses for only a selection of perceptions—those with which we have to concern ourselves in order to preserve ourselves. (WM 505)

If we sharpened or blunted our senses tenfold, we would perish [. . .]—our conditions of existence prescribe the most general laws under which we see, are *permitted* to see, forms, shapes, laws [. . .] (KGW VIII.1.6.8)

Some of Nietzsche's own arguments in favour of such an interpretation of the status of our beliefs as means or tools for the 'preservation of life' seem to be straightforwardly empirical: 'Morphology shows us how the senses and the nerves, as well as the brain, develop in proportion to the difficulty of finding nourishment' (WM 494). Although this may seem rather crude as an argument, it conforms to the general pattern characteristic of the Darwinian, naturalized approach to epistemology. To quote Lorenz again: 'one looks first at our cognitive apparatus, then at the things which it reflects in one way or another and [. . .] on both occasions one obtains results which throw light on one another.'[7]

---

[5] C. Darwin, *The Origin of Species* (Harmondsworth, 1968), 135.
[6] Lorenz, *Behind the Mirror*, 7.   [7] Ibid. 13–14.

Modern scientific research has led to the discovery of what may be thought to be mutually illuminating correlations between the nature of our cognitive apparatus and the 'things which it reflects' far beyond those which could be established in Nietzsche's time. To give only one suggestive example, we now know that only radiation with wavelengths of between 400 and 800 nm (and radio waves) penetrates the atmosphere of the earth and reaches the level of our eyes. This specific penetrability of the atmosphere by radiation is approximately matched by the sensitivity of our visual apparatus, which registers only radiation with wavelengths of between 380 and 760 nm.[8] It appears, therefore, that human visual capacities are adapted fairly precisely to the nature of our environment and do not extend beyond what is required to survive in it.

Now, it would seem that such arguments from natural science, which are strictly analogous to Nietzsche's own argument quoted above, can only lend support to his thesis on the understanding that the laws established by the natural sciences, and the observable consequences deducible from them in conjunction with statements of the relevant initial conditions, are not only biologically useful, but also true in the traditional sense of 'corresponding to' or 'adequately representing' the nature of the relevant part of reality in itself. If one did not either accept them as true in something like this sense, or alternatively simply equate biological utility and truth, it would be possible to reply to examples like the one given above that, while it may be biologically useful for us to believe that our perceptual capacities do not extend beyond what is required for our survival, we have no reason to think that this belief is *true*. Most advocates of evolutionary epistemology do not simply define the truth of a judgement in terms of its biological utility, but, while distinguishing these concepts, argue that we can infer from the biological utility of certain beliefs that they probably are at least approximately true: 'the fact that animals and human beings are still in existence proves that their forms of experience correspond, to some degree, with reality.'[9] Some of our beliefs are useful for the manipulation of our environment and mediately for the survival of

---

[8] Vollmer, *Evolutionäre Erkenntnistheorie*, 98.
[9] L. von Bertalanffy, 'An Essay on the Relativity of Categories', in *Philosophy of Science* (1955), 256–7. Cf. also Vollmer, *Was können wir wissen?*, i. 281: 'It is so obvious that correct beliefs [*Erkenntnisse*] are in principle more advantageous than errors [. . .] that I have not been able to find any counter-examples.'

the species because they reflect that environment, or at least the relevant aspects of it, to a sufficient extent as they really are. My belief that there is a hole of such-and-such a size a few yards ahead of me helps me to avoid falling into it by walking round it because there really is a hole of roughly the size I had estimated which I can avoid by walking a few steps to the left. My belief is useful, it seems, because it is (approximately) true.

In order to form an adequate assessment of this position, and of Nietzsche's contrary claims, we would do well to establish first what exactly is meant by the term 'utility'. Nietzsche mentions two related applications of it which are directly relevant to this context. First, our conceptualization of data, involving as it does abstraction from the qualitative differences of numerically distinct particulars and their subsumption under the same concept, is useful in making possible an effective form of communication and serves 'the purpose of mutual agreement and dominion' (WM 509; cf. WM 513). Secondly, Nietzsche speaks about beliefs as useful when they enable an agent to maintain himself in existence and to increase his power—to gain 'mastery' over his environment. In the case of human agents, this mastery tends to involve their capacity to calculate and predict the behaviour of the 'external reality' they seek to master (cf. WM 480). Not surprisingly, Nietzsche identifies science as the tool *par excellence* for providing human agents with the means for the mastery of their environment through the prediction of events:

Science—the transformation of nature into concepts for the purpose of mastering nature—belongs under the rubric 'means'. (WM 610)

Science has to establish to an ever greater extent the *one-after-another* of things in their succession, so that events become practicable for us [. . .] (GOA xii.4)

'Science' (as it is practised today) is the attempt to create a common sign language for all phenomena for the purpose of an easy *predictability* and, consequently, manipulability [*Beherrschbarkeit*] of nature. (GOA xiii.83)

Evidently, this second usage of 'utility' involves the first. The very formulation of scientific theories and experimental laws involves 'mutual agreement' on the meaning of terms, and the notion of prediction as it is generally understood and employed in science requires agreement among different observers on the occurrence and the description of the observed or observable events which a theory helps to predict. The testing of a theory or an experimental law is indeed partly defined in terms of such agreement. In the present context, we shall concentrate on this sense of 'utility' in which it is applied to scientific theories, experimental laws, and common-sense generalizations which make it possible to predict events and thus, to some extent, to manipulate our environment and to become masters over it.

Given this application of 'utility', we may rephrase the question posed earlier more precisely as follows: is it not plausible to maintain that beliefs which enable us to predict events are not only biologically useful, but that they are useful *because* they are at least approximately true on a minimal realist construal of truth? Such a construal involves the correspondence, in some sense, of what our judgements assert with the nature of 'real', ontologically independent items of some sort, a nature that they are assumed to have in themselves, whatever our beliefs about them may be. Nietzsche emphatically denies this claim. Here, as in his sceptical arguments discussed earlier, he proceeds as if such a notion of metaphysical, or absolute, truth made sense, granting the premiss of his opponents:

All our organs of knowledge and our senses are developed only with regard to conditions of preservation and growth. Trust in reason and its categories, in dialectic, therefore the valuation of logic, proves only their usefulness for life, proved by experience—*not* that something is true. (WM 507)

The categories are 'truths' only in the sense that they are conditions of life for us: as Euclidean space is a conditional 'truth' (Between ourselves: since no one would maintain that there is any necessity for men to exist, reason, as well as Euclidean space, is a mere idiosyncrasy of a certain species of animal, and one among many—.) (WM 515; cf. JGB 11)

Not only with respect to empirical properties, but also regarding the general 'categorial' framework to which all our (conceptualized) experience conforms, we have no reasons to believe that they correspond to the constitution of reality in itself. Unlike Kant, Nietzsche does not give a definitive, exhaustive list of what he takes to be the universal and necessary features of the experience of subjects like us, but he mentions in this context one of the Kantian forms of intuition—Euclidean space—as well as the axioms of classical logic, specifically the laws of identity and non-contradiction, and also our construal of objects as clusters of attributes inhering in substances (WM 522).[10] We shall deal with Nietzsche's remarks on these 'categories' at a later stage. At present, let us confine ourselves to the more limited claim contained in the quotations above: that our beliefs concerning the properties of objects and concerning their relations to each other in time and Euclidean space—which arguably is the only kind of space picturable by us[11]—are manifestly useful 'for life', helping us to find our way in our environment and enabling us to predict its behaviour, but that this utility does not render it even probable that the beliefs in question are true, or approximately true, in a metaphysical sense. In fact, Nietzsche's formulations suggest, on the contrary, that, for him, the relative utility of beliefs renders them proportionately more likely to be 'a mere idiosyncrasy of a certain species of animal', bearing no significant relation of correspondence to a putative metaphysical reality in itself.

What is the reasoning, if any, which lies behind this radical dissociation of utility and truth that is so obviously at odds with the views espoused by most orthodox evolutionary epistemologists and, it appears, with common sense? While this reasoning is never presented by Nietzsche in a fully explicit manner, it can nevertheless be gleaned from numerous passages scattered throughout his writings. Perhaps he comes closest to an explicit formulation in the following note from the *Nachlass*:

How is truth proved? By the feeling of enhanced power—by utility—by indispensability—in short by advantages (namely, presuppositions concerning what truth *ought* to be like for us to recognize it). But that is a prejudice: a sign that truth is not involved at all— (WM 455)

The argument here seems to be that a belief which we hold on account of the benefits we derive from it—certain advantages and utilities in practical life which either consist or result in 'pleasure' (a 'feeling of enhanced power')—are by virtue of that very fact unlikely to be metaphysically true. This is the core of what I shall

---

[10] The inclusion of this Aristotelian conception among the categorial features of our experience in one note is surprising, given Nietzsche's own criticism of the concept of substance *qua* substratum and his attempt—to be discussed later—to develop an alternative construal of objects as clusters of events or processes. Note that Nietzsche does not regard the Kantian form of intuition of time as 'subjective' or perspectival in the sense that the other categorial structures of experience are (see WM 1064 and KGW VII.1.1.3).

[11] Cf. Strawson, *The Bounds of Sense*, 283.

call the sceptical *argument from utility*. In addition to the previously discussed sceptical considerations deployed by Nietzsche against various metaphysical conceptions—things that persist self-identically through time, atoms, substance *qua* substratum, an efficacious will, etc.—he frequently, though often implicitly, advances this argument to throw doubt on their adequacy in first philosophy.[12]

To understand the import of the argument from utility, it is important to realize that it is used in the first place against certain religious and moral ideas—such as that there is a benevolent God, or a moral law, or a Kantian *summum bonum*. As early as 1878, in the first book of *Menschliches, Allzumenschliches*, he objects to what he calls the 'proof from pleasure':

The proof from pleasure—The pleasant conviction is assumed to be true: this is the proof from pleasure (or, as the Church says, the proof from strength), of which all religions are so proud, while they should be ashamed of it. If the faith did not make blessed, it would not be believed: hence, how little will it be worth! (MAM i.120)

According to the argument implicit in this and in many other passages, those who believe in the existence of a benevolent God or in a moral law have no other evidence for the truth of the relevant propositions than a feeling of 'pleasure' associated with, or resulting from, supposing them to be true. (For a discussion of Nietzsche's further analysis of pleasure as the 'feeling of power', see Chapter 5.1.) This pleasure or feeling of power is for them a 'criterion' of the truth of these thoughts:

It appears that there is a criterion of truth among Christians called the 'proof from strength'. 'The faith makes you blessed: *hence* it is true.' [. . .] could blessedness—speaking more technically: *pleasure*—ever be a proof of truth? So little that it constitutes almost the refutation, at least the greatest suspicion against 'truth' if feelings of pleasure have a say on the question 'what is true?'. (AC 50)

We shall attempt to establish precisely what Nietzsche means by a 'criterion' later. But we can already surmise, when considering passages like WM 455, quoted above, that he transfers his prima facie not implausible objection against the 'proof from strength/pleasure' from the context of religious and moral beliefs to beliefs

---

[12] Cf. R. Schacht, *Nietzsche* (London, 1983), 136–7 and 147.

of any sort whose acceptance has desirable consequences for the believer. In this generalized form, the argument from utility is formulated well by R. Schacht: 'to the extent that acceptance of any notion may be seen to serve some practical purpose associated with contingent factors of our manner of existence, the supposition that its actual status is merely that of a useful fiction is rendered more compelling'.[13]

How cogent is this argument? When applied to certain kinds of religious belief, it seems to carry some force, at least if one considers Nietzsche's description of these beliefs to be accurate. If one accepts, for instance, that Christian faith is typically a characteristic of weak and oppressed people who expect to be granted 'eternal' pleasure in another life and to see their enemies and oppressors punished by a supremely powerful agent (God), and if one accepts that their evidence to support this belief consists indeed in nothing other than the anticipatory pleasure they experience from supposing the relevant thoughts to be true, then one may be inclined to reject them as unlikely to be true—for past experience suggests that such pleasure or satisfaction afforded to a believer by the propositions he supposes to be true constitutes no evidence for their truth.

The believer might reply, drawing on one of Nietzsche's own distinctions, that this inductive argument is invalid, since it involves two different senses of 'truth'—'conditional' in the known instances, 'metaphysical' in the case in dispute. Let us consider this response in some detail. In most everyday and scientific contexts, truth claims are expected to be supported by evidence provided by 'rational' epistemic procedures. Such procedures typically involve the independent agreement of what we take to be different observers upon sensorily observable states of affairs, as well as inductive inferences based upon them. Clearly, claims which are accepted on no other evidence than feelings of pleasure experienced by those who suppose the relevant propositions to be true would fall foul of these validatory standards. Moreover, these procedures give us good inductive grounds to regard such claims, when their subject matter is empirical, as unlikely to be true.

However, Nietzsche himself suggests elsewhere that we have no good (rational) grounds to assume that any of the kinds of evidence

13 Ibid. 136–7.

we consider relevant in everyday and scientific discourse have any purchase on the question of truth in a metaphysical sense at all (cf. Chapter 2.3). Consequently, no amount of confirmation or disconfirmation of the adequacy of some type of ostensible evidence (e.g. 'pleasure') in a non-philosophical context renders it inductively either more or less likely to provide adequate grounds for any metaphysical beliefs.

But there are further reasons to doubt whether Nietzsche's argument from utility has much force even when directed against the religious convictions against which he originally deploys it. Its cogency would seem to depend partly on the degree of certainty with which the believer can expect 'blessedness' (or as Nietzsche would say: pleasure) once he has embraced a given religious doctrine. In some religions—some Christian traditions being cases in point—believers have often not been encouraged to feel confident, and have usually been discouraged from feeling certain, about 'beatitude' being granted to them after this life. Evidently, Nietzsche's argument from utility, whatever its other shortcomings may be, is bound to be very much weaker against such religious systems than it is against others which encourage or even require a sense of certitude in this regard from their adherents.

The force of the argument also depends crucially on whether it is accurate to describe the believer's 'criterion' of truth as pleasure. Presumably the pleasure in question here is primarily one of anticipation at the thought of future pleasures in store for the faithful. But it is not obviously the case that the thought of such future pleasures is indeed essential in eliciting assent to religious doctrines. However, this is a rather difficult and complex issue which we cannot enter into in detail at this stage. I shall return to it when discussing Nietzsche's analysis of the 'Christian ideal' (Chapter 5.3). In any case, to the extent that the attainment of a future state of happiness is both regarded as uncertain and as conditional upon precisely the *reining in* of many ordinary human desires for pleasurable experiences—as it is in 'ascetic' religions—it is far from obvious that the believer's present state is one of (anticipatory) pleasure.

If we now turn to the application of the argument from utility to beliefs other than moral and religious ones, it seems that Nietzsche's reasoning here is as follows. Most common-sense beliefs about the physical world are useful in our practical dealings with the world. Scientific theories are useful in helping us to predict the course of our experience in the future—indeed the adequacy of a scientific theory is partly defined in terms of its predictive success. Moreover, we have seen that, according to Nietzsche, the meaning of 'objectively real' involves the concerns and interests of subjects (Chapter 3.1). Hence, which judgements we normally consider to be true (or likely to be true) in the sense of representing objective reality as it is, also depends ultimately on the practical interests of subjects like us. Thus, practical interests may be said ultimately to delimit the range of judgements we would normally regard as true in this sphere. But, so the argument seems to continue, we know from experience that where our interests and considerations of advantage determine and delimit the evidence we are prepared to acknowledge and the methods of investigation we employ, the results of the latter are unlikely to be true—it is probable that, in such cases, 'truth is not involved at all' (WM 455).

This argument, if it is indeed Nietzsche's, clearly has several defects. If the beliefs and religious interests of a biologist who happens to be a fundamentalist Christian determine what evidence—compatible with these interests—concerning the theory of evolution he is prepared to consider, then we may well have doubts about the results of his investigations. For his interests here *interfere* with the methods of his science in a manner which we have inductive reasons to expect will lead to false results. However, this is quite different from the guiding interests which, arguably, *establish* a scientific methodology in the first place (such as the interest in prediction). These constitutive interests, unlike the interfering ones mentioned previously, we have absolutely no inductive reasons to suppose lead us astray *in metaphysicis*. Nietzsche's apparent argument to this effect rests on an equivocation. But, as with the religious beliefs against which he uses the argument from utility, there is a further equivocation here on two senses of 'truth' which he elsewhere distinguishes. It may indeed be rational, in terms of generally accepted standards of rationality, to suppose that what I have called interfering interests will lead to beliefs which are *conditionally* false. But what he wishes to show here is that interest-determined beliefs are likely to be *metaphysically* false. If his own sceptical argument discussed earlier (Chapter 2.3) is at all plausible, this conclusion does not follow.

2. EXPLANATIONS OF OBSERVATIONAL SUCCESS

The argument from utility is intended to establish the conclusion that beliefs are *unlikely* to be metaphysically true which enable us to manipulate our environment by 'explaining' the behaviour of objects encountered in it through subsumption under so-called nomic universals (describing 'laws of nature'). I have suggested that the argument fails. It has already been pointed out that proponents of various forms of naturalized epistemology often maintain, to the contrary, that beliefs which are useful in this sense are *likely* to be true, a claim which commands some intuitive plausibility. Since arguments to this effect, if they could be sustained, would clearly neutralize the sceptical strand of Nietzsche's thinking, and since the issue is of considerable independent interest today, I shall discuss it in some detail.

The meaning of 'true' in a metaphysical sense which emerged from our discussion in Chapter 3 might be paraphrased roughly as follows. A judgement is true in this sense if it attributes structures to reality, or some part of it, which it 'really', or 'in itself', has. If we add to this the requirement that it possess these structures independently of whether I—the respective subject of the inquiry—am aware of them, our conception of metaphysical truth will be what might be called a minimal realist one.[14] It is usually at least in this minimal realist sense that many adherents of naturalized epistemology hold that certain beliefs which are useful—here: predictively successful—are likely to be (at least approximately) true. Now, the term 'structures' in the above formulation is susceptible to a number of different interpretations. I should like to consider three of these which might be thought most relevant.

1. On the first and weakest interpretation, the claim that successful scientific hypotheses and theories are likely to be metaphysically true (or approximately true) in proportion to their predictive success does not involve the tenet that such hypotheses and theories attribute intelligible *qualitative features* to whatever entities they assume to exist which these entities really possess (e.g. solidity).

---

[14] This is to be distinguished from the 'strong' realism referred to in Ch. 3.1, according to which reality, or parts of it, possesses a structure or constitution irrespective of any subject's awareness of them. Berkeley was a minimal realist, Locke a strong realist.

Nor does it assert that the numerical indices by means of which scientific theories and hypotheses quantify the relevant properties of the entities they postulate and the relations and dependencies between them—this quantitative method being the hallmark of modern science—are, or are likely to be, identical with or closely similar to such formal, mathematical structures subsisting in reality. Rather, it is merely claimed that there is a relatively weak *isomorphism* between the elements of a successful theory—such elements being, for example, certain variables interpreted in terms of some more or less picturable model—and the elements making up reality or some part of it, such that to every instance of any distinct element-type A assumed by the theory there corresponds one and only one instance of some distinct element-type B of the latter. Evidently, two systems—here: a theory and a facet of reality—can be isomorphous in this way even though there are no interesting qualitative similarities betweeen the elements of each, nor any illuminating mathematical similarities between the quantitative relations predicated by the theory and the relations instantiated in reality. Thus, for example, there may be an isomorphism of this sort between messages sent via telegraph and certain sounds we emit when speaking.[15] Such isomorphisms do not entail that, in each case, the relevant qualitative features of each of the isomorphous 'systems' are similar, or that there obtain the same, or similar, mathematical relations between the suitably identified and quantified corresponding properties in each system.

Some realist construals of the 'truth' of those scientific propositions which, *ex hypothesi, are* true, are so exceedingly general as to be compatible with this interpretation.[16] It is in fact so general that not even the Cartesian sceptical scenario is ruled out by it—for it might after all be the case that to every instance of a specific kind of *cogitatio* A of the deceived subject, there corresponds one and only one instance of a distinct type of manipulative act B of the deceiving demon, whatever properties these acts might possess in themselves.

Nietzsche's own ideas in the early essay 'On Truth and Lie in a Non-moral Sense', which are clearly regarded by him as sceptical in

---

[15] Cf. G. Simmel, 'Über eine Beziehung der Selektionslehre zur Erkenntnistheorie', in *Archiv für systematische Philosophie*, 1 (1895), 37–8.
[16] e.g. W. Newton-Smith, *The Rationality of Science* (London, 1981), 29: 'to be true is to be true in virtue of how the world is independently of ourselves'.

nature, envisage precisely such an isomorphous—in his terminology: metaphorical—relation between our perceptual beliefs and reality in itself:

A nerve stimulus is transferred into an image: first metaphor. The image, in turn, is imitated in a sound: second metaphor [. . .]. One can imagine a man who is totally deaf and has never had a sensation of sound and music. Perhaps such a person will gaze with astonishment at Chladni's sound figures; perhaps he will discover their causes in the vibration of the string and will now swear that he must know what we mean by 'sound'. It is this way with all of us concerning language: we believe that we know something about the things themselves when we speak of trees, colours, snow, and flowers; and yet we possess nothing but metaphors for things— (PT 82)

It is questionable whether a realist construal of the truth of a theory which can, in principle, accommodate, with the exception of solipsism, *any* of the traditional metaphysical positions (including 'Cartesian' scepticism), can be considered a very informative one in our context. It is arguably not a very interesting one.[17]

2. A second interpretation of the kind of claim rejected by Nietzsche (i.e. hypotheses or theories are likely to approximate to metaphysical truth in proportion to their predictive success) is more restrictive. It does not maintain that the theories in question attribute intrinsic qualitative properties to the entities postulated by them which the items making up reality actually possess. But it does hold that, whatever the properties of the latter may be in themselves, there obtain quantitative, functional relations between them which are identical with, or closely similar to, the quantitative relations obtaining between the properties of the entities assumed by the theory (which entities and properties, in turn, are identified in practice by correlating elements of the mathematical calculus— e.g. certain variables—with features of a non-mathematical model and/or with observable phenomena by means of appropriate rules of correspondence). Thus, for example, the hypothesis that 'every particle of matter attracts every other particle with a force directly proportional to the product of the masses of the particles and inversely proportional to the square of the distance between them' is approximately true *not* in the sense that it tells us anything about

[17] It is perhaps with such a construal in mind that Vollmer makes the otherwise rather mysterious assertion that 'whoever is not a solipsist has to be a realist, more precisely, a hypothetical realist' (Vollmer, *Was können wir wissen?*, i. 50; cf. also 12–13).

the qualitative nature-in-itself of the entities or properties ('force', 'mass') it purports to refer to, but rather in the sense that the functional relations it asserts as holding do actually obtain between real properties and entities, whatever the intrinsic qualitative nature of the latter may be (whether their nature is, for example, essentially subject-implying—i.e., in a sense, 'mental'—or not).[18]

3. The third and strongest interpretation of the claim we are discussing states that predictively successful hypotheses or theories are likely to be approximately true in the sense of asserting the existence of both qualitative features and of functional relations between these suitably quantified, numerically indexed, features which do indeed characterize reality or the relevant facets of it. In contrast to the two positions previously mentioned, it is maintained here that scientific theories make statements about the qualitative features of the entities they postulate, and that these characteristics are likely to be, in the case of successful theories, similar (or materially analogous) to their counterparts in reality.

In the following, we shall only be concerned with the last two variants of a realist metaphysical interpretation of scientific propositions. While version (3) is probably no longer commonly held, I shall conjecture that most contemporary realists would wish to defend a variant which is at least as strong as (2), although this is rarely made explicit. If this conjecture is correct, then adherents of a naturalized theory of knowledge can be interpreted as commonly arguing for some such version of realism on the grounds that it is a 'well-supported hypothesis' or, at any rate, the 'best explanation' of a number of empirical facts.[19] It is pointed out, first, that the very fact that some theories enable us to make successful predictions, placing us 'in a better position to manipulate the world', while other theories are refuted by experimental tests, constitutes itself inductive evidence for the truth of the realist 'hypothesis'.[20] Another ostensible piece of evidence is the 'phenomenon of convergence', whether it be of theories, or of the results achieved by

---

[18] Some of Pierre Duhem's remarks suggest that he held a view of this kind. See his *The Aim and Structure of Physical Theory* (Princeton, 1954), 299 f.

[19] Vollmer, *Was können wir wissen?*, i. 28, 72, 204. See also Newton-Smith, *The Rationality of Science*, 195–6, and M. Devitt, *Realism and Truth* (Oxford, 1984), 228.

[20] Newton-Smith, *The Rationality of Science*, 196. Also Vollmer, *Evolutionäre Erkenntnistheorie*, 35–9.

different methods of measurement of some phenomenon, or the empirically discoverable convergence of the receptive capacities of cognitive apparatuses with the nature of the respective environments their owners find themselves confronted with.[21] Thirdly, it might be thought relevant that the realist 'hypothesis' offers the *simplest* explanation of the manifest predictive success of some of our theories.[22] Fourthly, it is pointed out that scientists usually work on realist assumptions and that this belief in the explanatory nature of their work seems to be a powerful stimulus for further successful research.[23] Finally, one might mention the *psychologische Evidenz*, that is, the intuitive plausibility of this approach, which seems to accord best with our 'natural', commonsensical, cognitive attitude to the world.[24]

Let us consider these points from a Nietzschean perspective. Is the assumption of the (approximate) metaphysical truth of what certain theories assert the 'best explanation', in some quasi-scientific sense of this phrase, of the fact that the theories in question 'work', i.e. that they lead to successful predictions? It would appear that the very description of the realist interpretation of some beliefs or theories as a 'hypothesis' which could be 'inductively supported' by 'evidence', and which could hence be regarded as the best explanation available of certain facts, is misguided. As we observed earlier (Chapter 2.2), in the usage of the term 'explanation' by most modern scientists, an explanation is, roughly, a statement or group of statements of certain presumptively universal regularities and dependencies in a system ('nomic universals'), from which, in conjunction with a statement of the state of the system at some given point in time, predictions (either determinate or probabilistic) about its state at other points in time can be deduced. An occurrence is explained in this sense if it can be identified as an instance of some specified nomic universal. What makes an explanation better or preferable to another in this scientific context? Several criteria are usually mentioned. The two most relevant here are observational success and degree of confirmation. A scientific explanation may be said to be better than a rival one if the domain of facts it explains—its scope of prediction—is greater than that of its

---

[21] Vollmer, *Evolutionäre Erkenntnistheorie*, 35–9.   [22] Ibid.
[23] Ibid. Also Popper, *Objective Knowledge*, 40.
[24] Vollmer, *Evolutionäre Erkenntnistheorie*, 35–9, and Popper, *Objective Knowledge*, 39.

rival, or if its predictions are more accurate, provided that its scope of prediction encompasses that of its rival. An explanation of this kind may, secondly, be held to be preferable to an alternative one if, *ceteris paribus*, it has a better record of experimental confirmation.

Clearly, the realist 'hypothesis' is not the best explanation available of any empirical facts in any such sense. The realist interpretation of the observational success of some of our scientific and common-sense generalizations does not, *qua* metaphysical interpretation, imply any predictions at all, any more than 'Cartesian' scepticism or indeed solipsism do. The domain of facts 'explained' by, say, a non-teleological physicalist interpretation of empirical data is no larger than that accounted for by Berkeley's spirits and ideas, by Leibniz's teleological monadology, or by the malicious activity of Descartes's demon. As to inductive probability, there are no tests which could possibly corroborate or support any of these rival metaphysical interpretations as against another, since *none* of them *disputes* that there are certain regularities among phenomena and that, consequently, some scientific theories 'work' and others do not. In view of the unavailability of any tests the results of which might support, say, a teleological monadology against a non-teleological physicalist realism, or the latter against Cartesian scepticism, it is somewhat misleading to speak of any of these metaphysical approaches as a 'hypothesis' ('hypothetical realism'), thus suggesting an affinity to the methods employed by science. To maintain that any of these metaphysical interpretations of observational success might themselves be argued for 'inductively', or 'corroborated' in a quasi-scientific manner, involves an *ignoratio elenchi*.

Similar considerations apply to the second set of facts allegedly pointing to a realist interpretation of scientific findings as their best explanation. Consider, for instance, the empirically discoverable 'fittedness' of the cognitive equipment of various organisms to their environment, which is pointed out by Nietzsche, too (WM 494). Does not the observation of different forms of adaptation to different aspects of the same system of law-like occurrences confirm our belief in the (metaphysical) reality of these occurrences and laws, just as the belief of a judge in the truthfulness of a witness is confirmed by the fact that different independent witnesses give mutually congruent (although not identical) descriptions of the incident under investigation?[25] Again, the argument fails, as neither the solipsist nor the Cartesian sceptic (nor, for that matter, the Berkeleian idealist or the monadologist) is committed to denying that there may be such congruences suggested by investigations at a highly theoretical level. The congruences by themselves do not 'support' any of the different possible metaphysical interpretations of them. They only appear to do so if we have *previously* tacitly adopted the interpretation which they are supposed to support. This becomes very clear in the judge/witness analogy. The analogy holds only if we have already decided to regard the putative witnesses as indeed independent observers of a world which is in turn independent of, but in principle accessible to, each of them. The sceptic will insist that our situation is better compared to that of a judge (or, more likely, of a police officer) who examines an incident for which there is no circumstantial evidence and only one witness. But this witness, about whose background he knows nothing, claims that many other people witnessed the same event and would confirm his own version of it—only they can, unfortunately, not be contacted personally.

But might not the simplicity of the realist interpretation of certain scientific and common-sense beliefs be counted as a point in its favour? After all, the simplest 'explanation' of the fact that we detect certain mathematically describable regularities in nature— and that our theories work to the extent that they describe these regularities fairly accurately—would appear to be that there *are* these regularities in reality as it is in itself. One might retort here that the notion of simplicity *per se* is a rather questionable one, that, as Wittgenstein pointed out, one can only speak of simplicity in certain definite respects, and that there are undoubtedly some relevant respects in which, say, a sceptical interpretation of our conditional truths is simpler than a realist one. But, waiving this objection for the moment, it is not clear why the criterion of simplicity should even be relevant in this context. To be sure, in science, when we are faced with a choice between rival theories, the relatively greater simplicity of one theory may incline us in its favour, other things being equal. But can it by itself be more than a pragmatic criterion of theory choice in science? Do we have any reason to believe that the relation between an assumed metaphys-

[25] Lorenz, 'Kants Lehre vom apriorischen im Lichte gegenwärtiger Biologie', in *Blätter für deutsche Philosophie*, 114.

ical nature of reality and our awareness of it is such as to appear simple, even relatively simple, to us? Clearly we have not, unless we make various additional assumptions—like Descartes, in his supposition of the veracity of God and the immutability of his decrees—which themselves stand in need of further justification. Indeed, there is much to be said for Nietzsche's observation, to be discussed in greater detail below, that it is the mind's ever-present desire to reduce the unfamiliar to the familiar, the complex and puzzling to the surveyable and simple, which gives rise to the belief that what appears to be a 'simple explanation' is always more likely to approximate to the real nature of things than a more complex, idiosyncratic or seemingly outlandish one. We are 'always full of tacit pre-judgements as to *how* truth would have to be constituted so that [we], [we] of all beings, could accept it' (MR 539). But it seems questionable whether this circumstance by itself is evidence for anything other than certain features of our psychology.

A similar rejoinder might be made to the fourth argument. It may well be the case that many scientists interpret their endeavours along realist lines and that the belief to be approaching truth in a metaphysical sense in practice has exerted a powerful impetus on their efforts to extend, refine, and unify their theories. But the presumed stimulating effect of realist beliefs on scientific research goes no further towards supporting the truth of these beliefs than the arguably considerable propitiousness of shared religious beliefs for social cohesion goes towards confirming their truth. It is of course a very interesting psychological question why there should be this—to a certain extent clearly culture-dependent[26]—desire or tendency on the part of some practitioners of science to give particular metaphysical interpretations to their theories, and why the acceptance of such interpretations should at least sometimes have a stimulating effect on scientific work, given the fact that modern scientific theories do not imply or presuppose any particular metaphysical view—they are in principle compatible with physicalism, idealism, the essentials of Thomism, Cartesian scepticism, and so forth. I have already given Nietzsche's answer to this question in general terms in the previous chapter; we shall address its more detailed development later on.

There remains a last point to be mentioned: the plain intuitive

[26] This was one of Duhem's chief claims in *The Aim and Structure of Physical Theory*.

plausibility of a realist interpretation of those common-sense and scientific beliefs which 'work'. The suppositions that, for example, our perceptions are ultimately produced by a deceiving, demonic mind manipulating us, or that we really are not affected by external, material objects at all, but rather are quasi-mental Leibnizian monads that only appear to themselves as interacting with one another in space—such suppositions may seem considerably more fantastic and 'implausible' to the non-philosophical layperson than the thesis that we perceive what appear to be 'external', subject-independent objects interacting in particular ways because, by and large, there really, metaphysically, *are* these objects thus related to one another and to us. One may, however, wish to ask whether alleged *psychologische Evidenz*, or intuitive plausibility, is not rather too variable, too relative to cultures and indeed individuals to be considered a *rational* support—in some non-culture-bound, universal sense—for any philosophical doctrine. After all, as Schopenhauer was fond of remarking, the Buddhist and Hindu religions testify that a large section of the world's population appears to find a view of the nature of things 'intuitively plausible' which is in important respects rather like his own, to most modern Westerners perhaps 'counter-intuitive', version of transcendental idealism. It is highly questionable whether there is any one metaphysical interpretation of our experience that appears, as a matter of fact, as the intuitively most plausible one to most people, or that would appear so to them if it were clearly set before them. Indeed, such a supposition must seem quite *irrational* to anyone who has ever seriously ventured outside the confines of his or her particular subculture—which may be a very large one, such as the secularized, industrialized, 'Westernized' parts of the modern world.

But even if there were such an interpretation, Nietzsche's more fundamental objection against this kind of thinking would still remain unanswered. It is a symptom of either naïvety or hubris to regard what spontaneously appears most 'plausible' or appealing to *us*, in other words, 'an anthropocentric idiosyncrasy as the measure of things, as the rule for determining "real" and "unreal"' (WM 584; cf. WM 565, WM 455, MR 539). Indeed, it is clear that, in Nietzsche's terms, the argument that some proposition about the world is to be regarded as metaphysically true for no other reason than that there is psychological evidence in this sense for it represents one version of the 'proof from strength' criticized by him. It amounts to accepting it solely on account of the (relative) psychological satisfaction or acquiescence one feels when yielding to its intuitive 'force'.[27]

All the above considerations have been directed against the claim that a realist interpretation of many of our ordinary and scientific beliefs can be shown by means of a naturalized epistemology, i.e. by a kind of reasoning which is purportedly in some way similar to the reasoning employed in science itself, to be more plausible or better supported than rival interpretations, such as Cartesian scepticism or solipsism. These critical considerations have been based, not on any particular objections against specific theories, but rather on the sceptical strand of thought in Nietzsche which we discussed at length in Chapter 2.3.

But it may be noticed that a realist construal of the propositions of science on the third and strongest interpretation we have mentioned would be subject, in addition, to the sceptical argument advanced by Nietzsche against the ostensibly explanatory nature of certain central concepts in the modern scientific paradigm. To the extent that science characterizes its objects in terms of 'force' or 'energy', it does not actually attribute any intelligible qualities to them at all, but only mathematically describes certain patterns of phenomenal, directly or indirectly observable 'effects', employing to this purpose variables which, while we label them with substantival terms ('force', 'energy'), cannot themselves be given any interpretation in terms of an intelligible non-mathematical model or analogy (cf. Chapter 2.2). From a Nietzschean point of view, the very notion that a realist construal in the strong sense of scientific generalizations should be the 'best (metaphysical) explanation' of the fact that these generalizations hold, or have held hitherto, is

---

[27] As was pointed out earlier (Ch. 2.3), something like this 'proof from strength' or intuitive plausibility has also been a popular move against Cartesian scepticism. It seems to have been at the back of G. E. Moore's thinking when he averred that, while he could not *prove* that 'here's one hand, and here's another', he nevertheless knew this proposition to be true when holding up his hands. If it *were* the case that a certain metaphysical interpretation of the objects of experience were in fact accepted as intuitively plausible by most or all competent human inquirers, it would, on some of the criteria mentioned in Ch. 2.3, be rationally justified and therefore, as far as this condition is concerned, qualify as knowledge. It is clear, therefore, that the conception of justification and of knowledge implied by the remarks presently under consideration is more demanding and less humanist ('anthropocentric') than the rather generous construal conceded in the sceptical arguments discussed earlier.

misconceived from the outset. For a characteristic feature of much of the substantival vocabulary of modern science is precisely that it is not explanatory in the relevant sense at all. The reply often made to this kind of objection—usually in the context of more recent scientific developments, such as quantum physics and its well-known anomalies—is that there is no reason to believe that the submicroscopic items constituting the medium-sized objects of ordinary experience should be 'like' these objects or indeed in *any* sense materially analogous to the entities we are familiar with in our experience. We may surmise that Nietzsche would quite agree on this point, but would add that, in so far as this is true, the terms apparently referring to these 'entities' are not explanatory in the sense of telling us anything intelligible concerning their intrinsic qualities (their nature). This does of course by no means affect our ability to make predictions about their behaviour—i.e. about their relations to other entities—by correlating each type of theoretical 'entity' to observable phenomena.

What is the relevance of these remarks to evolutionary epistemology? One of the latter's constitutive claims is that the development of our 'cognitive apparatus' and its characteristics are themselves to be made the objects of scientific investigation and that they are, as a matter of fact, explicable by its results. Any such claim would appear to conflict with these Nietzschean sceptical reflections—although he does not explicitly apply them to it—if, and to the extent that, central concepts used in the relevant branch of scientific investigation fail to be explanatory in his sense of the term.

The sceptical points made above against certain metaphysical claims ('hypotheses') often associated with the attempt to naturalize the theory of knowledge are all based on, indeed they are applications of, Nietzsche's own sceptical deliberations discussed earlier. But we have also pointed out that the 'evolutionary' line in his thinking and the sceptical argument from utility which he develops from it are logically quite distinct from those. Without doubt, he regards what I have called the argument from utility as an additional and, judging by its pervasiveness in his writings, perhaps even more important objection to metaphysical endeavours than the other sceptical considerations I have focused on. I have concluded above that the argument fails. Perhaps a more general conclusion can be drawn from its failure. It is questionable whether any argument proceeding from empirical premisses of the kind

Nietzsche adverts to—here, the empirically observable 'struggle for survival' and the greater utility in this respect of certain beliefs over others—can support the comprehensive scepticism he apparently thinks it supports.[28] For it seems clear that his argument presupposes the (metaphysical) truth of these empirical premises. If the relativity of our beliefs and of the more general, categorial features characterizing them is in any way to be argued for from the premiss that they are practical tools conducive to the 'preservation of the species' in given 'conditions of existence', then it must be true in a metaphysical sense that there *are* these conditions of existence, affecting individuals of certain kinds in certain ways. A belief can only *be* useful (rather than mistakenly appear to be useful) for the survival of individuals or species if the world really possesses those features—otherwise it is simply incomprehensible what could be meant by the terms 'preservation', 'survival', and 'conditions of existence' here, all of which Nietzsche uses.

It thus emerges, unsurprisingly, that the naturalizing, 'evolutionary' line of scepticism is not just different from, but incompatible with the Cartesian line to the extent that its premises concerning conditions of existence and so forth are assumed to be known in any sense which involves rational justification.[29] According to the

---

[28] Nietzsche possibly found his model for this kind of argument in Lange's *Geschichte des Materialismus* (p. 473). Lange held that if it could be shown that different species of animals perceive different phenomenal *Umwelten*, this would make it likely that our sense-based beliefs are (metaphysically) false.

[29] It seems that every form of naturalized epistemology, if it has metaphysical pretensions, has to make the assumption at the outset that some of its empirical premises are (at least approximately) true in a metaphysical sense. This presupposition can neither be argued for nor subjected to any criticism *within* naturalized epistemology. It may be objected that the empirical premises in question are in fact open to criticism within the naturalized approach. We all know, after all, that in the historical development of a science, many of its original assumptions may be jettisoned or revised at a later stage. (In the light of this fact, Vollmer calls the procedure of naturalized epistemology 'virtuously circular'; *Was können wir wissen?*, i. 176–7.) However, a science can only undergo a fruitful development—as opposed to perpetual new beginnings from scratch—if some of the assumptions and discoveries at an earlier stage are at least approximately correct when compared with those of the mature science which has developed from the earlier one and is parasitic on its results, or if the former are special cases of the latter (this relation obtains, for instance, between Newtonian physics and the theory of relativity). If the results of a mature science are to be given a metaphysical (realist) interpretation, then the earlier results on which it is parasitic obviously have to be assumed to approximate to some degree to what is metaphysically the case. In other words, epistemological considerations such as those suggested by Cartesian scepticism have to be excluded from the outset.

latter kind of scepticism we do not know them, for we have no rational grounds to believe in the metaphysical truth of any such specific propositions about what we call the external world.

3. THE TELEOLOGY OF THE WILL TO POWER

I remarked at the beginning of this chapter that Nietzsche's thoughts on the practical utility of some of our beliefs, and on the selective function of 'conditions of existence' with respect to the survival or disappearance of 'organisms' and their respective forms of experience and belief are quite different from the Darwinian version of this thesis, despite the partial affinities we have noted. In fact, what we find in those statements of Nietzsche's which are related to his interpretation of human beliefs as practical tools fitted only to certain conditions of existence is a combination of various lines of thought and of various intentions which are not easily reconciled with one another.

To begin with, the naturalistic interpretation of our beliefs as practical tools for the manipulation of a hostile environment prima facie commits him to some, albeit rather general, metaphysical tenets. In at least some passages he shows himself to be aware of this implication.

Secondly, we shall see below that he attempts to develop these ideas in such a way as to render them consistent with both his critical observations on various traditional metaphysical concepts (substance, the self, mechanical causation, etc.) and with his anti-essentialism. The result of this is what has been called the 'metaphysics of the will to power', which, so it has been alleged, can be construed from the *Nachlass* and from some passages in the later works. In the present Chapter, I shall only discuss the aspects of these apparently metaphysical ideas which bear directly on the status and the nature of what we ordinarily take to be our knowledge of the world.

Thirdly, Nietzsche appears to put forward certain psychological tenets concerning the motives underlying people's acceptance of different notions as to what counts as evidence for the truth of a belief, and their consequent espousal of a variety of different, often mutually incompatible, metaphysical systems and doctrines. These tenets are, or at least seem to be, intimately connected with his idea that our beliefs are to be understood as practical instruments whose primary function it is to help us to manipulate, and thus to exert a certain degree of power over, our 'conditions of existence'.

The reader can hardly fail to be somewhat surprised that Nietzsche should be making what are, on the face of it, metaphysical claims. After all, one would have thought that his sceptical and anti-essentialist objections rendered metaphysical assertions either (rationally) unsubstantiable or incoherent, respectively. On the following pages, I shall attempt to give an exposition and explication of some of his apparent positive claims. While addressing the question of their internal coherence, I shall leave the complex problem of their 'validation'—i.e. the arguments, if any, by which they are arrived at—as well as the equally difficult question of their ultimate status within his philosophy as a whole to be discussed later.

We have noted that behind the limited affinities between some of Nietzsche's statements and those of 'Darwin and his school' lurk very substantial differences, only some of which have been pointed out so far. What distinguishes the Darwinian account of the adaptation of individual organisms to their environment and of the development of species from most of its predecessors—notably the Aristotelian tradition—is its abandonment of teleology. In the Darwinian vision, the appearance and the extinction of species as well as the remarkable fittedness of different kinds of organisms to their habitats so admired of old is to be explained no longer by the benevolent purposes of an omnipotent creator, nor by some world-immanent teleology, but rather through causal laws which account for these facts in terms of the mutations in the hereditary make-up of organisms and of a similarly non-teleological process of 'natural selection'. The external environment of a given species of living beings is either favourable or destructive to it in a purposeless manner, depending on the survival-relevant features of the organisms. Thus, external circumstances represent an inexorable constraint on the existence of individual organisms and, in the long run, of species. These circumstances are ontologically independent of the naturalistically conceived subjects of evolution and alterable by them only within certain limits. They cannot, by sheer act of will or otherwise, undo the basic laws which govern the phenomena they encounter—they are either well adapted to them, thus being able to manipulate them to their advantage, or else become extinct.

From a Darwinian perspective, the relation between human cognitive faculties and their objects is clear. There is a world existing independently of the human 'mind', causally affecting it according to certain patterns which can at least partly be discovered by it. Furthermore, the mind—or its physical substratum—is subject to the very conditions which it endeavours to know. It is itself a party to the 'struggle for existence' that it observes, a party which flourishes if it identifies a sufficient number of the survival-relevant features of its environment correctly, but perishes if it fails to do so.

Nietzsche's conception of the relation between the 'subject'—including its 'organs of knowledge'—and its 'conditions of existence' appears to be quite different. This becomes clear, for example, from his statement that the general, psychologically necessary, forms of our experience—the 'categories'—are not the results of a process of mutation and natural selection according to non-teleological causal laws, but rather, as he somewhat quaintly puts it in one note, have been 'invented', presumably at some stage in pre-history, by individuals 'in the service of our needs' (WM 513). Since he also maintains that these 'categories' for us represent a universal 'scheme that we cannot throw off' (WM 522), this would seem to imply the notion of a hereditary transmission of acquired character-istics, an idea which he indeed seems to embrace explicitly in some places.[30] The general nature of the profound difference between Nietzsche's ideas and those of the Darwinian tradition can be gleaned from the following notes:

> The influence of 'external circumstances' is overestimated by Darwin to a ridiculous extent: the essential thing in the life process is precisely the tremendous shaping, form-creating force working from within which *utilizes* and *exploits* 'external circumstances'. (WM 647; cf. WM 70)

> Life is not the adaptation of inner circumstances to outer ones, but will to power, which, working from within, incorporates and subdues more and more of that which is 'outside'. (WM 681)

> Life [. . .] strives after a *maximal feeling of power*; [. . .] striving is nothing other than a striving for power; (WM 689)

While these statements are far from clear, it emerges from them that Nietzsche, in contrast to the Darwinians, derives the various

---

[30] Cf. G. Stack, *Lange and Nietzsche* (Berlin, 1983), 138.

characteristics of any kind of 'subject' (or 'organism') by recourse to teleological concepts. The nature of human activity, including the activity of cognition—or, as he prefers to say, of interpretation—is explained in terms of a teleological principle: the will to power.[31] The precise meaning of this notorious phrase will occupy us in one way or another for most of the rest of this study. First, however, let us specify what we mean by a teleological principle of explanation here. This term is not taken to imply that there is some overall common *telos* towards which all change tends and by reference to which it is to be accounted for. Nietzsche in fact explicitly rules out such an interpretation (WM 1062). Nor are we using it to signify a directedness towards an ultimate, 'natural' end-state (Aristotle's place of 'rest') characterizing some or any particular kind of object or organism. Rather, we refer by it, more modestly, to a type of explanation of events in terms of 'the goal or result aimed at, "for the sake" of which the event is said to occur', in contradistinction to the ordinary causal kind of explanation in terms of '(logically) unconnected antecedent conditions'.[32]

The account Nietzsche ventures is teleological in this last sense, in that he characterizes the nature of human experience and activity as manifesting a 'striving for power', more specifically, for what he calls a 'feeling of power', on the part of the 'subject'.[33] When he speaks, as he often does, of a striving *for* a feeling of power (or indeed a will *to* power), the prepositional phrase indicates clearly that he resorts to a kind of explanation by purpose, that is, one which appeals to some moving force which is to some degree analogous to that which we ordinarily consider to be efficacious in intentional, volitional activity. Indeed, it is arguable that the very concept of *Macht* implies an account of this kind. The *exertion* of power (*Macht*) in any literal sense would seem to involve a (successful) purposeful activity on the part of an agent—for example, the successfully executed intention of physically overwhelming an op-

[31] The teleological character of this principle is also emphasized in A. Mittasch's well-researched study *Friedrich Nietzsche als Naturphilosoph* (Stuttgart, 1952), 199.
[32] C. Taylor, *The Explanation of Behaviour* (London, 1964), 5–6. Taylor also observes, rightly I believe, that teleological explanation involves the assumption that the 'striving' or the 'purposes' it refers to are efficacious, i.e. that they play a part in bringing about the changes which are explained with reference to them (ibid. 33).
[33] Cf. G. Abel, *Nietzsche. Die Dynamik der Willen zur Macht und die ewige Wiederkehr* (Berlin, 1984), 106.

ponent or overcoming an obstacle. Thus we speak of human beings exerting power over nature, say, by building a dam to divert a river. From the patient's point of view, we speak of an individual being *under* the power of someone or something in a certain respect if he is prevented from realizing a purpose which he has or might have. Thus a man is under the power of a drug if the drug renders him incapable of staying awake even if he *intended* to stay awake. If neither the 'agent' nor the 'patient' in a given situation is in principle capable of purposeful activity, then this is not a situation in which *Macht* is either exerted or suffered.[34] We do *not* speak— except in an anthropomorphizing metaphor—of a mountain exerting power over a river by standing in its way and diverting it.[35]

Nietzsche describes the exertion of power more specifically as 'appropriation and assimilation [. . .] a desire to overwhelm, a forming, shaping and reshaping' (WM 656). It is important to realize the exceeding generality of this definition if one is not to misunderstand his view by construing it too narrowly and crudely. For Nietzsche, 'shaping' not only refers to, for example, the activity of an artist who literally shapes an object, or to that of a mechanic, engineer, or carpenter, but also, among others, to that of a teacher or a lawyer who 'shape' the minds of students or of a jury on a

[34] A closely related point is made by Taylor: 'the notion of power or domination requires some notion of constraint imposed on someone by a process in some way related to human agency. Otherwise the term loses all meaning.' (C. Taylor, 'Foucault on Freedom and Truth', in *Philosophical Papers* 2, p. 174.)

[35] Even the somewhat less peculiar sentence 'the mountain exerts a power on the river in diverting it' would sound either slightly ungrammatical or bizarrely anthropomorphizing in German if one used Nietzsche's term *Macht*: 'der Berg übt (eine) Macht auf den Fluss aus, indem er ihn umlenkt'.

Kaufmann maintains that 'we speak of power even in physics, where consciousness has not been verified to exist' (*Nietzsche—Philosopher, Psychologist, Antichrist*, 226). While we do indeed apply the term 'power' to inanimate objects (e.g. the power of a machine), it tends to be translated in these contexts as *Kraft* or, sometimes, *Stärke*. Using the above example again, it would make perfect sense to say 'der Berg übt eine *Kraft* auf den Fluss aus'. The German term *Macht*—a cognate of the English 'might' and closely related in meaning to 'domination'—can indeed *sometimes* be applied to natural events or objects (e.g. 'die Macht des Schneesturmes war so gross, dass er einen Baum entwurzelte'—'the power of the snowstorm was such that it uprooted a tree'). However, such usages are relatively rare and are arguably animistic metaphors. This seems also to be confirmed by the fact that *Macht* (unlike 'power') is not standardly applied to artificial objects or contrivances which we take to be inanimate. A competent speaker would say 'die Kraft (or Stärke) des Motors' (the power of the engine), but not 'die Macht des Motors'. The latter would be taken as an unusual and self-consciously poetic locution. Thus, although *Macht* is generally translated as 'power', the two terms are actually not synonymous.

particular issue. Similarly, 'overwhelming', in his use of the term, not only designates the act of physically overcoming an opponent, but also that of overcoming an intellectual or emotional resistance, say, by argument or persuasion. As regards 'appropriation' and 'assimilation', these expressions also have a wide meaning for Nietzsche, encompassing such diverse acts as the taking possession of objects as one's property, the acquisition of a skill, and the 'appropriation' of experiential data through classification and through reducing new and unfamiliar items to familiar and (supposedly) well-known ones in our 'explanations'. The latter meaning is particularly pertinent to the present context:

The power of the mind to appropriate the unfamiliar manifests itself in a strong tendency to assimilate the new to the old [. . .] Its purpose in this is directed towards the incorporation of new 'experiences', towards the integration of new objects into old series—towards growth, in other words; more specifically, towards the *feeling* of growth, towards the feeling of increased power [. . .]—and indeed, 'the mind' resembles a stomach most of all. (JGB 230)

[. . .] what do ordinary people mean by knowledge? [. . .] Nothing more than this: something that is alien is to be reduced to something *familiar*. And we philosophers—have we meant anything *more* by knowledge, after all? (FW 355; cf. also GD, 'The four great errors', 5. Also KGW VIII.1.5.10 and KGW VII.3.34.246)

Thus, the 'grasping' and 'comprehending' of experiential contents by means of classification and explanation are analysed by Nietzsche as instances of appropriation and, hence, of the exertion of power (cf. WM 423, 501, 502). His understanding of the latter phrase is so wide as to apply in fact to any kind of effect or influence an agent exerts on the object of his activity. Nevertheless, he can hardly be accused of distorting beyond recognition the meaning of the term 'power', its dictionary definition being precisely the 'ability to do or to effect something or anything, or to act upon a person or thing'.

Now, the 'feeling of power', which, according to him, is the end of any of our activities, involves the recognition of a 'difference' which 'presuppos[es] a comparison' (WM 699; cf. WM 688) by the agent between the state of an object or opponent before the agent has acted on it and after, or during, his activity. Indeed, Nietzsche's concept of the 'feeling of power' could perhaps be defined as a cognitive state consisting in the awareness by a given agent of an obstacle or opponent as being overcome, assimilated, shaped, or transformed by him according to his will,[36] or as the *anticipation* of such a state, or, derivatively, as a disposition to experience such states. The 'feeling of power' in the primary sense is a certain sort of awareness of a transformative activity—of the acting on what appears as an 'opponent', an 'obstacle', as something 'alien' or 'other' (see e.g. WM 689, 693, 699; FW 355). In order for such an awareness of something *as* an 'object' or 'other' to be possible, the feeling of power also (logically) has to include some awareness of self, i.e. of that which acts or is taken to act. Far from abolishing the distinction between 'self' and 'other' (as is sometimes maintained), the experience in question requires it. To be sure, the self-awareness involved in the experience Nietzsche calls the feeling of power is different from introspection, for attention is focused here on the *object* of the activity. Nor, of course, is the 'self' at issue (the 'encroaching unit') the mental substance of the philosophical tradition (cf. WM 693 and Chapter 6.3). Only if self-consciousness is equated with attentive introspection, and if it is thought to involve belief in a substantial self, can it appear remotely plausible to maintain that, in the sort of awareness of transformative activity Nietzsche is speaking about, there is no phenomenological distinction between the self and what is 'external' to it. Nietzsche, rightly in my view, insists that such a distinction is necessary for the 'feeling of power' to be possible (WM 693).

The feeling of power, he insists, is essentially relative. It implies the awareness in the agent of a difference between two or more successive states and it can only be realized and maintained if the power of the individual is continually increased, that is, if the process—as it appears to the agent—of overcoming resistances, of exerting power, does not cease:

If one level of power were maintained, pleasure would have only lowerings of this level by which to set its standards, only states of displeasure—not states of pleasure—The will to grow is of the essence of pleasure: that

[36] In fact, Nietzsche is not quite clear as to whether this cognitive state itself is the 'feeling of power', or whether the latter consists in a specific kind of sensation which, as a matter of fact, always supervenes upon the agent's recognition of his superiority or power, or whether it is to be identified with the cognitive state being experienced with a certain kind of hedonic 'colouring'. Nietzsche's attempts at a definition (in WM 688, 695, 696, 699) do not clearly distinguish between these different conceptions. See also Ch. 5.2.

power increases, that the difference enters consciousness. (WM 695; 'plea-sure' is here used synonymously with 'feeling of power'. For the general relation between these concepts in Nietzsche, see Chapter 5.1.)[37]

How exactly do these statements concerning the determining factors of our experiences and activities apply to the nature of our beliefs and, more particularly, their relation to the 'external world'? The following notes offer some enlightenment on this point. Nietzsche questions the Cartesian standard for the evaluation of the truth or falsity of an idea—its clearness and distinctness—and asks:

> Could it not be otherwise? that it is the hypothesis that gives the intellect the greatest feeling of power and security, that is most preferred, valued, and consequently characterized as true?—The intellect posits its freest and strongest capacity and capability as criterion of the most valuable, conse-quently of the true. (WM 533)

This train of thought leads him to the conclusion that:

> The criterion of truth resides in the enhancement of the feeling of power. (WM 534)

One might perhaps, as some commentators have done, paraphrase these statements as proposing a *pragmatic* conception of truth, but unless this description is followed by some important clarifications and qualifications it is more likely to mislead than to inform.

Nietzsche's claims here are, first, not intended as prescriptions or injunctions as to what 'criteria' of truth we ought to adopt, but rather as attempts at an elucidation of the 'criteria' that do in fact determine what we accept as true. Secondly, he is certainly not saying that we regard (or ought to regard) beliefs as true which are 'useful' for furthering whatever projects we may have, or for main-taining ourselves in existence *qua* empirical individuals (self-preservation). Nor is he saying that 'true' is whatever we agree on, either now or at some future point in the process of inquiry.

To bring out the general nature of Nietzsche's supposed 'pragmatism', let us confine ourselves for the moment to beliefs

---

[37] The thesis that any level or intensity of the 'feeling of power' can only be maintained if the individual experiences himself as overcoming ever new resistances or obstacles involves a further, not implausible, premiss which Nietzsche does not actually state, namely that the feeling of power associated with any particular successful exercise of power does not last indefinitely, but decreases after some time (rather like the experienced intensity of a prolonged sensory stimulus recedes with time).

about 'objective', external, reality. We recall that he analyses this concept in terms of such notions as being of concern, resisting effort, and affecting a 'subject': 'So, "being" is grasped by us as that which acts on *us*, that which *proves itself through its efficacy*' (KGW VIII.1.5.19). In the notes and passages we are examining now, he relates these patterns of resistance which make up objective reality to the feeling of power:

> that it is the hypothesis that gives the intellect the greatest feeling of power and security, that is most preferred, valued, and consequently characterized as true?—[. . .] Thus it is the highest degrees of performance that awaken belief in the 'truth', that is to say, reality of the object. The feeling of strength, of struggle, of resistance convinces us that there is something that is here being resisted. (WM 533)

> The measure of power determines what being possesses the other measure of power; in what form, force, constraint it acts or resists. Our particular case is interesting enough: we have produced a conception in order to be able to live in a world, in order to perceive just enough to endure it— (WM 568)

According to these remarks and similar ones, the kind of 'external reality' which a given 'subject' experiences is dependent upon the kind and 'measure', or degree, of will to power (striving for the experience of power) which that subject commands.[38] In other words, Nietzsche appears to say that we experience the kind of 'external reality' we do, a reality which displays an array of relatively stable and re-identifiable particulars, because, in some sense, we have ourselves 'determined' its nature, indeed we have 'produced' or 'created' it (cf. WM 552 D). By 'we' he does not mean every individual 'subject' of a certain kind, but rather some such subjects at some point in time, who, as he says, 'invented' (WM 513) a certain mode of experiencing the world. Leaving aside for the moment the difficult question of how we are to understand 'creation' in this context, let us first try to clarify some other salient aspects of this rather puzzling view.

To begin with, Nietzsche's account seems to involve, not only the idea of the transmission through time, from one 'subject' to another, of acquired characteristics, but also the notion that a 'sub-

---

[38] This seems to imply that 'will to power' is used in this context in the sense of an *efficacious force*. We shall discuss this usage of the term in greater detail in Ch. 6.1. The problem of measuring the 'degree' of will to power *qua* efficacious force will be briefly addressed in Ch. 6.3.

ject' can purposefully acquire a certain mode of experiencing reality.[39] The possible objection that empirical research does not substantiate the idea that certain originally acquired characteristics may have been inherited by us arguably does not affect his 'transcendental' claim, which is, after all, intended to apply to (at least some of) those features of our cognitive make-up the deliverances of which are, he would maintain, *presupposed* in all empirical research. However, it hardly needs to be emphasized that his thesis, if it is to be taken at face value, is a speculative one. (The question of its coherence will be addressed in Section 5 of this chapter.)

Secondly, Nietzsche stresses that the end or purpose of the 'creation' of some such mode of experience and of the 'objects' encountered in it is not self-preservation but rather the feeling of power:

'Useful' in the sense of Darwinist biology means: proved advantageous in the struggle with others. But it seems to me that the feeling of becoming stronger is itself, quite apart from any usefulness in the struggle, the real *progress* [. . .] (WM 649)

A living thing wants above all to *discharge* its force: 'preservation' is only a consequence of this.—Beware of *superfluous* teleological principles! The entire concept 'instinct of self-preservation' is one of them. (WM 650)

It transpires from these remarks that, according to Nietzsche, it is only contingently the case that the experiential patterns and objects which have been 'created' by 'subjects' of a certain kind also serve this particular species to 'maintain itself and increase its power' by making its phenomenal *Umwelt* 'calculable' and thus being enabled to 'become master of it' and to 'press it into service' (WM 480). The activity of 'subjects' of this type is directed by this specific form and quantity of the will to power[40] which is such that they will tend to find the 'highest degree of performance'—and consequently the greatest feeling of power—attainable by them elicited through the engagement with the Kantian world of relatively enduring spatio-temporal objects, i.e. through attempting to comprehend or 'grasp' its nature (for example, in scientific 'explanation') and through

---

[39] We may as yet ignore the question of whether this purpose is necessarily a conscious one. (But see Ch. 5.2.)

[40] It would be more accurate to say that a 'subject' *is* an instantiation of a certain kind of activity and that this activity *is* a particular form and quantity of the will to power. In order to elucidate the present point, however, it seems more helpful to stay closer to traditional usage for the moment.

manipulating it in certain ways, thereby 'preserving themselves'. The important point here is that the 'feeling of power' is logically independent of what we normally refer to as the self-preservation of an individual. It, or the desire for it, do not logically imply the individual's success in, or desire for, manipulating and 'press[ing] into service' the objects of what Kant called the phenomenal world which, I presume, most of us experience as 'real'. Indeed, Nietzsche suggests that for some individuals whom we regard as very much like ourselves—as members of our own species—the greatest feeling of power is associated with a kind of activity which may result in self-destruction:

what, after all, is 'useful'? One must ask 'useful in relation to what?' E.g., that which is useful for the long life of the individual might be unfavourable to its strength and splendour. (WM 647)

[. . .] selection of the stronger, better-constituted, and the progress of the species. Precisely the opposite is palpable: the elimination of the lucky strokes, the uselessness of the more highly developed types, the inevitable dominion of the average, even the *sub-average* types. (WM 685; cf. WM 649)

Leaving aside the suggestion of a hierarchy of manifestations of the will to power, which will occupy us later, it is arguable that the phenomenon which Nietzsche here accounts for in his own rather unfamiliar terms is not as divorced from common experience as it may appear at first sight. Consider, for instance, the case of a martyr who disregards his desire for self-preservation for the sake of what he takes to be a 'higher reality' than that of 'the flesh'. Or consider the soldier who willingly risks death in battle for the sake of 'glory' or for some good which he believes his army to be fighting for. In both these cases it would be appropriate to say that the individuals concerned display a 'capacity for desiring not to preserve [themselves]' (WM 688) *qua* organisms in the Kantian phenomenal world. They often believe there to be a reality (the good, God) which is 'more real' than the entities constitutive of the ordinary 'conditions of existence' they choose to disregard. Of course, such a belief by itself is not sufficient for its objects to *be* real for them. If this were what Nietzsche meant by 'perspectivism', then it would amount either to a very implausible theory (*qua* analysis of 'real') or a somewhat uninteresting conceptual revision.

For it would amount to saying that every belief is 'true'. (This and related issues will be discussed further in Chapter 6.3.)

Nietzsche wants to say that propositions are believed by a 'subject' because assent to them is associated, in some way, with a greater feeling of power than belief in propositions incompatible with them. But he must concede, I have suggested, in order to avoid falling into irrelevance, that not all beliefs are 'true'. But is not this precisely what the conjunction of the above claim with the statement 'the criterion of truth resides in the enhancement of the feeling of power' commits him to? Whether it does depends, obviously, on how this sentence is to be interpreted. It seems to me that there is good textual evidence for understanding him to be saying two different things in this much-quoted dictum.

First, that the items of experience which a subject finds itself empirically confronted with and which it is prepared to count as real, are, in a sense yet to be clarified, 'created' by that subject, and that their nature thus depends upon the specific form and 'degree' of will to power—striving for the experience of power—which that subject *is*. The latter, consequently, also determines what a subject would consider, in practice, conclusive, indefeasible evidence for the truth of a belief.

Secondly, Nietzsche's statement—'the criterion of truth resides in the enhancement of the feeling of power'—concerns those beliefs for which we do not have what we consider to be indefeasible evidence. Most beliefs are of this kind, but the type I would like to investigate further in the following section comprises, in particular, beliefs which have or are taken to have metaphysical import. I shall interpret his argument as saying that it is the form and 'degree' of a subject's striving for the experience of power which determines what counts, for it, as relevant evidence for the metaphysical truth of such beliefs. The unresolved question of what he means by a subject's 'creating' its world will be returned to in the final section of this chapter.

4. POWER AND THE VARIETIES OF EVIDENCE

We have seen that, for Nietzsche, truth in an absolute or metaphysical sense is an incoherent concept ('nonsensical'). Nevertheless, often human beings, whether philosophers or not, have believed themselves to have attained to precisely such truths. Notoriously, even those who have been the fiercest critics of metaphysical, 'absolutist' assumptions have often adhered to such assumptions themselves in an implicit, or unwitting, or unacknowledged fashion. This fact raises a number of questions. One of them, which I should like to pursue here, is: on what grounds, or on what evidence, have people attributed metaphysically true beliefs to themselves? Nietzsche answers that, whether this is always fully conscious to the individual concerned or not, 'it is the hypothesis that gives the intellect the greatest feeling of power and security, that is most preferred, valued, and consequently characterized as true [. . .]' (WM 533). This we have interpreted as the claim that what specific beliefs about the world a given subject assents to (accepts as true in an absolute sense) is determined by the kind and degree of will to power (striving for the experience of power) that this 'subject' represents.

The mode in which the striving for the experience of power manifests itself is designated by Nietzsche as 'drives' or 'affects'. As we shall see more fully later, the reason why he prefers these terms to others like 'intentions' or 'desires' is primarily that they connote physiological affections rather than the conscious episodes which desires and intentions have traditionally been construed as. This does of course not preclude the possibility that a 'drive' *may* surface as a conscious intention. Nietzsche calls the particular type of the striving for the experience of power which characterizes an individual at any given time his 'ruling drive'. One might say that a ruling drive is a desire for a particular kind of the feeling of power predominating over other desires the individual may have[41]—although it will emerge that Nietzsche ultimately treats drives not as attributes of agents (like desires), but as agents themselves. He expounds his analysis of our (usually unacknowledged) 'criterion' of metaphysical truth as the feeling of power in a number of *Nachlass* passages, among them one note entitled 'To what extent interpretations of the world are symptoms of a ruling drive':

---

[41] Since Nietzsche also likens our consciousness to a 'ruler' or 'regent' at the head of a communality of drives (e.g. WM 492; KGW VII.3.37.4), it would appear from this that the 'ruling drives' of which he speaks, that is, our dominant desires, are accessible in self-consciousness.

The *scientific* view of the world [. . . .] The desire to make comprehensible; the desire to make practical, useful, exploitable [. . . .] Only value, what can be counted and calculated. How an average type of man seeks to gain the upper hand in this way [. . .]

The *religious* view of the world: critique of the religious man [. . .] the man of powerful exaltations and deep depressions [. . . .] Essentially the man who feels himself 'unfree', who sublimates his moods, his instincts of subjection.

The *moral* view of the world: The feelings of a social order are projected into the universe: [. . .] because they are valued the highest [. . .]

What is common to all: the ruling drives want to be viewed also as the highest courts of value in general [. . .] (WM 677; cf. WM 580)

We recall that he maintains in another passage that 'the intellect posits its freest and strongest capacity and capability as criterion of the most valuable, consequently of the true' (WM 533). What he seems to be saying in these notes is that what we consider to be true in a metaphysical sense is determined by what aspects, or contents, of our experience are 'most valuable' or, in another phrase, of the greatest 'interest' (cf. WM 423) to us. In this sense, it is ultimately a matter of our ruling drives which internally consistent metaphysical system—which 'interpretation of the world'—will appear most intuitively plausible or evident to us.

To illustrate his point, let me elaborate a little on two of the examples he gives in the passage cited—the 'scientific' and the 'religious' interpretations of the world. The reader will not find it difficult to think of other examples and to apply his analysis to them. One kind of individual, whose ruling drive is the 'desire to make practical, useful, exploitable' will regard as real only what can be 'counted and calculated'—i.e. quantified and employed in the prediction of events. He will adopt a particular type of view as to what counts as evidence for the (metaphysical) truth or falsity of beliefs which reflects these concerns and interests. Hence, we might suspect, expanding on Nietzsche's point, that such an individual may take the fact that different human observers tend to deliver mutually congruent perceptual judgements as evidence for the truth of these judgements. He may also be inclined to interpret the circumstance that some of our common-sense and scientific generalizations lead to successful predictions as 'best explained' by the claim that these generalizations are at least approximately true in a metaphysical sense—that they to some degree correspond to the structure of a perception-independent reality (cf. our discussion of evolutionary epistemology in section 2 above).

Alternatively, a person with this kind of ruling drive might confine the predication of truth altogether to those propositions which are 'testable' through the experimental prediction and control of phenomena, for it is these procedures which generally enable us to manipulate the objects of our experience—to 'use' or 'exploit' them, in Nietzsche's terminology. It is observational agreement among (what we take to be) different observers which functions as the relevant test of statements about the world, and an individual with this sort of ruling drive may therefore refuse to admit to the realm of potential truths any claims which are not either directly or in some indirect form verifiable or at least confirmable in principle by observational agreement. The metaphysical view this position would seem to imply—and which, as we know, is not always acknowledged as metaphysical—is a variant of ontological phenomenalism.

What the above example also illustrates is a point which pervades Nietzsche's writings from the very earliest phase onwards: that views involving quite different propositional contents may, and often do, express the same kind of 'ruling drive'. This is arguably one of the main reasons why he rarely engages in the sort of detailed criticism of particular doctrines or systems which is the daily bread of more traditional philosophers. For even if one succeeds—a very rare feat indeed—in what is generally agreed to be a conclusive refutation of a particular philosophical doctrine or position, the same 'ruling drive' merely tends to reappear in a new philosophical guise. But, for Nietzsche, what matters about philosophical doctrines is primarily what 'drives', what values, they give expression to. And this can, if at all, only be established through a method which we might call hermeneutic, and which he himself often refers to as 'psychological' (cf. JGB 23). His sense of the futility of 'mere' philosophical criticism—which, needless to say, is itself expressive of certain values—is well conveyed in an early letter to Paul Deussen, who had urged him to write a critique of Schopenhauer's metaphysics:

Dear friend, 'writing well' [. . .] truly does not entitle one to write a critique of the Schopenhauerian system: [. . .] for I hope you mean by a critique [. . .] not merely the emphasizing of some defective passages, of unsuccessful proofs or of tactical clumsiness [. . . .] Anyway, one doesn't write the critique of a world-view: rather, one comprehends it or one doesn't; a third point of view is unfathomable to me. Someone who can't smell the fragrance of a rose certainly has no right to criticize it.[42]

To return to our examples. In contrast to the 'scientific view of the world', the 'religious man', the man of 'powerful exultations and deep depressions', whose ruling drive is the 'instinct of subjection',[43] will incline towards a metaphysical account of things which allows primarily for the satisfaction of this particular kind of desire (although he may make allowance for other, subordinate interests by a conception of reality which allows explicitly for a gradation among orders of reality). He, too, will accept canons of evidence which supposedly validate or support the truth of his beliefs, but these canons—which I shall henceforth call standards of validation—will at least partly differ from those of the 'scientific' man mentioned above. According to Nietzsche, the religious man's evidence involves the 'proof from power' in its most explicit form:

'The proof from power': i.e. an idea is proved true by its effect [. . .] what inspires must be true [. . .]. Here, the sudden feeling of power that an idea arouses in its originator is everywhere accounted proof of its value [. . .] the first predicate with which it is honoured is the predicate 'true'—How otherwise could it be so effective? It is imagined [to have emanated] from some power: if that power were not real, it could not be effective—The idea is understood to have been inspired [. . .] (WM 171)

For the religious individual, the reality of God is confirmed through the presence of certain experiences in which he believes himself to come into contact with the Absolute. The feeling of 'unfreedom' and the 'instincts of subjection' of which Nietzsche speaks manifest themselves more specifically in the experience of an 'infinitely valuable whole' external to the individual (WM 12), of an ontologically real (or, as some philosophers would say, objective) good, a 'superhuman authority' (WM 20) which he feels bound by and 'dependent on' (ibid.). He will characteristically describe

---

[42] Letter to Paul Deussen, October 1868. This attitude towards the futility of 'mere' logical criticism by means of a more or less proficient handling of the traditional *instrumentarium* of philosophers persists also throughout the later writings. Cf. the preface of *Zur Genealogie der Moral*: 'What have I to do with refutations!'

[43] The question of the compatibility of what Nietzsche here calls the instinct of subjection with the striving for the feeling of power will be discussed in Ch. 5.3. The religious belief in question here is of course of the 'narrow' kind distinguished earlier.

this experience of compulsion as cardinally distinct from that exerted by prudential considerations or by the threat of force, and as comparable rather to the sense in which, say, a courtly lover feels himself 'bound' by and called to obedience to, and reverence for, his beloved on account of what he perceives as her real virtue and excellence (cf. Chapters 5.1 and 5.3). In so far as he takes such experiences as evidence for the corresponding metaphysical beliefs (e.g. in an ontologically real *summum bonum*), he might be said, in a sense, to interpret *'inner* realities as realities, as "truths"—[. . .] he [takes] everything else, everything natural, temporal, spatial, historical, only as a sign, as an occasion for parables' (AC 34). Hence, his standard for the evaluation of judgements involves also some kind of empirical confirmation, although what counts as a corroborating experience for him does not satisfy the crucial conditions of intersubjectivity and repeatability (i.e. predictive power) associated with this concept by a person subscribing to the 'scientific view of the world'.[44] The latter is, therefore, likely to denounce the standard of validation employed by the religious man as purely 'subjective'—but this charge cannot quite escape the suspicion of begging the question. For he can only validate his criticism by reference to precisely those standards—intersubjectivity, repeatability—the exclusive validity of which his opponent calls into question. Philosophical argument reaches a deadlock when one of the disputants does not accept the evidential framework of the other, but simply insists on another set of standards of validation which is in crucial points incompatible with the former. For a genuine disagreement to be possible, it is of course necessary that the disputants understand each other—which requires that a sufficiently large number of the terms in which the argument is stated have agreed empirical conditions of application. As was pointed out above, standards of validation, as I have tried to characterize them, are usually distinct from the criteria (in a non-Nietzschean sense of this expression) which, if satisfied, would, for a given individual, entail the truth of some sentence asserted by him. Two people may consequently agree concerning the sort of experience,

---

[44] As distinct from the type of evidence described above, the believer is likely to possess, at least implicitly, a criterion or set of criteria which, if satisfied, would entail the truth of his beliefs. Given the nature of these beliefs, these criteria can of course not involve a method or technique of verification, since if there were such a method, it would imply the falsity of his beliefs (because it would imply the self-contradictory statement that a supposedly omnipotent God can be forced to 'reveal' himself by an appropriate technique deployed by finite agents).

or the state of affairs, which, if it occurred, would make a certain sentence metaphysically true—hence they would understand each other's claims in this respect—but disagree about what, for us, constitutes good evidence for its truth in this sense. It is also a consequence of this distinction that a person who has hitherto subscribed to some given standard of validation may later come to regard it as inadequate or erroneous—for example, on account of some experience in which he believes himself to have come into direct contact with reality, and which conflicts with the kind of experience his previously held standards of validation would have led him to expect. So Nietzsche's religious man may conceivably revise his view that certain experiences of his which he used to interpret as affections by an 'objective' Good were in fact such, and may come to attribute them to other causes instead. It should be clear from this that the present reading of Nietzsche's remarks does not imply that individuals accepting different standards of validation or evidence live, by virtue of this fact, in 'different worlds'.

Thus, to continue this reconstruction of Nietzsche's train of thought, we see that the different 'ruling drives' of different individuals lead to their acceptance of at least partly diverging notions either as to what counts as good grounds, as evidence, for the metaphysical truth of a belief or as to what relative weight various types of ostensible evidence ought to be accorded. Ruling drives, representing the type of desire dominant in an individual for some variant of the feeling of power, are therefore 'criteria' in the sense of being the psychological factors which, not always explicitly acknowledged by the individual, determine his adoption of any particular standard of validation (cf. WM 423).[45] A remark from an early notebook—which is very much in keeping with

[45] Nietzsche applies this analysis also to the sceptic who typically attempts to undermine the metaphysical beliefs of others by showing that they fail to satisfy some given standard of rationality which is generally accepted in other contexts and which they themselves profess to subscribe to (cf. Ch. 2.3). The sceptic himself may, but need not, refuse to subscribe to any of the standards of validation advocated by different schools of metaphysicians. This refusal is of course also motivated by a ruling drive which, according to one of Nietzsche's notes, is often the desire to remain free from the commitments which acceptance of some metaphysical doctrine might involve (see WM 963). But scepticism may also be the result of and subservient to other desires. For instance, it may be used as an instrument by those who desire to persuade others to set aside 'unavailing reason' and instead simply to accept and live by some faith, authority, or custom (historical examples might be Erasmus and Hume), or by those who are motivated by resentment against some powerful group or institution which claims to derive its *raison d'être* from some particular set of metaphysical truths (WM 455, 457).

the logic of the later views we are currently discussing—suggests that Nietzsche regards none of these various and at least partly incompatible standards as more or less 'rational' than their rivals: 'it is just as rational to take man's moral, artistic, and religious wants as the basis of the world as it is to take his mechanical wants' (PT 31).

I have indicated that it is a consequence of his view—which he does not explicitly draw himself—that individuals with different 'ruling drives' will find it difficult, perhaps impossible, to convince one another of what each regards as the falsity or indeed 'irrationality' of the other's beliefs. Since they either do not accept the other's standards of validation or the exclusivity of those, neither will regard the other's arguments as persuasive, let alone conclusive—their standards of what is 'rational' in this context might be said to differ.[46] Thus, for example, the quasi-Humean argument that it is unlikely to be true that there are or ever have been miracles because most people testify to certain regularities in nature to which they have never experienced any miraculous exceptions involves the assumption that, at least in the 'external' sphere of medium-sized objects, only such items are to count as real which are ('in principle') accessible to observation by any 'normal' observer. If one then proceeds to justify this assumption by recourse to what we have, supposedly, good reasons to believe to be real from the testimony of the vast majority of human beings, the circularity of this procedure is obvious. The acceptance of this (or any other) standard of validation for substantive claims by a given individual depends ultimately on whatever happens to be 'intuitively plausible' to her, and this, as Nietzsche observes, may vary from one individual to another or for the same individual at different times. What such basic assumptions have in common is that they are variants of the 'proof from strength' most explicitly encountered in religious discourse, but among philosophers frequently disguised behind a mask of 'cold, pure, divinely unconcerned dialectics' (JGB 5).

Even someone sympathetic to Nietzsche's account may feel that his thesis of the determination of an individual's standards of validation, hence of his or her metaphysical beliefs, by 'ruling drives' (desires, interests, values) does not sufficiently distinguish

---

[46] My discussion of this point is indebted to L. Kolakowski's analysis in his *Religion* (Oxford, 1982), 78 f.

various significantly different ways in which such determination may occur. There are cases where our acquaintance with a person's general attitudes and values may lead us to suspect that his metaphysical beliefs, and the standards of validation concomitant with them, are subservient to, and adopted in the light of, other (e.g. political or theological) interests or preoccupations he has, and that therefore the interest-bound nature of these beliefs may, if pointed out or attended to, be recognizable to himself. (Hume's views on miracles or Berkeley's conception of 'real things' may be cases in point here.)

However, there are other instances in which a person arrives at his beliefs through what insistently appears to himself as a perfectly disinterested, 'objective' inquiry. He is not at all aware of any particular interests or values determining the results of his investigations. Indeed, he may even think that he is conducting the latter without consideration for his own desires. The 'heroic posture' of many Enlightenment and post-Enlightenment atheists, also sometimes of Nietzsche himself, is perhaps a good example of this. Nevertheless, Nietzsche would argue, the outcome of such an apparently 'cold, pure, divinely unconcerned' inquiry, while it may indeed be conducted without consideration of, or in opposition to, *some* desires, is no less subject to 'ruling drives'—the inquirer's dominant values. For it is these values—which may be culturally transmitted and not even recognizable to the individual as anything less than self-evident and unquestionable—that render certain positions, or certain standards of validation, 'intuitively plausible' to him.

It was noted earlier that some philosophers maintain on behalf of their preferred form of realism that it is the 'best explanation' of the fact that things appear to us the way they do; indeed, sometimes they aver that it is precisely this 'additional explanatory power' which is the best argument in favour of such a metaphysical position. I have argued that this claim, in the sense in which it is intended, is misconceived. But it might be thought that a similar claim could be made with rather greater cogency on behalf of Nietzsche's conjecture that the standards of validation held by an individual are determined by his or her ruling drive—leaving aside for the moment his rather more problematic reduction of various 'drives' to the striving for the feeling of power. Does not this thesis, in conjunction with the sceptical argument discussed in Chapter

2.3, provide the best explanation of a fact which certainly seems to be in dire need of one, namely the notorious proliferation of mutually incompatible metaphysical systems and positions in the history of philosophy and the continuing failure of philosophers to reach consensus on most of the central questions of their discipline? In order for the thesis to have any empirical content, the 'ruling drives' it refers to would of course have to be identifiable independently of the philosophical beliefs they are claimed to determine. On Nietzsche's characterization of them there is no reason why this should not be possible—in fact we do it all the time in everyday life. His conjecture might arguably be considered a good explanation of various persistent philosophical disagreements if empirical research provided evidence to confirm (or—if we are falsificationists—no evidence to disconfirm) the hypothesis that independently identifiable 'ruling drives' of certain types are necessary conditions of people's holding metaphysical or quasi-metaphysical beliefs which share relevant 'evaluative' characteristics (e.g. logical empiricism and some variants of scientific realism, or Spinozism and Hegelianism). Nietzsche himself would of course not recognize the discovery of such correlations to be by itself genuinely explanatory—his concept of explanation is rather more demanding, as we saw earlier.

Even if a strong case could be made for his remarks concerning the connections between 'ruling drives' and metaphysical belief, caution would be required not to draw unwarranted conclusions from them which he himself is not quite able to resist. He maintains in a different context, but in a passage which can also be taken to apply to our discussion, that:

opinions with all proofs, refutations and the entire intellectual masquerade are only symptoms of [. . .] taste and most certainly *not* that which they are still so frequently declared to be, its causes. (FW 39; cf. WM 458 and 580)

This might partly and usefully be read as a rhetorical statement of the claim that the canons of rationality which are generally accepted in other areas of inquiry, such as natural science, have no purchase on metaphysical questions (cf. Chapter 2.3) and that the standards of validation we *de facto* employ in these matters differ from those canons and vary from one individual (or group) to another, depending on their respective 'drives', i.e. their interests or values ('taste').[47] However, the passage also seems to inform us that any standards we do employ here are '*only* symptoms of [. . .] taste' (my emphasis). Clearly, such a conclusion goes beyond what Nietzsche's argument licenses if it is meant to suggest that the various metaphysical views people hold are in fact *false* and that their standards of validation are always misleading. For all that has been said so far—leaving aside the anti-essentialist remarks mentioned in the previous chapter—it might be the case that some metaphysical claims are true and that the standards adopted by their adherents are in fact the appropriate ones. It would seem to require an additional argument on Nietzsche's part to rule out this possibility. In the next chapter, we shall examine his attempt to supply such an argument against one particular sort of metaphysical theory.

Perhaps our discussion has clarified to some extent what Nietzsche means when he makes such cryptic remarks in the published works as '*intellegere* [. . .] is merely a certain relation between drives' (FW 333). He obviously does not mean that some type of what is sometimes called a propositional attitude (and what Husserl calls the quality of an intentional act, e.g. a judgement that *p*) is in fact another type of propositional attitude (e.g. a desire that *p*). What we can ascribe to him, I have suggested, is rather a psychological hypothesis asserting the determination of a person's standards of validation by his ruling drive or by a combination of ('relation between') such drives.

According to Nietzsche, all human drives are ultimately directed towards ends of one generic kind, the 'feeling of power', whose instances are of various more specific forms. The standards of validation an individual accepts and, consequently, his conception of the nature of reality 'in itself', are determined by, indeed are partly constitutive of, the specific kind of the striving for the feeling of power characteristic of that individual. Now, we may want to know in what manner a 'feeling of power'—which here presumably must be construed as a disposition to experience such 'feelings'— may be associated with a person's adoption of some view of the nature in itself of reality (some 'world interpretation'). Nietzsche's

---

[47] Despite his general focus on the differences in the ruling drives of *individuals*, Nietzsche sometimes seems to acknowledge that standards of validation historically seem more commonly to have varied between different cultures and subcultures than among individuals within the same cultural setting (cf. WM 423).

remarks suggest that there is a variety of such ways. To begin with, construing the world in accordance with one's ruling drives clearly is by itself an instance of what he variously calls the familiarization, and thus assimilation or appropriation, of the alien or 'other', which is one of his favoured examples of the striving for the experience of power (cf. JGB 230 and my discussion in the previous section).

Another way in which a 'feeling of power' may be associated with the adoption of some (metaphysical) 'world interpretation' can be brought out by recalling a psychological phenomenon which, according to Nietzsche, is typically concomitant with the 'will to truth', avowedly for its own sake (cf. Chapter 3.2). It consists in the belief that 'reality' in some sense calls for, or requires, or justifies certain sorts of actions and attitudes, or a particular mode of life or range of such modes. As we saw, he suggests that this belief that particular modes of life, unlike others, are legitimized or justified and in this sense better than, or privileged over, the latter by virtue of 'what is (really, metaphysically) the case', is frequently found—even if unadmittedly—not only among value-realists, but wherever the 'will to truth' is in evidence. The relevant psychological disposition is thus not bound to any particular view as to what the nature of reality actually is. The belief in the 'objectivity' of values is, in fact, only its most visible, explicit manifestation.

If these ideas are conjoined with the claim that an individual's 'ruling drives' determine which metaphysical beliefs, if any, she inclines towards, it is not difficult to infer how such beliefs might be associated with a 'feeling of power' in the believing subject. If Nietzsche is right in his observation that a characteristic function of metaphysical beliefs is to engender in the believer a sense of legitimation, or justification, of some set of values, or notion of the good, or mode of life (as being in accordance with and recognizing 'the way the world is'), and if such beliefs are in any given case determined by the believer's dominant values, then clearly, the metaphysical conception of reality which an individual subscribes to will be such as to produce a sense of the legitimacy or justification of just those values which led to its adoption in the first place. The individual, in adopting some set of metaphysical beliefs, might be said, in Nietzsche's language, to assimilate the world to herself. However, given that the 'feeling of power' which results from the adoption of an appropriate metaphysics consists here in the subject's consciousness of her 'ruling drives' being in some sense justified, legitimized, and privileged over others by 'the nature of reality', it would perhaps be more apt to say that the feeling of power is attained here through assimilating, or attuning oneself to, the world, rather than vice versa. For Nietzsche, this self-assimilation to what is apprehended as a superior power, authority, or agent (e.g. God, reality), is one of the most pervasive manifestations of the striving for the experience of power (the will to power). We will return to it when examining his analysis of the Christian ideal (Chapter 5.3).

We may ask: who or what is power perceived or imagined by the subject as being exerted *over* here? There are a number of conceivable answers to this question. One of them is, presumably: over other actual or possible agents with opposing values or 'ruling drives'. In other words, what I have called the self-assimilation to reality—the embracing of a 'world interpretation' in accordance with one's ruling drives—may serve to give an individual the sense of strength or power which, for such individuals, is associated with the belief in being 'justified' (in the sense explained), in a struggle against other individuals or institutions who represent conflicting interests or values.

We also remarked earlier that often the adoption of a particular standard of validation may be subservient to an individual's extraneous (e.g. political) interests in a manner that is apparent to himself. It would, I think, be wrong to speak of such an individual being subject to the 'ascetic ideal' in Nietzsche's sense at all. Rather, I suspect he would say that, in such cases, metaphysical doctrines are merely used or deployed against opponents who *are* subject to that ideal and whose sense of the justification or legitimacy, i.e. of the 'righteousness', of their ruling drives depends on other, incompatible, metaphysical views. Thus, a given standard of validation and the metaphysical doctrines it supports may be, and often are, adopted as weapons of war in a struggle for power or supremacy. (This reverses the traditional view that such struggles may be, at least in part, *caused* by people's adhering to different metaphysical doctrines which, while having different and conflicting *implications* with respect to 'the good', are supposedly arrived at by considerations wholly independent of such values and practical interests— by 'cold, pure, divinely unconcerned dialectics'.)

Nietzsche's own sceptical attacks on various metaphysical positions might usefully be read in the light of our exposition of his views above—that is to say, one might plausibly interpret them as weapons deployed by him in his struggle against the adherents of the ascetic ideal. But it is not yet clear whether such a self-referential application of these ideas to his own views is possible without incoherence, nor whether Nietzsche himself would be prepared to accept it *en tout*. Even on a cautious interpretation of his main point, it raises well-known self-referential difficulties. The genesis and the 'justification' of metaphysical beliefs is said to depend causally—in a non-Humean sense—on certain psychological factors on the grounds of a psychological hypothesis which, it seems, itself aspires to (metaphysical) truth. Nietzsche's thesis seems to imply that it cannot itself lay claim to superiority over rival views on the strength of rational, that is, (at least) generally accepted standards of validation (cf. Chapter 2.3), and that it may be quite legitimately (on its own terms) rejected as 'purely subjective' by anyone whose 'ruling drives' are different from his and whose intuitions, consequently, as to what is an 'acceptable' or 'plausible' position on these matters differ from his.

The seemingly universal and, hence, self-referential nature of Nietzsche's remarks creates an impasse to which there are several possible solutions. He might, first, deny that his psychological thesis—the determination of an individual's standards of validation by his or her ruling drives—represents a claim to truth in an absolute or metaphysical sense. In other words, he might hold it to be true in some other, idiosyncratic sense, defined in terms of the satisfaction of some set of (subjective) evidential standards, so that the question of these standards being possibly inadequate could not even arise. Whether he does embrace such a view will be examined in detail in Chapter 6.3. We may notice already, however, that while such a move would avoid the present self-referential difficulties, it would also prima facie deprive his thesis of its critical force—for its truth in the new, Nietzschean sense would then be quite compatible with its metaphysical falsity (unless, of course, there are other considerations which do effectively dispose of the latter notion altogether).

Secondly, and contrary to some of his apparent claims discussed in Chapter 3.2, he might not deny that there are absolute or metaphysical truths in some domains of discourse (e.g. those relating to mental states), but might simply abandon the traditional philosophical ambition to convince one's opponents of the superiority of one's own tenets by recourse to standards of validation on which there is prior agreement. What a given individual (or, more frequently, a given culture or subculture) acknowledges as 'plausible' in these matters is, as we saw, defined in terms of such standards, but they themselves, if they differ from one's own, can only be altered by means of non-rational (though not *eo ipso* irrational) means, such as persuasion or force. The highly rhetorical, often inflammatory, and *ad hominem* style of many of Nietzsche's published writings has often been thought to express precisely this conviction.

Thirdly, he might exempt some types of statements from the scope of his analysis (and from the sceptical arguments considered in Chapter 2.3), according them a privileged epistemic status. The type of statement which has most often been granted such a status in the history of modern philosophy is of course that which refers to (one's own) states of consciousness. In the words of Wilhelm Dilthey's formulation of the Cartesian position, there is a 'decisive advantage which inner perception has over external perception. In becoming conscious of our own (inner) states, we perceive them without the mediation of external senses, in their reality, as they are'.[48] According to this view, 'inner perception' is privileged in this way over external perception because the in-itself of a state of consciousness consists precisely in its being apprehended as having a certain determinate quality or set of qualities. There is no distinction between the subject and the object of knowledge in inner perception. We shall address Nietzsche's analysis of 'inner experience' in the subsequent chapter to see whether, or to what extent, he accedes to this line of argumentation.

5. THE MEANING OF 'CREATION'

Nietzsche sometimes speaks of the reality experienced by a subject as 'created', 'produced', or 'shaped' by that subject (WM 552 D, WM 568, KGW VII.3.34.247). In the case of subjects like ourselves—or perhaps, of the subject(s) constituting, or corresponding

---

[48] W. Dilthey, 'Ideen über eine beschreibende und zergliedernde Psychologie', in *Gesammelte Schriften*, v. 198.

to, the psycho-physical individuals we ordinarily conceive ourselves to be—this creation is not, generally, a conscious activity. With respect to the 'external' reality of relatively enduring spatio-temporal objects there is no such act of 'creation' which enters our consciousness. We think of ourselves as discovering these objects rather than as 'shaping' them. It can be inferred from Nietzsche's remarks that the shaping of the objects of our experience is supposed to be a process attributable to certain features of our constitution of whose activity we are not conscious. In a number of passages it is strongly implied that many of these features were acquired at some stage of evolution, but have since become constitutive characteristics (cf. WM 513, 516, 522). They circumscribe the limits within which we are capable of shaping the world of our experience and determining the nature of that experience. Some of the characteristics we believe the world to possess are thus predetermined by 'our' constitution in such a manner as to render us unable even to imagine a world which would not display them. These most general and psychologically necessary characteristics of the objects of our experience Nietzsche calls the 'categories'.

It remains to be clarified how we are to understand the term 'creation' in this context. In some places he appears to maintain that the creativity in question consists primarily in what he calls our 'organs of knowledge' simplifying and coarsening the qualitative complexity that is really 'out there' in a perceiver-independent world characterized by properties it possesses in itself. Such passages suggest that the subject of knowledge 'simplifies' (KGW VII.3.34.247), 'adapts' (WM 569), and hence to some extent 'falsifies' (ibid.) the data which impinge upon it, thereby rendering them classifiable (WM 532, 517) and becoming able to discover as much regularity in experience (WM 480, 517) as is required for the satisfaction of practical needs. The very terms Nietzsche uses here—especially of course the notion that we 'falsify' a complex reality in cognitively apprehending it—would seem to imply, if taken literally, that there is *something*, some items or objects in the widest sense of this word, existing independently of the perceiver and capable of being described truly or falsely.

If this were indeed what Nietzsche is saying, we might detect again a limited analogy with mainstream evolutionary epistemology at this point. For it also concedes a certain degree of creativity, metaphorically speaking to be sure, to the cognitive apparatus of an organism, a creativity that consists primarily in its selectively operating on the data that impinge upon it. The mind (or the central nervous system, in the idiom of contemporary Darwinians) 'selects' for our conscious awareness those aspects or features of our environment which are most relevant to our survival.[49] Indeed, according to a theory widely accepted among biologists, the nature of the cognitive apparatus of an organism of one species often renders it incapable of becoming aware of environmental stimuli apprehended by organisms of another species. Thus, members of different species often have different phenomenal environments or *Umwelten*. We are told that the *Umwelt* of the paramecium is one-dimensional,[50] that bees perceive ultraviolet light invisible to humans,[51] while the visual contours of objects and their tactual solidity perceived by us represent no more than 'a phenomenal emphasis on the one physical discontinuity most usable by man [. . .] to the neglect of other discontinuities identifiable by the probes of modern experimental physics'.[52]

So it might appear that contemporary evolutionary epistemo-logists agree with Nietzsche when he says: 'there are many kinds of eyes[. . .]—and consequently there are many kinds of "truths" ' (WM 540). However, they tend to qualify the significance of the species-relativity of these phenomenal *Umwelten* by pointing out that

In the face of the immense diversity of these perceiving apparatus one fact emerges as of paramount importance, i.e. that messages pertaining to one particular environmental aspect never contradict each other.[53]

Consequently, proponents of an evolutionary epistemology tend to declare confidently that 'each of the separate contours diagnosed in these *Umwelten* are also diagnosable by a complete physics, which in addition provides many differentia unused and unperceived by any organism'.[54] Each species may selectively discriminate and highlight only some features of the whole canvas of reality which

---

[49] e.g. A. Shimony, 'Perception from an Evolutionary Point of View', in *Journal of Philosophy*, 68 (1971), 577–8. Cf. WM 532: 'There could be no judgements at all if a kind of equalization were not practised within sensations [. . .]. Before judgement occurs, the process of assimilation must already have taken place; thus here, too, there is an intellectual activity that does not enter consciousness.'

[50] Lorenz, *Behind the Mirror*, 9–10.   [51] Shimony, 'Perception', 577.

[52] Campbell, 'Evolutionary Epistemology', 448.

[53] Lorenz, *Behind the Mirror*, 12.

[54] Campbell, 'Evolutionary Epistemology', 448.

are of particular use to it, but these features remain nevertheless only aspects of one and the same reality that possesses an objective structure no matter whether it is perceived or not.

Nietzsche's conception of the 'created' character of the objects of our experience seems to be not only more far-reaching, but in fact incompatible with this naturalistic view. In some places he suggests that the 'external world' which we appear causally to act upon and be acted on by is literally produced by us *qua* 'subjects' of knowledge and would cease to exist if we subtracted our perception of, or 'perspective' on, it:

The apparent world, i.e. a world viewed according to values; ordered, selected according to values, i.e. in this case according to the viewpoint of utility in regard to the preservation and enhancement of power of a certain species of animal.

The perspective therefore decides the character of the 'appearance'! As if a world would still remain after one deducted the perspective! [. . .]

But there is no 'other', no 'true', no essential being—[. . .] The antithesis of the apparent world and the true world is reduced to the antithesis 'world' and 'nothing'. (WM 616; cf. also GD, 'How the "true world" finally became a fable'; KGW VII.3.38.10)

According to the view expressed here, the 'subject' does not merely arrange and simplify an objective qualitative complexity existing independently of it, but actually brings forth the 'external' reality it experiences.[55] As Nietzsche says in another note:

The entirety of the organic world is the juxtaposition of beings [*Wesen*] surrounded by fabricated [*erdichteten*] small worlds: in that they project [*setzen*] their strength, their appetites, their habits of experience outside themselves, as their *external world*. The capacity to create (shape invent fabricate) is their basic capacity [. . .]. (KGW VII.3.34.247)

The *Wesen* spoken of here create their experiential realities in a special sense of that verb in which it does not imply—as it usually

---

[55] Cf. J. Figl, *Interpretation als philosophisches Prinzip* (Berlin, 1982), 114–15: 'The only world that is given, according to Nietzsche, is a phenomenal one, i.e. it "is" only to the extent that it appears to some individual "being" [*Wesen*]. [. . .] That which understands determines not only the nature [*Art*], but also the "existence" of that which is understood.' Also Grimm, *Nietzsche's Theory of Knowledge*, 185–6: 'The external world is not something simply and univocally present, apart from any observer [. . .] It could be maintained that "I" am my "external world", since I am identical with my interpretative, creative activity.'

does—that what is thus 'created' has an independent, 'substantial', existence—rather, its *esse est percipi*, we might say. It is not difficult to detect a correspondence between these remarks and Nietzsche's analysis of 'objective reality' discussed earlier (cf. Chapter 3.1). We recall that, on that analysis, 'something that is of no concern to anyone is not at all' (WM 555). But if he indeed means to say that the patterns of resistance which constitute a subject's external reality are created by that subject, then we are forced to understand his use of terms like 'falsification' and 'simplification' as either rhetorical or confused. It also becomes rather mysterious how we are to interpret those 'conditions of existence' which our cognitive efforts are supposed to serve to master and which bring about the extinction (cf. FW 111) of those kinds, or species, of beings ill-fitted to survive in them. It would seem that 'conditions of existence' can only act upon 'organisms' in this manner if they exist independently of them, possessing determinate properties which, while being possibly manipulable by those organisms to some extent, are not in their entirety created by them.

How are these two seemingly incompatible elements in Nietzsche's thought to be reconciled? Clearly, if the determinate structure of all 'external' reality is itself the product, or creation, of the subject *for* which it is real, the conclusion appears inescapable that the only constraints conceivable upon the latter must ultimately be exerted by itself on itself, and that these constraints may be such as to bring about its perishing—effectively its self-annihilation. But why should an entity whose very *raison d'être* is, so we are told, the striving for the experience of power, annihilate itself? Any solution to this difficulty requires at least that the will to power be defined in a way which does not involve essentially the notion of success in a 'struggle for survival', i.e. which does not imply that any entity instantiating the will to power necessarily succeeds, or even strives to succeed, in maintaining or preserving itself. This condition seems to be met by Nietzsche's conception of the will to power. As we observed earlier, he does not define individuals characterized by the will to power as necessarily striving for self-preservation as this is ordinarily understood. Their *telos* is the feeling of power (cf. WM 643, 649, 685; JGB 230), which is quite compatible with their not desiring to maintain or preserve themselves (cf. WM 647, 648, 688). Nietzsche actually suggests that the greater the internal complexity[56] of an 'organism', the greater is the likelihood of its quickly perishing or disintegrating (WM 647, 684, 685). He contrasts types of organisms whose internal organization is conducive to stability and 'long life' (WM 647) with other, 'higher' types whose form of existence involves 'danger' and 'rapid wastage', expressing the 'strength and splendour' of the organism in possibly quite short-lived eruptions of intense activity. Here again, the analogy that perhaps illustrates his point best in the sphere of human behaviour is that of the heroic way of life where the agent seeks glory in battle, willingly accepting the likelihood of his own death. A particular kind of the experience of power is associated with this mode of action, and for Nietzsche it is this experience which is the *telos* of that type of agent. Activity of this kind involves by its very nature the likelihood of the destruction or disintegration of the individual which we call death, or, if it befalls a whole species, extinction.

Thus, the idea of subjects 'creating' their external reality and perishing or disintegrating in what appears to them as a struggle against some aspect of that reality is not incompatible with the will to power as conceived by Nietzsche. Are we, then, to attempt to solve the puzzles this conception gives rise to by interpreting 'organisms' or creative agents as quasi-monadic entities who are not acted on at all by anything ontologically independent of them, but some of whose auto-produced representational contents *appear* to them as ontologically independent objects acting on them?[57]

Such an interpretation is tempting, but Nietzsche's own formulations in the *Nachlass*, while being neither final nor entirely unambiguous, appear to rule it out. This becomes particularly evident once one examines his remarks concerning the most fundamental, psychologically inescapable, structural features of our experience, specifically those formulated in the axioms of logic. The 'categorial' structures—Nietzsche mentions explicitly the law of identity and the law of non-contradiction (WM 516)—are required for us to be able to classify the contents of our experiences and, ultimately, to make them predictable and manipulable; they are practical tools in the service of our vital needs (cf. WM 515, 520; FW 111). Here,

---

[56] The kind of complexity involved here will be discussed in greater detail in Chs. 6.1 and 6.2.

[57] Cf. WM 715: 'we may venture to speak of atoms and monads in a relative sense'.

too, Nietzsche appears to reason (although he does not do so explicitly) according to what I have called the argument from utility, and he seems to conclude that the very practical utility of these items of belief renders them unlikely to be 'adequate' to reality.

Another more explicit argument he adverts to in order to show this starts from the premiss that the existence of enduring particulars, or 'things' (*Dinge*), is a 'precondition' for the applicability of the laws of logic to the world (WM 516). In a world without persisting things (i.e. without substances, in one sense of this term), that is, in a world of 'flux' or continuous rapid change, the laws of logic would not apply. But there are no substances, indeed we do not even properly know what we mean by 'substance' (cf. Chapter 2.1). Consequently, the laws of logic apply only 'for us' and 'falsify' reality (WM 512, 515): 'The world seems logical to us because we have made it logical' (WM 521).[58]

If this is indeed Nietzsche's train of thought—and it has to be borne in mind that it is largely extracted from the provisional notes in the *Nachlass*—then it clearly rests on a fallacy. This can be seen even if one looks only at the major premiss of his argument. (The minor premiss is obviously also rather problematic—not only is it unclear how Nietzsche could justify the negative existential claim it makes,[59] it also involves an equivocation on two meanings of 'substance'.) The applicability of the axioms and rules of inference of logic does *not* presuppose the existence of even relatively enduring particulars. The law of non-contradiction asserts that 'no statement is both true and false' (we might add: in the same sense of 'true' and 'false'). This would hold even in a world of rapidly changing and chaotic constellations of qualities (Nietzsche's world of 'becoming', or of the 'chaos of sensations').

To be sure, it could be argued that if our *experience* were solely constituted by a succession of chaotic, instantaneous or near-in-

---

[58] This argument is paraphrased and endorsed by M. Djuric, *Nietzsche und die Metaphysik* (Berlin, 1985), 26–7. It also appears to be accepted by Grimm (*Nietzsche's Theory of Knowledge*, 118) and by W. Müller-Lauter ('Nietzsches Lehre vom Willen zur Macht', in *Nietzsche-Studien*, 3 (1974), 54–6 n.).

[59] Cf. R. Bittner, 'Nietzsches Begriff der Wahrheit' in *Nietzsche-Studien* 16 (1987), 75: 'what is the evidence suggesting that there are no such things [persisting for some time], but only becoming? The basis for this metaphysical claim cannot be discerned. Moreover, [. . .] if our language is inadequate to that which truly is, i.e. becoming, how can we even take cognizance of this inadequacy? Nietzsche himself speaks about the becoming of which, according to him, one cannot speak.'

stantaneous stimuli or sense-data of this kind—which it manifestly is not—we might not be able to detect those regularities enabling us to predict and successfully manipulate our environment. Nor would we in such a case be able to recognize numerically different sequences of marks as expression-tokens of the same type of statement (for there would, *ex hypothesi*, be no patterns of recognizable phenomenal similarities among those data). It might also be maintained, along moderate Kantian lines, that at least some relatively stable patterns in experience are necessary for any self-ascription of experiences and thus for experience *tout court*. But, since our experience is *not* entirely chaotic, we can know that even in a world consisting of an irregular (chaotic) succession of extremely short-lived, or even near-instantaneous, clusters of qualities, it would be necessarily true that not-(p and not-p). Put in first-order language, *if*, in such a world, there is some property F located within some spatial region S and within some temporal interval T (however brief), then it cannot also be the case that there is no F at S,T. Otherwise, Nietzsche would not even be able to say that reality is characterized by 'flux', or incessant rapid change (WM 616), since this is only intelligible as an assertion, one would have thought, if it excludes its contradictory, namely 'it is not the case that reality is characterized by change'. Contrary to what Nietzsche and those who follow him in this point seem to think, the question of whether there really are relatively enduring things has no bearing whatsoever on the applicability of the laws of logic to reality.[60] A universe characterized entirely by ceaseless, chaotic, and rapid change— assuming that it is possible at all—is not *ipso facto* a universe to which logical axioms do not apply (although, if the actual universe were like this, there would be no one who could know and apply these axioms).[61] Nietzsche, however, treats a universe to which the

---

[60] Nor does another point brought up by Nietzsche, namely that the general terms we predicate of grammatical subjects may lead us to believe unjustifiably that there are 'identical cases' in reality (WM 521). Even if, as other philosophers (like Leibniz) have also argued, there are no 'identical cases' in reality, this does not affect the logical point that each item has some determinate property or properties (at any one time), however insufficient our conceptual net may be to pick out its differences from other items adequately, and irrespective of the fact that different languages may classify them differently (another point sometimes made in this context, the relevance of which is criticized succinctly by Bittner, 'Nietzsches Begriff der Wahrheit', 78–9).

[61] Not surprisingly, Nietzsche himself explicitly appeals to the axioms of logic in his own interpretation of regularities in nature, quite disregarding his own claim that

laws of logic apply and a universe characterized by chaotic, rapid change or 'flux' as mutually exclusive (thereby, of course, applying the law of non-contradiction). He appears to say in these notes that a certain kind of 'subject' creates its own objects of experience, including the fundamental logical structures which characterize them (e.g. WM 501, 510) for practical purposes, that is, for enhancing its experience of power in 'conditions of existence' which are alogical (FW 111; WM 517, 521), i.e. which are, according to him, conditions of chaotic flux, rapid change, or 'becoming'. It would seem to follow from remarks like these that for Nietzsche, as for Kant, something, some reality in itself, does indeed 'remain after one deducted the perspective' of the 'subject', although this something would not be susceptible to classification and, hence, to propositional knowledge (cf. WM 520).[62]

. I have argued, by contrast, that even in a world of 'flux' some of the classical laws of logic would generally hold. A world to which these laws do not apply at all—assuming for the sake of the argument that such a hypothesis makes sense—would be one in which nothing would have any determinate property (at any moment in time, if it is a temporal world).[63] It is difficult to see how such a completely indeterminate *Etwas*, even were it conceivable—which would seem to be a necessary condition for it even being capable of being referred to—could constitute 'conditions of existence' that

these axioms are only part of 'our' perspective. This has also been noted by Danto (*Nietzsche as Philosopher*, 171).

[62] Nietzsche's apparent claim, in the notes currently under discussion, that the application of concepts and propositional knowledge are *in principle* impossible if the object-domain is one of 'flux', i.e. rapid change, is, I have tried to show here, mistaken (although a conceptualization and knowledge of items in such a domain might be impossible for some knowers in practice, due to their contingent cognitive limitations).

There is a venerable philosophical tradition which distinguishes between conceptualized objects of experience on the one hand, and 'prime matter' or 'stuff' or 'content' or 'sensations' on the other, and which has it that the conceptual 'form' is somehow 'imposed' on the latter, while the content is 'in itself' not structured in any way which might be in principle conceptualizable. It has often been argued that this picture is itself highly questionable: the 'dualism of scheme and content, of organizing system and something waiting to be organized, cannot be made intelligible and defensible.' (Donald Davidson, 'On the Very Idea of a Conceptual Scheme', in *Inquiries into Truth and Interpretation* (Oxford, 1984), 189.) See also Ch. 6.3.

[63] This is how Stack, among others, interprets Nietzsche's remarks: 'In Nietzsche's conception of *Wirklichkeit*, nothing is ever identical to itself from moment to moment or even, in a strict sense, at any given moment.' (*Lange and Nietzsche*, 215 n.)

cause the extinction of some 'subjects' (or instantiations of the will to power), while submitting to, or being mastered by, others. Reality can only 'select' well-fitted individuals for survival and condemn others to extinction if it has *determinate properties* which the respective individuals either are or are not capable of mastering.

Nietzsche's tentative remarks on logic and on the 'falsification' of reality by our perceptual faculties and by the conceptual grid we impose upon it contain elements of two distinct positions which are incompatible with one another, although each of them would be coherent by itself, or might at least be developed in such a way as to be coherent.

He appears to conjecture, on the one hand, that the objects represented by any subject, including their most fundamental, categorial structures, are 'created' by the subject. Such a view leads to a conception of subjects as uncaused quasi-monadic entities unaffected by anything genuinely external to—ontologically independent of—them, but appearing to themselves to be affected by an 'external' reality which they in fact 'produce' themselves by virtue of their very nature (they *are*, in part, this creative activity). These quasi-monads have to be uncaused, as otherwise one would have to assume some reality with determinate properties which pre-exists them, while *ex hypothesi* it is only *qua* objects of their experience that anything has determinate properties at all (the laws of logic belonging to the perspective of some of these subjects). They would resemble in this respect the God of the Christian philosophers, in that they would not be constrained by any reality or any formal structures instantiated independently of them and *discovered* rather than created by them or derived from their own nature (cf. WM 552 D).

On the other hand, there are elements of a quite different view in Nietzsche's thinking. This view could be formulated as follows. We, *qua* 'subjects' of knowledge, are confronted with an external reality which has determinate properties independently of our imposing any conceptual frameworks or theories on it. These properties are instantiated in highly complex and rapidly changing collocations in which there are no patterns which we could identify if we had undistorted sensory access to them. External reality is, in this sense, in a condition of chaotic 'flux' or 'becoming'. However, our cognitive organs, when affected by this ontologically independent external reality, do not process all the separate stimuli impinging on them, but rather censor them, unknown to us, in such a way as to register some of these data and ignore others, as well as to emphasize some of them, and the continuities or discontinuities between them, at the expense of others. As a result, we perceive a highly simplified and, in a sense, 'falsified' excerpt of the reality external to us, an excerpt, however, in which we are able to detect relatively enduring particulars (things) and patterns or regularities. This circumstance in turn renders us able to predict events and, to some extent, to manipulate external reality according to our needs. It may even make it possible for us, eventually, to arrive at some insight into the actual complexity of things when compared with the simplified objects of our perceptual experience.

As we have seen, the central elements of the second position bear some resemblance to the views of evolutionary epistemologists and other adherents of a naturalized theory of knowledge. Could we not consistently interpret Nietzsche's reflections in these terms, reading his remarks on logic as no more than slightly misleading formulations of the view that reality in itself does not consist of 'objects' qualitatively identical over periods of time long enough for us to attribute 'being' in the sense of qualitative persistence to them?[64] I do not think such an interpretation would do justice to Nietzsche's own ideas as expressed in his writings. Consider what it would imply. It would mean that there are metaphysical truths concerning an objective external reality independent of us *qua* subjects of knowledge. Of course, we might not know that reality adequately ('as it is in itself'), but nevertheless our simplified conceptions of it would be approximations to what would be metaphysically the case. For otherwise, 'operation with such a "conception of reality" could not have proven conducive to our preservation and development, and could not have facilitated our attempts to "master" and "press into service" even "a certain amount of it"'.[65] Every simplification captures something of the truth, albeit in a defective and inadequate manner. On such a view, it is difficult to see why it should be ruled out in principle that our conception of reality should become ever more adequate through the improvement of our theories and the development of more sophisticated instrumental aids to observation. Indeed, many

---

[64] Such an interpretation is strongly implied by Schacht, *Nietzsche*, e.g. 178, 185, 198.

[65] Ibid. 198.

people believe that this is precisely what has happened: as science has advanced, it has revealed a reality far more complex, far more in a condition of 'flux' than the plain evidence of our unaided senses would suggest (cf. Eddington's 'two tables').

But Nietzsche insistently argues against such suppositions. For him, our perspectival interpretations of reality may change to some extent, but they 'never get [. . .] near the truth: for—there is no "truth" ' (WM 616). The 'evolutionary' reading of his thoughts can only appear acceptable if one is prepared to ignore all his arguments and polemics against the very notion of metaphysical truth. Nevertheless, it is easy to see why such a reading should have been tempting to some of his students. It would permit us to reinterpret his fallacious and, in fact, incoherent ideas about the applicability of logic to the world in an intelligible manner and to eliminate the inconsistency which results from his combining of elements from incompatible metaphysical positions.

Our discussion has not, as was hoped, led to greater clarity about Nietzsche's anti-essentialist ideas. Indeed, the conclusion which has emerged from it is that these ideas, leaving aside for the moment other difficulties they may involve, conflict with his perhaps equally vigorous insistence on 'conditions of existence' which exercise constraints on the world-interpretation of any 'subject'. We shall pursue this problem further in our exposition of the 'metaphysics of the will to power' in the final chapter. Meanwhile, let us turn to address the question of the *validation* of some of the apparent positive claims discussed here.

5

The Nature of 'Inner Experience'

In the course of the previous two chapters, a number of questions have emerged regarding the relation between, on the one hand, Nietzsche's denial that it is in the last resort intelligible to speak of 'facts' which make our statements (metaphysically) true or false—'there are no facts' and, consequently, 'there is no "truth"'—and, on the other hand, his apparently quite confident advocacy, in the writings of the last period, of certain psychological theses which seem to imply that there *are* facts, at least in the domain of psychology.

The theses in question are primarily the following: first, that our standards of validation for metaphysical beliefs are determined by our 'ruling drives'—our dominant interests, values, and desires—and that any of these are reducible to the will to power. Secondly, there is the more general thesis that any human action or activity, whether 'instinctive' or 'voluntary', can be adequately accounted for in terms of an inherent tendency or 'striving' towards the enhancement of the experience of power of the agent. Thirdly, Nietzsche seems to assert in many places that there is something like an objective scale of power or force which allows us to refer to many actions, dispositions, and systems of belief as symptoms of relative weakness, i.e. lack of power (for example, the ascetic ideal and, specifically, Platonism and the 'Platonism for the people', Christianity) and to identify others as indicative of relative strength (e.g. what he calls the noble soul's reverence for itself, certain kinds of self-discipline, the 'virtue of bestowing', indifference towards traditional metaphysical questions).

There is obviously a tension between these pronouncements, if they are indeed to be understood as assertions, and Nietzsche's claim that it is incoherent to suppose that reality, or any part of it, has, at any one time, a constitution in itself which characterizes it as what it is at that time. For if this supposition is indeed 'nonsense', what are we to make of such Nietzschean propositions as that 'pity is essentially[!] [...] a pleasant motion of the drive for appropriation' (FW 118), or that 'life itself is *essentially* appropriating, violating, overpowering of the alien and of that which is weaker [...] because life is simply will to power' (JGB 259)? As any reader of Nietzsche knows, pronouncements like these abound in his writings, and indeed it is these remarks for which he is probably best known to non-philosophers (and also to some philosophers). It is one of the aims of the present chapter to determine if, or in what sense, these remarks are compatible with the anti-essentialism figuring so prominently in the writings of the last period.

1. THE FATE OF THE HIGHER SELF

Most of Nietzsche's observations on the nature of mental states—of 'inner experience', as he puts it—concern those beliefs, emotions, desires, and intentions which pertain to what would normally be called moral and religious practices. This emphasis is, of course, partly due to Nietzsche's own chief interests, but also derives from his assumption that an investigation of the psychological characteristics of the 'moral' and the 'religious' (and, to a lesser extent, of the 'aesthetic') will reveal most clearly certain important aspects of the mental—of beliefs, emotions, desires, and so forth—in general.

In order properly to understand his position on these matters in his later writings, and why they occupy such a prominent position in them, it is necessary to have a (regrettably brief) glance at the corresponding statements in his early work up to 1876. The writings I shall be referring to are *Die Geburt der Tragödie* and *Unzeitgemässe Betrachtungen*, as well as the notebooks of that period. The latter are a fascinating source which, unfortunately, has hardly been extensively studied.

In a notebook entry of spring 1874, Nietzsche declares that the lasting significance of Schopenhauer's philosophy consists in its warning to us 'above all not to play down and to obscure that indifferent [*tauben*], merciless, indeed evil original constitution of being' (KGW III.4.34.21). The desires and actions of human beings in their ordinary state—what Schopenhauer calls natural man in one passage[1]—invariably partake of, and manifest, this 'evil' consti-

---

[1] Schopenhauer, *The World as Will and Representation*, i. 404.

tution of being. Thus, human history is a 'compendium of factual immorality' (UzB II.306/105) and 'the history of nations is the history of the egoism of the masses and of the blind desire [. . .] to live' (KGW III.4.29.73. Cf. UzB II.255/68).

As in the case of Schopenhauer, one is perhaps tempted to presume that expressions like 'evil' and 'immoral' are used by Nietzsche in a 'descriptivist' sense and that they are intended to refer, say, to whatever causes human suffering. But Nietzsche shows this presumption to be wrong more unambiguously than Schopenhauer does (see e.g. UzB III.368/153 and KGW III.4.19.93). For him, natural man owes his evil 'original constitution' to the fact that his motivations are invariably 'egoistic' and that the type of motive he calls egoistic is *inherently* evil, irrespective of its consequences:

In Christian idiom: the devil is the lord of this world and the master of success and of progress; he is in all historical forces the real power [. . .] mankind seems to be close to the discovery that egoism [. . .] has been the lever of historical movements at all times; but at the same time one is by no means worried about this discovery, one rather decrees: egoism shall be our God. (UzB II.317/114)

The Lutheran flavour of this, as of many of the young Nietzsche's pronouncements, is difficult not to notice. Setting aside for the moment the question as to the precise meaning of 'egoism', we have to ask, as with Schopenhauer, whether the supposition of an evil or immoral 'original constitution' of man is a coherent one. Is it not contradictory to assert, on the one hand, that human beings are *wholly* involved in an 'evil' mode of existence and to maintain, on the other hand, that they can recognize and refer to it as such? The early Nietzsche, like Schopenhauer, attempts to resolve this apparent contradiction through the notion of a 'complete upheaval and overturning of [. . .] nature' (UzB III.367/152).[2] This overturning or destruction of nature occurs in a few exceptional individuals (the genius and the saint) who experience 'the meaning of [their] activity as a metaphysical one, explicable from the laws of another and

---

[2] For Schopenhauer, this overturning of nature cannot be willed by the individual; it 'comes suddenly, as if flying in from without', and is comparable to what Christians call the effect of grace. 'For what [the church] calls the *natural man*, to whom she denies all capacity for good [!], is that very will-to-live that must be denied if salvation is to be attained from an existence like ours' (*The World as Will and Representation*, 404–5).

higher life [. . .], although everything [they] do appears as a destroy-
ing and breaking of the laws of this life' (UzB III.368/153). Through
what kind of feeling and conduct does nature 'overturn' itself in the
genius and the saint? 'Where the individual starts to think little of
himself [*geringschätzen*], there the realm of the virtues [. . .] begins'
(KGW III.3.19.185). A number of virtues are specified by Nietzsche
in this context, such as 'justice, magnanimity, courage, [. . .] and
compassion with human beings' (UzB II.307/106). In another place,
he speaks of 'kindness, mercy, love and self-denial' (UzB I.191/30).
But, as *Die Geburt der Tragödie* illustrates, it is also in art that the
genius overcomes nature, either through the 'Apollonian' transfiguration (*Verklärung*) of phenomena in beautiful objects (the 'negation of misery'; cf. KGW III.3.7.27), or through the inducement in
his audience of a quasi-mystical state of 'oneness' with the ground
of being in 'Dionysian' art (GT 68–9/37–8).

Nietzsche insists that the justice, magnanimity, courage, etc. of
an individual are not good in virtue of their furthering the self-
interest of others (cf. KGW III.4.19.93), nor because they promote
the self-interest of the agent in any ordinary sense. Rather, actions
to which these words are appropriately applied are, for Nietzsche,
good on account of the fact (and only to the extent that) they are
expressive of the emotion of 'love' (ibid.). In love, we experience
that 'miracle of transformation' in which nature is redeemed from
itself (UzB III.378/161). In love, man 'despises himself and longs to
go beyond himself' (UzB III.365/151) and his life is experienced
'almost no longer individually' (UzB III.378/161). The object of
love is, ultimately, 'metaphysical': the 'law [. . .] of another and
higher life' (UzB III.368/153) which is apprehended as 'the perfect
and the just' (UzB II.292/95), or as the 'ideal': 'To think of oneself
gives little happiness: but if one feels much happiness in doing so,
this is because one is really not thinking of oneself but of one's
ideal' (KGW IV.1.3.75).

We can infer from the statements I have drawn attention to so far
that the early Nietzsche distinguishes between two levels or strata
in the self (explicitly so in KGW IV.1.9.1). There is what one might
call the natural self, which man comes to think little of, indeed
'despise', when illuminated by love, and which is associated with
the 'egoistic' desires Nietzsche also refers to as 'the passions'. On
the other hand, we find, at least in some exceptional individuals,
what he variously describes as a 'true', 'proper', or 'higher' self

which can only be identified through reference to the object of its love (cf. UzB iii.336/129). This object is regarded as external to, or independent of, the subject and its experiences—i.e. it is certainly not to be equated with any present or future 'pleasure' or 'happiness' of the subject—and as the 'perfect and the just', or the 'ideal'.[3]

The very expressions that Nietzsche uses here, unspecific as they are ('perfect', 'just', 'metaphysical', 'law of [...] a higher life'), make it nevertheless clear that the object of the love of the higher self is apprehended by it as valuable in itself—it is not called good because it happens to be desired, but is desired because it is taken to be inherently good. In other words, the object of love is considered to be real or, as some philosophers put it, 'objective'. There are many well-advertised difficulties with realist construals of value which we need not enter into here. When someone claims some values to be real or 'objective' as opposed to 'subjective', at least the following two assertions seem to be made. First, they, or at least some of them, are taken to exist (to be actual) independently of being experienced by the subject making this claim. Second, whenever they *do* become objects of experience, they are experienced as somehow calling for, or meriting, or deserving to be loved, even if such love should necessitate 'self-denial' or perhaps (in some cases) even the 'sacrifice' of the self *qua* empirical individual. It is precisely this possibility of 'heroic' self-denial—underlying much premodern discourse on values and also central to a dominant strand in German culture—which profoundly impressed and perplexed Schopenhauer and the young Nietzsche. I would go so far as to maintain that it is the focal preoccupation of the early Nietzsche and, in a somewhat different way, also of his later writings. In any case, it could be claimed, not implausibly, that it is primarily this phenomenological characteristic of a certain sort of experience which has been the main reason why those familiar with it have wanted to call values 'real' (in this respect, values are analogous to the resistance to the subject's will essential to 'real objects' discussed in Chapter 3.1). By contrast, the objects of what Nietzsche calls egoistic desires or passions—say, a sufficient income or a

---

[3] There is a partial affinity between Nietzsche's distinction of two levels within the self and the distinction between 'first-order' and 'second-order' desires drawn by Charles Taylor ('Responsibility for Self', in G. Watson (ed.), *Free Will* (Oxford, 1982), 111–26).

larger house—are not presented in the same way as meriting, or calling for, a particular kind of response, but rather, simply, as 'being wanted'. Furthermore, characterizing these objects does not, phenomenologically, require reference to anything ontologically independent of the valuing subject and the contents of its experiences. This is why the end of such desires may more readily be described as an experience on the part of the desiring subject, for example 'pleasure'.[4]

Now, the early Nietzsche's distinction between the passions and the higher self ('love') faces major difficulties arising from his continued acceptance of the essentially Schopenhauerian doctrine that the 'original constitution' of things is 'evil' and that *'nothing in the nature of things correspond[s] to morality'* (KGW III.4.19.185)—in other words, that the belief in real or 'objective' value, or even in a Platonic or Christian good *ante res*, is illusory (KGW III.4.19.132). Nietzsche, perhaps aware of the tension between those Schopenhauerian tenets and what he wishes to say about the virtues of the genius and the saint, sometimes maintains that man is virtuous to the extent that he *longs* for there to be a 'metaphysical' ideal, is dissatisfied with and 'denies' his natural self (UzB III.367/153), and acts *as if* an 'eternal' order of reality which is 'perfect and [. . .] just' and the appropriate object of love and reverence existed (cf. UzB II.315/112 and KGW III.4.19.185). Human virtue, according to these passages, is only to be found in the struggle of some exceptional beings—the genius and the saint—against the recalcitrant nature of things. It is, as it were, a protest

---

[4] As the later Nietzsche explicitly agrees, this does not imply that the pleasure which is the end of such 'egoistic' or self-directed desires can be satisfactorily analysed as analogous to brute sensations, as some of the classical utilitarian theories would have it. It is, in other words, quite compatible with the rather more plausible view that an adequate description of many such desires needs to make reference to certain 'objects' or representational contents the 'possession' of which in one's experience is desired in them. What I desire when I desire to listen to Mozart's *Krönungsmesse* is not some brute, unstructured sensation which that particular sequence of sounds only happens to be a suitable means of bringing about, but rather an experience which is pleasurable in being an experience *of* that sequence of sounds. The pleasure here cannot be characterized in its specificity without reference to its ('intentional') object.

Another misconception to be avoided is that the end of what I have called self-directed ('egoistic') desires is *eo ipso* a *self-conscious* state of the subject. The person who desires to get drunk certainly has a self-directed desire in the present sense of this expression—if asked, he would say that he desires the state of inebriation for *himself*, not, say, for someone else. But he does not desire a self-conscious state—quite the contrary.

against reality, an unending heroic quest for intimations of the 'ideal' which, given the way the world is, can never be rewarded by success. It hardly needs to be pointed out that this view was very influential in late nineteenth and early twentieth century European culture.

The problems encountered by such a position are analogous to those of Schopenhauer's corresponding views. For one thing, it is not clear how, if the 'original constitution' of things is 'evil', the denial of the natural self (in Schopenhauer's case: the self-denial of the will-to-live) is even possible. The notion of an 'overturning of nature' ultimately cannot escape the charge of being a euphemism for contradictory metaphysical assumptions. Put in Schopenhauerian terms: *if* the will-to-live can deny itself, then it is not adequately, or fully, described as will-to-*live*.

Moreover, neither Nietzsche nor anyone else can *both* love the 'ideal' (or, apparently more modestly, have a supposedly non-egoistic desire for there to be such an ideal to love), *and* believe that the ideal is illusory. For the higher self, which alone is ostensibly capable of such love and desire, is *defined* through its intentional relation to a good which, when apprehended, is experienced as 'real', which means, in this case, ontologically independent of the individual and calling for or meriting such an affective response and the appropriate actions for its own sake. But if the belief in the reality of the good (the ideal), in this sense, is seen as illusory, then the higher self, as defined by Nietzsche, evidently disappears with it. The enjoinder to act *as if* there were such a good can then only be justified, in Nietzsche's own terms, by appeal to the individual's 'egoistic', self-directed desires—that is, desires for experiences of certain sorts. Thus, the belief that one can deny the 'passions' (UzB III.367/153) and *desire*, non-egoistically, for there to be real goods, in the sense suggested by Nietzsche, already involves the belief that there *are* such goods, and this is incompatible with the conviction that 'nothing in the nature of things correspond[s] to morality'.

Nietzsche realizes this inconsistency in his earlier views in or about 1876. It is, in my opinion, this realization which is the origin of many of the characteristic features of his later philosophy which distinguish it from his earlier beliefs. In his writings after *Unzeitgemässe Betrachtungen*, he abandons his earlier dualistic conception of human desire. 'Love' is no longer cardinally distinct from, and opposed to, 'self-interest' or 'egoism'; it is rather a manifestation of the latter, while 'egoistic' desires themselves are ever more comprehensively subsumed under one general description: the desire of the agent to experience his power or superiority.[5] Similarly, behaviour which has traditionally been regarded as virtuous in the culture of Europe, a culture that was shaped by Judaeo-Christian, Platonic, and Aristotelian moral thought, is now no longer considered by Nietzsche to be brought about by the desire-entailing emotional state of love having as its intentional object a good which is conceived as real, i.e. as independent of the subject apprehending it and of its experiences. According to the Nietzsche of the middle and late periods, nothing external to the self in this sense is loved 'for its own sake'. Rather, we desire whatever objects we desire because we regard them as conducive to our own 'pleasure'. Hence, what he, in the pre-1876 writings, called the higher or true self which, at least in some individuals, was supposed to be capable of acting contrary to the 'passions' of the natural self ('self-denial'), is absent from the works written after that turning-point. 'Good', for any given individual, now designates either certain experiences of that individual—who therefore has only 'passions'—or whatever is considered to be conducive to them. Consequently 'there are no self-denying actions' (KGW VII.2.25.93), for 'the only motives which knowledge can admit to exist are pleasure and displeasure, advantage and disadvantage' (MAM i.34).

So far, there is nothing very revolutionary in Nietzsche's new position. A major tradition in modern philosophy, going back to Thomas Hobbes, had advocated essentially the same view before him.[6] However, for Nietzsche, pleasure and, indeed, happiness are not final explanatory concepts regarding human actions and their ends. Already in *Morgenröte* (1881), he generalizes the naturalizing psychological observations and analyses of *Menschliches, Allzumenschliches* and remarks that 'happiness, conceived as the

---

[5] Cf. Kaufmann, *Nietzsche—Philosopher, Psychologist, Antichrist*, 152: 'The basic difference between Nietzsche's earlier and later theories is that his final philosophy is based on the assumption of a single basic principle, while the philosophy of his youth was marked by a cleft which all but broke it in two'.

[6] Cf. Thomas Hobbes, *Leviathan* (Oxford, 1957), part I, ch. 6: 'But whatsoever is the object of any man's appetite or desire, that is it which he for his part calleth good: and the object of his hate and aversion, evil [. . . .] For these words of good, evil, and contemptible, are ever used with relation to the person that useth them; there being nothing simply and absolutely so.'

most vivid feeling of power [*Gefühl der Macht*], has perhaps no-where on earth been greater than in the souls of superstitious ascetics' (MR 113). Later, he says more explicitly and more generally:

that it is notably enlightening to put [*setzen*] power in the place of individual 'happiness' (after which every living thing is supposed to be striving): 'there is a striving for power, for an increase of power';—pleasure is only a symptom of the feeling of power attained, a consciousness of a difference [. . .] (WM 688)

and:

— no one had the courage to define the typical element in pleasure, every sort of pleasure ('happiness') as the feeling of power: for to take pleasure in power was considered immoral [. . .] (WM 428)

Nietzsche is perhaps a little disingenuous here in his claim to novelty. We find the explicit identification of 'happiness' with a consciousness of power, for instance, in a passage in Schopenhauer, who says there:

For there is really no other pleasure than the use and feeling of our own powers, and the greatest pain is when we are aware of a deficiency of our powers where they are needed.[7]

To be sure, this conception of pleasure is at odds with Schopenhauer's dominant view, on which pleasure is to be understood purely negatively as the absence of pain. A view reminiscent of Nietzsche's is, however, integral to the philosophy of Spinoza, who analyses pleasure as follows:

When the mind regards itself and its own power of activity, it feels pleasure: and that pleasure is greater in proportion to the distinctness wherewith it conceives itself and its own power of activity.[8]

But although there are these precedents for Nietzsche's equation of the consciousness of power with happiness as the end of human

---

[7] Schopenhauer, *The World as Will and Representation*, i. 305.

[8] B. Spinoza, *The Ethics*, in *Works of Spinoza* (New York, 1955), vol. ii, part 3, prop. 53. Cf. also part 3, prop. 55. Nietzsche expresses his approval of some of Spinoza's views in a letter to F. Overbeck (30 July 1881): 'I am quite astonished, quite delighted! I have a *predecessor*, and what a predecessor he is! I hardly knew Spinoza: [. . .] in five main points of his doctrine I recognize myself, [. . .]: he denies the freedom of the will—; final ends—; the moral world order—; anything unegoistic—; evil—[. . . .]'

activity, he elaborates it with much greater specificity and a rather more probing attention to the minutiae of the phenomenology of 'inner experience'.

We saw in the previous chapter how he interprets even cognitive activity itself, the attempt to 'grasp' or to comprehend a given subject matter, in terms of the desire for (the experience of) power. But he more commonly argues for this view in the context of an analysis of those human desires and practices which are prima facie most recalcitrant to such a construal, namely the moral, aesthetic, and religious ones which he formerly attributed to the 'higher self'. Clearly, his monistic analysis of the affective and appetitive aspects of the mental will gain in plausibility and strength if he is successful in reducing to the will to power even those emotions, desires, and intentions which seem least hospitable to such an account. Let us therefore examine the various arguments Nietzsche musters in favour of it. In the course of such an examination it will also emerge—or so we may expect—whether or in what sense, he recognizes the existence of ultimate facts and essential natures in 'inner experience'.

In *Menschliches, Allzumenschliches*, we find Nietzsche claiming that

the entire concept 'unegoistic action' vanishes into thin air under strict investigation. Never yet has any human being done anything solely for others and without any personal motive [. . .] in fact, how should he be *able* to do anything [. . .] without inner compulsion (which surely would have to have a personal need as its cause)? (MAM i.133)

The soldier wishes to die on the field of battle for his victorious nation: for in the victory of his nation his highest wishes are also victorious [. . . .] But are any of these states unegoistic? Are these moral deeds *miracles* because they are, in Schopenhauer's expression, 'impossible and yet real'? [. . .] The *inclination towards something* (wish, drive, desire) is present in all cases; to yield to it, with all consequences, is at any rate not 'unegoistic'. (MAM i.57)

The argument here seems to be that the kind of action which Nietzsche in his earlier writings attributed to the higher self is in fact *logically* impossible (cf. KGW VII.2.26.224). Every action is *qua* action susceptible to an explanation in terms of a desire, an 'inner compulsion' towards, or 'personal need' for, a certain end. Thus, any action, in aiming to realize a certain state of affairs, is *ipso facto* an attempt to satisfy a desire of the agent. Hence, by the very definition of action, there can be no action in which the desires of the agent are left out of account, as, Nietzsche implies, 'unegoistic' actions are supposed to do.

Evidently, this argument rests on an equivocation and merely begs the question against his former view, which recognizes a cardinal distinction between kinds of desires. For, obviously, such a view is not committed to the claim that the soldier who voluntarily risks his life in battle does so without desiring to do so. It is not in *this* sense that his own experiences are supposed not to enter into the description of his action. Rather, a view like that held by Nietzsche before 1876 insists on a distinction within the self which permits us to speak of actions performed in disregard of certain kinds of desires, a specification of the objects of which requires reference to the subject's expected future experiences, on the strength of desires of another kind whose objects cannot be so specified. It is such a distinction which seems to be presupposed in the traditional moral parlance of 'self-denying' and 'virtuous' action.

Nietzsche's attacks on this conception are extraordinarily manifold in character and are not always mutually compatible. While the argument above, if valid, would show that an agent cannot even coherently think of his or her desires as 'unegoistic', there are other passages where Nietzsche readily concedes this, but insists that they can be 'explained' in naturalistic terms:

'To deny morality'—that can mean, *first*: to deny that the moral motives which people *avow* have really moved them to their actions [. . . .] *Secondly*, it can mean: to deny that moral judgements are based on truths. Here, it is admitted that they really are motives of actions, but that in this way *errors*, as the basis of all moral judgement, move men to their moral actions. This is my point of view [. . .] (MR 103; cf. MAM ii,2,20)

What are the 'errors' which give rise to the desires and, ultimately, intentions that are characteristic of 'moral' actions? Nietzsche explains in another passage in *Morgenröte* that 'man, under the spell of morality and of the moral, [. . .] ties all his more elevated feelings (of reverence, of sublimity, of pride, of gratitude, of love) *to an imaginary world*: the so-called higher world' (MR 33). This imaginary 'higher world' is of course identical with what he earlier called the ideal, in particular with its foremost historical manifestation in the intellectual history of Europe: the Christian

God. But while Christian theism and the evaluative judgements apparently grounded in it are the primary targets of his attacks, he states quite generally that 'never yet has a religion contained a truth, neither mediately nor directly, neither as a dogma nor as a parable. For each one of them is born from fear and need, and has crept into existence on aberrations of reason' (MAM i.110). In the writings of the last period, he explains this in more detail (and with greater stridency):

In Christianity, neither morality nor religion touch reality at a single point. Only imaginary *causes* ('God', 'soul', 'self', 'spirit', 'the free will'—or also 'the unfree will'): only imaginary *effects* ('sin', 'salvation', 'grace' [. . .]). A communion between imaginary *beings* ('God', 'spirits', 'souls'); an imaginary science of *nature* (anthropocentric, total lack of the concept of natural causes); an imaginary *psychology* (only self-misunderstandings [. . .]); an imaginary *teleology* ('the kingdom of God' [. . .]). (AC 15; cf. FW 151)

Having previously discussed Nietzsche's various sceptical arguments, and having also mentioned his anti-essentialism, we can readily see that most of these assertions—if they are assertions—are highly problematic on his own terms. If his own quasi-Humean observations on causality are accepted, then the causes and effects postulated by theologians can hardly be regarded as any more imaginary—in the sense of: unknown in their efficacious nature—than the 'natural causes' of science. In fact, considering Nietzsche's own indecision concerning the efficacy of the will (see Chapters 2.1 and 6.1) and his rather more determined critical remarks about ostensible non-teleological efficient causes, one would expect him to consider the final causes of the theologians to have, in one sense, greater empirical warrant than these (see WM 551).

Of course, he could object against theistic metaphysics that even if its basic concepts—such as a Spirit as cause—have some empirical basis (if only by analogy), such a metaphysics is still open to the more general, Cartesian, sceptical doubts about the 'external world' discussed in Chapter 2.3. But this would be a double-edged criticism, for in the passages quoted above and in many similar ones Nietzsche himself seems to assert that certain moral and religious beliefs do not 'touch reality at a single point'. In the light of his own sceptical arguments we may ask: how does he know this? Clearly, if those arguments hold, he cannot know it on any understanding of 'knowledge' which involves rational justification. Hence, the theologians may well turn the tables on him and reply to those criticisms that they will only possess any force to someone who has already accepted certain standards of validation which correspond to a particular set of 'ruling drives', and simply fail to engage a disputant who does not share these. Now, it may turn out in the course of these investigations that Nietzsche would actually concur with this reply (in fact, he anticipates it; see JGB 10). But the point to be made here is simply that passages like the ones I have cited insinuate something different, namely that there are shared, generally accepted modes of argument by means of which it can be demonstrated, or shown to be probable, that 'neither morality nor religion touch reality at a single point'. If our observations are correct, such passages can only be understood as either expressive rather than assertoric, or as rhetorical devices whose force depends crucially on the reader's either not being convinced by, or not being aware of, other things Nietzsche says.

We may also note, in parenthesis, that remarks to the effect that certain judgements 'do not touch reality' or are not 'based on truths' go very uneasily with his statements elsewhere that 'there is no "truth"'. They are not necessarily incompatible with his analysis of 'objective reality', but they are difficult to square with his anti-essentialism, i.e. with the view that it is incoherent to suppose that reality, or any part of it, is, at any moment, characterized by any intrinsic properties which constitute it as what it is (at that moment). However, since this anti-essentialism is itself highly problematic (see Chapter 6.2), one should perhaps not place too much emphasis on the apparent incompatibility with it of the remarks presently under scrutiny.

We may conclude that Nietzsche, by virtue of his sceptical arguments, cannot consistently object to the kind of traditional account of human desire and action, of which his own earlier philosophy represents one version, that it describes the phenomenology of the relevant desires correctly, but that belief in the 'higher world' which figures in this description represents a rationally demonstrable (or probable) 'error'. He might, of course, raise objections against the very intelligibility of theistic metaphysics, drawing on his anti-essentialist ideas. But, as it happens, he does not generally rely on these ideas when attacking 'narrowly' religious doctrines in particular.

It would thus appear that the only remaining line of criticism open to Nietzsche with respect to the alleged occurrence of actions which do not have the experience of power as their end lies in calling into question the phenomenal reality or the efficacy of the motives that are purportedly characteristic of such actions. In other words, he might question the adequacy of the descriptions which, say, the courageous soldier ('for the sake of my country/family') or the allegedly charitable man ('for the sake of God') give of their actions, and conjecture that the real causes of these actions are different from the avowed motives. And this is indeed his approach in most of his reflections on human action. In the majority of these remarks, he does not seek to establish the falsity or unintelligibility of a Christian or otherwise 'narrowly' religious account of virtuous action by arguing for the falsity or incoherence of their metaphysical items of belief (e.g. the belief in a 'perfect and [. . .] just' God), but rather attempts to discredit these beliefs by showing that the only arguments in their favour which seem to carry any force are based on inadequate interpretations of 'inner experience'. In fact, many of his remarks indicate, not surprisingly in the light of his ideas on the will to truth, that the question of the truth of theistic *metaphysics* is an entirely secondary one for him:

> The question of the mere 'truth' of Christianity, either as regards the existence of its God, or the historicity of the legend of its origin, not even to speak of Christian astronomy and natural science—is an entirely secondary matter, as long as the question of the value of Christian morality has not been touched upon. Is Christian morality any *good*, or is it an infamy and a disgrace [. . .]? (KGW VIII.3.15.19. See also AC 56)

What addressing the 'question of the value of Christian morality' of course presupposes is a *description* of that morality (cf. JGB 186), and that is precisely what Nietzsche embarks upon. What he also, crucially, assumes is that the 'question of value' *can* be addressed without incurring any—or at least any controversial—metaphysical commitments: indeed, on the present interpretation, this is an essential aspect of his critique of the will to truth. The above passage and other similar ones (e.g. AC 56, JGB 4) show very clearly what I regard as a central feature of his later philosophy, which is sometimes obscured by his own formulations on a careless reading, and which is also not always sufficiently appreciated by his interpreters, namely the priority, when all is said and done, of phenomenology—in particular of the phenomenology of value—over metaphysics and indeed over historico-genealogical 'explanations'.[9] The claims of theistic metaphysics, like all other metaphysical claims, are symptomatic of the 'ruling drives' of their advocates and, like these other conflicting claims, they cannot be 'rationally' disproved (provided they are not obviously incoherent). But they can be rendered irrelevant and obsolete, that is, deprived of their function, by showing the falsity of the psychological interpretations and self-interpretations which both are the only real 'evidence' for them and which, if accepted, appear to the believer himself to be his only, or at any rate by far the most important, *motive* for wishing these metaphysical doctrines to be true: 'one cannot refute conditions of existence, one can only—not have them' (KGW VII.1.1.2, cf. MR 95, WM 157). Ultimately, Nietzsche's most interesting arguments against the metaphysics of *homo religiosus* consist in his attempt to show that the inner experiences—emotional or 'affective' states and the desires entailed by them—which alone suggest and seem to require the truth of such metaphysics, are either self-deceptive misinterpretations or epiphenomena which do not have any causally operative role in human action.

2. UNCONSCIOUS MENTAL STATES

The claim that conscious emotions, desires, and intentions are epiphenomena seems to be either expressly asserted or implied in a considerable number of Nietzsche's remarks (e.g. WM 478), and it entails an account of human agency according to which the efficacious antecedents of human behaviour—both 'voluntary' and 'involuntary'—are not to be discovered in consciousness, i.e. they are *unconscious*. Thus he says that

Every action that we '*will*' is definitely only represented [*vorgestellt*] by us as the appearance of a phenomenon [*Schein der Erscheinung*].—All consciousness is only a *secondary manifestation of the intellect*. (KGW VII.1.12.34)

---

[9] 'Genealogy [*die Geschichte der Entstehung*] does not explain the qualities. The latter must already be known. *Historical* explanation is reduction to a conjunction *familiar* to us: by means of analogy' (KGW VII.3.34.69; cf. the beginning of GM ii.9).

In keeping with this, he attacks the Cartesian assumption that consciousness is transparent to itself—that in 'inner experience' there is no distinction between appearance and reality:

Critique of modern philosophy: erroneous starting point, as if there existed 'facts of consciousness'—and no phenomenalism in introspection. (WM 475; 'phenomenalism' is here evidently related to the Kantian dichotomy between phenomena and things in themselves, not to the standard modern usage of this expression [P.P.].)

Especially in the *Nachlass*, we find time and again the claim that emotions, desires, and intentions—understood as conscious mental occurrences—are appearances of a hidden reality, often described by Nietzsche as consisting of 'drives', 'instincts', or 'affects', and that it is these latter which determine our actions, while conscious desires and intentions are quite irrelevant to their real origin and nature: 'Unconscious deception is also possible: [. . . .] Ultimately, this is what *always* happens, with all our actions. The essential things happen unconscious to us' (KGW VII.1.1.31; cf. KGW VII.1.1.20 and WM 676). Our avowals of conscious motives constitute 'deceptions', yet they are deceptions in a rather wide and novel sense of the word in that we cannot help committing them, being in ignorance of the unconscious real springs of action. Nietzsche's statements are, of course, particularly directed against the notion that there are 'unselfish' desires which give rise to actions. The idea of the unconscious origins of actions allows him to acknowledge the phenomenology of such desires—their appearance as non-self-interested to the agent himself—and yet to insist that 'moral actions are in reality "something different"' (MR 116):

the falsity does not become conscious. It is a sign of a broken instinct when man sees the driving force and its 'expression' ('the mask') as separate things—[. . . .] Absolute innocence in bearing, word, affect, a 'good conscience' in falsity, the certainty with which one grasps the greatest and most splendid words and postures—all this is necessary for victory. (WM 377; cf. MAM ii.96)

In what precise sense are the efficacious antecedents of human behaviour conceived of as 'unconscious' by Nietzsche? Unfortunately, here too his statements are not without ambiguities at crucial points. He sometimes describes the unconscious drives and instincts which bring about our actions, and of which our consciousness of 'motives' is only a highly interpreted and 'falsified' epiphenomenon, in quasi-physiological language. But he also emphasizes that the complex system of functions which we call the body is only an 'image' (*Gleichnis*) or appearance of these drives and the complex relations between them (KGW VII.3.37.4; cf. also GM iii.16, where he distinguishes his concept of 'physiology' from that of the adherents of 'materialism').

It is sometimes not sufficiently appreciated in the literature that, when it comes to specifying the actual mode of operation or agency of these drives, which he in fact seems to conceive of as the ultimate agents, Nietzsche invariably uses intentional–mentalistic terms. We learn that they jointly constitute a 'higher, comprehensive intellect' (WM 676), that they have experiences and interpret them (MR 119, KGW VIII.1.1.58; KGW VII.3.37.4), that they have a kind of reason (WM 387), that they feel (KGW VIII.1.1.58), that they desire and have wants (WM 676 last para., WM 377), indeed that they choose, command, and obey (KGW VII.3.40.21; KGW VII.3.37.4). It could be argued with some plausibility that most of these terms, in their ordinary meanings, imply the presence of consciousness. Can one be said, for example, to be 'interpreting' a text—other than in an obviously metaphorical and derivative sense—unless one is aware of there being a text to be interpreted? Similarly, the having of wants or desires, even if analysed as dispositions, would seem to imply, at *some* stage, consciously experienced inclinations towards certain objects, persons, or whatever. And it is prima facie difficult to conceive how a being can be said literally to be able to command or to obey unless it can be aware of the meaning of a command. However, Nietzsche occasionally conjectures that 'thinking, willing, feeling' as well as 'acting' are possible without corresponding mental episodes *ever* occurring in *any* consciousness:

For we would be able to think, feel, will, remember, we would equally be able to 'act' in every sense of the word: and yet all of this need not 'enter our consciousness' [. . . .] Life in its entirety would be possible without, as it were, seeing itself in the mirror [. . .] (FW 354)

And he praises

Leibniz's incomparable insight [. . .] that being conscious is only an *accidens* of representation [*der Vorstellung*], not its necessary and essential attribute, i.e. that what we call consciousness is only one state of our mental and psychic world [. . .] and does *by no means constitute it as such* [*sie selbst*]—. (FW 357; cf. KGW VII.1.7.25 and KGW VIII.1.1.52)

According to the statements we are currently examining, it is our 'drives' which, unknown to us, determine our actions. The activity of these drives—which he sometimes also refers to as a hierarchy or 'oligarchy' of 'organic beings' (*Wesen*) constituting our 'body'—is described in anthropomorphizing and mentalistic terms. However, the passages cited above suggest strongly that we are nevertheless not to understand these agents, or constitutive *Wesen*, as themselves conscious of their activity—of their desiring, interpreting, willing, commanding, and obeying. This raises a number of questions, both concerning Nietzsche's own philosophy and its cogency, and of a more general kind.

The anti-Cartesian supposition that 'consciousness is only one state of our mental and psychic world', rather than being an essential attribute of the mental, has found wide acceptance in our own century, owing largely, albeit not exclusively, to the writings of Freud. Freud, it is useful to remember, developed his ideas during the heyday of Nietzsche's influence in German-speaking countries and he explicitly acknowledged his debt to Nietzsche's 'educator' Schopenhauer. Since much of the philosophical discussion of the notion of unconscious mental states has centred around Freud's theory, it is convenient for a discussion of Nietzsche's corresponding views briefly to note both their analogies with, and their differences from, Freud's.

In terms which are strikingly reminiscent of Nietzsche's, Freud describes the 'soul' as 'a hierarchy of superordinated and subordinated agents, a labyrinth of impulses striving independently of one another towards action'.[10] These agents are more precisely characterized as 'drives' consisting of an idea or representation (*Vorstellung*) together with a 'quantity of affect' or 'feeling' (*Affekt, Gefühl, Empfindung*).[11] Under certain circumstances, the idea-component of a drive is 'repressed' from consciousness by an obscure entity, the 'censor', and, crucially, 'continues, after repression, as an actual formation in the system Ucs [Unconscious]'.[12] Yet, while ideas may thus exist *qua* ideas unconsciously, the 'affect or

---

[10] Cited in I. Thalberg, 'Freud's Anatomies of the Self', in R. Wollheim and J. Hopkins (eds.), *Philosophical Essays on Freud* (Cambridge, 1982), 243.
[11] S. Freud, 'Die Verdrängung', in *Gesammelte Werke* (London, 1942), x. 255.
[12] Freud, 'Das Unbewusste', in *Gesammelte Werke*, x. 277.

feeling'[13] as which a drive 'appears'[14] is necessarily conscious. For it is of the essence of a feeling that it is felt or 'perceived' (*wahrgenommen*).[15] On this account, an unconscious desire would be a desire which is represented by a 'quantity of affect' together with a conscious idea of an object or end which is, however, not its real object or end, while the latter (the 'ideational representation' of its real end) persists in the unconscious. Moreover, in order to give any force at all to the claim that the unconscious idea of the object of the desire is indeed the idea of its *real* object, one has to assume that it is, unknown to the individual, 'efficacious in shaping and giving meaning to [the individual's] conscious experiences'.[16]

Two points should perhaps be added. First, if one takes Freud's utterances seriously, it is clearly impermissible to construe the Freudian notion that a person has unconscious desires or memories as simply the disposition to behave in certain ways.[17] Freud is not merely saying that the person to whom he attributes unconscious desires and memories tends to display behaviour—including verbal behaviour—which can be interpreted by an observer as following an apparently intelligible pattern, just *as if* that person has all along been having certain desires and memories, while in fact no claim is being made that he really *has* been undergoing distinctly mental episodes, i.e. states which, if conscious, would have a certain phenomenal character (a certain what-it-is-likeness). In introducing unconscious mental states, Freud is not merely offering a slightly misleading behaviourist analysis of the mental. Secondly, it should be emphasized that Freud rejects the assumption of there being a plurality of separate 'centres of consciousness' in an individual. There is not another consciousness within us which is aware of the ideas in what is *our* unconscious; there are, rather, 'psychic acts which are devoid of consciousness'.[18]

Nietzsche's claims, in the passages we have quoted from *Die fröhliche Wissenschaft*, seem if anything even more radical than Freud's. For he seems to recognize not only unconscious

---

[13] Ibid. 276.   [14] Ibid. 275.   [15] Ibid.

[16] M. Fox, 'On Unconscious Emotions', in *Philosophy and Phenomenological Research* 34 (1973/4), 170.

[17] Cf. I. Dilman, *Freud and the Mind* (Oxford, 1984), 26.

[18] Freud, 'Das Unbewusste', 269. Freud's reason for this rejection, namely that the assumption of more than one consciousness in an individual rests upon a doubtful 'inference', is somewhat peculiar, given the highly inferential nature of his own alternative theory.

Vorstellungen, but also unconscious 'feeling' and 'willing'. It may of course be asked what should prevent us, once we recognize *essentially* unconscious ideas or representations, from acknowledging the existence of unconscious feelings as well. For is not the (conventionally) literal or central meaning of 'idea' logically tied to its referent's having what I have called a phenomenal quality or what-it-is-likeness, just as the concept of a feeling is? If this is so, then the traditional objection against the notion of unconscious yet distinctly *mental* states—that it is a contradiction in terms—would be relevant both in Freud's and in Nietzsche's case.

To clarify this point, consider what is implied by the assertion that drives 'interpret', 'estimate', 'command', and 'obey' each other unconsciously (that is, being themselves unconscious agents). Nietzsche says, for example:

From each of our basic drives there is a different perspectival assessment of all events and experiences. Each of these drives feels itself to be either impeded or assisted with respect to each other drive [...] (KGW VIII.1.1.58)

All basic drives are, as ultimate agents, variations of the will to power, that is, the end of their activity is the 'feeling of power' (WM 649, 643, 689 last para., KGW VIII.1.1.30, KGW VIII.1.40.61). This involves, as we have seen in the preceding chapter, the appropriation or subjection or the imposition of a certain form or character upon other agents by a given agent, as perceived by that agent (i.e. a given 'drive' or 'quantum of force'). Now, the 'assessment' by the agent of an object (or an opponent) which is involved in this process would seem to require, first of all, an awareness of it, an observation of its behaviour, and a comparison with other objects and/or with the agent himself. Moreover, as we pointed out in Chapter 4.3, talk about the exertion of power or domination (*Macht*) implies purposes, either in the agent who exerts power, or in the patient over whom it is exerted, or in both.

If the activity of the ultimate agents (of 'affects', 'drives', or 'power-centres') on the pattern outlined above is to be thought of as strictly unconscious, we would have to say that they recognize, compare, intend, and feel, without necessarily ever being aware of doing any of these things. It is very important to remember that, since we have reached the most fundamental level of psychological explanation here, we are not entitled to assume any physiological substrata of these drives[19] in which certain processes, describable in a physicalist vocabulary, are going on and the results of which we might call 'recognition', 'intention', etc.[20] Nor is there, on Nietzsche's account, a yet deeper psychological level where any of the mental states in question might be present to a consciousness in what is our unconscious.

Once these reservations are made, it becomes mysterious what could be meant by saying that the ultimate agents have unconscious ideas (e.g. recognizing some quality in an object), feelings, and intentions. As for ideas, it is difficult to understand the meaning of the assertion that an idea exists or occurs *qua* idea (rather than as, say, a series of events in a physiological substratum) without it, or more precisely its *content*, being contemplated, perceived, or attended to by anyone. How can a *Vorstellung* exist without it being *gestellt vor*—present *to*—a consciousness to which it displays a certain array of phenomenal properties?[21] Irving Thalberg's criticism of Freud's concept of unconscious ideas seems just as relevant to the corresponding claims by Nietzsche:

Our puzzlement should not diminish because now we are talking about unconscious ideas. What could we mean if we supposed that they unfold or persist, although neither the person in whom they occur, nor any agency within him [. . .] takes note of them? Surely the unconscious idea [. . .] did not contemplate itself![22]

---

[19] Nietzsche's criticisms of the putative explanations of physics (cf. Ch. 2.2) of course also apply to physiology in the ordinary, as opposed to his own idiosyncratic, sense of the word. Cf. GOA xiv. 353.

[20] Somewhat as we occasionally speak of a sophisticated machine as recognizing something, or intending to do something. But it is worth bearing in mind that, in such cases, these terms are applied by *us*, that is, by conscious subjects who *interpret* the behaviour of the machine as being, in certain respects, analogous to their own.

[21] In saying that mental representations, in the literal sense, have to be present to a *consciousness*, one is of course not committing oneself to a belief in a *res cogitans*—contrary to what is sometimes suggested by philosophers influenced by Heidegger. To understand the meaning of a term like 'consciousness' as it is used here, all one needs is an ability to tell the difference between states of consciousness of a certain sort occurring (e.g. a tactile awareness of an object), and their not occurring (e.g. when one is anaesthetized).

[22] Thalberg, 'Freud's Anatomies of the Self', 261. A similar point is made by J.-P. Sartre in *Being and Nothingness* (London, 1958), 52–3: 'it is not sufficient that [the censor] discern the condemned drives; it must also apprehend them as to be repressed, which implies in it at the very least an awareness of its activity. In a word, how could the censor discern the impulses needing to be repressed without being conscious of discerning them?'

While it might be suggested that the anthropomorphizing language regarding 'drives' in both Nietzsche and Freud may be metaphorical, it should be noted that such metaphors can only be elucidatory at all in proportion to the degree of intelligible similarity between the metaphorical description and the thing described.[23] If one says, for example, that some occurrent is just like an episodic desire, except that it is wholly unconscious and possibly entirely inaccessible to any consciousness, one merely succeeds in denuding the concept of its empirical content and thus of it explanatory power (in Nietzsche's sense; see Chapter 2.2).

It is arguable that the expression 'unconscious idea' can only appear meaningful either if one is really thinking of processes in an assumed material base of the mental, or if, unlike Nietzsche, one uses the term loosely to signify a behavioural disposition, or if one hypothesizes that there is one or more 'hidden consciousness' in an individual, or, alternatively, if one confusedly 'reifies' ideas, thinking of them as objects contained in a receptacle, the 'unconscious'. (Freud encourages the latter confusion through his frequent use of topological metaphors.) But there is perhaps yet a further possible sense in which the expression 'unconscious ideas' may be understood. It may be used as a functional *chiffre* for some entity or process which is in fact unknown in its nature, but which we talk about *as if* it could be assimilated to 'ideas'—thereby rendering the fragmentary data of behaviour and consciousness more coherent and thus 'intelligible' and predictable—without claiming that it ultimately, and literally, can be thus assimilated.[24]

What has been said here about unconscious ideas applies also to the notion of unconscious feelings. The case of unconscious intentions seems perhaps more problematic. It has often been pointed out that a person can be said to be engaged in intentional activity without there always being, either concomitantly or immediately preceding the activity, a conscious episode in his mind of a particular identifiable kind to which the name 'intention' might be applied.

[23] See also Thalberg, 'Freud's Anatomies of the Self', 245.

[24] This agnostic position is suggested by some of Freud's statements: e.g. *An Outline of Psycho-Analysis* (New York, 1949), 106; and *The Interpretation of Dreams* (New York, 1938), 542: 'The unconscious is the true psychic reality; in its inner nature it is just as much unknown to us as the reality of the external world'. At other times, Freud conjectures that the various psychic functions may eventually be reducible to a physicalist paradigm. As should be obvious by now, this option is not open to Nietzsche.

On the other hand, it can also plausibly be maintained that an agent can only be described as engaged in intentional activity at a given moment if, at that moment, he is able to give an account of what he is doing. In other words, being engaged in intentional behaviour (action) implies the accessibility, hence recognizability, of the intended end of the action by the agent at the time of his engagement.

This is, of course, precisely what is denied by the theory of unconscious intentions. According to it, an agent may be said to act, i.e. to behave intentionally, without the end or 'point' of his behaviour being recognizable by, or accessible to, him. On the present interpretation of Nietzsche's remarks which seem to suggest the possibility of strictly unconscious intentional behaviour in this sense, we are of course not entitled to construe this claim as asserting the existence of one or more conscious agents *within* the individual who act 'through' him without his being aware of their agency. But if this reading is ruled out, the theory in question seems again to disappear into the realm of the unintelligible.

Nietzsche, in the passages we are referring to, simply states the claim without elaborating it. If we turn for enlightenment to those who, usually in the Freudian tradition, have argued for the theory at length, we tend to find that it involves, not surprisingly, a dissociation of the concept of intention from any actual or possible experiences of the agent, and its association, instead, with his observable behaviour and with certain external circumstances, which factors, if they jointly form a certain putatively self-evident pattern, are alleged to be sufficient to justify the ascription of an intention to an agent:

Normally he can say 'I am doing so-and-so'. But this is neither necessary nor sufficient. What is crucial is how he goes on with what he is doing at present.[25]

My wife asks me to bring her the scissors from the bedroom. I go to fetch them. But I am thinking of something else and open the drawer absent-mindedly. I ask myself, 'What did I come here for?' and cannot answer [. . . .] I continue to rummage about in the drawer while absorbed in thought. I then sight the scissors, pick them up and take them to my wife. Before I sighted the scissors I did not know what I was doing. Had I been asked I would not have been able to answer. But was I not looking for the

---

[25] Dilman, *Freud and the Mind*, 77. Cf. ibid. 65–6.

scissors all the same? Do not the circumstances give us good reasons for saying that I was?[26]

They clearly do not. The example, which is meant to illustrate the contrary, in fact illustrates our point. Everyone has probably at some time had the momentarily disorienting experience of having forgotten the purpose of the activity he has just been engaged in. At such a moment, even if one absent-mindedly ('mechanically') goes through certain motions, one is literally not performing any *action* (except possibly that of trying to remember what one was doing). It is only when one remembers and thus re-acquires the ability to give an account of one's behaviour that one can again be said to be resuming the previous intentional activity.

Having found good reasons to have doubts about the intelligibility of the construal of unconscious ideas, feelings, and intentions as distinctly *mental* occurrences which are neither present nor immediately accessible to any consciousness, it remains to be asked if there is not another interpretation of Nietzsche's insistent claim that the origins of our actions are unconscious. We have seen that he credits Leibniz with the 'incomparable insight' that there may be states which can properly be called mental while not being conscious. If we turn to what Leibniz actually says, we find, apart from highly disputable a priori arguments,[27] also some rather interesting empirical illustrations of what he means by 'insensible perceptions'. Thus he says that 'habituation causes us not to notice the motion of a mill or waterfall, after we have lived near by for some time.' Also, 'when we are not admonished, so to speak, and warned to pay attention to certain of our present perceptions, we let them pass without reflexion and even without noticing them.'[28] In both cases, it appears incontestable to Leibniz that we do have experiences, yet they do not 'attract our attention and memory' and thus fail to be apperceived by us. Clearly, these perceptions are not examples of unconscious experiences in anything like a strict (Freudian) sense, that is, of mental events which are absolutely inaccessible to con-

---

[26] Dilman, *Freud and the Mind*, 77. Cf. ibid. 70–1.

[27] The 'most conclusive' of these (B. Russell, *The Philosophy of Leibniz* (London, 1937), 156) involves a conception of the mental as always involving an act directed towards an object. We cannot be conscious of every act of perception or thought, because this would require yet another act of perception or thought by which we know the former, and so on *ad infinitum*.

[28] G. W. Leibniz, *New Essays on the Human Understanding*, in G. H. R. Parkinson (ed.), *Philosophical Writings* (London, 1973), 155.

sciousness in ordinary circumstances. Rather, they might be described metaphorically as experiences on the threshold of consciousness; or, in another metaphor, they provide the backdrop against those experiences which we focus our attention on at a given moment. Characteristically, they can always themselves become the objects of full conscious attention whenever we choose to concentrate on them.

Are we, then, to interpret Nietzsche's claims in this rather harmless Leibnizian sense? Is he saying that the intentions, desires, and so forth of the ultimate agents are like those of our own experiences which we do not 'thematize', that is, focus our attention on? While such an interpretation may be tempting, some of the statements cited earlier certainly suggest that he means something stronger than this when he speaks of unconscious experiences. On the other hand, I have already indicated that many of his remarks on this issue are ambiguous. And against those we have discussed so far, there are others which lend themselves to an interpretation according to which there exists a plurality of what one might call centres of consciousness within an individual:

But the most important thing is: [. . .] that wherever we see or suspect motion in the body, we learn to infer, as it were, an accompanying subjective invisible life. Motion is only a symbolism for the eye; it suggests that something has been felt, willed, thought (KGW VII.3.40.21).

Thus there are in man as many 'consciousnesses' as there are beings [. . .] which constitute his body. The special thing about the 'consciousness' which we usually think of as the only one, the intellect, is precisely that it remains protected and secluded from the innumerable multiplicity in the experiences of these many consciousnesses and [. . .] is presented only with a selection of experiences, moreover with experiences that are rendered clear and comprehensible, i.e. *false* [. . .] (KGW VII.3.37.4; cf. KGW VII.2.25.401)

These notes are illuminating in various respects. First, they make it entirely explicit that when Nietzsche speaks of unconscious feeling, willing, and thinking, he means occurrent mental states (a 'subjective invisible life'; cf. WM 619: 'an inner event'), and is not merely offering a behaviourist analysis of the mental.[29] Secondly,

---

[29] In JGB 287, he explicitly contrasts his own account of certain mental states or dispositions with what would now be called a behaviourist analysis. Asking what constitutes 'nobility', he replies: 'it is not his actions which prove [the noble man]— actions [i.e. observable behaviour] are always ambiguous, always unfathomable

they suggest very strongly, unlike the passages quoted earlier, that the real purposes of our actions are unconscious to us in the sense that we are constituted by a plurality of conscious *Wesen*, each of whose intrinsic modes of existence is that of a 'feeling, willing, thinking' consciousness (which appears to perceivers of a certain kind as spatial movement)[30] and whose purposes determine 'our' actions in such a way as to be inaccessible to that ' "consciousness" which we usually think of as the only one'.[31]

Yet, while this construal of unconscious, yet distinctly *mental* states and acts (such as interpreting, perceiving, and intending) is, I believe, an intelligible one, there remains a problem. After all, unconscious motivation was meant to account for the possibility of a person's sincerely avowing certain desires and intentions, particularly in purportedly non-self-interested actions, while being unaware of the quite different real purpose of the action in question, i.e. being unconscious of the real nature of the action itself. More specifically, Nietzsche's thesis was that the ultimate end of any action is the 'feeling of power', irrespective of whether the agent herself is aware of this in every case.

But if the determining antecedents of our actions are indeed unconscious in any of the strong senses discussed so far, it is unclear what could be the evidence for such a thesis. Observable behaviour

---

[. . . .] It is not the works, it is the *faith* which is decisive here [. . .], to adopt an old religious formula in a new and more profound sense: some basic certainty which the noble soul has about itself [. . .]'. Nietzsche's point here anticipates more recent criticisms of behaviourist analyses of the mental. It seems impossible to provide an account of, for example, purposeful behaviour or belief, in terms of a finite set of statements about externally observable behaviour which would succeed in capturing what we are saying when ascribing purposes and beliefs. See Taylor, *The Explanation of Behaviour* (esp. 76–82) and H. H. Price, *Belief* (London, 1969) (esp. 250–66).

[30] Cf. also KGW VII.3.37.4.

[31] Figl has urged that Nietzsche's ascription of consciousness to those ultimate agents which jointly constitute an individual 'should not mislead us into supposing that these [. . .] beings have consciousness and intellect in the proper [*eigentlich*] sense of the word. They are pre-conscious and also supra-conscious [. . .]' (Figl, *Interpretation als philosophisches Prinzip*, 129). I am not sure what exactly is meant by 'pre-conscious' and 'supra-conscious' here, but it is true that Nietzsche remarks that the 'willing, feeling, thinking' characteristic of the ultimate agents which are the real 'force' behind our actions is not entirely of the same kind as their corresponding phenomena detectable in self-consciousness, but only, to an unspecified degree, analogous to them—'a primitive form of those' (KGW VII.3.40.37). However, if Figl means to say that the ultimate agents are, strictly speaking, not conscious at all, we are again saddled with all the conceptual problems we have discussed above.

by itself clearly cannot validate it (Nietzsche implicitly acknowledges this by never drawing merely on externally observable behaviour as evidence); physiological evidence—in the traditional,
rather than the Nietzschean, sense of 'physiology'—is neither available nor is it clear how it could, even in principle, establish a thesis
of the kind he is suggesting. What is more, Nietzsche would dismiss
it as no more genuinely explanatory than the theories of physics. It
might therefore appear that his psychological theory of the will to
power is either purely speculative, or that it is asserted to be 'true'
in a novel sense in which evidence and the future course of our
experience are simply irrelevant to the 'truth' of a statement. For
example, it might be claimed that when Nietzsche says that all
'drives are reducible to the will to power' (KGW VII.3.40.61) he is
merely saying that thinking this proposition is associated with what
appears to him to be an enhanced feeling of power and that this is
what it *means*, for him, to say that it is 'true'. I have already
suggested that a reading of this sort is highly unattractive, both
from a philosophical and from a textual point of view.

Philosophically, it would entail that none of Nietzsche's apparent
criticisms of the inadequacies of various traditional accounts of
human action are really criticisms at all—they would merely
amount to rejecting the traditional question concerning an adequate, or even a relatively more adequate, account of action. From
a textual point of view, it is very conspicuous that just as Nietzsche
is concerned to undermine, in one very specific sense, the distinction
between 'text' (that is, subject-independent, non-perspectival, facts)
and 'interpretation', so he insistently *emphasizes* the importance of
a distinction between 'facts' and 'interpretation' in 'inner experience'. The very least that is implied by this is that, for him, there is
some reality in the sphere which we ordinarily refer to as the mental
which our explicit, propositional interpretations are *of* and of
which they are sometimes true and, more often, false (see e.g. WM
229; KGW VII.3.38.1; GD, 'The four great errors', 6). This
strongly suggests that an interpretation of, say, a desire which,
when entertained, is associated with a feeling of power, is not
thereby 'true'. Otherwise, *every* interpretation of our desires which
makes us feel good would be 'true'. To the extent that Nietzsche
himself is concerned with saying something rather different and
more interesting about mental states—as he clearly is, if we take his
explicit statements seriously—he cannot simply ignore questions of

validation and evidence. And, not surprisingly, we find that he is very much occupied by, and troubled by, them:

There are no immediate facts! It is the same with feelings and thoughts: in becoming *conscious* of them, I am making an excerpt, a simplification, an attempt to organize: *becoming conscious is just this*: a very *active making up*.

How do you know this?—

we are aware of the *labour* when we want to grasp a thought, a feeling clearly—with the aid of *comparison* [. . . .] A thought and a feeling are signs of processes of some kind [. . .] (KGW VII.2.26.114)

In this highly revealing fragment, a persistent dilemma of Nietzsche's is condensed in a few sentences. His conjecture, in *some* passages, that fully explicit, conceptualized, and propositionally structured self-consciousness does not put us into contact with ultimate facts—because in 'grasp[ing] a thought, a feeling clearly' we 'simplify' the data—confronts him with the question: '*how* do you know this?'. His reply here, however self-contradictory it may seem in the light of the first paragraph of the note cited, is characteristic of his general 'method'—it is, in the end, a Cartesian appeal to qualitative contents that can be discovered introspectively: he maintains that conceptualized, 'clear' self-consciousness involves an active organization of material *on the evidence that we are conscious of the labour* we are performing when attempting to get a mental item into conceptual focus. This answer implies, of course, that Nietzsche does in the end accept, in spite of occasional statements which appear to say the contrary, that it *is* possible to grasp the general nature of certain 'facts of consciousness' broadly correctly (in this case, the experience of effort or labour).

In fact, throughout Nietzsche's later writings, and alongside his denials of 'immediate facts' of consciousness, we find statements in which he appears to admit that it is possible, at least for some people ('good philologists') at some times, to 'read off' the facts of consciousness without 'interposing an interpretation':

'I feel unwell'—such a judgement presupposes a great and late neutrality of the observer—; the simple man always says: this or that makes me feel unwell—he makes up his mind about his feeling unwell only when he has seen a reason for feeling unwell.—I call that a *lack of philology*; to be able to read off a text as a text without interposing an interpretation is the last-developed form of 'inner experience'—perhaps one that is hardly possible— (WM 479)

Referring to the first lines of a famous poem by Heinrich Heine, he makes the same point more concisely and decisively: 'The *fact* is "that I am so sad"; the problem "I do not know what it means . . ." [. . .]' (KGW VIII.3.15.84; cf. also WM 229). The distinction drawn here within an emotional state between a factual aspect ('being sad', 'feeling unwell') and a (usually unwarranted) *interpretation* of this fact as having been *caused by* some 'intentional object' present to the individual's awareness (the object of his emotion, e.g. a 'sinful act which I committed yesterday') recurs throughout the writings of the last period (e.g. GD, 'The four great errors', 4; GM iii.16; KGW VII.3.38.1; KGW VIII.2.15.84). It is a *fact* that a person feels 'unwell'; she *interprets* this fact as a particular emotion, for example as the emotion of guilt which has as its intentional object a 'sinful deed' committed by her. In other words, she interprets her belief that she performed a certain action and that that action was sinful as the causal antecedent of her feelings, and it is only *through* this interpretation that her state can acquire the character of the emotion of guilt.[32]

In WM 479, cited above, Nietzsche implausibly contrasts 'read[ing] off a text' and 'interpretation' as being mutually exclusive. But in many passages, he does not oppose interpretation and 'reading a text' (or 'the facts') in this manner, but rather suggests, more convincingly, that there may be true or false interpretations of the facts of 'inner experience'. While he occasionally surmises in the *Nachlass* that the real causes (hence the real nature) of our emotional and affective states are entirely unknowable by us (e.g. KGW VII.3.34.46)—which implies that *any* interpretation of them in terms of their causal antecedents is equally speculative and conjectural—his attitude frequently is less agnostic. He often says, for example, that the causal interpretations that we typically give of our mental states—especially moral or religious interpretations of the kind exemplified above—are in fact *false* (WM 229; KGW VII.3.38.1; GD, 'The four great errors', 6). The real causes,

---

[32] For an analysis of the difference between feelings and emotions, and of the relation between emotions and their objects, see W. Lyons, *Emotion* (Cambridge, 1980), 6–8, 99 f., 133, 138. One of Nietzsche's own examples for the factual aspect of an emotion—'feeling sad'—is, on Lyons's criteria, badly chosen. 'Feeling sad' refers to a full-blown emotional state, i.e. a state which involves a judgement by an individual about an 'object' and the belief, on the part of that individual, that it is some property correctly attributed in this judgement to the 'object' which is the cause of his present state (e.g. 'I feel sad, because I was betrayed by an old friend').

while 'not yet statable with precision' (GM iii.16), are rather 'physiological' ones (WM 229; KGW VII.3.38.1; GM iii.15, 17).

The basic 'physiological' properties which determine our conscious states 'remain partly unconscious, and [partly] become conscious as *drives*' (KGW VII.2.27.27). The general nature of these drives, Nietzsche suggests in various places, *is* accessible to attentive self-reflection. How else, indeed, are we to understand his claim, reiterated and applied time and again, that exposing the psychological 'falsity' of various traditional accounts of the 'moral' requires good 'philology' and 'most subtle observation'? He proposes, in short, that 'nothing else is "given" as real than our world of appetites and passions, that we cannot get up or down to any other "reality" than the reality of our drives' (JGB 36). The parallel passages in the *Nachlass* read:

Motions are symptoms, thoughts are equally symptoms: the appetites are detectable[!] behind both, and the basic appetite is the will to power. (KGW VIII.1.1.59)

Our drives are reducible to the will to power. The will to power is the ultimate fact[!] that we reach down to. (KGW VII.3.40.61; also KGW VIII.1.2.88)

According to these statements, it is indeed possible to discover 'facts' in our interpretions of inner experience, or at least to grasp through them the general character of an aspect of reality which is sufficiently analogous to the agencies responsible for most of our conscious mental states and our actions to be rightly used as a guide towards their nature. This does not mean that all the moving agencies ('motives') behind our actions are conscious. However, what it does imply, in Nietzsche's view, is that we can only understand the agencies behind those instances of our behaviour whose origins are strictly inaccessible to consciousness—i.e. the majority—as *similar* to those 'drives' or 'appetites' which are ' "given" as real' in self-consciousness, and all of the latter are variations of the will to power.

While this interpretation of Nietzsche's remarks on the so-called facts of consciousness in terms of a cautious and qualified Cartesianism is not compatible with all of his statements, it is compatible with most. It is also, I think, the only reading which can save the psychological analyses that make up so much of his work from the charge of either being entirely arbitrary and speculative, or expressing predilections on Nietzsche's part, and hence simply failing to engage rival accounts of human experience and action in a philosophical-critical sense altogether. If the present reading is accepted, then the accessibility of the will to power in self-consciousness can be seen as the fulcrum on which Nietzsche ultimately rests the philosophical levers in his attempt to dislodge the metaphysical enterprise from its traditional position of pre-eminence. What is more, it enables us to understand what has often remained a mystery to his readers: the rationale or point of his philosophical and psychological *tour de force*.

3. SELF-DECEPTION AND THE CHRISTIAN IDEAL

> In every philosophy there comes a point where the philosopher's 'conviction' appears on the scene: or, to put it in the language of an ancient mystery:
> *adventavit asinus*
> *pulcher et fortissimus.*
>
> (JGB 5)

One consequence of the claim that 'nothing else is "given" as real' in inner experience than the will to power is that those who assert the existence of emotions, desires, and intentions with intentional objects of a different sort, far from being misled by the phenomenology of experience, deceive either others or themselves. The genuine 'priests' and believers of the various religious and ethical creeds—Nietzsche of course has again particularly Christianity in mind—are not innocently mistaken; they are in some sense self-deceived.[33] They characteristically do 'not *want* [. . .] to know what is true' about themselves (AC 52): 'I call lie: *not* wanting to see what one does see[!], not wanting to see it *as* what one sees it. The most common lie is the one with which one lies to oneself' (AC 55). Let us not dwell here on the relatively unimportant point of whether Nietzsche is justified in extending the concept of lying to cover self-deception also. It is clear that he can only do so by ignoring an aspect of self-deception on which he is quite emphatic

---

[33] The claim that the Christian ethos in particular involves self-deception is stated explicitly in many places, e.g. GM i.13 ('sublime self-deception') and GM i.14. More generally, self-deception is (logically) involved in all *ressentiment* attitudes. It is evidently impossible to state Nietzsche's *ressentiment* hypothesis without a concept of self-deception (see Ch. 3.2).

in other passages (e.g. GM iii.19), namely the aspect of sincerity which distinguishes it from ordinary lying. It is a rather more interesting and important question whether his analysis is a plausible one. This may best be examined with reference to the central case of self-deception as diagnosed by him—that of the 'good Christian'.

A prominent place in the Christian's conception of virtue is occupied by the idea of humility—the enjoinder to have little self-regard or pride, to think little of oneself, not to impose one's will on others, not to exact revenge for offences committed against oneself. Indeed, the Christian is asked to go beyond *humilitas* and show *caritas* even to those who offend against him (to 'love his enemies'), as indeed to anyone, but especially to the suffering and oppressed. On his own testimony, the Christian does this not for his own sake—the object of his desires is not the realization of certain possible experiences to be had by himself—nor for the sake of the other person in an unqualified sense (for no human being, due to man's creaturely, imperfect nature, is to be loved *qua human being* without qualifications), but, ultimately, for the sake of the perfectly good, all-powerful, ultimately real Deity.[34] On one doctrinal variant, the good Christian 'universalizes' his love of man because, and in so far as, every human being is the creation of God and participates in an imperfect degree in His goodness. In another (Lutheran) version of Christianity, the genuine believer loves other human beings (although there is nothing at all in them which makes them deserving of love) because he is filled by God's grace—God literally acts through him and gratuitously bestows His love on human beings.

For Nietzsche, such self-interpretations are either simply mendacious or else involve self-deception. His alternative analysis of the Christian's actions and of the emotional states giving rise to them ('love') starts from the assumption that 'sincere' (i.e. self-deceived) Christianity is to be found, at least 'originally', only with individuals who are weak or powerless. As his examples make clear, the senses of 'weakness' relevant here are the first two mentioned in Chapter 3.2—what he calls physical ill-constitutedness and/or the property of being a member of the 'lower orders' in a society dominated by an aristocratic ruling class espousing the (Homeric or

---

[34] Thomas Aquinas, *Summa Theologiae*, Ia IIae, 2. 7. Also: Augustine, *The City of God* (London, 1945), xix. 1.

Roman) virtues of excellence. Thus he says that Christianity originated from 'the instincts of the subjugated and oppressed—originally from the lower social orders of a subjugated people: it is the lowest orders who look for their salvation in it' (AC 21). In one sense, the 'self-denying' virtues of Christianity are simply the rules of prudence of the physically or socially powerless:

we, the weak, cannot help being weak; it is good if we do nothing *for which we are not strong enough*; but this bitter fact, this prudential rule of the lowest rank [. . .] has arrayed itself in the splendour of [. . .] virtue, as if the weakness of the weak were [. . .] a voluntary achievement [. . .], a *merit* [. . .] (GM i.13)

The Christians self-deceivingly interpret their powerless passivity in the face of violence as self-denying 'righteousness', indeed as 'love', and their prudent submission to those who are more powerful as voluntary submission, not to their actual superiors, but to a purportedly supremely powerful authority whose 'children' they regard themselves as and whom they call God.[35] This authority, they say, enjoins charity and humility on them. In fact, Nietzsche replies, by glorifying a God who allegedly demands of them precisely those 'virtues' which they are alone capable of exercising, they merely attempt to elevate themselves, His 'elect' (AC 44).

The Christian's 'love' of God, for the sake of whom he claims to be acting, is analysed by Nietzsche as being analogous to one of two types of erotic love among humans, while *eros* itself is accounted for in terms of the striving for the 'feeling of power'. Erotic love, for

---

[35] Nietzsche's account here of the Christian virtues of self-denial as being prudential rules enabling the 'weak and oppressed of any sort' to preserve and to *affirm* themselves (GM i.13)—to believe in their own worth—stands in a relation of tension to some of his claims in the second essay in *Zur Genealogie der Moral* (GM ii.16–22). He argues there that an instinct towards cruelty, allegedly inherent in humans, turns inward when the individual is prevented from discharging it onto outer objects, and becomes a desire to torment *oneself*. Thus, the 'will towards self-torture constitutes the presupposition for the value of the unegoistic', of 'selflessness, self-denial, self-sacrifice' (GM ii.18). The apogee of this will to self-torture is reached in Christianity where, supposedly, nature—and hence the individual himself, also—is regarded as 'worthless as such' (GM ii.20). It is evident that this conflicts with the above account of Christian virtues as 'prudential' and as designed to make possible the 'self-affirmation' of the weak. The two views are, however, not necessarily contradictory, since they may be intended to apply to different types of Christian believers. Since the genuinely self-tormenting type is arguably rare by comparison, and since the 'prudential' account both preponderates in Nietzsche's writings and has had a far wider influence on subsequent writers as well as on popular notions, I shall concentrate largely on it.

Nietzsche, is or entails frequently a desire to possess another person, to dominate her and to 'shape' her according to one's own wishes. This 'strong' and characteristically masculine form of love is an expression of the will to power in a very obvious sense. However, there is another form of love—characteristic of the weak, especially of women—which submits to the superior strength of another and which finds its happiness in obedience and devotion to him: 'A man's happiness is called: I will. A woman's happiness is called: he wills' (Z 81/92). The ultimate aim of this form of *eros* is also (the experience of) power, which, however, in the case of a weak individual, can only be attained vicariously through identification with a more powerful will. As Nietzsche puts it in *Also sprach Zarathustra*:

Wherever I found living things, there I found the will to power, and even in the will of the servant I found the will to be master. That the weaker one should serve the stronger, unto this persuaded him his will, who wills to be master over yet weaker ones [. . . .] And where there is sacrifice and service and looks of love: there, too, is the will to be master. On furtive paths the weaker steals into the castle and into the heart of the powerful—and there steals power. (Z 143–4/137–8; cf. MR 145)

It is not difficult to think of analogues to this 'feminine' attachment of a weaker to a stronger will, agent, or authority for the purpose of an indirect enjoyment of power through an identification with, or assimilation to, it. One example—not used by Nietzsche himself—that suggests itself in this context is a certain type of nationalism, an attachment to one's nation in which the real or imagined importance and power of the latter is identified with by the individual, who experiences a sense of personal power and grandeur through assimilating himself in this manner to 'something greater'.

We encountered another such analogue, much more central to Nietzsche's thought, in Chapters 3.2 and 4.4. It consists in the sense, characteristic of the devotees of the 'ascetic ideal', that the nature of reality in itself calls for, or provides a legitimation of or authority for, some practices or pursuits, or some modes of life, privileging and rendering them superior over others. We referred to this basic psychological phenomenon as the 'self-assimilation to reality', a tendency which, according to Nietzsche, is associated for a certain type of individual with an increased feeling of power:

'whoever is incapable of laying his will into things [. . .] at least lays some *meaning* into them, i.e. the belief that there is a will in them already [. . . .] The philosophical objective outlook can therefore be a sign that will and strength are small' (WM 585 A).

Returning to Nietzsche's analysis of the Christian mentality, we may want to know in what way the specific Christian doctrines give rise to experiences of power in the believer and are believed— unavowedly, to be sure—for this reason. His answer here is complex. First, and most importantly, the Christian expects 'eternal beatitude' in the life to come, as an extravagant recompense for his sufferings in this world. This expectation of beatitude is essentially one of pleasure (WM 221). The Christian notion of a *contemplatio Dei*—the ultimate end of man, the 'complete good which satisfies his desire altogether'[36]—is analysed by Nietzsche as comprising two elements. On the one hand, there is the 'hypnotic feeling of nothingness', the 'liberation from any goal, any wish, any activity' and the absence of pain (GM iii.17). When Christian moralists and metaphysicians speak of the unchanging vision of God in paradise, they have in fact no real positive conception at all, but a purely negative one: 'all pessimistic religions call nothingness God' (ibid.). In this respect, Christian beatitude is like Schopenhauer's 'pleasure', a state characterized negatively as the absence of pain. However, unlike Schopenhauerian pleasure, beatitude is supposed to be a changeless ('eternal') state from which all *desire* for change is absent and which is therefore, in a sense, a condition of final rest. As we saw in Chapter 3.2, this conception of 'happiness' is one of the characteristics of the ascetic ideal in general—it is also typically found among individuals who avowedly desire truth 'for its own sake'.

Why does Nietzsche analyse the *contemplatio Dei* as a purely negative notion and the aspiration towards what it refers to as a desire for 'nothingness'? After all, traditional theology has generally ascribed various positive characteristics to God—if only by analogy—and has described beatitude as the unchanging contemplative 'grasping' of these. Not only would this contemplative state thus seem to have a positive quasi-perceptual intuitive content, it also has certain apparently positive affective features, namely the 'love' which supervenes upon the contemplative act.

[36] Aquinas, *Summa Theologiae*, Ia IIae, 2. 8.

The reason why the *contemplatio Dei* has traditionally been conceived as an 'unchanging' state by philosophical theology is not difficult to discern. It lies in the conceptual necessity that the souls of the blessed, if indeed they *are* blessed, cannot *desire* any change in their state. For every desire for such a change presupposes an experienced lack or deficiency in one's present condition. If beatitude is indeed the 'complete good', no such desire can arise here. (This does not by itself imply that the blessed state cannot consist in a certain kind of activity or process, but this activity would have to be entirely uniform and hence, in the sense relevant here, an unchanging and 'static' condition of 'rest'—the traditional image for it is the motion of the planets, which was taken to be circular and uniform.)

In order to understand why Nietzsche denies that any positive specification of the content of the *contemplatio Dei* can be given, we need to recall Schopenhauer's contention—which Nietzsche continues to accept—that we are utterly unable concretely to envisage any state which 'so [...] fulfil[s] a man's whole desire that nothing is left beside for him to desire'.[37] Whichever concretely imaginable positive specification of the good we may care to adduce—be it sensual pleasure, or aesthetic contemplation, or the enjoyment of friendship, or whatever—we can see upon reflection that none of the states in which these ostensible goods are realized is such that no desire for change would eventually arise in us. Humans cannot conceive of any positive good the unchanging possession of which would not eventually terminate in boredom and in a desire for change. Consequently, no positive characterization of the Christian 'beatific vision' can be given.[38]

---

[37] Aquinas, *Summa Theologiae*, Ia IIae, 1. 5.

[38] Christian philosophers and writers have, of course, tended to acknowledge that, in this life, we can have no *adequate* positive conception of the beatitude promised to the faithful. But they have traditionally attributed this incapacity to the imperfections of the human mind and have usually suggested that there are at least imperfect and temporally limited intimations in this life of the beatitude to come. For Dante, his encounter with Beatrice was such an intimation. As the pilgrim's journey in Dante's *Paradiso* illustrates, human nature has to undergo a transfiguration, a process of 'perfection', in order even to understand in a non-analogical way what the blessed state might be. Schopenhauer, on the other hand, refers to the *Paradiso* as an example precisely illustrating our total inability to imagine an unchanging state of complete 'happiness', and therefore rejects that notion altogether (Schopenhauer, *The World as Will and Representation*, chs. 58 and 59, esp. p. 325). The radical point of Schopenhauer's 'pessimism' is not just that we cannot *get* what we ultimately want, but that we have not even the slightest idea of anything we might 'ultimately' want while yet desiring for there to be such a thing.

According to Nietzsche, a conception of 'happiness' which, however confusedly, thinks of the latter as a 'coming to rest' (GM iii.17), a static condition in which all pain, desire, and change are absent, is symptomatic of ill-constituted, suffering, and oppressed individuals. Only to them can such a vision spontaneously appear as the most desirable end, the *summum bonum* (cf. Chapter 3.2). But he insists that the desire for pleasure in this sense is nevertheless a special case of the will to power. It is the confused articulation of the will to power of those who are too weak to hope for anything beyond deliverance, or 'salvation', from suffering. For a healthy and well-constituted individual, the prospect of eternal Christian 'beatitude' merely evokes a sense of utmost tedium.[39]

There is a second element in the Christian conception of ultimate happiness in which the will to power is more clearly recognizable. The Christian envisages the judgement of the unrepentant sinners— of those who refuse to embrace his faith and his 'virtues' of weakness—and their consignment to the eternal punishment of hell. The ostensible belief in God's justice is in fact an expression of the desire for revenge against the strong, and the expectation of happiness is, in its positive aspect, the expectation of seeing one's enemies and oppressors suffer through the divine power with which the Christian identifies himself. Any positive conception of happiness or pleasure we have consists, we recall, according to Nietzsche in the perception of a difference in power, in a more or less subtle form of enjoyment of superiority. As evidence for his exposure of the ostensible Christian belief in divine justice as an expression of a disguised desire for revenge on an 'other', and hence as a paradigm case of *ressentiment* (cf. Chapter 3.2), he quotes Aquinas's remark on the blessed souls in heaven: '*Beati in regno coelesti [. . .] videbunt poenas damnatorum, ut beatitudo illis magis complaceat*' (GM i.15).[40]

It should not be forgotten that he also stresses the various ways in which the Christian without admitting it seeks the experience of power in *this* world—for example, through attempting to induce a sense of guilt in the strong and 'noble', or through exhibiting the

[39] Cf. J. de Gaultier, *From Kant to Nietzsche* (New York, 1961), 166: 'The secret sensibility of human nature rejects the insipidity of that perfect felicity.' Also Kaufmann, *Nietzsche*, 238: 'The question is whether, as long as we retain our human nature, a perfectly painless "heaven" would seem like a heaven to us—or whether such an abode would only be a subtle version of hell.'

[40] 'The blessed in the heavenly kingdom will see the punishments of the damned, so that their beatitude may be even more pleasing to them.'

condescending 'compassion' of the superior for those who are not 'saved' like himself, or simply through feeling, or wanting to feel, more 'righteous', i.e. better, than the 'unregenerate sinners'. Our reconstruction of Nietzsche's analysis of Christian 'otherworldliness', brief though it is, may suffice to convey his essential point. The 'love of God' is not a desire cardinally distinct from ordinary self-directed ones that are reducible to the desire for the experience of power. Rather, it is a self-deceptive cloak over the prudent obedience to a power who, the Christian hopes, will 'in another world' procure the gratifications of his self-directed desires, a gratification which he is unable to attain for himself in this world (cf. KGW VIII.2.10.200). For Nietzsche, we may surmise, the true nature of Christian belief is expressed in the reflections of the theological utilitarians who asserted bluntly that the motive behind so-called moral actions such as keeping one's word is 'the expectation of being after this life rewarded, if I do, or punished for it, if I do not [. . . .] Therefore private happiness is our motive, and the will of God our rule.'[41]

Nietzsche's analysis has had a wide popular influence far beyond those who would consider themselves Nietzscheans in any other respect, and it can be encountered, though not always in as explicit and undiluted a form, in many anti-religious writings. In assessing its plausibility, I shall confine myself to three salient problems it raises.

To begin with, the description of one aspect of the Christian desire for beatitude as a longing for a state of rest from which pain is absent appears to conflict with Nietzsche's claim that the will to power, defined as a striving or tendency towards the experience of power, is the 'ultimate fact we reach down to' in inner experience, the sole 'given' reality in the appetitive part of our nature. That description seems to amount to the acknowledgement that there is in fact at the phenomenological level a genuine desire for a state which is not characterized by the individual's awareness of a favourable difference of strength or power between himself and an opponent or obstacle. To be sure, Nietzsche *interprets* this desire

---

[41] W. Paley, *The Principles of Moral and Political Philosophy*, in L. A. Selby-Bigge (ed.), *British Moralists* (Oxford, 1897), vol. ii, para. 1020. There is obviously a contrast between this and the corresponding statements, say, by Augustine or Aquinas. For Nietzsche, the real meaning of their reflections is identical with that of Paley's, yet, unlike Paley's, veiled by self-deception.

as symptomatic of a certain kind of subject with a weak will to power (e.g. WM 703, GM iii.17). But since this interpretation seems to go beyond what is ' "given" as real' in inner experience cleansed of self-deception, it could be argued to be, by virtue of his own strictures on interpretation in this context (see WM 479), as speculative and unsubstantiable as any alternative interpretation.

Nietzsche could meet this objection in two ways. He could, first, limit the scope of his account of human desires and actions, in terms of a striving for the experience of power, to those desires and actions which, at the phenomenological level, are presented to a given agent as of particularly great importance, taking precedence for him or her over other desires and other possible courses of action. This qualification would permit Nietzsche to concede that there may indeed be human desires which may be experienced by a non-self-deceived subject—by a 'good philologist' capable of the 'most subtle observation'—as not having as their generic object the experience of power, while still maintaining that such desires are invariably of relatively minor importance to the individual in question. He could then argue that the believer's desire for beatitude is of this kind, and that it can be recognized as such by the believer.

If the Nietzschean account of human experience is to command any plausibility, some distinction of this kind would appear to be essential. For while at least the great majority of desires are susceptible to *some* description which would be compatible with his analysis in terms of a striving for the feeling of power—due to the very breadth of his definition of the will to power—it seems clear that in many cases this is not the kind of description we would choose to give of our desires, even when genuinely attending, with Nietzschean honesty (*Redlichkeit*), to their phenomenal nature. A person's desire to indulge in an elaborate meal at an expensive restaurant may be described as a desire to impress his friends with his good taste or his wealth, or as a desire to replenish his physical strength for the tasks ahead of him, but it seems hardly contestable that in at least some instances the honest description given by the agent himself will simply be that he desires a certain kind of sensation on his palate. Nietzsche could arguably accommodate such instances by maintaining that such desires, when the individual attends to them, are recognizable as of comparatively lesser

significance to him or her and that, by contrast, those desires which
are genuinely of great importance to the individual *can* be characterized in terms of the will to power.

But it is doubtful whether the Christian's desire for beatitude
through the contemplation of the divine essence would, were he
asked to perform such a test, fall into the first of these categories.
For, surely, the *unio mystica*—for Nietzsche, the contemplation of
'nothingness' (GM iii.17), a final state of rest free of pain and
further desire—*is* central to the Christian's aspirations. This means
that Nietzsche's account of inner experience can only be rendered
consistent with the presence of a desire for such a state if it can be
shown that its more precise description does indeed involve a
'comparison' of the sort required by that account. He would have
to argue that the Christian, in desiring the *unio mystica*, does not
actually envisage that state *per se* (in isolation, as it were), but
rather that (contrary to what the Christian claims), his envisaging
of it includes *essentially* an awareness of those unsatisfactory
worldly conditions which it is expected to supersede. In other
words, it is only desired because it is imagined *in contrast* to that
unsatisfactory reality of 'life' which the Christian experiences as
oppressive. It is desired not, as is claimed, for and *as* what it is itself,
but rather '*as* [. . .] a liberation, *as* a getting away from [. . .]' (ibid.,
my emphases) the overpowering forces of 'life'. An awareness of the
latter thus has to be present in any occurrent desire for Christian
beatitude. (The Christian's confusion—apart from not explicitly
recognizing or not admitting to himself the relational character of
the object of his desire—would then lie in supposing that in that
state of 'liberation', once attained, no further desires would arise.)
Nietzsche's own formulations, elusive as they are, provide some
confirmation for such a reading of his view, and if it is interpreted
in this way it is, I believe, consistent with his general analysis of
human desire.

A second problem in Nietzsche's analysis of the Christian ideal as
based on self-deception is the ostensibly empirical claim providing
its point of departure. According to it, that ideal and its conception
of virtue 'originate' among the physically or socially weak and
powerless. If by this is meant that it is only to be found among
individuals of whom this description might be thought appropriate,
it is subject to many prima facie counter-examples. To name but
one, Francis of Assisi was a scion of a wealthy and powerful family

and appears to have been, according to the sources, what Nietzsche would probably call physiologically well-constituted. It is of course possible that the sources are misleading, or that there was some 'physiological' defect in him which we do not know about. But there is absolutely no evidence of this.

But if, as many remarks indicate (e.g. JGB 199), Nietzsche's claim is rather that, while the Christian ideal *originates* with the weak, it may eventually also infect ('convert') the strong, and that it has done so in Europe, a new problem arises. The type of Christian mentality we might find among them would presumably have to be—drawing on our earlier distinction—of the self-tormenting rather than the prudential kind. But if one looks at Nietzsche's genealogy of such self-torment, in the form of a sense of guilt (*schlechtes Gewissen*), it is quite clear from his exposition that it also originates among the subjugated and oppressed (GM ii.17). It represents the turning inward of all the aggressive instincts whose outward discharge has been prevented through the creation of the state and its system of laws and punishments (GM ii.16). But the cage of the state itself is supposed to be the product of the violent subjugation of some 'amorphous, [. . .] nomadic population' by a 'race of masters and conquerors', that is, by individuals whom Nietzsche would call strong. It is they who create that 'terrible tyranny', that 'oppressive and ruthless machinery' which enforces the turning inward of the aggressive instincts of the subjugated populace. It is mysterious how such internalization could occur among strong individuals, for they do not, according to Nietzsche, possess the cautious and prudent disposition—the propensity towards self-preservation—which might prevent them from discharging their instincts against external opponents, even if there *were* opponents powerful and overbearing enough to render such internalization expedient to more prudent (i.e. weaker) individuals.

Alternatively, Nietzsche might argue that those apparent followers of the Christian ideal to whom his socio-physiological analysis does not seem to apply—such as St Francis—did not in fact embody that ideal in its pure form, but rather in an adulterated, 'paganized' version, or even transformed that ideal altogether as, according to him, the princes of the Renaissance church did. If this hypothetical rejoinder suggests that the ethos of a figure like St Francis was, either consciously or unknown to him, different from an ethos which can also be found in the main texts of the Christian tradition and their interpreters, then it would require evidential support, which Nietzsche fails to provide.

A third difficulty, and probably the most important, of Nietzsche's analysis is connected with his concept of self-deception. According to it, human beings have, as a matter of fact, only desires of the sort that have traditionally been characterized as 'self-interested'. Nietzsche, as we saw, also refers to them as 'passions' or 'appetites' and subsumes them under the generic concept of the will to power. The Christian deceives himself and others into be-lieving that there are desires other than those for the experience of power, namely desires that are directed towards—have as their intentional object—a reality external to, and ontologically inde-pendent of, the individual and her experiences, which reality is allegedly apprehended as being good or to be loved in itself, *irre-spective* of any relation it may stand in to the particular individual making this judgement. According to this self-deceptive belief, the 'happiness' of the individual experiencing desires of this kind is not itself their intentional object, but is, as it were, an indirect result of the recognition by her of an 'other'—of an independently real good and of the love of it 'for its own sake'. (Defenders of this view sometimes point out that this phenomenon is neither rare nor confined to what is conventionally regarded as the religious sphere. They argue that there are many kinds of 'happiness' which are only attainable by a subject if they are not *intended* in the subject's desires and actions—if they do not constitute the *objects* of her desires and actions.)

The crucial question raised by Nietzsche's account is this. Can self-deception of the sort he imputes actually occur if the subject to whom it is imputed does not ever really (non-self-deceivedly) have desires of the kind it self-deceivedly interprets itself as having on a particular occasion? It is difficult to reject the observation that, in order to deceive myself (rather than merely to deceive *others*) about the nature of my desires or emotional states, it is a necessary condition that I have, at some stage, really (non-self-deceivedly) experienced the desire or emotional state I wrongly ascribe to myself in the act of self-deception. But this would seem to be ruled out by Nietzsche's monistic anthropology, according to which 'nothing else is "given" as real than our world of appetites and passions' (JGB 36), and all of these 'are reducible to the will to power' (KGW VII.3.40.61).

Consider the following example. A man *a* has recently acquired a great amount of money through successful speculations. Since then, his old friend *b* has taken a noticeable dislike to him. Those who are well-acquainted with *b*'s character from his past utterances and actions suspect that *b*'s sudden dislike of *a* is due to his being envious of *a*. But *b* protests that he by no means begrudges *a* his newly acquired wealth, but that he is appalled by what he considers the dishonourable manner in which it has been gained. He insists that the kind of speculations *a* has engaged in, though not illegal, are immoral and reprehensible, since they involved as a necessary corollary of their success the impoverishment of others.

What is involved in the claim that *b* is self-deceived about his motives, and that the real motive of his dislike is envy? Let us assume that he does not really believe in the 'immorality', in the required sense, of any action at all. He does not really understand what people mean when they talk of good or bad actions other than in the sense of their being conducive or disadvantageous to the satisfaction of whatever happen to be the agent's self-interested desires at any given time. It would appear that, given the limits of *b*'s comprehension (or experience), it is impossible that he should genuinely deceive himself into believing that he disapproves of *a*'s actions because of their putative immorality—the latter being defined without reference to self-directed, 'egoistic' desires. Yet this is precisely what Nietzsche's analysis asks us to accept. Human beings are constituted in such a way as to experience exclusively desires which fall under the general description of the will to power, yet some of them *pretend* to themselves (not merely to others) to have, sometimes, desires of a cardinally different kind. The dubiously coherent nature of this theory becomes starkly apparent in a very interesting and pertinent passage from the *Nachlass*:

If the suffering, oppressed individual *lost the belief* to have a *right* for his contempt for the will to power, he would enter the state of hopeless despair. This would be the case if this trait were essential to life, if it turned out that even that 'will to morality' is only this 'will to power' in disguise, that even that hatred and contempt [for the will to power] is still a will to power. The oppressed person would [then] realize that he stands *on the same ground* as the oppressor. (KGW VIII.1.5.71)

Here Nietzsche implies, quite in keeping with his general position as we have outlined it above, that the belief in 'moral', that is, not self-directed, motives/desires, such as *caritas* or the desire for justice or the Kantian motive of 'respect' for some purely formal 'moral law'—e.g. the principle, which Kant thought constitutive of morality, to 'act only according to a maxim which you can will at the same time to become a universal law'—is a characteristic result of the need of the wretched and oppressed to feel in some manner superior to those who oppress them. If they realized that all desires are essentially homogeneous, and that they consequently have no 'right' to despise the will to power, they would despair.

One problem with this genealogical account is that the invention of a spurious (self-deceived) 'morality' could only have fulfilled its alleged real purpose—of preventing or staving off the despair of those who are weak and suffering by giving them a 'right' to look down upon 'immorality'—if they were already, *prior* to this invention, acquainted with the relevant 'moral' intuitions. For clearly the right in question here is not legal or conventional, but itself a *moral* right. As an explanation of the genesis of the belief in distinctly moral motives and actions, Nietzsche's thesis, like so many theories of a similar kind (e.g. Freud's genealogy of guilt), seems to involve a circle. It amounts to the claim that an 'amoral' person who in reality only desires power invents some conception of what is 'moral' (which he does not originally or naturally possess) *in order* then to be able to persuade himself (self-deceivingly) to have a distinctly *moral* right to despise other persons who also desire only power and whom he perceives as his oppressors. Clearly, the *explanandum* ('morality') is here already presupposed in the *explanans*. For only if the person *already* recognizes 'moral' values and desires could he possibly have a motive for self-deceivingly inventing such values and desires with the unacknowledged purpose of procuring for himself the 'right' to despise the will to power.

While the points made above constitute, in my opinion, a very fundamental criticism of Nietzsche's philosophical anthropology, they do not necessarily invalidate all of the many psychological analyses of particular cases that he offers in his writings. Nietzsche is strikingly ingenious and not seldom subtly perceptive—albeit also somewhat monotonous and obsessive—in tracing self-deception, veiled self-interest, and the will to power in allegedly charitable or 'altruistic' actions and attitudes. Our argument here has been that, if certain kinds of self-deception in particular instances are possible, as indeed they are (*vide* our example above), then it seems that the correct analysis of human desires and emotional states cannot be a monistic one of the sort Nietzsche suggests.

A few more words ought perhaps to be said about his assertion that the Christian ideal, even when it demands—in traditional terminology—self-denial and self-sacrifice, amounts ultimately to a self-interested policy of prudence, as it does explicitly in Paley's version. The plausibility of this position hinges largely on the more specific claim that the Christian *in fact*, but without acknowledging this to himself, defines the good (including the goodness he ascribes to God) in terms of the conduciveness of an object (or of a person) to the satisfaction of desires of his which are characterizable without ineliminable use of 'moral' notions such as justice, generosity, honesty, and so forth, as the Hobbesian tradition has done. It follows from this that, to the Christian, it is *really* (although sometimes contrary to his own self-deceived beliefs) a matter of indifference whether God is just in anything analogous to the ordinary, 'human' (or 'natural') conception of justice. God's being just in this sense would seem to involve (putting the matter somewhat crudely) taking into favourable account in His final judgements—although not necessarily in guiding the fortunes of men in this life, as the story of Job illustrates—the efforts made by any human being towards Christian virtue and their sincere intentions in conformity with such virtue (including, of course, the theological virtue of faith). Eschewing both Pelagianism and the various theological controversies around the question of free will, we might say, more cautiously, that it would involve at least favourably taking into account efforts and intentions in this regard which normally *appear* to humans to be their own. Moreover, if justice can be ascribed to God at all, this would seem to require that the grace (or punishment) accruing to different individuals in the afterlife is generally in some intelligible way proportional to 'their' respective sincere efforts and intentions (or lack of such)—i.e. those efforts and intentions which normally appear to them to be theirs—towards or in conformity with Christian virtue. (The 'generally' indicates a proviso which I shall return to presently.) This obviously does not mean that the beatitude or otherwise that is eventually granted to them is of the same specific kind(s) as the goods or ills which they themselves exemplified, or (as we say) brought about, in this life, or, assuming that these things can be thought of as quantifiable, that their eventual beatitude or punishment is of the same or a comparable amount as, and proportionate to their 'merits' in, *this* sense. We should also note that justice is not necessarily abrogated if God chooses to grant, as it were, additional favours to some individuals but not to others, for no reason which could be explained in terms of justice. To use a familiar analogy: an employer may choose to bestow gifts *over and above* standardly agreed wages on some of his labourers but not on others, for no reason which might be intelligible to us—yet no one would be tempted to say that this makes the employer *unjust*.

However, according to Nietzsche, the believer's concept of God exhausts itself essentially in the following determinations, although, if he is self-deceived, he will not admit this to himself. God is an infinitely powerful agent who, if I have 'faith' (i.e. trust) in Him and if I obey whatever commands He is pleased to issue,[42] will grant happiness to ('save') me—which happiness involves knowing my enemies punished—and confidence in whose power and favour towards me engenders in me a sense of superiority over my enemies even in this world. If our earlier remarks are correct, it is in fact, on Nietzsche's anthropology, *impossible* that the Christian should possess a concept of God very significantly different from this, or that he could even deceive himself (rather than others) into believing this. This conception of God and of God's 'goodness' is, of course, quite compatible with the belief that God elects or rejects other humans—those who are in no way connected with the respective believer and of whose existence he is perhaps not even aware—according to criteria which, even if they were revealed to him, would remain incomprehensible to him in that they would appear to his best (human) understanding as entirely arbitrary. God is still God, even if he is unjust in the sense explained above.

There can be little doubt that Nietzsche's analysis, or parts of it, fit the actions and convictions of some adherents of Christianity through the centuries. Literature, for example, provides numerous

---

[42] The role of obedience to God's commands through one's 'works' has, to be sure, been interpreted differently in different variants of Christian doctrine. In some versions, it is seen as making the individual, generally speaking, more acceptable to God—it as it were facilitates salvation, although it is not invariably and in all cases a condition of the latter. In other versions, such obedience expressed in action is regarded as a *consequence* of having already been elected for salvation.

psychologically convincing portrayals of 'the Christian' which illustrate Nietzsche's point or at least certain aspects of it.[43]

Leaving aside for the moment the question of what nominal Christians have actually believed, it is interesting to consider to what extent Nietzsche's characterization of Christianity accords with what they are doctrinally *supposed* to believe. It is arguable that *some* of his claims in this regard are actually compatible with various explicit tenets of some versions of doctrinal Christianity, in particular of versions which insist strongly on the utter incomprehensibility of God's sovereign will, that is, on the total *incompatibility* of His counsel with our ordinary, revelation-independent, and therefore 'merely human' or 'natural' conception of justice, or which accord central importance to the believer's subjective feeling of certainty about his own salvation. Nietzsche's personal acquaintance with Christianity was, of course, primarily with a doctrinal variant—Lutheranism—in whose theological foundations both of these elements are very prominent. The importance of Lutheran theology for Nietzsche's conception of Christianity has often been noted. Walter Kaufmann goes so far as to maintain that '[Nietzsche's] whole conception of historical Christianity hinges on Luther.'[44] This claim would be questionable if it were intended to suggest that the *attitudes* Nietzsche describes, or certain aspects of them, have always or exclusively or predominantly been characteristic of adherents to Luther's interpretation of Christianity. On the other hand, Kaufmann's statement seems to me to contain an element of truth, which is that Nietzsche's understanding of the *doctrines* of Christianity is strongly, although by no means exclusively, influenced by Luther. In his main theological work, Luther not only emphasizes the crucial importance of a person's feeling of certainty regarding his own salvation, but actually suggests that such supreme confidence is both a necessary and a sufficient condition for him to *be* saved—'for as a man believes, so it is with him'.[45] He also asserts there, in effect, that God's 'righteousness' is

---

[43] For instance, the character of Madame Stahl in Tolstoy's *Anna Karenina*, or Brigitte Pian, the protagonist of Mauriac's *La Pharisienne*.

[44] Kaufmann, *Nietzsche*, 298. Kaufmann's point has also been made by other Nietzscheans—at some length by Gerd-Günther Grau, *Christlicher Glaube und intellektuelle Redlichkeit* (Frankfurt, 1958), 33–81.

[45] M. Luther, *On the Bondage of the Will*, in E. G. Rupp and P. Watson (eds.), *Luther and Erasmus: Free Will and Salvation* (Philadelphia, 1969), 309. See also 329.

not merely different from, but incompatible with, human conceptions of justice.[46] The latter tenet is a consequence of his radical opposition of nature (including natural man as conceived by Aristotelian philosophy) and grace, and his insistence that nature is entirely evil[47]—a doctrine frequently emphasized by Nietzsche in his characterization of Christianity (e.g. GM ii.20, WM 786). This entails that any apparent goods which natural man may recognize independently of Christian revelation—whether it be pagan 'justice', 'beauty', or indeed 'reason'—are not so much imperfect in varying degrees, but rather stand equally in total opposition to God's will (cf. WM 283).

On the face of it, Nietzsche's analysis is more difficult to square with the doctrines of mainstream Christianity. According to them, God is to be loved 'for His own sake' and His will is to be obeyed because He is the *summum bonum*—His goodness, while infinitely surpassing the goodness of any created thing, being understood in a sense which is analogous to human goodness (as conceived by the Christian, of course). This theology sees divine goodness as the perfect exemplar of the imperfect virtue which it is possible for natural man to exercise, and it therefore has to make room for,

---

[46] 'By the light of grace it is an insoluble problem how God can damn one who is unable by any power of his own to do anything but sin and be guilty. Here both the light of nature and the light of grace tell us that it is not the fault of the unhappy man, but of an unjust God; for they cannot judge otherwise of a God who crowns one ungodly man freely and apart from merits, yet damns another who may well be less, or at least not more, ungodly. But the light of glory tells us differently, and it will show us hereafter that the God whose judgement here is one of incomprehensible righteousness is a God of most perfect and manifest righteousness.' (Ibid. 331–2; cf. 231) Note that Luther is not merely saying that God may appear unjust to us because we lack knowledge of His providential plan—no Christian thinker, including the Renaissance humanist Erasmus, who is his immediate opponent here, has disputed this. Rather, God's plan *is* radically unjust if measured by human, 'natural' standards. 'Many things as seen by God are very good which as seen by us are very bad [. . .] how things can be good in God's sight which are evil to us only God knows, and those who see with God's eyes, that is, who have the Spirit.' (Ibid. 231. On the necessary and radical 'offensiveness' of God's will to the idea of justice of 'natural reason', see also ibid. 244.)

[47] 'These are the facts which prove that the loftiest virtues of the heathen, the best things in the philosophers, the most excellent things in men, which in the eyes of the world certainly appear to be, as they are said to be, honourable and good, are nonetheless in the sight of God truly flesh and subservient to the kingdom of Satan; that is to say, they are impious and sacrilegious and on all counts bad' (ibid. 275–6; cf. 317). Luther emphatically includes among the 'most excellent things' mentioned here 'natural [Aristotelian] reason' (cf. 299). *All* of natural man is 'truly flesh and subservient to the kingdom of Satan'. In fact, for Luther there is strictly

rather than be incompatible with, ordinary human notions of just-ice in its conception of God. This means that for a believer in this doctrine, contrary to what is implied by Nietzsche's analysis of the 'Christian ideal', it should not be acceptable that God should save or reject men in a manner which is incompatible with human (natural, revelation-independent) ideas of justice, *even if* the respective believer himself should happen to be among the 'elect'. For this kind of believer, on his own self-interpretation, God is only God because He is just, which involves His taking into account every individual's desires and efforts (or lack of such) towards the good. If God were unjust, the 'beatitude' promised by Him would, as it were, not be worth having, since beatitude, in this theology, is conceived of precisely as the eternal contemplation of God's perfec-tion, which includes His justice. Nietzsche, as we have seen, replies that this conception of the nature of God is the result of self-deception, i.e. that the perfections ascribed in it to God (such as justice in the sense indicated) are not *really* valued by the believer for their own sake. But we have also seen that such a reply is itself problematic to the extent that it is either based on, or intended to establish, a monistic philosophical anthropology of the kind suggested by him.

A further question that could be raised about Nietzsche's account is whether the desire for an other-worldly reward—salvation con-ceived as the satisfaction of various self-directed desires—is quite as essential to Christianity as he maintains. In fact, many saints and *homines religiosi*, of various doctrinal persuasions, declared that they would still love Christ even if they had to forgo all the 'rewards' promised to them by their religion. Meister Eckhart, for instance, says that he 'would rather be in hell with Jesus than be in heaven without him'. While Eckhart might be thought to be un-

---

speaking no such thing as *human* agency—it is always either Satan or God who acts through human beings (180, 219: humans are 'impelled, as a saw or an axe is wielded by a carpenter'). God's agency therefore has to 'cast out' or 'break' nature— the 'kingdom of Satan'—rather than 'perfect' it—a notion which in Luther's the-ology is either meaningless or a blasphemy. This is not to say that the believer, once he *is* 'justified' by faith, may not in good conscience *use* the resources of nature as he pleases (183), or indeed enjoy 'natural' pleasures—as a fallen human being he cannot avoid being drawn to them while he lives in this world. But he is only justified in this enjoyment because God's freely bestowed grace has enabled him to acknow-ledge that there is really nothing whatsoever that is intrinsically good about these 'natural' pleasures or indeed about nature in general, which has been corrupted *in toto* by the Fall (see cit. above).

representative, we find similar sentiments expressed by a more orthodox figure like Teresa of Avila: 'Did I not hope as I do hope, I would still love as I do love'.[48] The inadequate participation in God's perfection which, according to mainstream theology, is possible for human beings in this life, seemed desirable to these believers, if their words are to be given credence, independently of any further 'benefits' or 'rewards' they might expect. In fact, these rewards themselves were conceived by them as a fuller participation in God's perfection and as not characterizable without reference to it. None of this is intended to suggest that the notion of salvation as a 'heavenly reward' has not played a very important part in historical Christianity, or that it has not been a crucial motive for many people for assenting to its metaphysical doctrines. The questions we have raised here concern, rather, whether this notion can, in all its historical manifestations, be adequately analysed in the way Nietzsche proposes, and whether it has always been as central to all major aspects of the Christian ethos as he asserts.

We have dwelt at such length upon Nietzsche's analysis of the Christian ideal for two reasons. First, because it seems to imply either that he does not intend his scepticism, nor indeed his anti-essentialism, to be relevant to 'inner experience',[49] or that he is not aware of the objections which either of these strands in his thinking give rise to with respect to his psychological claims. If these claims were plausible, they would provide evidence for his more general assertion that the essence or nature of the affective and appetitive aspects of inner experience consists exclusively of 'passions' involving an individual's awareness of a certain power-difference between himself and a perceived opponent or obstacle, and of 'appetites' for experiences of power. As an analysis of putative self-deception, those claims imply that the real nature of our affective and appetitive states is accessible in self-consciousness. As Ludwig Klages, along with many others, has pointed out, Nietzsche's 'unmasking' of the Christian ideal in all its ramifications requires that 'we are capable of becoming conscious of the fact of self-deception

---

[48] Both quotations taken from Scheler's discussion of this matter in *Das Ressentiment im Aufbau der Moralen*, 46n. Along similar lines, L. Kolakowski has pointed out that the *resignatio ad infernum* is quite a common theme in Christian mystical thought (*Religion*, 114–15).

[49] Cf. Eugen Fink, *Nietzsches Philosophie* (Stuttgart, 1960), 128.

and of its motives'.[50] Indeed, the very concept of self-deception presupposes the accessibility of an individual's real emotions, desires, intentions, and so on, in self-consciousness:

> If a subject *persuades* himself to believe contrary to the evidence *in order to evade*, somehow, the unpleasant truth to which he has already seen [!] that the evidence points, then and only then is he clearly a self-deceiver.[51]

Nietzsche's position as we have outlined it above would, if plausible and coherent, not imply that the efficacious antecedents of our actions are *themselves* always present in self-consciousness—indeed, he frequently maintains that they usually are not—but it *would* imply that we are to understand these antecedents as being similar in kind to the 'appetites and passions' which appear to a self-consciousness cleansed of self-deception and which invariably fall under the concept of the will to power (cf. KGW VII.3.40.37).[52]

Let us first turn to the question of the compatibility of these views with Nietzsche's sceptical arguments (see Chapter 2.3). In the light of the massed evidence of the texts, it would seem wilfully obtuse to deny that he assumes that there are other 'subjects' who 'have' what he calls inner experiences or a subjective invisible life, that is, mental occurrences characterized by a certain phenomenal character or what-it-is-likeness which are not directly accessible to other subjects in the way objects are. He also assumes that these states of other subjects do, in fact, have the phenomenal characteristics he imputes to them, namely characteristics falling under the concept of the will to power. His sceptical arguments, if accepted, imply that none of these suppositions can be rationally justified. For Nietzsche, of course, this objection would not by itself provide a reason for relinquishing them. His sceptical arguments and his psychological theories are, at any rate, not mutually contradictory.

According to the anti-essentialist strand in his thought, no part of reality has, at any time, a nature in itself (a set of intrinsic

[50] L. Klages, *Die psychologischen Errungenschaften Nietzsches* (Leipzig, 1926), 46. Cf. K. Jaspers, *Nietzsche—Einführung in das Verständnis seines Philosophierens* (Berlin and Leipzig, 1936), 115. On the importance of the possibility of self-knowledge for Nietzsche, see also Volker Gerhardt, 'Self-grounding: Nietzsche's Morality of Individuality', in K. Ansell-Pearson and H. Caygill (eds.), *The Fate of the New Nietzsche* (Aldershot, 1993), 286–9.

[51] H. Fingarette, *Self-Deception* (London, 1969), 28. Cf. AC 52, 55.

[52] In some notes, Nietzsche suggests that non-cognitive pleasurable or painful *sensations* are also results of 'intellectual' occurrences which are unconscious to us, i.e. which presumably are to be ascribed to those drives of ours of which we are not

properties), constituting it as what it is at that time. We recall that Nietzsche's formulations in the notebooks suggest very strongly that he believed this to follow from the insight that all properties are 'perspectival'—they are what they are only *for* a 'subject' (see Chapter 3.1). Nevertheless, in his psychological analyses he emphatically draws a distinction between reality and appearance ('text' or 'fact' versus 'interpretation'). He argues, time and time again, that the self-interpretations of the self-deceived person are false and that her mental states are 'in reality "something different"' (MR 116) from what those fully explicit, propositionally structured, self-interpretations allege them to be. Note that this claim by itself is not in any way inconsistent with saying that all truth is 'perspectival'. For, after all, it is part of what is meant by talk of mental, subjective states ('inner experiences') that they are what they are only from a certain point of view or perspective— that of the first person. Every such state exists, by definition, only for a 'subject'. However, the idea, omnipresent in Nietzsche's writings, that a subject's explicit self-interpretation may, and often does, fail to capture the 'facts' (or 'text') of her own mental states does seem to imply that such states do have an intrinsic nature, a set of phenomenal qualities, which constitute them as what they (*qua* subjective states or 'inner experiences') really, or in themselves, are. Self-deception, in Nietzsche's words, consists in '*not* wanting to see what one does see, not wanting to see it *as* what one sees it' (AC 55). How such a state is possible has often puzzled philosophers. In keeping with Nietzsche's remarks, I would suggest the following tentative analysis. Self-deception usually involves an incipient, fleeting apprehension of a certain description or characterization of some occurrent or dispositional mental state, or of some event or action—a characterization which, as it were, obtrudes itself (somewhat analogous to objects obtruding themselves in one's visual field). However, it is then avoided, or refused attention, because it is, for whatever reasons, painful or disquieting to the individual. Instead, a more acceptable alternative description, which seems at least possibly correct or not wildly implausible to the individual, is fastened upon, or attended to. Only *through* this attention does it become possible to make it fully explicit and to assent to it. By

aware, but whose activity is analogous to our conscious 'passions', 'appetites', and 'judgements' (cf. WM 699). It is the outcomes of their struggles for power which sometimes become conscious to the individual merely as brute sensations.

contrast, the characterization which is 'avoided' or refused attention, precisely for this reason, can neither be consciously and explicitly assented to nor initiate the sort of enquiry on the part of the self-deceiver which might provide good reasons for him to consider it to be true. Hence it is indeed the case that the self-deceiver usually does not know the truth of the description of the matter which he tries to evade. Sometimes, when a person who has been in a state of self-deception is afterwards inescapably confronted with the truth he has been avoiding, he defends himself by protesting 'but I did not *know* that this was the case'. In a sense, this may well be correct: he may really not have 'known'. But, if he was in a condition of self-deception, the main reason for this lack of knowledge is likely to have been the purposeful refusal to inquire into the situation precisely *because* such an inquiry might have confirmed the description of it he has been trying to evade. This refusal—what Nietzsche calls a 'not wanting to see'—that is, a certain quality of evasion, of compulsive avoidance, remains present in the self-deceiver's consciousness. But it also is never sufficiently attended to to be made entirely explicit and held, arrested as it were, 'before' the mind in a propositionally structured judgement. Thus it is, phenomenologically, a characteristic of states of this kind that certain qualities are present in them which are not explicitly acknowledged by the subject; indeed such states consist partly in this peculiar evasive character, this refusal to acknowledge or state their presence.[53]

There are indeed many kinds of mental states the presence of which is arguably incompatible with 'objectifying' or 'thematizing' or 'contemplating' them, as philosophers from Spinoza to Heidegger have insisted. An intense state of fear or anger or love will disappear, at least momentarily, when I concentrate on the attempt to 'contemplate' it—to observe myself being in this state. One cannot both be in a state of intense fear of something and successfully attend to, or 'thematize', one's state at the same time. But in general such an objectifying of what then becomes one's

---

[53] At least some, but often not all, of the relevant unacknowledged contents of the self-deceiver's experience tend to be what Michael Dummett calls proto-thoughts; they do not have the structure of linguistically expressed thoughts, but do nevertheless represent an awareness of something *as* something, an awareness moreover which involves a characteristic type of evasive 'behaviour' or, more accurately, activity, on the part of the subject. (For the notion of proto-thoughts, see Michael Dummett, *Ursprünge der analytischen Philosophie* (Frankfurt, 1992), Ch. 12.)

immediately preceding occurrent emotional state has no tendency at all to destroy or mitigate it permanently. One's fear or anger or love can resume unaltered, or even intensified, after one has ceased to attend to it self-reflexively. Self-deception, by contrast, tends not to survive such self-reflexive acknowledgement. It requires those elements in the self-deceiver's mental state which constitute his self-deception to remain unacknowledged.

Self-deception, to continue Nietzsche's visual analogy, is like catching a fleeting glimpse of an object (thus 'seeing' it), and then immediately and purposefully averting one's eyes and one's attention from it, that purposefulness being itself a characteristic one tries to avoid 'seeing', i.e. attending to and thereby becoming able to state the presence of. Hence one cannot sincerely state that one is self-deceived while being self-deceived.[54] It is only afterwards, when recollecting the peculiar character of that psychological condition, that such explicit acknowledgement becomes possible.[55] There is a well-attested phenomenological change in a person's experience when she ceases to be self-deceived. The quality of compulsive avoidance disappears, and it is the person's awareness of this change which enables her to acknowledge the character of her previous psychological condition. Self-deception is to some extent like dreaming: in many instances one cannot acknowledge that one is dreaming while dreaming, but one can do so afterwards, when awake and recollecting that state with sufficient attention. The analogy is only partial, however. For one has, in many dreams, no awareness at all that one is dreaming, while there is, indeed there must be, a certain kind of fleeting, 'fugitive' awareness of one's condition in typical states of self-deception.

It may be asked, in the light of what has been said here, whether a person can ever have good non-behavioural grounds to believe that she is not self-deceived at the present moment. Nietzsche would certainly have to answer this question affirmatively, for he

---

[54] One consequence of this is that it is impossible to convince a person that she is self-deceived while she continues to be self-deceived. On the other hand, one's success in creating this conviction does not entail that it is justified.

[55] It may be objected that in thus 'recollecting' and putting a certain verbal or otherwise symbolic interpretation on a prior psychological state, one necessarily radically alters or distorts its character, rather than ever recovering and acknowledging its 'real' nature. I do not think that this point adds anything of substance to old-style memory scepticism. Interestingly, Nietzsche himself shows no significant concern with this kind of scepticism.

operates with a concept of self-deception very much like the one outlined here. Conspicuously, he never resorts exclusively to behavioural or otherwise public criteria for ascribing self-deception to individuals, although he would certainly admit that observable behaviour, including verbal behaviour, may often provide strong *evidence* for the correctness of such ascriptions. In the case of the self-deception involved in *ressentiment*, for instance, he suggests that its presence—the merely apparent character of an individual's commitment to certain 'positive' values, and their actual negative, detractive intent—is generally confirmed by behaviour which indicates the constitutive, but usually unacknowledged, tendency on the part of the subject of *ressentiment* to be preoccupied with his 'enemy': in particular, with the qualities of the latter which are interpreted negatively by him. He has, as Nietzsche puts it, 'to construct his happiness artificially through gazing at [his] enemies' (GM i.10). The non-self-deceived—in particular, the 'noble'—individual by contrast tends to avoid dwelling on the (to him) negative qualities of his 'opposite', at least in normal circumstances when he does not find himself in a situation of inescapable and irresolvable conflict with that 'opposite'. The latter is for him normally merely a 'faint contrasting image' which he either barely notices or from which he 'impatiently' 'looks away' (ibid.). The observations Nietzsche is making here are themselves phrased somewhat carelessly and impatiently, but they are quite subtle and permit, I think, further explication. One type of symptom which often—not always—indicates the presence of *ressentiment* is the manifestation of a characteristic inclination on the part of the subject to attend frequently or even predominantly to supposedly negative qualities of other individuals who are apprehended as 'different' from him in some significant respect. This inclination may, for example, manifest itself in frequent explicit criticism or blame of others who are regarded as 'different', or in other kinds of detractive reactions (sarcasm, *Schadenfreude*, etc.) which therefore, if they are sufficiently pervasive, constitute prima facie evidence for the presence of *ressentiment*. Such evidence is the stronger the less restrictive the subject behaves in his or her selection of the 'differences' which elicit these detractive reactions, and the less the latter are tied to immediate, present occasions of actual practical confrontation—in other words, the more habitual such reactions are and the less 'stimulation' is required for them to occur. There are, furthermore, symptoms which sometimes indicate the characteristic tendency of the subject of *ressentiment* to focus, when some representational content ostensibly recognized as 'good' by him is presented to him, not on those aspects of the content which we would normally ('naïvely') regard as intrinsic to it, but on a certain alleged value-*relation* of it to some *other* content, namely the object of *ressentiment*. The former content will, for example, tend to be described not as 'courageous', or 'harmonious', or 'just', etc., but as 'more rational than *x*', or 'more just than *y*', or 'at least as good as *z*', and so forth, or it will predominantly be described in ways which more subtly imply such comparisons, but which nevertheless indicate the subject's continuing actual or dispositional awareness of and preoccupation with the 'other' who is resented. Nietzsche maintains, of course, that for any object to be regarded as 'good', this requires at least an implicit, unthematized awareness of a 'difference' (WM 699, see Chapter 4.3), but not necessarily a comparison of *this* sort.

For Nietzsche, neither an individual's 'observable' weakness nor his public behaviour is ever logically sufficient for the correct ascription of *ressentiment* to him. Nor are public symptoms like those mentioned above usually entirely unambiguous and conclusive even in practice.[56] Moreover, even the identification of such symptoms *as*

---

[56] We can perhaps appreciate the difficulty of interpreting such evidence if we recall that Nietzsche's own writings (especially in the very last phase) manifest a pervasive, some would say obsessive, concern with the psychology of his 'antipodes'. Does this not, given his own analysis, at least create the suspicion of the presence of the very phenomenon he has ostensibly exposed? There are, of course, alternative explanations of this prominent feature of his work, some of them suggested by himself. He may have seen himself—as many of his remarks suggest—as so inescapably engulfed by slave morality that 'looking away' from it more often and looking towards 'friends' (or 'good enemies') became almost impossible. Or he may have fallen victim to that perennial temptation to diagnose the perceived unsatisfactoriness and the specific limitations of the present human condition as resulting from one identifiable cause—here, the historical victory of slave morality—which can be seen as external to the diagnoser and whose elimination would also eliminate that which it is supposedly the sole cause of. Whatever the best explanation of that feature of his work, the problems arising from the possibility of a self-referential application of the *ressentiment* theory to Nietzsche's own writings suggest the idea, which seems to me to be in the spirit of his analysis, if perhaps not entirely in accord with his practice, that the ascription of *ressentiment* to others on the basis of their verbal or non-verbal behaviour is least likely to fall under the suspicion expressed by the theory, or to other misgivings, if it is made sparingly and reluctantly, as a hypothesis of last resort as it were, if all other available hypotheses seem to fail to account adequately for the behaviour to be explained. Those misgivings and suspicions are of course less likely to befall the application of the

relevant evidence relies ultimately on 'psychology' of a certain kind which involves, among other things, extrapolating from the 'most subtle observation' in 'one's own case'. In JGB 186 he explicitly declares the task of moral psychology to be the correct 'description' and 'classification' of 'moral facts' and 'value-*feelings*' (my emphasis). That at least some of his most important grounds for his psychological claims are of an introspective rather than a publicly observable kind emerges very clearly from a large number of passages (e.g. JGB 36; WM 479; KGW VII.3.40.61; KGW VII.2.26.114). It is also obvious from his pronouncements to the effect that one has to have *experienced* a mode of relating to the world—a 'world-interpretation' and its associated ruling drives—in order to understand it and to be in a position to criticize it (see e.g. JGB 220—he himself had, of course, been very much subject to the 'ascetic ideal' in his earlier phase). He emphasizes that in order to understand, for example, an evaluative expression such as 'common' it is not sufficient that one uses it in a way which other people would regard as linguistically competent: 'to understand one another it is not sufficient that one uses the same words; one also has to use the same words for the same kind of inner experiences [!], ultimately one has to have the same experience' (JGB 268). Finally, it is clear from the whole tenor of his work that he does not rely on socially agreed and publicly accessible criteria for the ascription of mental states to others—in particular, from his relentless insistence on the solitary and 'unsocial' character of his enterprise. He self-consciously and belligerently *refuses* to accept the publicly accessible grounds which are in practice most widely accepted in his society for the ascription of certain mental states (like 'altruistic' desires) to others. Consequently, these grounds cannot have the status of criteria, but at best of misleading evidence, for him.

In order to forestall at least some of the objections against his approach which are to be expected in a twentieth-century philosophical context, it is worth stressing what Nietzsche is *not* claiming. He is obviously not saying that an individual's explicit (e.g. verbal) identification, in his own case, of the absence of the characteristic features of self-deception is self-guaranteeing, or that it can never be overruled, for that individual himself, by other evidence. Nor is he saying that a person's actions are simply *irrel-*

challenge posed by the theory to *oneself* as a test of one's apparent evaluative commitments.

evant to determining whether he is self-deceived or not. This would indeed be an odd assumption, given that human affective and appetitive states *normally* issue in actions of some sort if the conditions are judged appropriate. Nietzsche is also not committed to the claim that we would be able to attribute specific mental states to others (or for that matter, to acquire a language to speak about them) even if such states did not have typical behavioural manifestations.

Can one, then, ever have good 'introspective' grounds to ascribe self-deception or its absence to oneself? It is true that one cannot acknowledge in a propositionally structured judgement the presence of the quality of avoidance which is experienced in characteristic states of self-deception while experiencing it (i.e. while being self-deceived). This inability is in part what self-deception consists in. However, it could be argued—and Nietzsche, I suggest, would accede to this—that it is possible, in some cases, and for some people ('good philologists'), to be aware of the absence of those features of consciousness which are constitutive of self-deception. The qualification 'in some cases' is important here, because, among other things, self-deception is a matter of degree, and there are obviously many instances in which a person may find it impossible to feel confident as to whether she is presently in a state of self-deception or not. It is by no means ruled out by what has been said here that, with some individuals, the phenomenological difference between the mental state of compulsive avoidance which is involved in self-deception and its absence is never experienced. Nietzsche would, indeed, say that this is a fairly frequent case. Such an individual would not possess Nietzsche's concept of self-deception.

It seems to me that some such account, suitably elaborated, enables us to make sense of Nietzsche's distinction between 'fact' and 'interpretation' in inner experience. However, as I have indicated, this distinction is incompatible with his anti-essentialism, according to which no part of reality has an intrinsic character (a 'constitution in itself', WM 583 A) constituting it as what it is, for 'we possess the concept "being", "thing", only as a relational concept' (ibid.). His universal application of this view not only to 'things', but to any kind of content of awareness, bespeaks his continued adherence, in some of his moods, to Schopenhauer's doctrine—not consistently upheld by Schopenhauer himself—that every state of awareness involves a distinction between an 'object' (or content) and a transcendental subject standing 'outside' of, but being related to, that object. Consequently, no mental content of any kind can have an intrinsic non-relational character. Such a view is, however, not only difficult to square with Nietzsche's own psychological analyses, it is also inconsistent with his criticisms of various traditional conceptions of the subject, including Schopenhauer's (see Chapters 2.1 and 6.2).

When Nietzsche says that people often fail to distinguish between 'fact' and 'interpretation' in inner experience, and that their interpretations of their own mental states are frequently false, he is claiming, according to the present reading, the following things. He believes it to be true (for him, or 'perspectivally') that there are other 'subjects' who have a 'subjective invisible life', that is, mental states with a certain phenomenal character. He also believes that this character or what-it-is-likeness can be, in its affective and appetitive aspects, described correctly in terms provided by his notion of the will to power. He moreover holds—despite occasional prevarications—that the 'correctness' of this description means that it could be recognized, with sufficient attention (i.e. in the absence of self-deception), as being correct by those other subjects to whose states it refers.

The fact that his psychological analyses concern subjective (mental) states might be expressed by saying that their truth is, in one sense, 'perspectival'. What is less clear is whether he would regard it as being perspectival in the much stronger sense according to which these analyses might be true for a certain perspective or point of view, while actually *being* false for other such perspectives (in whose existence Nietzsche himself believes). In other words, the question is whether Nietzsche is saying that there may be other 'subjects' (perspectives) for whom nothing would ever count, in principle, as establishing that there are subjective states—states having a certain phenomenal, perspectival character—other than their own,[57] and that, since for him all truth is perspectival (and absolute truth 'nonsense'), we literally could not intelligibly say that such solipsistic subjects are mistaken.

---

[57] An example of this would be someone who genuinely holds that what it means—for him, or members of his language community—to say that someone else, *x*, believes that *p*, or desires that *q*, is that *x*'s behaviour is of a certain level of complexity and that it is 'interpretable' in the sense of predictable.

Certainly, if something analogous to his analysis of 'objective reality' as dependent on the concern of some subject(s) could be applied to the sphere of the subjective, or perspectival, itself, it would follow that the very existence or reality of subjective perspectives is logically dependent upon, and relative to, some *other* subject acknowledging these perspectives different from its own. While some of Nietzsche's remarks do tend in this direction, it seems to me that one only has to state this position to appreciate its untenability. While it is at least arguable that what can intelligibly be said to be a 'real object' depends upon some subject for whom it is real, it is not even remotely plausible to claim that, on reflection, what I mean when I speak of the reality of 'other minds' is: subjective states other than my own whose existence is relative to, and ontologically dependent on, my interests and concerns. What this in turn suggests is that the perspectival or subjective and the absolute or metaphysical are by no means as mutually exclusive as Nietzsche is often tempted to assert. We shall see in Chapter 6.2 that his succumbing to this temptation is particularly evident in the passages sometimes referred to as the 'metaphysics of the will to power'.

As mentioned earlier, Nietzsche's denial of the very intelligibility of 'metaphysical truth' (his anti-essentialism) is, psychologically, connected with his conviction that the apparent desire for knowledge of reality as it is in itself 'for its own sake', just like the belief in God, results from a particular—weak and often self-deceived—constitution or position of the individuals experiencing this desire. Nietzsche's own values—what he unapologetically calls his taste—are diametrically opposed to this aspiration of the weak and suffering for an 'other-world' of pure contemplation—a 'return and homecoming to the ground of things, as breaking free of all delusion, as "knowledge", as "truth", as "being", as liberation from any goal, any wish, any activity' (GM iii.17). As we also saw, he believes that the ascetic ideal frequently involves self-deception, in particular the self-deception of *ressentiment*. A typical element of the latter is, according to him, the conviction that (metaphysical) truth authorizes, justifies, or enjoins on all human beings a certain range of pursuits or modes of life, and in this sense privileges them over others. His own attitude—what he would undoubtedly call his 'instinctive' response—to the self-deception of *ressentiment* is a contempt the profundity of which is generally conveyed in images of aesthetic revulsion (from 'uncleanliness' and 'bad air', to mention some of his milder images). His rejection, or disavowal, of weakness in general, and his contempt for the weakness of *ressentiment* in particular, furnish us with a psychological explanation of why he is so obsessively concerned, in his later writings, with showing that 'reality in itself' is unintelligible and that, even if it were not, knowledge of it—*qua* true, rationally justified belief— is unattained by us. Thus, Nietzsche's anti-essentialism and the polemical flavour of his scepticism become psychologically comprehensible once we realize that in his own psychological theories, summarized in the slogan of the will to power, he is ultimately neither sceptical (in the sense of uncommitted or doubtful) nor anti-essentialist: 'I am telling the *genuine* history of Christianity' (AC 39).

This brings us to the second reason why we have elaborated upon Nietzsche's analysis of the 'Christian ideal' and the 'ascetic ideal' of which the former is a special case, as well as on his alternative conception of the end of human actions and beliefs as the experience of power. Together with his passionate and largely unwavering commitment to certain 'values', they enable us to understand the mainsprings, not merely of his thought on epistemology and metaphysics, but of the peculiar nature of his entire philosophy and its polemical and, in the very last writings (1888), intensely personal and sometimes hysterical idiom.

What are these values and 'virtues' (cf. JGB, part 7) which Nietzsche espouses? (It goes without saying that any such commitment, given his rejection of the notion of a good ontologically independent of the valuer, cannot but be a matter of subjective 'taste', in accordance with his 'ruling drives'.)[58] One of them,

---

[58] It is to these basic values, and only to these, that the following remarks apply: 'I have a taste, but no reasons, no logic, no imperative for this taste' (letter to Peter Gast, 19 November 1886). It should be mentioned here, in parenthesis, that not all of the emotions and desires Nietzsche calls noble can easily be analysed on his own non-realist model of value. This is particularly the case with the 'noble' emotion of reverence (*Ehrfurcht*). He says, for example: 'it is possible that today there is still more *relative* nobility of taste and tactful reverence to be found among the people— among simple people, especially among peasants—than among the newspaper-reading *demi-monde* of the spirit, the educated classes' (JGB 263). It is statements such as these which are most difficult to reconcile with an emotivist meta-ethic, a variant of which Nietzsche is often taken to espouse. For it is essential to the concept of reverence that its object be taken by the valuer (the 'subject') to be worthy of such a response (i.e. good), irrespective of its relation to the valuer and irrespective of

prominent in most of the writings of the last period, but particularly in *Also sprach Zarathustra*, is the virtue of self-overcoming.[59] What does self-overcoming mean in Nietzsche? Walter Kaufmann has pointed out its apparent affinities with important aspects of both Aristotelian and Kantian ethics.[60] He also concurs with Ludwig Klages's observation that the 'motif of self-overcoming' in Nietzsche, ironically, has close parallels in Christianity.[61]

Now, it is true that Nietzsche shares with these traditions a rejection of hedonism, for which his contempt is only slightly less pronounced than for *ressentiment* (see especially the section on the 'last man' in the prologue of *Also sprach Zarathustra*). By hedonism we may understand, in this context, a disposition with the following characteristics. It involves, first, the refusal to draw qualitative distinctions[62] between desires, so that, in the vocabulary of the hedonist, terms like 'higher' and 'lower', 'noble' and 'base' have no application to desires. Secondly, the dominant desires of the hedonist have as their end a state of satisfaction characterized by the absence of pain, including of course the pain frequently concomitant with internal struggles—such as those often resulting from a conflict between desires in a framework of qualitative distinctions[63]—but also with external opponents or obstacles. This

whether he—*qua* series of conscious states—even exists. Its 'goodness' therefore cannot be understood by the valuer as being constituted by, or dependent upon, his approval of it. Similarly, it is difficult to see how reverence is even possible if, ultimately, the object of one's desire is always a state of oneself (the feeling of power). Nietzsche, perhaps aware of this problem, attempts to overcome it by saying that '[t]he noble soul has reverence *for itself*' (JGB 287; my emphasis). It is safe to assume that he is not talking here about a sense of self-importance, or about complacency or feeling pleased with oneself. But if he is not, it is doubtful whether his formulation is coherent as it stands, or whether an elaboration of it can solve the difficulty. Unfortunately, an adequate discussion of this aspect of Nietzsche's 'ethics' would require rather more space than it can be given in the present context.

[59] As has often been observed by commentators, this emphasis on self-overcoming, which is also an overcoming of the 'human' (cf. KGW VII.1.16.41, and *Also sprach Zarathustra, passim*), is at odds with his praise elsewhere of 'harmony of soul' (WM 283), of Goethean serenity and contemplative 'repose', and of the latter's 'trusting fatalism' in accepting the world—including oneself—as it is (see e.g. WM 95, KGW VIII.2.9.179).

[60] Kaufmann, *Nietzsche*, 183 and 329.

[61] Klages, *Die psychologischen Errungenschaften Nietzsches*, 203–10. Cf. also de Gaultier, *From Kant to Nietzsche*, 207.

[62] For the relevant sense of 'qualitative distinctions', see Taylor, *Sources of the Self*, part 1.

[63] e.g. when a person strongly desires a certain good—say, money—but judges the means available to him for attaining it to be 'ignoble'.

state of satisfaction is, thirdly, conceived by the hedonist as, at the ideal limit, a state of rest from which all desire is absent, i.e. no change is wished for.

While there is, in Nietzsche's rejection of hedonism and in his advocacy, instead, of self-overcoming, a partial affinity with the Aristotelian, Christian, and Kantian ethical traditions, it is mistaken to say, as Kaufmann does, that his conception of virtue displays no significant differences from the conceptions found in these traditions.[64] For what is distinctive of Nietzschean *Selbstüberwindung* is that he considers it to be 'great' and 'noble' irrespective of any ulterior end—irrespective of what it is 'for'. Indeed, it seems as if, for Nietzsche, self-overcoming has the most nobility when it is itself desired by the agent—if *it* is the end of his desire or his action. This contrasts obviously with the more traditional notion of an 'overcoming of the passions'—in Aristotelian, Christian, and Kantian ethics—as being good not because it is an *overcoming*, but because of the specific nature of what is being overcome. For Kant, for example, a will in accordance with the moral law would be *better* if it was so spontaneously, without having to struggle against and 'overcome' the passions. But the highest good in Aristotelian and Christian philosophy (less clearly so in Kant) is conceived as a contemplative state of 'happiness' which, in Aquinas's words 'so [. . .] fulfil[s] a man's whole desire that nothing is left beside for him to desire'.[65] For Nietzsche, such a conception of the highest good, far from being opposed to hedonism, shares the latter's essential features. While it appears to make qualitative distinctions between desires as higher or lower, noble or base, it does, at least in its Christian version, on Nietzsche's analysis not really do so. Moreover, it sees the *summum bonum* as a final state of rest, free of pain, conflict or struggle, in which all desire is stilled (cf. WM 221, 696, 781; KGW VII.1.16.88).[66] Thus, for Nietzsche, central elements of the Christian—and, more generally, the ascetic—ideal expose them as really variants of hedonism. But

---

[64] Kaufmann, *Nietzsche*, 92–3. Kaufmann's view clearly also involves rather too great an emphasis on the similarities among these more traditional views, ignoring the significant differences among them.

[65] Thomas Aquinas, *Summa Theologiae*, Ia IIae, 1. 5.

[66] For Nietzsche, by contrast, pain, discomfort, and change are integral to 'happiness' as analysed by him (i.e. the feeling of power), since it is only through ever again encountering and overcoming resistances to our will, manifesting themselves as 'unpleasurable stimuli', that we can attain it at all (WM 695, 699).

it is not only because of his distaste for the latter that he so relentlessly attacks those ideals. They also involve self-deception and, usually, *ressentiment*, both of which are 'vices' for Nietzsche who, in most of his moods, extols honesty and generosity—the 'virtue of bestowing'.[67] It is conspicuous that both of these virtues have close parallels in the self-interpretation of the very Christian–Aristotelian tradition which he accuses of being 'really' devoid of them. Similarly, his distaste for *ressentiment* has its parallel in the (according to him, only apparent) Christian condemnation of the related sin of envy.

What arguably remains as the most interesting, revealing, and original element in Nietzsche's own table of values is the notion of self-overcoming as an end in itself. One important question it raises is, of course: what is the 'self'—what are the drives, in his terminology—which is to be overcome? Nietzsche's formulations, especially in the notebooks and in *Also sprach Zarathustra*, make it clear that the drives to be overcome include, first, those which become conscious as desires for pleasurable sensations or for the restful repose of 'comfort'. But secondly, in a very significant reversal of his earlier views, they also include all those desires which involve an apparent recognition of goods or values in the world which are, when apprehended, taken to be ontologically independent of the subject recognizing them. In other words, 'self-overcoming' involves the subjugation of all those desires which the young Nietzsche thought to be constitutive of the 'higher self'. I take this to be quite clearly implied by statements like the following:

Of course, one must get rid of that clumsy old psychology which taught of cruelty only that it originates in the sight of the suffering of others; there is also an abundant and over-abundant pleasure in one's own suffering, in making oneself suffer—[. . . .] Consider, finally, that the man of knowledge

---

[67] Nietzsche's *schenkende Tugend*, which he sometimes also calls 'the great love' (KGW VII.2.26.262), bears a considerable resemblance to some aspects of Christian *agape* on one interpretation of this term. His *Übermensch* is like God in so far as he 'loves' and 'gives away' from a plenitude of power. But his love is fully sovereign in the sense that it is, judged by ordinary human standards, arbitrary. It is not, that is, either dependent on, or in any way proportional to, relative values in the respective objects of love, values which are taken to be real even if they are not apprehended by the lover. The 'virtue of bestowing', in keeping with Nietzsche's general philosophy of value, arbitrarily *bestows* value in every act of great love, rather than ever recognizing it as already existent in its object. (For a Christian version of this concept of 'sovereign' or 'creative' love, see Anders Nygren, *Eros und Agape*, i, esp. 60 and 185 f.)

disposes as an artist and transfigurer of cruelty in *forcing* his spirit to know *against* its inclination and often enough also against the wishes of his heart—saying No where he wants to affirm, love, worship—(JGB 229, cf. Z 144/138)

Has ever yet a man searched on the path of truth as I have done hitherto—namely struggling against and contradicting everything that gave comfort [*wohl that*] to my most intimate feeling? (KGW VII.2.27.81)

Heroic = that is the striving for one's total destruction [*Untergang*] into one's opposite, the recasting of the devil as God: that is *this degree* of cruelty [. . .] (KGW VII.1.1.67; cf. WM 417; KGW VII.1.16.4; KGW VII.1.5.1)

In the light of such remarks and many similar ones it is difficult to avoid the conclusion that Nietzsche's attacks on Platonic or Christian 'heavenly goodness' and 'divine justice' (KGW VII. 3.34.5) are as persistent (and later as vitriolic) as they are partly because these ideas give 'comfort' to his own 'most intimate feeling'. This also seems to be borne out by the fact that he continues to describe a world from which the Christian God is absent as 'terrible' (ibid.). But why should self-overcoming in this sense—as 'cruelty against oneself'—become the supreme virtue for Nietzsche?[68]

A satisfactory answer to this question is as difficult as it is central to an understanding of his philosophy. Any plausible attempt at answering it has to take as its basic datum Nietzsche's consistent detestation, throughout his career, of what he calls the 'vulgar' form of egoism (KGW VII.2.26.262). For a certain kind of human sensibility, value resides primarily in certain states of oneself which might be characterized as states of pleasure in the sense of comfortableness or agreeableness, from which any pain as well as any sense of struggle, threat, danger, or insecurity are absent. Hedonism as defined above is one variant of this sensibility. This is what Nietzsche means by 'vulgar' egoism. It has, of course, been a target of criticism for various traditional theories of value, expressing quite different sensibilities, which have insisted that there are greater goods than states of pleasure in this sense. Usually, these objections have taken the form of realist construals of value. What those who have held that there are real, or 'objective', values have generally wanted to say is, partly, that they acknowledge goods in comparison with which their own pleasure or comfort (or, for that

---

[68] De Gaultier, *From Kant to Nietzsche*, 243.

matter, that of others) is of lesser importance. They have also wanted to say that, when we desire to act 'for the sake of' such goods, the intentional *objects* of our desire are normally not possible future states or experiences of ours. We do not, in such cases, act *in order* to have certain experiences ('pleasure'). Yet, our 'well-being' lies, according to such theories of value, at least partly in having desires and performing actions of this kind.

Now, Nietzsche, as we have seen, shares one basic intuition generally underlying this sort of view: a distaste for the 'vulgar' sensibility for which states of pleasure or comfort are the highest good. The embodiment of this sensibility in *Also sprach Zarathustra* is the 'last man'—'the most contemptible man who can no longer despise himself' (Z 13/46). Nevertheless, according to him, all human desires are 'egoistic' (e.g. KGW VII.2.26.224). That is to say, there are, as a matter of fact, no desires whose intentional objects are not states of the desiring subject or elements of such states. For the value realist, happiness or well-being accompanies, or is an aspect of, ostensibly non-egoistic desires and actions, but it is not *intended* in them if the relevant desire is genuine. Nietzsche, by contrast, has to say, given his analysis of human motivation, that happiness is in fact the object of such desires and actions, although the subject may be self-deceived about this. Hence, supposedly non-self-directed actions, even where they are not enjoined with the promise of an extrinsic reward (as in Christianity), nevertheless have as their object the happiness of the agent. The particular kind of happiness which Nietzsche alleges to be desired in such cases he thinks it correct to describe as 'comfort' (KGW VII.2.27.81)—hence the apparent love of external goods 'for their own sake' is in fact a form of 'vulgar' egoism. It is an interesting question what the 'comfort' might be which accrues to the believer in real goods which are to be loved for their own sake. Nietzsche would presumably say that it lies in the very fact of his being able to view the world, not as disenchanted or as 'merely' a resource for the satisfaction of self-directed desires, but as a locus of independent value.[69] In any case, it follows from this train of thought that desires and actions which are 'noble' and 'heroic'—i.e. which Nietzsche approves of or, more accurately, admires—must 'deny' not only hedonistic impulses but also those goods which are ostensibly

---

[69] If this *is* Nietzsche's view, it leads to difficulties similar to those discussed above in connection with KGW VIII.1.5.71.

apprehended as valuable in themselves, independently of the subject's recognizing them. This is what he means when he says that heroism lies in 'recasting [. . .] the devil as God' and in 'cruelty' against oneself, or self-overcoming. It also explains statements like this:

But even religions are still results of that instinct for beauty (or: being able to endure it all): the ultimate consistency would be—to grasp the absolute ugliness of man, existence without God, reason, etc. [. . .] It is this most extreme form of world-denial which I have been seeking. (KGW VII.2.25.101)

This strand of thought in Nietzsche, which pervades the later writings (although, to repeat, it does not exclusively dominate them), evidently manifests a deliberate 'struggle' against his—and, in his view, mankind's—'most intimate feeling'. His much-quoted dictum that 'man is something to be overcome' can only be understood in the light of it. It represents an uncompromising revolt against nature—against man as he (supposedly) is. It also is arguably the most radicalized and interiorized form of an ethic of work and striving, according to which seemingly futile labour and the absence of beauty are to be welcomed, if not positively to be sought—to chastise the 'weakness of the flesh' and to destroy what is 'merely nature' in us. As Klages, Löwith,[70] and others suspected, in both of these respects Nietzsche, like many rebels, had perhaps not travelled quite as far as he thought from *some* aspects of the tradition which shaped him. It is not without a certain irony that he who, in his more serene moods, wished to celebrate 'harmony of soul' (WM 283), human 'flourishing' and 'its expression: beauty, joy' (GM iii.11), and to defend it against what he saw as the infectious sickness of *ressentiment* should nevertheless in the end have succumbed to that craving for the radical subjugation of 'internal' and 'external' nature which, in a myriad of shapes and transformations—philosophical, economic, and technological—has been one of the driving forces of modernity since its inception.

---

[70] 'All this superlative "highest" and "ultimate" willing [. . .] is as anti-natural as it is un-Greek. It originates in the Judaeo-Christian tradition, in the belief that the world and man are created by God's omnipotent will, and that God, and man who is created in His image, are essentially will.' (K. Löwith, *Nietzsches Philosophie der ewigen Wiederkehr des Gleichen* (Stuttgart, 1956), 126.)

6

The Will to Power: Nietzsche and Metaphysics

In this final chapter, I shall attempt to draw together, so far as the unsystematic nature of Nietzsche's thinking permits this, some of the main threads of the previous discussions. While there are many aspects of his thought which we have not been able to explore as extensively as they would merit, there is one very central problem which perhaps has remained more puzzling than any other—the exact import and scope of what I have called Nietzsche's anti-essentialism.

This question is probably most usefully discussed in the context of what is sometimes referred to as the 'metaphysics of the will to power', extensive sketches of which are to be found in the *Nachlass* of the 1880s, and some aspects of which we have already encountered in Chapter 4. These sketches have sometimes been portrayed as providing a metaphysical basis for Nietzsche's attacks on other, 'traditional', metaphysical claims and for his rejection of the notion of essential natures.[1] Perhaps it is more appropriate, however, to regard them as attempts to spell out the *implications* of his various critical reflections and of his psychological theories, all of which he attempts to take account of and to incorporate in the 'metaphysics of the will to power' (I shall use this conventional label as a convenient shorthand for the *Nachlass* sketches in question, without intending to prejudge thereby the issue of whether they are indeed to be interpreted as outlines of a metaphysical system in the usual sense of that expression). One might say, in a preliminary fashion, that the 'metaphysics of the will to power' is a model of reality which attempts to do without the various concepts— Boscovichean force, efficient mechanical causation, substance, soul, the will of faculty psychology, essential natures, and so forth—that have previously been criticized by Nietzsche as unintelligible (that

---

[1] e.g. by Danto, *Nietzsche as Philosopher*, 80.

is, as either incoherent or empirically empty; cf. WM 635). We can therefore expect that, among other things, an investigation of it will provide some insight into the precise meaning of his anti-essentialist utterances. We shall address the problem of the 'metaphysics of the will to power' in three stages: first, how is it arrived at?; secondly, what exactly does it say?; and, thirdly, how are we to interpret what it says in the context of Nietzsche's philosophy as a whole?

1. ANALOGY AND THE WILL

We have seen that Nietzsche considers the term 'explanation', when applied to the practice of Newtonian and post-Newtonian science, to be a misnomer: the alleged explanations offered by science are in fact not explanations at all but abbreviated descriptions, in the form of mathematical equations, i.e. of functional correlations among phenomena.[2] The concept of explanation presupposed by Nietzsche's criticism is, I have suggested, in agreement both with most traditional philosophical discourse and with everyday usage: according to it, we have explained an event in the proper sense if we have comprehended the nature of the efficacy which brings it about. Hence, explaining events involving unfamiliar entities would consist in correctly establishing their efficacious nature as similar or materially analogous to efficacious natures (powers) with which we are experientially acquainted (cf. Chapter 2.2). Putative instances of this kind of explanation are Boyle's and Locke's corpuscles, Berkeley's ideas and spirits, Leibniz's monads, and Schopenhauer's will. As Nietzsche puts it: 'to "understand" means merely: to be able to express something new in the language of something old and familiar' (WM 479).

Modern natural science does not even pretend to explain in this sense. A force which acts neither through a material medium (i.e. by contact) nor in some 'mental' mode is not familiar to us (only its 'effects' are). Moreover, following Boscovich, natural science has increasingly analysed matter itself in terms of fields of force, thereby dissipating the simple verities of the atomists. Science leaves

---

[2] Strictly speaking, these correlations do not hold between phenomena, but between variables in a calculus which are interpreted in terms of certain theoretical notions or models, some of the latter being in turn correlated by correspondence rules to observable phenomena.

us with a universe of which we lack comprehension in the sense in which Nietzsche, and many others before and after him, have used this term: 'The development of science resolves the "familiar" more and more into the unfamiliar:—it desires, however, the reverse, and proceeds from the instinct to trace the unfamiliar back to the familiar' (WM 608).

The epistemological starting-point from which Nietzsche proceeds to develop the 'metaphysics of the will to power' is thus rather similar to Schopenhauer's, and so is the argument from analogy, which he appears to propose as a means to escape from ignorance:

The victorious concept 'force', by means of which our physicists have created God and the world, still needs to be complemented: an inner will must be ascribed to it, which I designate as 'will to power', i.e., as an insatiable desire to manifest power [. . . .] Physicists cannot eradicate 'action at a distance' from their principles; nor can they eradicate a repellent force (or an attracting one). There is nothing for it: one is obliged to understand all motion, all 'appearances', all 'laws', only as symptoms of an inner event and to employ man as an analogy to this end. (WM 619; cf. WM 689; KGW VII.3.40.37)

The will to power in human beings, it emerged in the preceding chapter, can become self-conscious in a consciousness purged of self-deception as the 'ultimate fact we reach down to' (KGW VII.3.40.61), and it involves, in this fully conscious form, the desire for the experience of power and action towards this end (cf. WM 663). Nietzsche declares repeatedly that all human behaviour, even when its efficacious antecedents are unconscious to us, is to be comprehended in analogy to this model. Given his concept of comprehension, this would seem to imply that, when acting in a non-self-deceived manner, we are indeed acquainted with the real force which brings about our behaviour, or at least with something rather like it. In a number of notes, he straightforwardly asserts 'that all driving force is will to power, that there is no other physical, dynamic or psychic force except this' (WM 688), for 'we cannot imagine any change that does not involve a will to power' (WM 689; cf. also WM 490, 658). What this seems to imply is that we *can* imagine, i.e. comprehend in Nietzsche's sense, a change involving the will to power and this in turn implies, given his view of 'comprehension', that we are familiar with (have experience of) the nature of an efficacious power in at least some of our actions.

The problem with this is, as was pointed out earlier (Chapter 2.1), that there are other passages in which he seems precisely to deny this. To be sure, nearly all of his criticisms of the concept of the will and of the idea that we are acquainted with volitional efficacy are aimed either at particular psychological theories of volition which he considers to be false (e.g. WM 689), or at Schopenhauer's notion of a blind, aimless 'striving'.[3] But there remains at least one note in which he explicitly denies that we have any experience at all of efficacy in volition (WM 664). This might still be considered a freak, a provisional and later discarded assumption in the experimental, tentative development of Nietzsche's thought on the matter. But even in his presumably less provisional reflection on the issue in JGB 36, he still declines to assert unambiguously that there is an experience of efficacy in willing, and he recommends the supposition that there is as no more than an admissible, while still rather doubtful 'hypothesis'.

The question as to his final position on the matter cannot be settled confidently on the basis of Nietzsche's own utterances and perhaps all we can say is that he does not reach a final conclusion on this central point, but that he is at least tempted to acknowledge the presence of an experience of efficacy in volition and to conclude that willing, as analysed by him, is at any rate the most promising candidate for furnishing such an experience.[4] He is arguably rather more convinced that all conscious human desires and intentions can be analysed monistically in terms of the desire/intention to bring about a state in which the experience of power or superiority is enhanced, than that we actually experience any *efficacy* of these desires and intentions. However uncertain our intuition may be on this point, there is, according to Nietzsche, no better available

---

[3] A point emphasized by L. Giesz, *Nietzsche—Existenzialismus und Wille zur Macht* (Stuttgart, 1950), 7, and by Mittasch, *Friedrich Nietzsche als Naturphilosoph*, 227. Stack, by contrast, claims that Nietzsche's criticisms are directed against the idea of volitional causality in general (*Lange and Nietzsche*, 245).

[4] Despite his prevarications on this issue, Nietzsche is in fact, whether willingly or not, committed to the view that we do have some contentful idea of efficacy, *if* indeed his analysis of objective reality is to make sense. As I argued at some length in Ch. 3.1, he equates objectivity with the interpretation, by some subject, of certain representational contents as acting on it, this 'efficacy' (KGW VIII.1.5.19) manifesting itself in the awareness of a resistance to the subject's will.

model on which we can make causal power comprehensible to us, and he consequently 'ventures the hypothesis' that the will is indeed efficacious and thus explanatory in a way no scientific theory is—it is on the basis of this hypothesis that the 'metaphysics of the will to power' is erected.

Nietzsche gives a fairly elaborate, if not entirely clear, account of what is involved in his concept of the will and of its differences from previous psychological or metaphysical conceptions. 'Willing' an action, he explains, is a complex occurrence in which at least three kinds of elements can be distinguished: first, a number of feelings;[5] secondly, a thought, image, or 'representation'; and thirdly, what he calls the 'affect of commanding' (JGB 19).

In the first category, we find a 'feeling' which characterizes the state which we are about to leave, an anticipatory feeling of the state we hope to enter by our action, as well as a feeling which accompanies, and is characteristic of, that transition itself. Furthermore, there are additional accompanying muscular feelings or sensations, which may even occur, on account of long habitual association, before the physical movement itself commences. In Chapter 2.1, we mentioned yet another *Gefühl* involved in action according to Nietzsche, namely the deceptive 'feeling of force' which is occasioned by 'the sight of an enemy or an obstacle to which we feel ourselves equal' (WM 664) and which we sometimes mistakenly regard as the effective force by which the movement is brought about. (We may of course rightly wonder whether we really always experience as many distinct and identifiable 'feelings' in our actions as Nietzsche claims to detect.)

As for the thought, image, or representation involved in willing, it represents either the goal of the action or some aspect of the bodily movement through which that goal is to be attained. Often it consists in an anticipatory 'idea of the movement' or, in another formulation, an 'image of the movement within us' (WM 671;

---

[5] The term *'Gefühle'* which Nietzsche here uses is ambiguous. On the most plausible construction of his view, he sometimes intends it to refer to sensations—as when he speaks of an 'accompanying muscular feeling'—and sometimes to a certain hedonic quality or 'colouring' with which some state of affairs, actual or anticipated, is experienced (cf. JGB 19), or to the experience of a determinate 'direction' of desire which arguably can be present even when the goal of the desire—the state of affairs aimed at—is not yet specifiable. (For an analysis of this elusive pre-representational awareness of a certain 'direction' of desire, see M. Scheler, *Der Formalismus in der Ethik und die materiale Wertethik* (Bern, 1980), 51–64.)

GOA xii.151). But in contrast to, for example, William James's ideo-motor theory of action, Nietzsche maintains that it is never this representation itself which effects the movement (GOA xiii.133; WM 671), although it may function, through repeated association with the movement, as a 'triggering stimulus' (GOA xii.151). Nevertheless, as against Schopenhauer, he insists that a thought, image, or representation is an essential ingredient of 'willing', without the presence of which we would not be entitled to speak of willing at all: 'We can only "will" what we have *seen* [. . . .] We cannot do anything without previously projecting a *free image* of it' (GOA xii.150; cf. also WM 692). But if this representation is not actually the force effecting the movement, but only a disinhibiting factor 'triggering it off' (*auslösen*) by virtue of frequent previous association, what *is* the power which does bring about the movement? Nietzsche suggests in a number of places that this force is located in the third ingredient in volition—the 'affect of commanding':

The only force that exists is of the same kind as that of the will: a commanding of other subjects which thereupon change. (WM 490)

Willing t[hat is] *commanding*: but commanding is a particular *affect* (this affect is a sudden explosion of force)— (KGW VII.2.25.436)

there is a 'thou shalt' for the individual organs which comes down to them from the commanding organ [. . . .] Some tasks are commanded that cannot be fully *performed* (because the strength is insufficient). But often the most extreme tension [. . .]—an *exertion* of the will, as we know this in ourselves in the case of difficult tasks. (GOA xiii.170)

These sketches of an account of the efficacy of the will seem to comprise two elements, or rather, two models by way of which the notion of efficacious force is given empirical content. The first is the psychic compulsion we experience when faced with a command which we perceive as authoritative and which makes us feel 'compelled' to obey. This is how I would interpret Nietzsche's statement that we can think of the way in which an organism functions as involving something analogous to moral injunctions ('thou shalt'). This model of force is thus, strictly speaking, not drawn from our putative experience of efficacy in volition, but rather from the experience of being the *recipient* of a command which one acknowledges as 'to be obeyed' and which one feels 'compelled' by (cf. esp. JGB 19). Nevertheless, the command Nietzsche refers to is presumably a potentially conscious occurrence in the willing 'subject', even if its compelling force is felt only by its recipient.

We may certainly doubt whether all or even most of the actions we consider voluntary are initiated by an occurrence which could plausibly be described as a command. But this is not Nietzsche's point in any case; all his argument requires is that an occurrence of the relevant kind is 'familiar' to us in some of our actions. And it is not implausible to maintain that in some circumstances, even when we are not aware of an *external* command or injunction, there does occur a mental event or act which could be characterized as a fiat that seems to us to initiate the movement. The very concept of a command implies, of course, what Nietzsche variously refers to as a thought, image, or representation of its object, for one can only command *something* (e.g. 'that such-and-such a state of affairs be brought about'; cf. WM 668). What it requires to be effective is the possibility of *understanding* that thought or representation on the part of a recipient.

There is a second model of efficacy or force which is strongly, if imprecisely, suggested by the notebook entry cited above (GOA xiii.170). It consists in an individual's experience of 'exertion' or effort when attempting to perform a 'difficult task'. It is tempting to interpret these remarks as referring to the 'mental effort' (as opposed to, say, a muscular effort) that we experience ourselves as making when attempting to execute an action which we also have a strong disinclination to perform. Arguably, Nietzsche's point is similar to that which William James formulated rather more explicitly and elaborately. James (whose work was unknown to Nietzsche) argued that we are sometimes aware of a 'force of consciousness', or a 'feeling of spontaneous psychic effort', by which we sustain the anticipatory idea of a movement against the intrusion of countervailing ideas, thereby enabling the idea of the movement in question to prevail and to result in the movement itself.[6] (To repeat, neither James nor Nietzsche claims that this is what happens in all actions; all they require is that something like this occurs in some instances which are preceded by a kind of internal struggle, the resolution of which involves the 'psychic effort' referred to.)

---

[6] James, 'The Feeling of Effort', esp. 190–204 and 213–17.

If force is to be understood on the twofold model of compulsion by a quasi-moral demand or injunction and psychic effort, then any change, if it involves a plurality of entities, requires these entities to be rather like subjects (WM 490), capable of willing and understanding (i.e. of interpreting certain symbols as representing specific commands). As Nietzsche puts it, 'there is absolutely no other kind of causality than that of will upon will' (WM 658).[7] As we saw in the previous chapter, he, quite consistently in this regard, conceives of the human individual that experiences itself as capable of agency and self-movement as a plurality of subjects ('drives', 'consciousnesses', 'living beings') variously commanding and executing commands, being related to one another in a quasi-political structure (see e.g. WM 490, 492, 660; KGW VII.3.37.4). The individual is a *Gesellschaftsbau*, a society or polity of such 'subjects'. Consciousness—our conscious representations, our reasonings, and, intimately tied up with these and partly directing them, our conscious appetitive and affective life—can be compared to a regent or ruler 'at the head of a communality' (WM 492). There may, however, be a number of such 'ruling drives' which alternate in, as it were, presiding over the 'communality', rendering it analogous to an oligarchy and accounting for the possibility of quite different, sometimes mutually incompatible, conscious desires and values or preferences of one individual at different times. While this view may not necessarily conflict with the possibility of different experiences being ascribed to 'the same' self—which, if we accept Kant's argument, is not just something we as a matter of fact do, but rather a necessary condition of subjectivity—nor with the prevailing belief in personal identity, or at least continuity, over time, Nietzsche certainly makes no attempt to show how either possibility can be accounted for on his assumptions.[8]

---

[7] It is not clear whether Nietzsche would consider the resistance posed by some representational contents, which we interpret as their acting on us, as a further independent mode of acquaintance with efficacy or power. But it is likely and in keeping with his general position that he would regard it as secondary, at least in one sense, to the primary idea of efficacy obtained from volition. He might argue, in other words, that we can only interpret objects as affecting us in so far as they are impervious to the 'commands' and 'exertions' of our will, the latter being conceived as potentially efficacious.

[8] The problem is highlighted by Christopher Janaway: 'Can a collection of subpersonal drives fabricate a unitary self that comes to regard those drives as its own? Or must there be a presupposed unitary self as author of the fiction?' (C. Janaway, *Self and World in Schopenhauer's Philosophy* (Oxford, 1989), 355).

He extends the analogy between a human individual and a state or polity beyond the features we have mentioned so far. Like the actions taken by a state, the actions of an individual can be initiated by the command ('will') of its ruler ('consciousness'). But this is obviously not sufficient for the action to take place. For one thing, the initial command is too 'indefinite' and 'imprecise' (WM 666) to determine the action in detail, and consequently requires multifarious specifications, interpretations, and applications by subordinate agents. This is the main reason why Nietzsche stresses time and again how little we really know of an action and all that is involved in its execution when we are conscious of its purpose (ibid.):

commands have to be given (and obeyed) time after time down to the most minute detail, and only then, when the command has been divided up into a myriad of small sub-commands, can the movement take place [. . . .] Here it is presupposed that the whole organism thinks, that all organic things participate in thinking, feeling, willing,—(GOA xiii.266).

In this respect, the body, with its multitude of coordinated, sub- and superordinated organs and functions, provides us with a better *Gleichnis* or analogy for an understanding of the nature of human agency than our relatively simple and paltry consciousness of 'ends'. Nevertheless, it is important to remember that each of these bodily functions or organs involved in action is itself ultimately interpreted by Nietzsche in a mentalistic idiom (see esp. WM 492; also Chapter 4.3).

There is yet another feature of the analogy between a state and an individual agent Nietzsche likes to emphasize. This is the fact that, in the former, many decisions are made and courses of action pursued by various social and political forces (by subordinate agents, in his terminology) of which the ruler is ignorant. In fact, Nietzsche's preferred *Gleichnis* for the human individual is that of a state in which the ruler is frequently kept in the dark about what is really going on by his scheming subordinates and unruly subjects who pursue their own particular interests (cf. WM 492). These interests, as was related at length in the preceding chapter, are in the last resort reducible to various specifications of one generic end: the 'feeling of power'. Each of the 'drives' or 'living beings' constituting the individual has to be conceived of as a complex of 'thinking, feeling, willing' (GOA xiii.170), a quasi-mental reality acting for the sake of the experience of power.

These entities enter into the hierarchically structured 'confederations' (*Zusammenschlüsse*) constituting individuals in a similar manner as these individuals in turn—according to Nietzsche—enter into relations, alliances, and dependencies with other individuals, namely, either because they are compelled to do so by more powerful individuals, or because they are themselves sufficiently powerful to 'annex' and rule over others by force, whether 'intellectual' or 'physical'. Most, however, belong to neither of these extreme categories, and enter into, or remain in, their respective *Zusammenschlüsse* for the sake of gaining power over individuals outside them. They become constituent parts subordinate to a more powerful whole, desiring to increase their 'feeling of power' by co-operating in and identifying themselves with the latter (cf. our Nietzschean analysis of nationalism in the previous chapter).

The essentially aggressive, expansionary, appropriating, and violating character—'physical', 'intellectual', or otherwise—of the human individual is, on this account, a result of the nature of its constituent elements, and it is not difficult to infer from this what Nietzsche considers to be the character of even larger communalities like the state. An individual, like a state, is engaged in a constant quest for power by virtue of its nature and, since (the experience of) power in Nietzsche's definition logically involves the experience of overcoming resistance, it is continuously either engaged in a struggle with opponents, or in search of such opponents and obstacles to be overcome. However, just as the wills of individuals hardly ever totally coincide with the common interests of the political structure to which they belong, but rather tend also to express particular interests as against other particular interests within the same communality, so there is also an incessant hidden struggle for power between the quasi-mental entities constituting the individual. But it is usually only the result of these struggles, or rather a particular interpretation of them, that emerges into the light of the individual's consciousness.

One question Nietzsche does not explicitly address is what differentiates a *Zusammenschluss* of entities constituting an individual, say a human being, from the apparently much looser 'confederations' these individuals in turn enter into with one another in their social and political relations. It seems, for example, that (to retain the physical idiom for the moment) an organ of the body like the heart is much more strongly integrated into, and dependent upon, the rest of the body than the human individual as a whole is with respect to the society or the state he or she lives in. Nietzsche would presumably reply that the difference here is precisely—and no more than—one of the degree of a *Wesen*'s integration into and dependence upon the command structure of a larger political or quasi-political entity.

2. QUANTA OF FORCE AND PERSPECTIVISM

Like Schopenhauer, Nietzsche proposes to 'employ man as an analogy' towards an understanding of the nature of things in general. Not only are we to conceive of other organisms—animals and plants—as constituted by analogues to the 'thinking, feeling, willing' entities making up a human individual (WM 619), but we are also to think of so-called inorganic nature in the same manner:

> If we translate the concept 'cause' back to the only sphere known to us, from which we have derived it, we cannot imagine any change that does not involve a will to power. We do not know how to explain a change except as the encroachment of one power upon another power [. . . .] Should we not be permitted to assume this will as a motive cause in chemistry, too?—and in the cosmic order? [. . .] the only reality is the will to grow stronger of every centre of force—not self-preservation, but the will to appropriate, dominate, increase, grow stronger. (WM 689; cf. JGB 36)

A. Psychological *starting point*:

- our thinking and valuing is only an expression of desires which are at work behind them.
- the desires specialize themselves more and more: their unity is *the will to power* [. . .]
- reduction of all basic organic functions to the will to power
- question whether it is not also the *mobile* in the inorganic world? For the mechanistic interpretation of the world a *mobile* is still needed.

  [. . .]

- mechanical *motion* is only an expression of an inner occurrence. (KGW VIII.1.1.30)

Nietzsche's 'hypothesis' is thus that there is no essential difference between organic and inorganic nature, that all motion, all change is a kind of agency:

> Should it not suffice to conceive of 'force' as a unity in which willing feeling thinking are still blended and unseparated? [. . .] Ultimately nothing is given as real but thinking and feeling and drives: is it not permitted to try whether this given material might be *sufficient* to construe the world? I do not mean as appearance: but as just as real as our willing feeling thinking is—but as a primitive form of the same [. . .] (KGW VII.3.40.37)

The parallel evoked by formulations like this is of course the organicist metaphysics of the ancestor of German philosophy in the modern era—Georg Wilhelm Leibniz.[9] For Leibniz, extended bodies are appearances of aggregates of simple, unextended monads (forms, entelechies, 'living things'[10]) whose intrinsic nature consists in 'perception' and 'appetition', neither of which necessarily involves apperception, i.e. self-consciousness. Organic beings are distinguished from what we normally regard as non-organic ones only in the sense that they are collections of monads that are, unlike the latter, subject to a dominant monad whose dominance consists in its having clearer and more distinct perceptions than its subject monads. In human beings, the perceptions of the dominant monad are, at least sometimes, so distinct as to be apperceived, that is, accompanied by self-conciousness. All active force (which gives rise to change) is, for Leibniz, a *conatus* or effort characterizing a monad like a quality at any given moment. Ultimately, this 'effort' is akin to a desire[11] and involves the 'perception' or 'mirroring' of the state of one monad by another,[12] although neither the effort nor the perception is necessarily self-conscious (in the case of aggregates

---

[9] One recent writer who has discussed in some detail the affinity of Nietzsche's ideas to Leibniz's monadology is Friedrich Kaulbach, *Nietzsches Idee einer Experimentalphilosophie* (Cologne, 1981), 49–58. See also his 'Nietzsche und der monadologische Gedanke', in *Nietzsche-Studien* 8 (1979), 127–56.

[10] G. W. Leibniz, *Metaphysical Consequences of the Principle of Reason*, paras. 7 and 8, in G. H. R. Parkinson (ed.), *Philosophical Writings* (London, 1973), 174–5.

[11] Cf. B. Russell, *The Philosophy of Leibniz* (London, 1937), 87.

[12] Leibniz, *Monadology*, paras. 14 and 15, in *Philosophical Writings*, 180–1.

of monads appearing to us as inanimate bodies, they are never apperceived).

While Nietzsche's account of force as a 'primitive form' of the complex act of 'willing', and his reduction of both the organic and the apparently non-organic to 'communalities' of 'living beings' (of which matter in motion is only an image or expression —a *Gleichnis* or *Ausdrucksmittel*), is indeed strikingly reminiscent in these respects to Leibniz's corresponding ideas, there are evidently also considerable differences between the views of both thinkers.

Perhaps the most obvious difference is that monads are not acted upon from without. It is their own appetitions which exclusively bring about the succession of perceptions in them, although some of these perceptions *appear* to them as effected by external objects. Nietzsche, on the other hand, generally maintains that his counterparts to the monads, quanta of force, genuinely act upon one another, although some of his statements, as we shall see, imply that this cannot be so. Finally, quanta of force are not to be conceived as self-identically persisting substances with potentialities (like monads), since this is ruled out by Nietzsche's criticism of substance. His alternative conception is perhaps best conveyed in his own words:

A quantum of power is designated by the effect it produces and that which it resists. The adiaphorous state is missing, though it is thinkable. It is essentially a will to violate and to defend oneself against violation. Not self-preservation: every atom affects the whole of being—it is thought away if one thinks away this radiation of power-will. That is why I call it a quantum of 'will to power' [. . . .] Subject, object, a doer added to the doing, the doing separated from that which it does: let us not forget that this is mere semiotics and nothing real. Mechanistic theory as a theory of motion is already a translation into the sense language of man. (WM 634)

[. . .] no things remain but only dynamic quanta: their essence lies in their relation to all other quanta, in a relation of tension to all other dynamic quanta, in their 'effect' upon the same. The will to power not a being, not a becoming, but a *pathos*— (WM 635)

My idea is that every specific body strives to become master over all space and to extend its force (—its will to power:) and to thrust back all that resists its extension. But it continually encounters similar efforts on the part of other bodies and ends by coming to an arrangement ('union') with those of them that are sufficiently related to it: thus they then conspire together for power. And the process goes on— (WM 636; the terms 'space' and 'body' here are presumably not to be understood literally).

It would be most apt to say that the ultimate 'entities' are in fact acts of will—analogous to the complex acts described earlier in this chapter—and perceptions or interpretations of such acts.[13] Nietzsche describes both of these as 'processes' (WM 655) or 'complexes of events' (WM 552 C), that is, as clusters of continually changing qualities without even relatively enduring substrata.

Every process of 'willing' and of reacting to impinging forces (i.e. other acts of will) has an effect on every other, and it exists indeed only as the sum of 'its' effects on (or relations to) other processes/ entities/quanta of force (cf. WM 556, 557, 558, 583 A).[14] This conception, in which any entity exists only in so far as it stands in certain relations to other entities, affecting them and being affected by them in turn, can be seen as a model of a reality of which the second-order statement 'no proposition about the world can ever correspond to, or represent adequately, the constitution in itself of any part of reality or of reality as a whole' would be 'true'. For in such a reality, nothing would have a constitution in itself:

A thing would be defined once all creatures had asked 'what is that?' and had answered their question. Supposing one single creature, with its own relationships and perspectives for all things, were missing, then the thing would not yet be 'defined'. In short: the essence of a thing is only an *opinion* about the 'thing'. (WM 556)

Before going on to comment on some of the problems of this 'perspectivist' model, it may be useful to recall Nietzsche's account of a 'subject's' knowledge of a world external to it as being itself an expression or manifestation of the will to power of that subject, and to consider this account now in the context of the 'metaphysics of the will to power' as a whole. I described in Chapter 4 how, for

---

[13] Cf. Grimm, *Nietzsche's Theory of Knowledge*, 154: 'The individual mind [. . .] is not the doer or the thinker: it is not the interpreter, but is itself an interpretation [. . .]' If this suggestive but somewhat cryptic remark is meant to say that Nietzsche wants to reject the notion of mental substrata or of transcendental subjects, it is, I believe, correct. On Nietzsche's radically empiricist approach, there is, at any given moment, nothing to any of the ultimate subjects—'quanta of force', 'drives', 'living beings'—other than the perspectival qualities characterizing them. However, Nietzsche is certainly not saying that such subjects do not or cannot distinguish between 'inner' and 'outer', 'self' and 'other' (cf. Chs. 3.1 and 4.3).

[14] Cf. A. Nehamas, *Nietzsche—Life as Literature* (Cambridge, Mass., 1985), 80–3.

Nietzsche, the external world we find ourselves in is literally shaped by us, although this creative process does not enter our consciousness. The Kantian phenomenal world of spatio-temporal objects changing their states according to apparently invariable laws is thus a product of 'us' *qua* will to power. We interpret, select, and 'falsify' any data impinging upon us in such a manner that the contents of our conscious perceptions exhibit a considerable amount of order, stability, and mutual resemblance. It is only through the creation of such a world of comparatively stable things and 'identical cases' that the contents of our experience assume the order and regularity necessary for prediction and control. The creative-interpretive processes in question are unconscious to the empirical individual, for they occur at the level of the 'hidden' drives or quanta of force, communalities of which constitute the individual and which appear as an extended body to external observers (and indeed, in one of its aspects, to itself). These ultimate agents are:

beings [*Wesen*] surrounded by fabricated small worlds: in that they project [*setzen*] their strength, their appetites, their habits of experience outside themselves, as their *external world*. The capacity to create (shape invent fabricate) is their basic capacity [. . .] (KGW VII.3.34.247)

It is not entirely clear whether these 'feeling willing thinking' *Wesen* are themselves aware of their creative activity by virtue of which they 'shape' the world we perceive and believe ourselves to act upon and be acted upon by. But Nietzsche surmises that they have only a 'falsified [. . .] simplified' awareness of their own activity (ibid.). This seems to raise again all the difficulties which we have grappled with in our discussion of unconscious ideas, desires, and intentions in the previous chapter. The world of willing and perceiving quanta of force is explicitly presented as an explanatory 'hypothesis' at the final level of explanation. It is also evident (e.g. from WM 619, WM 689, and JGB 36) that Nietzsche intends this model and its notion of efficacy to be, in his own terms, an intelligible one, taking us beyond the occult qualities of science. But if we are indeed to understand the ultimate agents as strictly unconscious (rather than as sometimes self-deceived, or dimly, inattentively, or confusedly conscious in a Leibnizian sense), then the model is not, on Nietzsche's criteria, an intelligible one, for the notion of something that is literally a perception or volition, but *totally* devoid of

and inaccessible to *any* consciousness, is, unsurprisingly, empirically empty (even if one grants that it is not strictly incoherent). It
can only be a manner of speaking about either physical events
(which it is evidently not in Nietzsche), or about a behavioural
disposition, or about something unknown in its nature—an occult
quality (see Chapter 5.2).

While Nietzsche denies any fundamental differences between the
realms of the organic and the apparently inanimate, he seems to
acknowledge (like Leibniz) that there is some basis for this distinction which we draw in ordinary discourse. He suggests that there is
a real difference in the 'certainty' and 'determinacy' of the activity
of the quanta of force constituting what we ordinarily refer to
as organisms and inorganic bodies respectively.[15] In 'inorganic'
nature, the 'perceptions' of the constituent entities are utterly determinate and without error, and their volitional activity invariably
brings about its ends (cf. KGW VII.3.41.11), while it is only in the
'organic' world that 'thought and perception' become subject to
indeterminacy and to 'illusion' and 'error' (cf. KGW VII.3.35.35;
KGW VIII.1.1.105).

Turning now to the question of the coherence of these claims
considered as an outline of a metaphysics, I shall confine myself to
one salient problem arising from them. If our interpretation so far
has been correct, Nietzsche asks us to think of reality as consisting
of a plurality of 'entities' which are in fact processes or subjective
(perspectival) episodes analogous to occurrent perceptions, judgements, desires, and volitions which, however, are present in these
processes 'blended and unseparated' (*gemischt und ungeschieden*;
KGW VII.3.40.37).[16] The model is therefore, according to
Nietzsche's intention, a pluralistic one—it is 'monistic' only in the
sense that it envisages all these 'entities' to share the same essential
features,[17] namely a certain kind of directedness of all their activities towards the end of the feeling of power. On the other hand, he
also appears to say that the ultimate entities/processes do not even
at any given moment, however short, have any essential constitution (or nature), that is, any intrinsic qualities that constitute their

---

[15] Cf. Figl, *Interpretation als philosophisches Prinzip*, 107–8.

[16] Leibniz also attributed to the monads 'simplicity' while yet ascribing to them a
plurality of properties in any given state. They are 'a plurality within the unity or the
simple' (*Monadology*, paras. 12–14, in *Philosophical Writings*, 180–1).

[17] This has also been emphasized by W. Müller-Lauter in his 'Nietzsches Lehre
vom Willen zur Macht' in *Nietzsche-Studien* 7 (1978), 19–20.

identity *at that moment in time*. Any quantum of force has its essence (at any moment) *exclusively* in its 'relation to all other quanta [. . .], in [its] effect upon the same' (WM 635). An entity exists only *qua* 'effect' upon other entities, so that it 'would be defined once all creatures had asked "what is that?" and had answered their question' (WM 556). I have argued that this view, which I have called anti-essentialism, is at the very centre of Nietzsche's thought in the last period, being the metaphysical counterpart to his epistemological claim that the concept of metaphysical truth as the mapping by a representation of a 'fact', a segment of reality as it is in itself, in its intrinsic nature, is unintelligible. He declares that 'there are only interpretations', none of which can be said to be 'objectively' better or to be more 'fitting' than any other, since it is not coherent to suppose that there is anything for any interpretation to fit in the required way.

The conjunction of these two aspects of the 'metaphysics of the will to power'—its assumption of a plurality of interacting 'beings' (*Wesen*) on the one hand, and its anti-essentialism on the other—is very problematic. This becomes evident if we imagine, by way of an illustrative example, a highly simplified Nietzschean world consisting at a given instant of two quanta of force acting on each other. Let us assume that the action of one quantum, *b*, gives rise, at the instant in question, to a certain perception in the other, *a*. As Nietzsche insists, the contents of this perception of *a*'s will be an *interpretation* by *a* of a certain stimulus. The character of this interpretation defines in fact partly the specific form and quantity of the will to power which *a is* (at that time). Let us also assume that *a*'s activity does not exhaust itself in perceiving (i.e. interpreting) what we have called, for lack of a more noncommittal expression, stimuli. Let us rather suppose that its activity is more complex, in particular, that it also strives to affect *b* in a certain manner, say, to bring about certain perceptions on *b*'s part. The quasi-volitional activity or 'force' of *a* will in its turn be given a particular interpretion by *b*, provided it affects *b* at all.

In this scenario, we would have to say that both *a* and *b* are constituted, at the time in question, by their respective activities and other experiences, that is, by interpretive activities and their contents, volitions ('commands') and desires—the latter being invariably versions of the desire for the experience of power directing the former. Yet, Nietzsche's anti-essentialism does not permit statements of the form that *x* is in itself constituted by qualities of whatever sort, whether they be Lockean primary qualities, Leibnizian entelechies, or the Nietzschean episodes of 'thinking feeling willing' illustrated by our example. According to the central anti-essentialist strand in Nietzsche's later thought, 'the properties of a thing are effects on *other* "things" [. . .] i.e. there is no thing without other things' (WM 557, my emphasis). If indeed 'the essence of a thing is only an opinion about the "thing"' (WM 556), then the 'essence' of the quantum of force *a* would consist in whatever is the content of *b*'s interpretation, which would therefore not really be an interpretation of anything ontologically independent of it, since *a*'s *esse* would consist in its being perceived (or 'interpreted') by *b* as an entity of a certain kind affecting it (i.e. *b*). If we follow this strand of Nietzsche's thinking, *a* would have no existence other than *qua* perceptual or 'interpretive' content *vorgestellt* by *b*.[18] But what are we to make of *b*, the second entity in this imaginary Nietzschean universe? Since his analysis of the essence of any entity as 'its' relations to (i.e. effects upon) other entities is universal in its scope, it has to apply to *b* as well. This means that, in our model, *b* is not identifiable separately from its effect on *a*; it *is* this effect, namely a certain perceptual content of *a*'s. Nietzsche's claims thus seem to force us to say that *a* exists only *qua* perception ('interpretation') of *b*, while *b* exists only as a perception of *a*—yet both are also required to be separate in some sense, since otherwise there would not be a plurality of quanta of force at all.

The two requirements are not compatible. On the one hand, Nietzsche's anti-essentialism, according to which 'the essence of a thing is only an *opinion*' about the thing leads him to the assertion that 'beings will have to be thought of as sensations [i.e. here: perceptual or 'interpretive' contents] that are no longer based on anything devoid of sensation' (WM 562), ruling out the independent existence of the objects of any given 'interpretation'. On the other hand, the concept of the will to power necessitates the assumption of a plurality of numerically distinct quanta of force, each being characterized by '*its own* particular valuation, mode of action, and mode of resistance' (WM 567, my emphasis). Each of

---

[18] It is the apparent affinity of this with the Berkeleian analysis of objects as ideas whose *esse est percipi* which has led Danto to see a close resemblance between Berkeley's conception and Nietzsche's (*Nietzsche as Philosopher*, 232).

them is a 'living being' which 'exists for some time' and is 'dependent and subservient and yet in a certain sense also commanding and acting from its own will' (KGW VII.3.37.4). But if a quantum of force is constituted at any given moment by a particular kind of valuation, action, and resistance, then it is *ipso facto* not reducible to sensations, perceptions, interpretations, or evaluations in another quantum of force. But even if it were consistently thus reducible, in a quasi-Berkeleian manner, then that *other* quantum of force would after all possess a constitution in itself (at that moment in time) consisting of the experienced contents of its interpretations and of its awareness of its own activity. In traditional language: it may be intelligible to say that this tree exists only as my 'idea', but I cannot also maintain that at the same time I exist only as an idea of some other mind or minds, and that other mind or minds in their turn exist only as an idea ('effect') in some yet further mind and so forth.

It is clear that on this interpretation of Nietzsche's anti-essentialism, which is the one most straightforwardly suggested by his explicit statements, we encounter an infinite regress. It is difficult to avoid the conclusion that if this is how we are to understand his assertion that nothing has a constitution in itself—i.e. that that notion is ultimately unintelligible—then this claim itself is an incoherent one.[19] Nevertheless, it is worthwhile to inquire whether there might not be some plausible construal of it which is both consistent with what Nietzsche says and internally coherent.

His remarks might, for example, be taken as suggesting nothing very different from Schopenhauer's analysis of 'representation'. It could be said that, for Schopenhauer also, there are neither (representing) subjects nor objects with intrinsic properties. Objects exist only relative to, or for, subjects, while the knowing subject is also exclusively characterized by its cognitive relation to the objects represented by it. Neither subject nor object can be thought independently of its relation to the other. The basic ontological item in Schopenhauer's phenomenal world (leaving aside the problematic case of the phenomenal will) is therefore neither the subject nor the object but the 'representation', which is a real relation between these terms, neither of which has any intrinsic properties such that

---

[19] At this point, the reply is sometimes made that, on account of Nietzsche's 'critique of logic', the charge of incoherence need not concern him. Such a response would be confused. See the discussion of Nietzsche's remarks on logic in Ch. 4.3.

it could conceivably exist independently. Nevertheless, it is clear that that real relation which Schopenhauer calls *Vorstellung does* have an intrinsic character (despite some occasional statements of Schopenhauer's which would seem to rule this out). If we think of it, for example, as a perceptual situation at a given moment in which, say, a mountainous landscape is perceived from a certain point of view, the intrinsic character of this representation will consist in the totality of phenomenal, perspectival properties as they appear at this moment. But when Nietzsche says 'the question "what is that?" is an imposition of meaning from some *other* viewpoint' (WM 556, my emphasis), this and similar remarks appear intended to apply to items of any sort, including Schopenhauerian representations. According to these remarks, a representation could *not* have an intrinsic character, but would be exclusively characterized by its relations to 'some other viewpoint' upon it. Consequently, I do not think that Nietzsche's ideas in this respect can with textual plausibility be construed along Schopenhauerian lines.

On another construal Nietzsche might be interpreted as dispensing with most, but not all, of the intrinsic natures admitted in realist metaphysics. One might meaningfully, if somewhat fantastically, speculate that the world as a whole is, in Nietzsche's language, 'posited' (*gesetzt*)—albeit without having a subject-independent existence—by a quasi-Fichtean subject whose being consists precisely in its representing to itself a world of apparent objects which it experiences as obstacles to the activity of the empirical self and as causally affecting it in various ways. The mode of being, or essence, of such a subject would consist in the character of its own activity and, presumably, in the representational contents encountered by, and partly constituting, the empirical self. We might even suppose drastic variations in the latter's experiences to occur—yet, at any one time, it would have a 'nature', i.e. intrinsic properties which constituted it as what it was at that time. In other words, it would have a constitution in itself, even if the latter was subject to incessant change.

In fact, as we saw in the preceding chapters, Nietzsche does not appear to be consistent in his anti-essentialism. We have found that he does assert a number of things about the intrinsic nature of beliefs, emotions, desires, and intentions—in particular, that all desires are variations of the desire for the experience of power and that the nature of our emotions, intentions, and even of our beliefs is at any time specified by the particular form which this desire takes, i.e. by the form of the will to power an instance of which we *are* at that time. (Strictly speaking, no two instances of any 'form' or 'kind' are ever exactly alike according to Nietzsche, who, somewhat more dogmatically than Leibniz, denies that there are actual 'identical cases' without giving any convincing reasons for this denial.) He thus seems to admit the existence of at least one 'stream' of experience which has its own intrinsic properties, or essence, even if these properties may change continuously within certain limits set by the definition of the will to power. Could we not then legitimately interpret his metaphysical sketches in terms of the solipsism adumbrated above, which would allow us to retain both (*a*) the claim that the objects of experience—and indeed other subjects—have no existence and nature in themselves, independently of their being 'my interpretation', and (*b*) the claim that 'I' do have a nature or essence which is correctly described as 'will to power' in the sense of this phrase elucidated earlier?

It does not seem to me that this attempt to synthesize the two conflicting strands in Nietzsche's apparent ontology is a plausible one. Too emphatic is his assertion of the plurality of what he variously calls 'living beings', 'drives', 'power-centres', 'quanta of force', each defined by its own mode of action and interpretation. Leaving aside various other difficulties a Fichtean or quasi-Fichtean solipsism raises—such as the unconscious nature of the subject's creative activity—the fact is that Nietzsche nowhere suggests that the entities/processes he refers to can ultimately be reduced, or ascribed to, a single subject 'creating' a world of representations which, *qua* empirical self, it perceives itself to be affected by and to act upon in turn.

The 'metaphysics of the will to power' appears intended as a model of a temporal reality which would be such that the second-order predicate metaphysical truth would be inapplicable to any statements expressed in the object-language used to refer to this reality. I have argued that this model is itself not a coherent one. It is worth reflecting upon what leads Nietzsche into this incoherence. As I indicated briefly in the previous chapter, it seems to be the transference of his relational, or perspectival, analysis of 'objective reality' to the sphere of the subjective or perspectival itself. For

Nietzsche, it makes no sense to speak of the intrinsic nature, the constitution in itself, of objects *qua* objects, independently of their being objects of awareness and concern for some 'subject'. Many of his reflections in the notebooks show that he universalizes his account of objects so as to apply also to any kind of mental content. Rather like Schopenhauer in some passages, he is thus led to the position that every content of awareness—every instantiation of phenomenal qualities having a certain perspectival what-it-is-like-ness—is what it is not intrinsically, but only *for* what perforce has to be a transcendental subject which, logically, cannot have any intrinsic properties. Consequently, there can be nothing which has intrinsic, non-relational properties, i.e. a 'constitution in itself'.

Ironically, this strand of thought conflicts with Nietzsche's own critique of various traditional conceptions of the subject as being separate from and not to be identified with any of the qualitative characteristics of 'its' activities or any of the contents of 'its' aware-ness. When he argues, to the contrary, that the subject simply consists of 'processes' or 'inner events', he clearly means to suggest that the subject is to be *identified* with (some of) those changing, perspectival, phenomenal qualities. (In the case of human subjects, these qualities will, in many contexts, include those which consti-tute what we normally call 'our' bodies.) Thus we can see that Nietzsche's own critique of various traditional accounts of the subject, and the alternative conception outlined in some passages, provide the philosophical resources which, even while holding on to his idealist premises, could have enabled him to avoid the incoherence of the 'metaphysics of the will to power'. If he had more consistently identified the subject with the qualitative what-it-is-likeness of some of 'its' experiences and their contents, he would have recognized that the (according to him) perspectival character of all reality and the notion of a constitution in itself—intrinsic properties which constitute something as what it is—are not mutu-ally exclusive. To be sure, such a radically empiricist conception of the subject would have to confront well-known Kantian, transcen-dentalist objections. But, ignoring these (as Nietzsche himself does), there seems to be at least nothing inconsistent in holding that the nature in itself of reality consists in the totality of all experiential (perspectival, subjective) episodes in their phenomenal nature or what-it-is-likeness. Contrary to the view which Nietzsche often expresses, which leads to the incoherence of his ontology of quanta of force, perspectival and metaphysical (or absolute) truth do not exclude one another.

3. THE PROBLEM OF SELF-REFERENCE: SOME CONCLUSIONS

There are no indications in Nietzsche's writings that he is aware of the incoherence which characterizes the 'metaphysics of the will to power'. On the other hand, he is quite conscious of the fact that his own strictures on truth prevent him from claiming anything other than 'perspectival' truth for it. In various places he explicitly acknowledges the relevance of these strictures to his own apparently metaphysical claims:

[. . .] the 'lawfulness of nature' [. . .] that is interpretation, not text; and someone might come along, [. . .] an interpreter who presented to you the exceptionless and unconditional character of everything that is 'will to power' in such a way that almost any word, even the word 'tyranny', would eventually appear as a softening and mitigating metaphor—as too human; an interpreter who nevertheless ended up asserting the same about this world that you assert, namely that it takes a 'necessary' and 'predictable' course, but *not* because there are laws, rather because laws are absolutely *absent*, and because every power goes to its ultimate limit at any instant. Granted that this too may be only an interpretation— and you will be assiduous to object this?—well, so much the better.— (JGB 22)

One seeks a picture of the world in that philosophy in which one feels freest; i.e. in which our most powerful drive feels free to function. This will also be the case with me! (WM 418)

When Nietzsche grants that the specificities of the ontology of interacting quanta of force are 'only an interpretation' such that, with it, his 'most powerful drive feels free to function', what precisely is he conceding? First, he attempts to take account of his own claim—itself incoherent, I have argued—that it is unintelligible to say that any proposition about the world might be true in the sense of corresponding to the nature in itself of reality or some part of it. Secondly, and somewhat less problematically, he is acknowledging that his apparently metaphysical doctrine is not rationally justifiable in any of the senses of 'rational' mentioned in Chapter 2.3. This does not *by itself* mean that it is irrational or anti-rational or that it does not make use of what can generally be recognized as arguments. It is only to say that the standards of validation it employs (such as the quasi-Schopenhauerian argument from analogy) will not be acceptable to someone who does not share similar 'ruling drives'—in this respect, it is on the same footing as the familiar metaphysical endeavours in the history of philosophy, although rather more self-consciously so than is usually the case with its more traditional rivals. Thirdly, Nietzsche concedes that there may conceivably be subjects for whom the details of his ontology of power-quanta may indeed be false. That is to say, such hypothetical subjects may not themselves possess the constitution or *modus operandi* he outlines in his ontological sketches, nor could anything even in principle establish, for them, that other subjects are constituted in the manner he conjectures. (What this means, of course, is that the apparent metaphysics of the will to power cannot really be a metaphysics, a comprehensive ontology, at all.) So it seems that Nietzsche, in effect, concedes that while he believes the apparent metaphysics of the will to power to be 'true for him', it may actually *be* false (rather than just mistakenly considered to be false) for other subjects or 'perspectives'. This is how Rüdiger Grimm, among others, interprets his pronouncements: 'Nietzsche's scheme can account for both contingencies: it can be both true and false [in his sense] for different individuals at the same time (or the same individual at different times).'[20] In other words, Nietzsche's view entails a form of relativism. Since it has often been maintained that such a position cannot be coherently formulated, it may be useful to pause a little at this point in order to draw some distinctions which are relevant in this context. This will in fact give us an opportunity briefly to recapitulate and to draw together some of the central points which have been made concerning Nietzsche's thought on truth and metaphysics in the course of this study.

Let us take the relativist position to be that 'many judgements about the world may be true for one individual or group of individuals and false for another (or true and false for the same individual at different times)'. Several of Nietzsche's ideas which we have discussed might be thought to imply such a view.

1. In Chapter 4.5, we investigated those remarks in the later writings in which he seems to maintain that even the axioms of

---

[20] R. Grimm, 'Circularity and Self-Reference in Nietzsche', in *Metaphilosophy* 10 (1979), 297.

logic are 'imposed' upon the world by a certain kind of will to power, and that it could at least meaningfully be conjectured that the world as it exists independently of that particular imposed form—for example, the world as it is interpreted by some other 'subject' or instantiation of the will to power—might not conform to these axioms, i.e. that, in such a perspective, it might be alogical. This could be taken to license the claim that 'outside' the human perspective even contradictory statements about the world might after all not exclude each other, but be equally 'true' (or 'false').

The precedents of such a view can be found in Schopenhauer, who argues that the validity of the 'laws of thought', being one form of the principle of sufficient reason, is restricted to phenomena, but that they do not apply to reality as it is in itself.[21] Schopenhauer's views, in turn, are a development of Kant's, who, while not explicitly relativizing the validity of logical axioms and rules of inference in this sense, declared that none of the 'concepts of the understanding' (including 'reality' and 'negation') apply to things in themselves. Notwithstanding the significant differences in detail and in intention within this family of views, the crucial features which they have in common (and which seem to me to license the label 'anti-rationalist' with regard to them)[22] is that they deny the applicability of the most fundamental categories of our thought to 'reality in itself' (or, in Nietzsche's case, to some phenomenal or perspectival reality other than the phenomena presented to us within our own perspective), while still considering it possible to *refer* to such a reality allegedly radically beyond our conceptual means of comprehension.

I have argued that this anti-rationalist assumption is mistaken. If indeed no predicate whatever can be legitimately applied to reality in itself such as to exclude its negation, then we cannot even refer to reality in itself. There is an ongoing debate in contemporary philosophy of language and thought as to whether one can use a name to refer to some item without being able to give a correct description of it. Without needing to interfere in that debate we may yet say that, unless a person can apply some predicate—

---

[21] See A. Schopenhauer, *Über die vierfache Wurzel des Satzes vom zureichenden Grunde* (Hamburg, 1957), paras. 29–33 (pp. 131–7).

[22] Kant, of course, would not have accepted the label of anti-rationalism. But I think he would have had no good grounds on which to object to it being applied to some of his pronouncements in the sense in which it is used here.

excluding its negation—to whatever she wishes to refer to, she literally does not know what she is talking about. And if none of our concepts could be appropriately applied to reality in itself, none of us could have any idea what we are speaking of when uttering the sounds 'thing in itself'. As far as our understanding is concerned, we would merely be making a noise, and to say 'we know nothing about things in themselves' would, for us, be equivalent to saying 'we know nothing about ——'—a non-statement which is neither very illuminating nor very troublesome. To put the same point differently: we cannot even conceive of the thing in itself as a *something*, an 'object in general', unless we are prepared to consider it as an item to which some predicates and, hence, some 'concepts of the understanding' apply, even though we may know none of its intrinsic properties adequately. In fact, of course, Kant and Schopenhauer as well as the later Nietzsche do apply certain predicates to 'reality in itself' (or, in Nietzsche's case, to perspectival realities other than our own), implicitly ruling out the applicability to it of literally contradictory predicates (e.g. Nietzsche's 'reality is in flux'). There has occasionally been a temptation—including, in some moods, for Nietzsche—to think of logic as a 'limitation' (WM 522) which fetters or inhibits thought. It is perhaps apposite to remind ourselves just how misleading this picture is. Without logic, neither Schopenhauer nor Nietzsche could even *distinguish* our own phenomenal perspective from either a thing in itself (Schopenhauer), or other actual or possible perspectives (Nietzsche). Far from being a limitation chaining us to 'our' perspective, logic *enables* us to think of other possible perspectives. Giving up logic only amounts to a liberation of thought if one considers the absence of thought, what might metaphorically be described as an undifferentiated blur, to be liberating.

2. Another line of argument, which is specific to Nietzsche, seeks to eliminate the notion of absolute or metaphysical truth by showing it to be ultimately unintelligible. This approach of Nietzsche's emerged in our discussion in Chapter 3.2 and it has been criticized in this chapter. According to it, no thoughts about the world can be true in the sense of standing for, representing, or corresponding to the intrinsic properties (the 'nature') of reality or of any part of it, since it is 'nonsense' to suppose that anything has such intrinsic features which constitute it as what it is. This argument, as we

pointed out earlier, is not only directed against timeless essences
(like the Platonic Forms), but also against the notion of an entity
having, or being constituted by, intrinsic properties at any one time.
It suggests that the being and the 'whatness' of *any* entity whatever
consists exclusively in its being interpreted as possessing certain
characteristics by one or more other entities. I have argued that this
claim, leading as it does to an infinite regress, is not a coherent one.

3. But does not Nietzsche's analysis of objective reality in terms
of the representational contents and the interests (desires, values) of
'subjects' entail a form of relativism? Clearly, if it is meaningful to
suppose that there may be different subjects of knowledge whose
experiences involve different, not mutually congruent, patterns
of 'affections', i.e. different types and constellations of what are,
relative to them, real objective properties, then, according to
Nietzsche's analysis, it would be correct to say that these hypothetical subjects live in distinct worlds. Consequently, at least some
judgements about objective reality would be true for some such
subjects but false for others. The statement, for instance, that there
are relatively enduring spherical objects might be true for some
such subjects while being illusory for other phenomenal, subjective
points of view or perspectives. If the relativist position is construed
in this manner, it is arguably coherent. However, it is usually not
thus understood. The 'individuals' referred to in our statement of
the relativist claim are generally taken to be the human subjects of
everyday discourse. When we speak of human individuals in everyday discourse, it seems that part of what we mean is that they are
independent subjects who are affected, by and large, by spatio-
temporal objects of the same sorts we are affected by, and in at least
partly the same manner. If and in so far as this is what we mean by
'individual', it is obviously not the case, even on Nietzschean
premises, that 'many judgements about objective reality may be
true for one individual and false for another'.

Our original question was to what extent Nietzsche's apparent
metaphysics involves a form of relativism. But in that 'metaphysics', we recall, there are, strictly speaking, no objects at all.[23] The

[23] As Rüdiger Bittner puts it: 'The statement "there are only interpretations"
means: there are no objects which in themselves have this or that nature. Our life and
our world are productive agency [. . . .] Just as the Great Fugue is only something
that is being played, so objects in general are only something that is being done. The
world is everything that is being done' ('Nietzsches Begriff der Wahrheit', 88).

world, according to it, consists of 'quanta of force' which are 'living beings' whose mode of existence is that of a 'subjective invisible life' (KGW VII.3.40.21)—of 'inner event[s]' (WM 619) or 'processes' (WM 655)—instantiating a 'primitive form' of 'willing feeling thinking' (KGW VII.3.40.37). Extended objects, to which Nietzsche's analysis of objective reality applies, are in this world (as they are for Leibniz) a *Gleichnis* or 'symbolism' (KGW VII.3.40.21)—in other words, a mode in which some 'communalities' of these *Wesen* appear to others or, in part, to themselves (KGW VII.3.37.4).

As I have suggested, Nietzsche's disclaimers for his apparent metaphysics amount, among other things, to the acknowledgement that the details of his own construal of the *modus operandi* of those other subjects may actually be false from their point of view or perspective. It may be even *in principle* impossible for them (or for those of them capable of the degree of self-awareness which can express itself in explicit judgements) to recognize Nietzsche's analysis of their states (their 'invisible subjective life') as correct—unless they *change* their character to such an extent that this analysis *becomes* true of it. But if that is so, it is not clear how Nietzsche's account could be said to be true, even 'perspectivally' true, of them at all in any interesting sense. When episodic subjective (perspectival) states constitute the ultimate stratum of explanation, as they do in Nietzsche, and when they therefore cannot be given a further analysis in, say, physicalist or behaviourist terms, then it is simply mysterious what could be meant by saying that these perspectival states, *qua* perspectival states, have a certain specific character without this character being recognizable from within the perspective in question. Consequently, if Nietzsche really does want to say that his account of the nature of other subjects' perspectives might be true only relatively, i.e. 'for him', but not for those other subjects, he would be saying—short of a radical revision of the meaning of 'true' (see below)—that it is not true at all. As has been argued at various points in this study, he is often (although not invariably) tempted to extend his account of 'real objects' to the sphere of subjective, perspectival states. But it is one thing to maintain that what counts as a real object is dependent on the interests and values of the subject(s) to whom it is, as he puts it, of 'concern'; it is quite another thing to say that the character of another's subjective states—whose existence one recognizes—is logically dependent in this manner on an external interpreter's interpretive stance.

Let me return once more to the question of self-reference. On the present interpretation, Nietzsche does not claim more than 'perspectival' validity for his apparent metaphysics of the will to power—he does not assert more than that it is true for him, a claim that is still distinctly problematic. But, in fact, the very cautious, tentative formulations which he frequently uses when presenting what he calls his 'hypothesis' suggest that he does not even unreservedly subscribe to it himself.[24] For example, he speaks of some of his assumptions not only as 'hypotheses' (JGB 36), but as 'heuristic principles' (GOA xiv.319) or 'basic probabilities, provisionally adopted principles' (KGW VII.2.24.2). Furthermore, the apparent ontology of quanta of force is, on the face of it, a proposal towards an explanation of phenomena by 'reducing the unfamiliar to the familiar' (cf. WM 619, 689). Indeed, according to Nietzsche, such a reduction is what we *mean* by the terms 'explanation' and 'comprehension' (cf. WM 619, 621, 627). But elsewhere he castigates the idea that reality should be comprehensible to us in this sense as inspired by human hubris (cf. MR 539) and, like Lange, repeatedly criticizes any attempt to conceive of it in analogy to some allegedly familiar content of our experience (be it 'matter' or 'will') as an unsubstantiable anthropocentric naïvety (e.g. WM 584). It is hard to believe, in the light of this, that he should have been convinced of the literal truth even in a 'perspectival' sense (i.e. as a 'truth for him') of his self-consciously anthropomorphizing ontological sketches.

Do all these reservations mean that he avoids the charge, often levelled against him, of self-referential inconsistency?[25] He would indeed avoid it if he claimed no more for his pronouncements than that 'this is how things appear to me now', or if he refused to lay claim to any greater adequacy of the statements in question over other, *apparently* incompatible ones, in any sense, or on any grounds, other than that 'this way of looking at things accords with

---

[24] Cf. K. Schlechta, *Der Fall Nietzsche* (Munich, 1959), 120.

[25] Nehamas has argued that Nietzsche is not self-referentially inconsistent, since his thesis according to which 'every view is an interpretation' does not preclude the possibility of some interpretations (e.g. Nietzsche's) being true (*Nietzsche—Life as Literature*, 65–7). But the real charge against Nietzsche seems to be rather that there is an inconsistency between his apparent claims (*a*) that 'there is no truth' and (*b*) that true statements can be made about human beliefs, desires, and intentions.

my taste at present' (cf. FW 39). In that case, the problematic items would in fact not be assertions about their ostensible referents at all, but rather first-personal reports (or perhaps expressive utterances). But our inquiries so far suggest that there are a number of tenets which, on any plausible reading of the whole body of Nietzsche's later writings, cannot be re-interpreted in this way.

1. As I argued in Chapter 5, Nietzsche asserts a number of things concerning our appetitive and affective life. Specifically, he maintains that all significant human desires, cleansed of self-deception, are in fact desires for the experience of power. Emotions and intentions are to be similarly analysed in terms of the will to power. In the light of a plethora of explicit statements and of the character of his philosophical work in general, it would require a truly heroic interpreter to argue that his analyses of 'inner experience' are not intended as assertions aspiring to truth at all. It seems considerably more likely (for the reasons given in Chapter 5.3) that he wishes to make true statements about the nature of his and other humans' experience, maintaining that, if we could eradicate our self-deceptions, and attend sufficiently to the phenomenological character of our desires, we would describe them—or at least those which are more important to us—as variations of the generic desire for the experience of power.[26]

2. Throughout the works of the middle and late periods and in the *Nachlass*, Nietzsche suggests that there is a scale of force or power which permits him to grade systems of belief, attitudes, and types of actions as indicative of varying degrees of force manifested in the individuals exhibiting them. He appears to maintain that there is an invariable correlation between certain properties of empirical individuals—such as their physical 'well-constitutedness' (*Wohlgeratenheit*) or the presence in them of *ressentiment*—and the quantity of efficacious force which they represent. This speculative

---

[26] This has been implicitly taken for granted by most commentators. Cf. e.g. Müller-Lauter, 'Nietzsches Lehre vom Willen zur Macht', 48–50. One exception appears to be Stack: 'All of man's urges are reducible to *Wille zur Macht* and this is the supposed "fact" at which we ultimately arrive [. . . .] But of course, Nietzsche knows that this is an *interpretation* of our psychic experiences' (*Lange and Nietzsche*, 299). Yet, in another passage, Stack also maintains that '[Nietzsche's] psychological theory that man is motivated primarily by a "lust of power" is a viable theory[!] that is based, alas, on an astonishing number of facts[!]' (ibid. 293).

supposition requires that the force in question be, in principle, capable of being measured, which implies that there would have to be, at the ontological level, re-identifiable opposing forces providing the standard (or unit of measurement) by means of which each instantiation of efficacious force could in principle be compared and graded. What this implies, in turn, is that the forces manifesting themselves in individuals can (again, in principle) be re-identified independently of what these individuals do at any particular time. While these suppositions are incompatible with Nietzsche's anti-essentialism (the rejection of the notion of a constitution in itself), they need not conflict with his analysis of objective reality. Nor are they necessarily incompatible with his sceptical arguments, as these merely attempt to establish that none of the beliefs we hold concerning the concrete nature of reality can be justified rationally as being metaphysically true. We may, of course, ask what should induce us to accept Nietzsche's speculative tenets concerning the degrees of power manifested in individuals if our 'ruling drives' differ from his.

3. The same question may be asked with respect to the very claim that certain beliefs we may hold about the world are 'symptomatic' of (WM 677), 'directed' by (WM 458), or 'consequences' of (WM 580) our ruling drives, our dominant desires and interests. The assertion that our adoption of various beliefs stands in a causal relation to certain desires or 'drives' seems to commit Nietzsche to the tenet that our desires and intentions, or at least some agencies which, while not necessarily conscious to us, are at least analogous to them, are indeed efficacious in shaping the nature and the course of our experience (in this case: our beliefs). As we have seen throughout this study, Nietzsche himself sometimes rather hesitates to make such a claim. Nevertheless, it is arguably central to most of his later thought—not only to the *soi-disant* metaphysics of the will to power, but also to his critical reflections, such as those discussed in Chapter 4.4.

4. In all the points mentioned above, reference was made to different 'individuals', to 'us', to 'our' desires, intentions, and beliefs. All of these locutions, which Nietzsche himself uses throughout, imply that he acknowledges the existence of perspectives other than his own. More than this, they imply a great number of assumptions concerning the nature of these perspectives. Not only are they regarded as involving (or being partly constituted by) beliefs

about 'objects', but they are also seen as loci of sensations, emotions, desires, and intentions, and indeed as exercising powers, thus affecting other 'subjects' or 'quanta of force'. Moreover, since most of Nietzsche's statements concern the beliefs, desires, etc. of human individuals, he seems to credit at least those objects of experience we normally think of as other human beings with representing separate subjective perspectives. None of these assumptions are—granting the force of his own sceptical arguments—rationally justifiable. They rather seem to rely on a 'proof from strength' similar in kind to those implicitly invoked, according to him, in all traditional metaphysics.

It might be objected that Nietzsche after all claims only 'perspectival' truth for any of these propositions. This may well be so, but if our interpretation of his concept of perspectival truth is correct,[27] then a claim to truth in this sense certainly goes considerably beyond what might be predicated of reports such as 'this is how things appear to me now' or even 'holding this belief increases my feeling of power at this moment'. Moreover, we have seen that the concept of perspectival truth in fact tacitly presupposes that of truth in a metaphysical sense. Perspectivism, if it is to be coherent, does not ultimately conflict with or rule out the latter notion, but rather itself involves a particular kind of metaphysics, although, if our reading is correct, this is contrary to Nietzsche's intention.

But is it not possible that we have misinterpreted his notion of perspectival truth? It could be argued that what Nietzsche means by a 'true' thought or proposition is quite simply one which is in some way associated with an increase of power (or, more plausibly, of the feeling of power) on the part of the thinker. This is perhaps what R. Grimm proposes when he says, somewhat vaguely: 'a statement, proposition, theory, etc. is regarded as "true" if it aids me in increasing my power [. . . .] Truth *means* power-increasing, falsity *means* power-diminishing.'[28] This could be interpreted as suggesting that, for Nietzsche, to say truly that there are different individuals or 'power-centres' representing various degrees of power or force is equivalent to saying that the entertaining of this thought involves (at the time of entertaining it) an increase of the feeling of power of the individual who has this thought (e.g. of

---

[27] Perspectival truth concerning objects was discussed in Ch. 3.1, concerning subjective states in Ch. 5.3.

[28] Grimm, 'Circularity and Self-Reference in Nietzsche', 295. See also my discussion of Grimm in Ch. 1.

Nietzsche himself). This and similar interpretations of Nietzsche as radically *redefining* 'truth' for his apparent positive claims seem to me neither exegetically convincing nor of independent interest. For one thing, they would not even permit one to say that an individual's attitude towards a given proposition is *causally related* to an increase in his or her feeling of power, since this would evidently involve a causal claim along traditional lines. Ultimately, one would be reduced to saying little more than this: a proposition is 'true' for an individual at a given time if entertaining it seems to that individual, at that time, to be associated with a feeling of power. Evidently, if Nietzsche intended to redefine truth in this manner, or something like it, the upshot of his reflections would consist in no more than the refusal to venture statements other than of the type 'x now appears within this ('my') perspective as f' and, perhaps, the enjoinder to what appears to him at that time as other individuals to refuse to do so as well. He would then not be saying 'there is a causal relation between people's beliefs and some of their interests and desires' or 'different beliefs are symptomatic of various degrees of power manifested in different individuals', but rather 'there now appears to me to be a causal relation between people's beliefs and some of their interests and desires', and 'different beliefs now appear to me as symptomatic of various degrees of power in what now seem to me to be different individuals'. Nietzsche, on this interpretation, would simply refuse to enter at all into the traditional 'discourse', which is rather more ambitious in its claims, not because he would have any generally recognizable *reasons* for such a refusal, but because he would have 'no taste for it'. We need not concern ourselves here with the question of whether such a refusal is, in general, even possible. Suffice it to say that it seems to me too reductive to be satisfactory as an interpretation of Nietzsche's arguably rather more interesting and complex, if highly problematic, stance.

It would mean, among other things, that none of the myriad of critical remarks in the published works and in the *Nachlass* concerning objectivist (realist) accounts of conventional moral language and practice could be understood literally as *criticisms* at all. For the utterances (i) 'a now appears within this ('my') perspective as F' and (ii) 'a is G' are obviously not mutually exclusive. If one heroically wished to argue that they are, or that statements like (ii) are impossible, one could only do so, self-defeatingly, by going beyond statements like (i). If Nietzsche really intended only to make statements of the latter kind, none of the traditional value-judgements, which involve claims of type (ii), would be affected in the slightest by anything he says. The passionate intensity with which he tirelessly attacks the 'lies' (self-deceptions) of Platonist, Christian, and indeed of any realist conception of the good would be completely bizarre if he were not convinced of the falsity, in a rather more substantial sense, of these conceptions. It would otherwise also be difficult to see why *all* his psychological analyses in the post-1876 writings should have consistently tended in one direction—the debunking of all 'ascetic ideals' as symptoms of weakness. This consistency of purpose and direction in his investigations could not have failed to strike a passionately self-critical mind like Nietzsche's as an *idée fixe* of the most narrow and limited kind— the sort he himself would call pathological—had he not regarded their results as perspectivally true in the sense elucidated in Chapter 5.3. Only an interpretation of the propositions listed above as claims to truth in such a more substantial sense makes it possible, in conjunction with a knowledge of Nietzsche's own values, to understand—i.e. to regard as more than a case study in compulsive pathology—the passionately, almost obsessively critical nature of his philosophical enterprise.[29]

A central question still remains concerning the 'metaphysics of the will to power'. We have seen that it is very doubtful whether even Nietzsche himself would have confidently embraced it in all its details as 'perspectivally' true. But, in this case, what *is* its status within his philosophical endeavour as a whole? Some critics have proposed that the apparently metaphysical sketches ought not to be understood literally at all, but rather as 'metaphors',[30] as 'signs',[31] as figurative or poetic 'truths'.[32] We are invited to read the will to power as a 'symbol' representing a reality not literally accessible to

---

[29] The consistency of direction in Nietzsche's philosophical work after 1876, behind the variety of his numerous 'masks', has always been noted by those who have studied his work in any depth. (See e.g. K. Schlechta's 'Nachwort' to his edition of Nietzsche's *Werke* (Munich, 1966), iii. 1435–6, and also Löwith, *Nietzsches Philosophie der ewigen Wiederkehr des Gleichen*, 19.) Schlechta went as far as to speak of the *Monotonie* of Nietzsche's *Gesamtaussage* (a fact which did not prevent him from devoting most of his scholarly life to Nietzsche's writings).

[30] Djuric, *Nietzsche und die Metaphysik*, 76. Mittasch, *Friedrich Nietzsche als Naturphilosoph*, 289.

[31] Grimm, *Nietzsche's Theory of Knowledge*, 24 n.

[32] Stack, *Lange and Nietzsche*, 219–20.

human language and thought. This approach assimilates Nietzsche to the position of Lange, who averred that, unconditioned reality being unknowable to us, any metaphysical view can at best aspire to the status of a symbol or metaphor for the ultimate nature of things.[33]

A reading of the 'metaphysics of the will to power' along these lines seems to me to be not very illuminating, for two reasons. First, a term used metaphorically is only informative if, in its non-metaphorical (i.e. standard) usage, it refers to some specific property (properties) which is (are) taken to be analogous to some property (properties) of the object to which it is applied metaphorically, even though we may not be able to specify the precise degree of this similarity. In *this* sense at least, metaphorical language is parasitic on literal language.[34] If someone says, for example, 'God is a father', then this utterance will only be illuminating if we understand there to be a literal similarity between God and a father in respect of some property, e.g. the property of (fatherly) love. 'Love', in this case, applies *literally* both to God and to a human parent, although its referents are not taken to be exactly similar, there being obviously several respects in which divine love and human love differ. Consequently, if *none* of the predicates which are applied by Nietzsche to reality in the 'metaphysics of the will to power' were intended to apply literally, it would remain a thoroughly unilluminating and, one would have thought, rather pointless exercise. This might, perhaps, recommend him to those few among his readers for whom the *jeu de mots* for its own sake is a matter of supreme *jouissance*, but it would render him rather less exciting to the rest, who have been inclined to think that there are more interesting activities. On the other hand, if it is replied that some of the predicates used in Nietzsche's apparent ontology are indeed intended to apply literally, although analogically, since metaphor is only a species of analogy in any case, a problem encountered earlier recurs: his sketches would then become just one more instance in the long history of metaphysical explanation by analogy—reducing the unfamiliar to the supposedly familiar—which he repeatedly attacks.

But, secondly, the interpretation we are discussing seems to ig-

---

[33] Lange, *Geschichte des Materialismus*, 539.
[34] Danto makes the same point, but for different reasons (*Nietzsche as Philosopher*, 43).

nore Nietzsche's claim—which we have criticized—that the notion of an unconditioned, metaphysical reality is entirely unintelligible. If this is so, we cannot talk about it, not even in metaphors or symbols. For Nietzsche to attempt to do so would be like arguing that the concept of God is 'nonsensical' and yet insisting that we can speak about God in metaphorical terms.

Nietzsche occasionally refers to his 'metaphysical' sketches as 'hypotheses', and this appellation is also sometimes echoed in the critical literature. But what exactly does this term mean here? Clearly, its use in this context is not the same as in modern scientific discourse, which is, in Nietzsche's view, in fact only concerned with elaborating calculi enabling us to correlate phenomena and to predict them. It rather, I would suggest, signifies one mode of conceiving of, or perhaps better, relating to, reality with which the 'heroic' man of whom Nietzsche would approve would be happy and feel at ease, and in which he would feel 'free to function'. It is 'provisional' in that such a man, unlike most traditional metaphysicians, would neither feel particularly committed to, nor concerned to defend, the details of its intellectual architecture, for he would not primarily be interested in 'knowledge' in that traditional philosophical sense at all. The point of the apparent metaphysics of the will to power, being what one might call an existential one, is precisely that it represents (in *intention*, at any rate) a way of thinking of the world such that, according to it, nothing could ever be 'known', held fast, and restfully contemplated in its intrinsic nature. The 'heroic' man would be 'strong enough' to live without any such place of rest or comfort, contemplative or otherwise, and indeed without anything eternal or sempiternal or entirely predictable—he would welcome 'his' world being without God, self-identical (unchanging) soul-substances, matter, invariant laws of nature, 'objective' value properties, and without any reality-sanctioned 'right' independent of might.

Does this mean that our criticisms of the incoherence of Nietzsche's apparent metaphysics would be, for him, entirely irrelevant? Not quite. For, as we have seen throughout this study, it is by no means the case that he is simply unconcerned with and uninterested in rational argument. This is evident even in his 'metaphysical' sketches. To be sure, given his views about the role of 'rationality' in philosophy—i.e. about people's motives for holding particular philosophical beliefs—it would obviously be absurd for

him to attempt to demonstrate the preferability in general of the
'metaphysics of the will to power' over other positions incompatible with it. However, his arguments to support it, as well as the
nature of this conception itself, clearly suggest that it is intended by
him as an intelligible and internally consistent 'hypothesis'. Thus he
argues for the 'will' as the only conceivable causal power in all
events by an argument of analogy derived essentially from
Schopenhauer. Furthermore, he takes care to exclude all those
concepts which he has criticized as unintelligible (whether in the
sense of 'empirically empty' or 'incoherent')—there are no mechanical causes, no Boscovichean forces, no substances or soul-
substrata, no simple unanalysable faculty of 'willing' in his
'metaphysical' sketches. That Nietzsche aims (unsuccessfully) to be
consistent in them is clear not only from this, but also from the fact
that he sometimes appeals explicitly to the principle of non-contradiction in his arguments (e.g. WM 631, 639). We may surmise that,
had he recognized the objections raised here against his scheme of
quanta of force, he would certainly have taken account of them by
making adjustments in it (for example, by abandoning the more
extreme aspects of his anti-essentialism). However, as with his
own early criticisms of Schopenhauer, he would have regarded this
merely as a correction of technical 'infelicities', relatively easily
accomplished, with ultimately little bearing on what, for him,
would have been important about that scheme: the mode of relating
to the world which it gives expression to. A view which pervades
his writings is that very similar modes of relating to the world
(ruling drives, values) can manifest themselves in different, even in
incompatible, philosophical tenets (although it is not the case that
any values whatever can express themselves in any philosophical
doctrine whatever). It would be surprising, in the light of this, if he
had found our criticisms of the doctrine of quanta of force, even
had he recognized them as valid, to be fatal to his wider project.
But, not being a simple irrationalist, he would certainly have
acknowledged them as *objections*.

   But his rejection of a simple irrationalism is even more evident,
and arguably more important to his philosophical enterprise as a
whole, in his negative, critical reflections. Traditional deductive and
inductive modes of reasoning are obviously crucial to the sceptical
strand of his thought. They are similarly indispensable to what we
have identified as the nucleus of his later thought on metaphysics

and epistemology, and of his attitude to philosophy in general: the subsumption of 'narrowly' religious values like those represented by Christianity and the philosophical will to truth 'for its own sake' under the wider concept of the ascetic ideal, and the identification of the latter as a symptom of weakness and, usually, as an expression of *ressentiment*. Nietzsche's own repudiation of that ideal rests—apart, of course, from his own values—on his belief in the correctness of his description of it and in the validity of the conclusions he draws from his premises. Neither the 'correctness' nor the 'validity' in question here are, we have argued at length, substantially different from what many traditional philosophers would claim for their reasoning. If they were, his thought could not even be recognized by those philosophers as constituting a critique of their activities and the values implicit in their pursuit of them.

There are indeed anti-rationalist (rather than just sceptical or anti-contemplative) elements in Nietzsche's thought. Two such elements are his rejection of the notion of absolute or metaphysical truth (anti-essentialism) and, in some notes, of the assumption that logical axioms like the principle of non-contradiction apply to reality independently of a particular kind of will to power 'imposing' them on it. But even here he believes himself to have good arguments, which can be assessed in traditional terms, for his conclusions. It seems to me, therefore, that Jürgen Habermas is essentially correct when he observes that Nietzsche here endeavours to show the 'inadequacy' of reason by ostensibly rational means, attempting, as it were, a *reductio ad absurdum*, or *Selbstaufhebung*, of reason itself.[35]

Most of the commentators who accept Nietzsche's anti-rationalist ideas accept them because they take him not merely to have considered or asserted them, but to have 'established' them.[36] In this study, we have come to the contrary conclusion that not merely the attempt to show or demonstrate, but even to state, an anti-rationalist position of the sort Nietzsche sometimes feels drawn to is bound to usher us into the realm of the meaningless. We fail to comprehend what could be meant by the statement that 'reality is not (or might not be) subject to the principle of non-contradiction', because any idea of 'reality' which we can form involves this

---

[35] Habermas, *Erkenntnis und Interesse* (Frankfurt, 1968), 353, 363.
[36] e.g. Djuric, *Nietzsche und die Metaphysik*, 74–5. Also Müller-Lauter, 'Nietzsches Lehre vom Willen zur Macht', 54–6 n.

principle. Nor do we understand what a person is saying when he claims that 'nothing has at any time intrinsic properties which constitute it as what it is at that time'. We may, of course, choose to 'throw off' the fetters of rational thought (WM 522) and to contradict ourselves, but we will not be able to state as a *reason* for such a decision that self-contradiction is literally more 'adequate' to reality than logical consistency. This is not to say that deliberate self-contradiction may not sometimes have a *point* or an intelligible *motive*. A person may express through it, for instance, the exceptional or (to him) incomparable character of some experience he has had (as, arguably, many mystics did) or it may be used for quite a different purpose, such as to offend or confuse one's interlocutor, or—an extremely popular motive in intellectual history—it may be employed in the endeavour to convince others that one has some special insight, not available to the *vulgus*, which transcends mere ordinary logic. This latter disposition, with its presumption towards cognitive elect-ness, its desire to 'transcend' common modes of knowledge—to be 'something else, somewhere else' (GM iii.13)—its peculiar form of other-worldliness, perhaps invites, and might repay, a Nietzschean analysis. In any case, he himself is generally no more enamoured of it than Schopenhauer was before him. He believes he has widely accessible and intelligible *reasons* for his anti-rationalism, and he thus cannot avoid ignoring time and again his own anti-rationalist statements and making use of both the axioms and rules of inference of logic, and of the notion of a constitution in itself (however much this constitution may be subject to temporal change)—for example, of quantities of force with determinate modes of action.

If, as we have argued, his views at least in this particular regard are not coherently statable, they give us no grounds to conclude that metaphysics in the traditional sense—the quest for the nature in itself of reality—is an impossible enterprise. Metaphysics remains a possible and legitimate endeavour, although, to be sure, it is in any of its manifestations subject to the sceptical objections of Nietzsche and others against its claims to rational validation. But if this is so, the question forces itself upon us, as it does on Nietzsche: given that metaphysics has never yet delivered answers to its questions which have been widely acceptable outside the confines of particular contingent traditions, constituted by practices and modes of life which involve specific ways of looking at the world, and given that this fact may plausibly be thought to be due to the very nature of the enterprise, why should we, indeed why do we, continue to concern ourselves with metaphysics at all?

The later Nietzsche's reply to this psychological question assimilates metaphysics to religion in a wide sense. The belief in the importance or value of metaphysics, i.e. of the attempt to attain knowledge ostensibly 'for its own sake' of the constitution in itself of that which is ultimately real, involves (1) the acknowledgement of a good the achievement of which is envisaged as a restful or inactive state of 'contemplation of being', and/or (2) the notion that 'being in accordance with the (presumed) nature of things' confers a special type of legitimation on human activities and modes of life which is distinct from and overrides the mere matter-of-factness of contingent human wants at any one time. It is these 'values' which Nietzsche identifies as the core of the ascetic, or religious, ideal. I have suggested here that, while his analysis commands, in my view, great plausibility for many cases where the 'will to truth' has been in evidence, it is unlikely to be the whole story. The argument in Chapter 5 indicates that there may be human dispositions and desires which involve certain ontological (metaphysical) commitments, although they are neither contemplative in the traditional sense nor essentially concerned with universalizability (i.e. expressive of *ressentiment*, on Nietzsche's view), nor with self-legitimation by some external authority or higher power. Nietzsche in his anti-metaphysical fervour arguably ignores the fact that metaphysical assumptions may be involved in the adequate phenomenological description of (in his terms) non-reactive and 'natural' desires, rather than being invariably a means to escape from, or a *ressentiment*-ploy to denigrate, the phenomenology of non-reactive 'life'.

BIBLIOGRAPHY

A. EDITIONS OF NIETZSCHE'S WRITINGS USED IN THIS STUDY

Nietzsche, Friedrich, *Werke: Kritische Gesamtausgabe*, 8 *Abteilungen*, eds. G. Colli and M. Montinari (Berlin, 1967–).
—— *Werke*, 20 vols. (Leipzig, 1895–1911, 1926) (*Grossoktavausgabe*).
—— *Historisch-Kritische Gesamtausgabe*, ed. J. Mette and K. Schlechta (Munich, 1933–40).
—— *Briefwechsel: Kritische Gesamtausgabe*, ed. G. Colli and M. Montinari (Berlin, 1975–).
—— *The Will to Power*, ed. W. Kaufmann (New York, 1968). Trans. W. Kaufmann and R. J. Hollingdale.
—— *Philosophy and Truth—Selections from Nietzsche's Notebooks of the early 1870s*, ed. D. Breazeale (Atlantic Highlands, NJ, 1979). Trans. D. Breazeale.
—— *The Birth of Tragedy and The Case of Wagner* (New York, 1967). Trans. W. Kaufmann.
—— *Untimely Meditations* (Cambridge, 1983). Trans. R. J. Hollingdale.
—— *Thus Spoke Zarathustra* (Harmondsworth, 1969). Trans. R. J. Hollingdale.

B. LITERATURE ON NIETZSCHE

Abel, Günter, *Nietzsche. Die Dynamik der Willen zur Macht und die ewige Wiederkehr* (Berlin, 1984).
Allison, D. B. (ed.), *The New Nietzsche* (New York, 1977).
Ansell-Pearson, K., and Caygill, H. (eds.), *The Fate of the New Nietzsche* (Aldershot, 1993).
Bäumler, Alfred, 'Nachwort' to his edition of Nietzsche's *Der Wille zur Macht* (Leipzig, 1930).
Bittner, R., 'Nietzsches Begriff der Wahrheit', in *Nietzsche-Studien* 16 (1987).
Breazeale, Daniel, 'The Word, the World, and Nietzsche', in *The Philosophical Forum* 6 (1974/5).
Clark, Maudemarie, *Nietzsche on Truth and Philosophy* (Cambridge, 1990).

Cooper, David E., *Authenticity and Learning* (London, 1983).

Danto, Arthur C., *Nietzsche as Philosopher* (New York, 1965).

Deleuze, Gilles, *Nietzsche and Philosophy* (London, 1983).

Derrida, Jacques, *Spurs. Nietzsche's Styles* (Chicago and London, 1979).

Djuric, Mihailo, *Nietzsche und die Metaphysik* (Berlin, 1985).

Figl, Johann, *Interpretation als philosophisches Prinzip* (Berlin, 1982).

Fink, Eugen, *Nietzsches Philosophie* (Stuttgart, 1960).

Gaultier, Jules de, *From Kant to Nietzsche* (New York, 1961).

Gerhardt, Volker, 'Die Perspektive des Perspektivismus', in *Nietzsche-Studien* 18 (1989).

—— 'Self-grounding: Nietzsche's Morality of Individuality', in K. Ansell-Pearson and H. Caygill (eds.), *The Fate of the New Nietzsche* (Aldershot, 1993).

Giesz, Ludwig, *Nietzsche—Existenzialismus und Wille zur Macht* (Stuttgart, 1950).

Grau, Gerd-Günther, *Christlicher Glaube und intellektuelle Redlichkeit* (Frankfurt am Main, 1958).

Grimm, Rüdiger H., *Nietzsche's Theory of Knowledge* (Berlin, 1977).

—— 'Circularity and Self-Reference in Nietzsche', in *Metaphilosophy* 10 (1979).

Habermas, Jürgen, 'Zu Nietzsches Erkenntnistheorie', in *Kultur und Kritik* (Frankfurt am Main, 1973).

Hayman, Ronald, *Nietzsche—A Critical Life* (London, 1980).

Heidegger, Martin, *Nietzsche* (Pfullingen, 1961), 2 vols.

Hollingdale, R. J., *Nietzsche—The Man and his Philosophy* (London, 1965).

Jaspers, Karl, *Nietzsche—Einführung in das Verständnis seines Philosophierens* (Berlin and Leipzig, 1936).

Kaufmann, Walter, *Nietzsche—Philosopher, Psychologist, Antichrist* (Cleveland and New York, 1966).

Kaulbach, Friedrich, *Nietzsches Idee einer Experimentalphilosophie* (Cologne, 1981).

—— 'Nietzsche und der monadologische Gedanke', in *Nietzsche-Studien* 8 (1979).

Klages, Ludwig, *Die psychologischen Errungenschaften Nietzsches* (Leipzig, 1926).

Köster, P., 'Die Problematik wissenschaftlicher Nietzsche—Interpretation', in *Nietzsche-Studien* 2 (1973).

Lea, F. A., *The Tragic Philosopher* (London, 1957).

Löwith, Karl, *Von Hegel zu Nietzsche* (Stuttgart, 1950).

—— *Nietzsches Philosophie der ewigen Wiederkehr des Gleichen* (Stuttgart, 1956).

Man, Paul de, *Allegories of Reading* (New Haven and London, 1979).

Margreiter, Reinhard, *Ontologie und Gottesbegriff bei Nietzsche* (Meisenheim, 1978).

Mittasch, Alwin, *Friedrich Nietzsche als Naturphilosoph* (Stuttgart, 1952).

Most, Otto, 'Das Selbst des Menschen in der Sicht des jungen Nietzsche', in *Philosophische Jahrbücher der Görres-Gesellschaft*, 1965/6.

Müller-Lauter, W., *Nietzsche—Seine Philosophie der Gegensätze und die Gegensätze seiner Philosophie* (Berlin, 1971).

—— 'Nietzsches Lehre vom Willen zur Macht', in *Nietzsche-Studien* 3 (1974).

—— 'Der Organismus als innerer Kampf. Der Einfluss von Wilhelm Roux auf Friedrich Nietzsche', in *Nietzsche-Studien* 7 (1978).

Nehamas, Alexander, *Nietzsche—Life as Literature* (Cambridge, Mass., 1985).

—— 'Immanent and Transcendent Perspectivism in Nietzsche', in *Nietzsche-Studien* 12 (1983).

Sallis, J. C., 'Nietzsche and the Problem of Knowledge', in *Tulane Studies in Philosophy* 18 (1969).

Schacht, Richard, *Nietzsche* (London, 1983).

Schlechta, Karl, *Der Fall Nietzsche* (Munich, 1959).

—— 'Nachwort' to his edition of Nietzsche's *Werke in drei Bänden* (Munich, 1966).

—— and Anders, Anni, *Friedrich Nietzsche—Von den verborgenen Anfängen seines Philosophierens* (Stuttgart-Bad Cannstadt, 1962).

Silk, M. S., and Stern, J. P., *Nietzsche on Tragedy* (Cambridge, 1981).

Simmel, Georg, *Schopenhauer und Nietzsche* (Munich and Leipzig, 1920).

Simon, Josef, *Nietzsche und die philosophische Tradition* (Würzburg, 1985), 2 vols.

Stack, G. J., *Lange and Nietzsche* (Berlin, 1983).

Stegmaier, W., 'Nietzsches Neubestimmung der Wahrheit', in *Nietzsche-Studien* 14 (1985).

Stern, J. P., *Nietzsche* (London, 1978).

—— *A Study of Nietzsche* (Cambridge, 1979).

Ulmer, Karl, *Nietzsche—Einheit und Sinn seines Werkes* (Bern and Munich, 1962).

Vaihinger, Hans, *Nietzsche als Philosoph* (Langensalza, 1930).

Wilcox, J. T., *Truth and Value in Nietzsche* (Ann Arbor, 1974).

Wood, D., and Krell, D. F. (eds.), *Exceedingly Nietzsche* (London, 1988).

C. OTHER LITERATURE

Alexander, Peter, *Ideas, Qualities and Corpuscles—Locke and Boyle on the External World* (Cambridge, 1985).

Aquinas, Thomas, *Summa Theologiae* (London, 1963–81), 61 vols.

Aristotle, *Categories*, in R. McKeon (ed.), *The Basic Works of Aristotle* (New York, 1941).

—— *Metaphysics*, in *The Basic Works of Aristotle*.

—— *Nicomachean Ethics*, in *The Basic Works of Aristotle*.

Augustine, *The City of God* (London, 1945), 2 vols.

Austin, J. L., *Philosophical Papers* (Oxford, 1961).

Bennett, J., 'Substance, Reality, and Primary Qualities', in C. B. Martin and D. M. Armstrong (eds.), *Locke and Berkeley* (Notre Dame, 1968).

Berkeley, G., 'Of Motion', in M. R. Ayers (ed.), *Philosophical Works* (London, 1993).

—— *The Principles of Human Knowledge*, in *Philosophical Works*.

Bertalanffy, L. von, 'An Essay on the Relativity of Categories', in *Philosophy of Science* 22 (1955).

Bieri, Peter, 'Scepticism and Intentionality', in E. Schaper and W. Vossenkuhl (eds.), *Reading Kant* (Oxford, 1989).

Boscovich, Roger J., *A Theory of Natural Philosophy* (Chicago, 1922).

Boyle, Robert, *The Origins of Forms and Qualities*, in M. A. Stewart (ed.), *Selected Philosophical Papers* (Manchester, 1979).

Brentano, Franz, *Psychology from an Empirical Standpoint* (London, 1973).

Broad, C. D., *Scientific Thought* (London, 1923).

Campbell, D. T., 'Evolutionary Epistemology', in P. Schilpp (ed.), *The Philosophy of Karl Popper*, i (La Salle, 1974).

Cohen, J. B., *The Newtonian Revolution* (Cambridge, 1980).

Darwin, Charles, *The Origin of Species* (Harmondsworth, 1968).

Davidson, Donald, *Inquiries into Truth and Interpretation* (Oxford, 1984).

—— 'A Coherence Theory of Truth and Knowledge', in E. LePore (ed.), *Truth and Interpretation* (Oxford, 1986).

Descartes, R., *The Philosophical Works of Descartes*, ed. E. S. Haldane and G. T. R. Ross (Cambridge, 1931–4), 2 vols.

Devitt, Michael, *Realism and Truth* (Oxford, 1984).

Dilman, Ilham, *Freud and the Mind* (Oxford, 1984).

Dilthey, Wilhelm, 'Beiträge zur Lösung der Frage vom Ursprung unseres Glaubens an die Realität der Aussenwelt', in *Gesammelte Schriften*, v (Leipzig and Berlin, 1923).

—— 'Ideen über eine beschreibende und zergliedernde Psychologie', in *Gesammelte Schriften*, v (Leipzig and Berlin, 1923).

Duhem, Pierre, *The Aim and Structure of Physical Theory* (Princeton, 1954).

Dummett, Michael, *Frege: Philosophy of Language* (London, 1973).

—— *Ursprünge der analytischen Philosophie* (Frankfurt am Main, 1992).

Fechner, Theodor, *Über die physikalische und philosophische Atomenlehre* (Leipzig, 1864).

Fingarette, Herbert, *Self-Deception* (London, 1969).

Foster, John, *The Case for Idealism* (London, 1982).

Fox, M., 'On Unconscious Emotions', in *Philosophy and Phenomenological Research* 34 (1973/4).

Freud, Sigmund, *The Interpretation of Dreams* (New York, 1938).

—— 'Die Verdrängung', in *Gesammelte Werke*, x (London, 1942).

—— 'Das Unbewusste', in *Gesammelte Werke*, x (London, 1942).

—— *An Outline of Psycho-Analysis* (New York, 1949).

Grayling, A. C., *Berkeley: The Central Arguments* (London, 1986).

Habermas, Jürgen, *Erkenntnis und Interesse* (Frankfurt am Main, 1968).

Hampshire, Stuart, *Thought and Action* (London, 1959).

Harré, H. R., and Madden, E. H., *Causal Powers* (Oxford, 1975).

Harrison, Bernard, *Inconvenient Fictions* (New Haven and London, 1991).

Hegel, G. W. F., *Phänomenologie des Geistes* (Hamburg, 1952).

—— *Vorlesungen über die Geschichte der Philosophie* (Stuttgart, 1965), 3 vols.

Heidegger, Martin, *Sein und Zeit* (Tübingen, 1986).

Hesse, Mary, *Forces and Fields* (New York, 1962).

—— *Models and Analogies in Science* (Notre Dame, 1966).

Hobbes, Thomas, *Leviathan* (Oxford, 1957).

Hume, David, *An Enquiry Concerning Human Understanding*, in L. A. Selby-Bigge (ed.), *Enquiries Concerning Human Understanding and Concerning Morals* (Oxford, 1975).

—— *A Treatise of Human Nature* (Oxford, 1978).

Husserl, Edmund, *Cartesian Meditations* (The Hague, 1977).

—— *The Crisis of European Science* (Evanstown, 1970).

James, William, 'The Feeling of Effort', in *Collected Essays and Reviews* (London, 1920).

—— *Principles of Psychology* (New York, 1950), 2 vols.

Jammer, Max, *Concepts of Force* (Cambridge, Mass., 1957).

Janaway, Christopher, *Self and World in Schopenhauer's Philosophy* (Oxford, 1989).

Kant, Immanuel, *Critique of Pure Reason* (Basingstoke and London, 1990). Trans. N. Kemp Smith.

Kolakowski, Leszek, *Religion* (Oxford, 1982).

Lange, Friedrich A., *Geschichte des Materialismus* (Iserlohn, 1866).

Leibniz, G. W., *Philosophical Writings*, ed. G. H. R. Parkinson (London, 1973).

Locke, John, *An Essay Concerning Human Understanding*, in *The Works of John Locke*, i (London, 1874).

Lorenz, Konrad Z., 'Kants Lehre vom apriorischen im Lichte gegenwärtiger Biologie', in *Blätter für deutsche Philosophie*, 1941.

—— *Behind the Mirror* (London, 1977).

Luther, Martin, *On the Bondage of the Will*, in E. G. Rupp and P. Watson (eds.), *Luther and Erasmus: Free Will and Salvation* (Philadelphia, 1969).

Lyons, William, *Emotion* (Cambridge, 1980).

Mackie, J. L., *The Cement of the Universe* (Oxford, 1974).

Moore, G. E., *Philosophical Papers* (London, 1959).

Nagel, Ernest, *The Structure of Science* (London, 1961).

Newton-Smith, William, *The Rationality of Science* (London, 1981).

—— 'Relativism and the Possibility of Interpretation', in M. Hollis and S. Lukes (eds.), *Rationality and Relativism* (Oxford, 1982).

Norman, R., 'The Primacy of Practice: "Intelligent Idealism" in Marxist Thought', in G. Vesey (ed.), *Idealism—Past and Present* (Cambridge, 1982).

Nozick, Robert, *Philosophical Explanations* (Oxford, 1981).

Nygren, Anders, *Eros und Agape* (Gütersloh, 1930).

Paley, W., *The Principles of Moral and Political Philosophy*, in L. A. Selby-Bigge (ed.), *British Moralists*, ii (Oxford, 1897).

Popper, Karl, *Conjectures and Refutations* (London, 1963).

—— *Objective Knowledge* (Oxford, 1972).

Price, H. H., *Belief* (London, 1969).

Putnam, Hilary, *Reason, Truth and History* (Cambridge, 1981).

Quine, W. V., *The Roots of Reference* (La Salle, 1973).

—— 'Reply to Stroud', in *Midwest Studies in Philosophy*, 6 (1981).

Quinton, Anthony, *The Nature of Things* (London, 1973).

Rorty, Richard, *Consequences of Pragmatism* (Brighton, 1982).

—— *Contingency, Irony, and Solidarity* (Cambridge, 1989).

Rosen, S. H., *Nihilism* (New Haven, 1969).

Russell, Bertrand, *The Philosophy of Leibniz* (London, 1937).

Ryle, Gilbert, *Dilemmas* (Cambridge, 1954).

Sartre, J.-P., *Being and Nothingness* (London, 1958).

Scheler, Max, *Der Formalismus in der Ethik und die materiale Wertethik* (Bern, 1980).

—— *Das Ressentiment im Aufbau der Moralen* (Frankfurt am Main, 1978).

—— *Erkenntnis und Arbeit* (Frankfurt am Main, 1960).

—— 'Idealismus-Realismus', in *Späte Schriften* (*Gesammelte Werke*, ix), (Bern, 1976).

Schopenhauer, Arthur, *Über die vierfache Wurzel des Satzes vom zureichenden Grunde* (Hamburg, 1957).

—— *The World as Will and Representation* (New York, 1966), 2 vols.

Shimony, A., 'Perception from an Evolutionary Point of View', in *The Journal of Philosophy* 68 (1971).

Simmel, Georg, 'Über eine Beziehung der Selektionslehre zur Erkenntnistheorie', in *Archiv für systematische Philosophie* 1 (1895).

Spinoza, Benedict de, *The Ethics*, in *Works of Spinoza*, ii (New York, 1955).

Sprigge, T. L. S., *Facts, Words and Beliefs* (London, 1970).

—— *The Vindication of Absolute Idealism* (Edinburgh, 1983).

Strawson, Galen, *The Secret Connexion* (Oxford, 1989).

Strawson, P. F., *The Bounds of Sense* (London, 1975).

Stroud, Barry, *The Significance of Philosophical Scepticism* (Oxford, 1984).

—— 'Transcendental Arguments', in *The Journal of Philosophy* 65 (1968).

Taylor, Charles, *The Explanation of Behaviour* (London, 1964).

—— 'Responsibility for Self', in G. Watson (ed.), *Free Will* (Oxford, 1982).

—— 'Foucault on Freedom and Truth', in *Philosophy and the Human Sciences* (Cambridge, 1985).

—— *Sources of the Self* (Cambridge, 1989).

Thalberg, Irving, 'Freud's Anatomies of the Self', in R. Wollheim and J. Hopkins (eds.), *Philosophical Essays on Freud* (Cambridge, 1982).

Trigg, Roger, *Reality at Risk* (New York and London, 1989).

Tugendhat, Ernst, *Der Wahrheitsbegriff bei Husserl und Heidegger* (Berlin, 1970).

Vollmer, Gerhard, *Evolutionäre Erkenntnistheorie* (Stuttgart, 1975).

—— *Was können wir wissen?* (Stuttgart, 1985), 2 vols.

Walker, R. C. S., *Kant* (London, 1978).

—— 'Transcendental Arguments and Scepticism', in E. Schaper and W. Vossenkuhl (eds.), *Reading Kant* (Oxford, 1989).

Warner, Martin, *Philosophical Finesse* (Oxford, 1989).

Williams, Bernard, *Problems of the Self* (London, 1973).

—— *Descartes—The Project of Pure Enquiry* (Harmondsworth, 1978).

Wittgenstein, Ludwig, *Philosophical Investigations* (Oxford, 1958).

INDEX